"*Mindfulness and the Art Therapies* is a wonderful an important contribution to the growing field that Laury Rappaport has masterly brought to the forefront the importance of mindfulness and art therapies."

—*Bob Stahl, Ph.D., Co-Author of* A Mindfulness-Based Stress Reduction Workbook, Living with Your Heart Wide Open, Calming the Rush of Panic, *and* A Mindfulness-Based Stress Reduction Workbook for Anxiety

"Applications of mindfulness and meditation are demonstrating their effectiveness with stress reduction, self-regulation, trauma recovery, and overall quality of life. Likewise, the expressive arts therapies are increasingly embraced as methods of transformation that enhance health and well-being. This impressive book is a timely and seminal contribution to both the current literature on mindfulness and the arts therapies. It incorporates everything helping professionals and students need to know, including the foundations of mindfulness and arts therapies, neurobiology and somatic perspectives, and pragmatic, integrative approaches to applying methods to a variety of populations and settings.

Mindfulness and the Arts Therapies brings together the basics of mindfulness and meditation in a practical, accessible way that invites not only arts therapists but also, all mental health and healthcare professionals to cultivate and apply its wisdom to both working with clients and as a personal wellness practice."

—*Cathy Malchiodi, Ph.D., ATR-BC, LPAT, LPCC, Trauma-Informed Practice and Expressive Arts Therapy Institute, and Lesley University*

"Mindfulness and the arts can play an important role in psychospiritual growth and the evolution of human consciousness. Is the complex consciousness that we call 'mind' and brain the same or different? If you are interested in this question, Drs. Jared D. Kass and Sidney M. Trantham provide a clear and comprehensive roadmap to your evolving understanding in their ambitious chapter in *Mindfulness and the Arts Therapies.*

The authors decipher the most current research in brain science— the autonomic nervous system, polyvagal theory and the stress response, human brain evolution, hemispheric lateralization, attachment theory, pleasure and pain, trauma and PTSD, addiction, self-awareness, empathy, memory, and emotion. They carefully link their discussion of these topics, fostering greater appreciation of the neuroanatomy and physiology of internal composure, resilience, and maturity —in contrast to that of aggression, violence, and destructive coping. Kass and Trantham's chapter, toward the end of this impressive volume, provides an integrative understanding for clinicians, researchers, and anyone interested in mindfulness, meditation, the arts, and the brain."

—*Lawrence Peltz, MD, Author of* The Mindful Path to Addiction Recovery: A Practical Guide to Regaining Control Over Your Life

"The integration of mindfulness practices and the art therapies is a natural and much needed evolution for clinicians and group facilitators. Dr. Laury Rappaport has brought together a remarkable group of practitioners in this timely book. The authors embrace a broad spectrum of approaches —authentic movement, Focusing-Oriented Arts Therapy, Person-Centered Expressive Arts, drama, poetry, and music therapies, and more—all finding enhanced results of combining deep meditation practices with their arts modality. Theories and concepts are carefully presented with meaningful case material. The last chapter, 'Perspectives from Clinical Neuroscience: Mindfulness and the Therapeutic Use of the Arts' describes how the healing, transformative work we are doing is validated by scientific research. This book contributes new and vital material to the humanistic practices of the arts therapies as enhanced by mindfulness methods."

—*Natalie Rogers, Ph.D., REAT, Author of* The Creative Connection for Groups: Person-Centered Expressive Art for Healing and Social Change *and* The Creative Connection: Expressive Arts for Healing

"Although I sincerely believed that I was a pretty thoughtful art therapist, this book has enabled me to realize that I have not been sufficiently mindful of mindfulness— at least not in the deepest sense of the word. As a painter I often experience an altered state of consciousness in the process of creating, something I value tremendously, but have not named. My psychoanalytic training allowed me to strive for 'evenly hovering attention,' trying to attune my entire self toward the other. Yet now, Laury Rappaport's marvelous collection of writings by expressive arts therapists who have experienced genuine mindfulness—and who know how to name and to promote such states—has opened my spirit to an even more profound way of being-in-the-world as a helper. There is no question that this book is both timely and timeless, as are the arts themselves, and the practice of mindfulness in all of its forms."

—*Judith A. Rubin, Ph.D., ATR-BC, HLM, Department of Psychiatry, University of Pittsburgh, Pittsburgh Psychoanalytic Center, Author of* Approaches to Art Therapy and The Art of Art Therapy

"Psychotherapists will find here a rich, practical guide for illuminating how mindfulness can be applied to a variety of art therapies. Rappaport has brilliantly assembled leading pioneers in their respective fields to clearly show how mindfulness offers a basis for healing, growth, and transformation. Her own chapters are notable for offering a clear, compelling integration of Gendlin's Focusing—a very specific kind of mindfulness practice —with the expressive arts. I highly recommend this refreshing and insightful resource."

—*John Amodeo, Ph.D., author of* Dancing with Fire: A Mindful Way to Loving Relationships

"*Mindfulness and Art Therapies* is a diverse yet cohesive collection of essays revealing the deep connection between mindfulness and the arts, and articulating the applications of this meaningful synergy to a range of clinical areas including pain, anger, trauma, etc. This multifaceted book also dives deeper into particular arts modalities such as dance and poetry with well-rounded contributions of a vast subject. It gracefully expresses the key pillars of the ancient mindful practice, and offers a solid academic foundation, while remaining accessible and highly useful."

—Leslie Davenport, MFT, Author of Healing and Transformation Through Self Guided Imagery, *founding member of the Institute for Health & Healing at California Pacific Medical Center in San Francisco, faculty of California Institute of Integral Studies, John F Kennedy University, and Five Branches University*

"Gathering together a rich array of creative arts therapists in a single volume, the various authors provide rich illustrations of how mindfulness and creative arts enhance and reflect each other. Readers are presented with a diverse range of practical application, and left with the space to imagine additional ways to apply these concepts in therapy, education and wellness."

—Jordan S. Potash, Ph.D., ATR-BC, REAT, LCAT, Lecturer, Centre on Behavioral Health and the Department of Social Work and Social Administration, The University of Hong Kong

"Finally there is a book that brings together leaders in the field of arts-based therapy, to impart their knowledge of mindfulness-based practice. This innovative and comprehensive book demonstrates the effective use of a 2,500-year practice within the framework of expressive arts for health and well-being. Mindfulness has been utilized in the lexicon through other names such as 'presence' or 'attunement' or 'flow' or 'witnessing' but here, through historical background, theory and current day mindfulness-practices, the authors gathered take contemporary psychological inquiry to a new wave of application and understanding. I am sure this book will have a great impact and be utilized in the training of practitioners for many years to come."

—Mitchell Kossak, Ph.D., Associate Professor, Expressive Therapies, Lesley University, Executive Co-Chair, International Expressive Arts Therapy Association

by the same author

Focusing-Oriented Art Therapy
Accessing the Body's Wisdom and Creative Intelligence
ISBN 978 1 84310 760 6
eISBN 978 1 84642 852 4

of related interest

Art Therapy in Asia
To the Bone or Wrapped in Silk
Edited by Debra Kalmanowitz, Jordan S. Potash and Siu Mei Chan
Forewords by Shaun McNiff and William Fan
ISBN 978 1 84905 210 8
eISBN 978 0 85700 449 9

Principles and Practice of Expressive Arts Therapy
Toward a Therapeutic Aesthetics
Paolo Knill, Ellen G. Levine and Stephen K. Levine
ISBN 978 1 84310 039 3
eISBN 978 1 84642 032 0

Shamanism and Spirituality in Therapeutic Practice
An Introduction
Christa Mackinnon
Published by Singing Dragon
ISBN 978 1 84819 081 8
eISBN 978 0 85701 068 1

The Ethical Space of Mindfulness in Clinical Practice
An Exploratory Essay
Donald McCown
Foreword by Kenneth Gergen
ISBN 978 1 84905 850 6
eISBN 978 0 85700 510 6

Mindfulness and the Arts Therapies

Theory and Practice

Edited by Laury Rappaport, Ph.D.
Foreword by Jakusho Kwong-roshi

Jessica Kingsley *Publishers*
London and Philadelphia

Rita Dove quote on p.129 has been reproduced with kind permission.
"These Days" by Charles Olson, in Chapter 9, has been reproduced
with kind permission from University of California Press.

First published in 2014
by Jessica Kingsley Publishers
73 Collier Street
London N1 9BE, UK
and
400 Market Street, Suite 400
Philadelphia, PA 19106, USA

www.jkp.com

Library of Congress Cataloging in Publication Data
Mindfulness and the arts therapies : theory and practice / edited by Laury Rappaport.
     pages cm
  Includes bibliographical references and index.
  ISBN 978-1-84905-909-1 (alk. paper)
  1. Art therapy. 2. Mindfulness-based cognitive therapy. I. Rappaport, Laury, editor of compilation.
  RC489.A7M56 2014
  616.89'1656--dc23
                           2013030413

British Library Cataloguing in Publication Data
A CIP catalogue record for this book is available from the British Library

ISBN 978 1 84905 909 1
eISBN 978 0 85700 688 2

Printed and bound in Great Britain

Contents

List of Figures, Tables, and Boxes

Figures

Tables

Boxes

Foreword

Original mindfulness is the actualization of humanity's inherent basic goodness. Mindfulness creatively joined with the new therapies offers a stream of helping and compassionate services for something very old. If the newness of this is taken beyond these words and disciplines, that very stream will become the ocean.

I am very grateful that Laury Rappaport is committed and has pursued this worthy endeavor that connects and shows us all the unseen work related to the benefit and healing of human beings. This book is an expression of love from our inherent basic goodness.

Jakusho Kwong-roshi
Author of No Beginning, No End: The Intimate Path of Zen
Co-founder and Abbot, Sonoma Mountain Zen Center —Genjoji
Santa Rosa, California

Acknowledgments

This book is written in honor of Thich Nhat Hanh and Jakusho Kwong-roshi—who nourish the seeds of mindfulness within me and in the world—and my first meditation teacher, Gurumayi.

I am deeply grateful to Jessica Kingsley for her deep belief in this work, immense wisdom and compassion, and trust in me. This book is as rich and deep as it is because of all the authors—immense gratitude to you for your unique contribution and heartfelt collaboration.

I honor my early teachers in the expressive arts—Shaun McNiff, Paolo Knill, Norma Canner, Peter Rowan, and Elizabeth McKim. To Spring Hill—home of the Opening the Heart workshop—your metaphors and teaching story live on in Chapter 1. Thank you to Gene Gendlin—whose Focusing process has been a teacher to me in mindful awareness, non-judgment, deep listening, and compassion; and to the Focusing community for all of your support and rich exchanges that cross with this work.

Much appreciation to those who offered their wisdom and support—Cathy Malchiodi, Shaun McNiff, Terri Halperin-Eaton, Jared D. Kass, Michael A. Franklin, John Amodeo, and Madelaine Fahrenwald. Thanks to Richard Carolan for the early conceptualization and collaboration on the book. Immense appreciation to my research assistants Emily Tara Weiner, Melanie Dorson, and Chessey Bird Henry. Thank you to Ron Zaidman and Joanna Zhao, colleagues at Five Branches University and the Sonoma Mountain Zen Center.

Most of all, boundless gratitude to my husband Wayne—whose day-to-day availability for consultations and support permeate the pages of this book, and whose compassion nourishes my soul; my daughter Zoe—a true supporter and mindfulness bell of what truly matters in life; and to my loving family, and dear friends.

Introduction

Breathing in, I am aware of breathing in
Breathing out, I am aware of breathing out.

(Mindfulness phrase used frequently by
Thich Nhat Hanh based on Buddha's teaching)

I am honored and excited to be a part of bringing this first generation of writing on the integration of mindfulness and the arts therapies into the world. All of the authors are pioneers who are bringing new thinking, creativity, and clinical approaches to the intersection of these two powerful transformative methods.

Over the past 40 years, methods and techniques from meditation and mindfulness practices have entered the fields of psychotherapy and mind–body medicine—with growing clinical evidence demonstrating their effectiveness in reducing stress, decreasing depression and anxiety, improving quality of life, enhancing well-being, improving immune function, lowering blood pressure and providing other benefits (see Chapters 1 and 21 for references). For the past 75 years, we have seen the increasing use of the arts in healing through the advancement of art therapy, dance/movement therapy, music therapy, drama therapy, psychodrama, poetry therapy, and integrated expressive arts therapy, in conjunction with their expanding clinical applications and research. Today neuroscientists are substantiating the positive benefits and healing changes that meditators and arts therapists have known from both their own experience and their work with others. Through the use of brain imaging, heart monitoring, and other physiological measures, neuroscientists are able to document specific changes that register the effectiveness of these approaches (see Chapter 21).

As mindfulness approaches are expanding into psychotherapy and health-related applications, and the arts therapies are continuing to bring positive results to a wide variety of clinical populations, this book explores the intersection of these two approaches. Each chapter in this book can be thought of as an exploration along the continuum between mindfulness and the arts therapies, emphasizing different aspects. It is interesting to see that there are ways in which the arts therapies cultivate mindfulness, present-moment awareness, compassion, and insight, and ways that mindfulness fosters awareness of and attunement with the creative pulse of life itself.

The interconnectedness between mindfulness and the arts is seen throughout cultures and religious and spiritual traditions. For example, sacred objects and art are imbued with qualities that serve as a focus for healing rituals, meditation, and prayer. Artisans creating these works undergo artistic and spiritual training so that the objects will possess the proper qualities. Mindfulness teacher Thich Nhat Hanh (1991) refers to this way of things existing within each other as "interbeing":

> If you are a poet, you will see clearly that there is a cloud floating in this sheet of paper. Without a cloud, there will be no rain; without rain, the trees cannot grow; and without trees, we cannot make paper. The cloud is essential for the paper to exist. If the cloud is not here, the sheet of paper cannot be here either. So we can say that the cloud and the paper inter-are. "Interbeing" is a word that is not in the dictionary yet, but if we combine the prefix "inter-" with the verb "to be," we have a new verb, inter-be. (p.95)

I noticed this interbeing when I first learned how to meditate over 30 years ago. I sensed there was something familiar about it, and I realized that I had a similar feeling during art-making. My daily concerns seemed to take a back seat as I became immersed in drawing, silk-screening, or painting, and also when I learned to notice, greet, and let go of thoughts and feelings while meditating. In both processes I felt a deep inner quiet and a sense of well-being, even if I was drawing a portrait of someone experiencing immense suffering or witnessing my own worried thoughts. Throughout meditation, I am always amazed to notice the continuous arising of something new within each moment and the falling away of the previous one, and the birth of something new as the cycle continues to unfold, moment to moment. To me, this is a microscopic view into the essence of creativity.

I began to express my meditation experiences in a journal and found that art and writing helped to capture what was essential from the experience; it also helped me to feel the experience as more grounded in my body. Art enabled me to express the subtle energies through shape, color, texture, and imagery. Writing clarified my experiences. Later I found that a gesture or movement helped me to express a sense of sacredness, and sound seemed to help the subtle inner energies expand, much like chanting.

Over the years, I began to teach mindfulness methods to clients and added the various arts therapies modalities. I usually integrate the arts after meditation, but sometimes introduce them before as a way to enhance focus and calm. Clients begin to learn how the breath serves as an anchor for centering and relaxation. They begin to find and deepen their connection to a peaceful center that later becomes known as a secure, internal nourishing home. Expressing the experience of mindfulness practices through the arts also provides clients with a concrete reminder affirming the positive states from the experience that they can later return to.

From personal experience and professionally working with a wide variety of clients for over 30 years, I resonated deeply with this balance between the inward direction of mindfulness and the outward expression through the arts therapies. Together, they help to develop skillfulness in being able to become more aware of various dimensions of inner experience—feelings, thoughts, sensations, and energies; and transform them through mindfulness practices and/or creative means, release them in constructive ways, access inner wisdom, and cultivate self-compassion and compassion toward others. All of the authors explore this interrelatedness between mindfulness and the arts therapies—emphasizing different aspects along this continuum using a variety of approaches.

How this Book is Organized

This book is divided into six sections that address different aspects of mindfulness and the arts therapies, including: (1) an overview of mindfulness and its development in psychotherapy and the arts therapies; (2) the role of the expressive arts in cultivating mindful awareness and presence; (3) approaches that add mindfulness to the arts therapies; (4) approaches that are inherently mindfulness-based; (5) the role of mindfulness in the training and education of arts therapists; and (6) the neuroscience underlying mindfulness and the arts therapies. Many of the chapters include clinical or training examples. The names and identifying information have been changed to protect the clients' confidentiality (unless otherwise requested with proper permissions). For gender neutrality in the writing, I have elected to use the singular plural (e.g. the client/their).

In Part I, Debra Kalmanowitz and I offer a definition of mindfulness at its essence, outside of any religious or spiritual tradition. We offer a brief glimpse into the Buddhist roots of mindfulness, and discuss how mindfulness practices are also found in other wisdom traditions, including Hinduism, Christianity, Judaism, and Islam. Our introductory chapter seeks to create an awareness of religious and culturally sensitive options for learning mindfulness, in addition to the secular methods offered in psychotherapy and stress-reduction programs. We identify the early influences of mindfulness in psychoanalysis, including the work of Sigmund Freud, Wilfred Bion, Karen Horney, and Erich Fromm—followed by its later development into contemporary approaches, such as Mindfulness-Based Cognitive Therapy, dialectical behavioral therapy, and acceptance and commitment therapy. The chapter concludes with a brief discussion about the relationship between mindfulness and the arts therapies, and the remaining chapters address the topic in depth.

Part II explores the role of the arts therapies in cultivating mindful awareness and presence. Shaun McNiff, the creator of the first expressive arts therapies program in the world, reflects on his early mentors and over three decades of clinical and training experiences that have led him to identify the role of the arts therapies in fostering mindful perception and witnessing consciousness. He discusses the use of creative space and articulates the components of arts therapy practices that foster mindful awareness, acceptance, and empathic understanding. I have witnessed and experienced McNiff's invitation for participants in his workshops to "pause" as both the sharer and witnesses deepen into mindful awareness and presence.

Pat B. Allen, creator of the Open Studio Process (OSP), describes the connections between mindfulness and the OSP practices of intention, writing, art, and witnessing. She shares a powerful example of applying this process to her work with adolescent boys that illustrates how intention, witnessing, and painting are practices of mindfulness in action and lead to insight and compassion.

Part III comprises nine chapters in which mindfulness practices are blended with the various arts therapies. Several of the authors' work derive from Kabat-Zinn's (1990) Mindfulness-Based Stress Reduction program (MBSR). Caroline Peterson integrated art therapy with Kabat-Zinn's model and created an eight-week program called Mindfulness-Based Art Therapy (MBAT). Peterson's and her colleagues research has demonstrated its positive impact on people living with cancer (Monti *et al.* 2006). In addition to describing her MBAT program, Peterson shares a newly developed program, Walkabout, that unites the natural environment, photography, and collage, and helps participants cultivate mindfulness in daily life. Patricia D. Isis, also a long-time pioneer in integrating the expressive arts with mindfulness, describes her creative application that joins intermodal expressive arts with MBSR at a community outreach program. She also shares a touching example from her own life that led to training in MBSR, affirming the importance for therapists to learn these practices from the inside out. Daniel Herring was inspired by Peterson's MBAT, Insight Meditation, and MBSR and pioneered the development of Mindfulness-Based Expressive Therapy (MBET) with people who experience serious and persistent mental illness. His chapter describes exercises that he developed with contributions from trainees and expressive therapists, as well as important considerations for working with this population.

From Germany, art therapist Jürgen Fritsche describes the approach he developed—inspired by his practice of Vipassana meditation and MBSR—that incorporates mindful awareness, body scanning, and art therapy. His chapter details the transformation of a woman with chronic pain who moves into greater aliveness and joy using this method in a studio art environment that allows for the creation of both small and very large paintings.

Part III also includes chapters on the application of mindfulness to drama therapy, dance/movement therapy, music therapy, and an integrated creative arts therapy silent retreat. Drama therapist Joel Gluck developed psolodrama, an integration of Insight meditation and drama therapy. After clarifying the theoretical constructs, Gluck demonstrates how teaching mindfulness practices, authentic movement, and methods from psolodrama help a client with uncontrollable rage decrease his outbursts, resolve inner and outer conflicts, and bring meditation into his daily life. Jennifer Frank Tantia, a dance/movement therapist, presents a theoretical model—somatic modes of attention (Csordas 1993)—that is especially helpful in working with trauma. After describing the distinction between attention to the body and attention with the body, Tantia demonstrates this sensitively attuned application of somatic awareness and dance/movement therapy with a client who has trauma.

Australian music therapists Carolyn Van Dort and Denise Grocke introduce a ten-session group approach that brings together music, imagery, and mindfulness for people with substance dependence. Their chapter illustrates the program's methodology and includes case studies that elucidate the healing benefits. In addition, they provide a rich resource for music for imagery work in Appendix 2. Poetry therapist John Fox transmits the powerful use of words and poem-making to harness mindfulness and presence in the moment. His chapter includes the healing power of poem-making for both staff and patients in a hospital setting.

Paola Luzzatto is one of the earliest art therapists to bring silence and meditation to the creative arts. She and her co-authors describe their international team's creation of a Silent Creative Retreat in Assisi, Italy, for people living with cancer. The retreat was offered for ten years to over 154 participants, including some family members. Their hope is that this chapter will serve as a guide for other professionals who want to offer this type of healing retreat.

Part IV presents five arts therapy approaches that are mindfulness-based, in that they integrate qualities of non-judgment, awareness, and witnessing within a theoretical and practice orientation. Zoë Avstreih, a pioneer in the development of Authentic Movement, illustrates the ways in which Authentic Movement is an embodied mindfulness practice. She describes the development and intentions underlying Authentic Movement and clarifies both the roles and forms of mover and witness. Based on 40 years of experience, Avstreih demonstrates how Authentic Movement cultivates the qualities of presence, acceptance, and compassion, and is linked to ancient mindfulness-awareness practices.

Hakomi Therapy (Kurtz 1990) is a body-oriented approach to psychotherapy that is based on Buddhist principles of mindfulness and non-violence. Merryl E. Rothaus provides an overview of Hakomi and describes the mutual benefits of combining it with art therapy. She offers a rich case study illustrating the moment-to-moment unfolding of Hakomi integrated with art therapy.

Fiona Chang from Hong Kong discusses how the values and underlying principles of Person-Centered Expressive Arts—based on unconditional positive regard, congruence, and empathy—are similar to those of mindfulness practice. She includes examples of expressive arts with a mindfulness orientation in an outpatient cancer support group.

Karin von Daler and Lori Schwanbeck developed Creative Mindfulness, an approach that integrates Dialectical Behavior Therapy (DBT) with expressive arts therapy. Their chapter includes an overview of DBT followed by the theoretical connections between DBT and the expressive arts, its clinical application, and a case study illustrating their approach. They provide a rich resource of creative exercises that are paired with traditional DBT exercises.

There are two chapters on Focusing-Oriented Arts Therapies (FOAT). The first, written by me, describes the parallels between Thich Nhat Hanh's teachings on mindfulness and FOAT. Examples are provided from the principal approaches of FOAT—expressing a felt sense through the arts; Clearing a Space with the Arts; Theme-Directed FOAT; and Focusing-Oriented Arts Psychotherapy. Emily Tara Weiner and I co-authored a chapter on mindfulness and FOAT with children and adolescents. The chapter presents an overview of theory and research on mindfulness, art, and FOAT with children and adolescents. The chapter includes a workshop design of a five-day summer camp group that Emily led at the Omega Teen Camp that integrates mindfulness practices with FOAT. Adaptations for younger children are also included.

Part V focuses on the significance of integrating mindfulness and meditation into the training of arts therapists. Michael A. Franklin is a groundbreaking leader in contemplative art therapy and is Director of the Art Therapy Program at Naropa University, where mindfulness practices are part of the curriculum. He offers insight into the significance of integrating meditation into arts therapy curricula and presents theoretical connections between meditation and art therapy. Franklin includes illuminating excerpts from interviews with four Naropa faculty on the importance of teaching meditation to counseling and art therapy students, as well as a case study illustrating the application of mindfulness and art from a student's perspective.

Nancy Beardall, a dance/movement therapist and Janet Surrey, founding scholar of the Jean Baker Miller Training Institute at the Stone Center, present the significance of mindfulness in relationship. They discuss and illustrate their theoretical and practice model based on relational mindfulness, relational movement, relational cultural theory, Insight Dialogue, and contributions from interpersonal neurobiology in training dance/movement therapists. Their chapter includes a description of their training exercises along with a thematic analysis of the benefits derived from students.

In Part VI, Jared D. Kass and Sidney M. Trantham, seasoned professionals in holistic psychology, provide a clear and comprehensive overview of the neuroscience underlying mindfulness practice and the arts therapies. They explain why and how the cultivation of internal composure is beneficial for resilient coping, and describe cutting-edge advances in polyvagal theory; the significance of attachment templates in both resilient and destructive coping; the mind–body dynamics governed by the autonomic nervous system, HPA axis, and triune brain; the role of mirror neurons in empathy; and emerging insights about the mind–body mechanisms underlying somatic memory. The authors then connect this neuroscience to mindfulness practices and specific applications to music, movement and dance, art, and dramatic enactment, including an emphasis on how a positive therapeutic relationship builds capacity for secure attachment. This important chapter provides a solid neuroscientific foundation for the clinical material in all of the preceding chapters. It will help clinicians understand and refine their use of mindfulness practices and the arts therapies as tools for cultivating internal composure and resilient coping.

A Mindfulness Bell

My hope is that the chapters in this book inspire you and your work, and bring benefit for healing in the world. I wanted this book to be written in such a way that it is easy to understand how mindfulness is cultivated in relation to all of the approaches presented here. I also wanted you, the reader, to be able to see the similarities and differences in each author's approach. While many methods or techniques that you read may look or sound as easy as "breathing in and breathing out," they are much more than that. All of the authors have been practitioners in the arts and/or mindfulness for many years. Applying the arts and mindfulness with different populations requires proper training and a willingness to learn it for ourselves first. We explore the terrain, learning how to breathe or walk mindfully as difficulties and unpredictable inner experiences float into awareness. We learn about different states of awareness and how the arts and the body can, at times, quickly bring up emotional material. We learn how to use mindfulness and the arts to bring about calm and self-soothing for ourselves and how they can be adapted to working with people of varying needs and ages. This is a gentle mindfulness bell to emphasize the importance in obtaining proper training and supervision when applying mindfulness and the arts in psychotherapeutic work with others.

Having shared this awareness with you, my hope is that this book will nourish the seeds of mindfulness and creativity to sprout in new ways for the benefit of all.

References

Csordas, T. (1993) "Somatic modes of attention." *Cultural Anthopology 8*, 2, 135–156.

Hanh, T.N. (1991) *Peace is Every Step: The Path of Mindfulness in Everyday Life.* New York: Bantam Books.

Kabat-Zinn, J. (1990) *Full Catastrophe Living: Using the Wisdom of Your Body and Mind to Face Stress, Pain, and Illness.* NewYork: Delacorte Press.

Kurtz, R. (1990) *Body-Centered Psychotherapy: The Hakomi Method.* Mendocino, CA: LifeRhythm.

Monti, D., Peterson, C., Shakin Kunkel, E., Hauck, W.W., *et al.* (2006) "A randomized, controlled trial of mindfulness-based art therapy (MBAT) for women with cancer." *Psycho-Oncology 15*, 5, 363–373.

PART I

Mindfulness and the Arts Therapies

Overview and Roots

Chapter 1

Mindfulness, Psychotherapy, and the Arts Therapies

Laury Rappaport and Debra Kalmanowitz

Mindfulness is a practice of bringing awareness to the present moment with an attitude of acceptance and non-judgment. Often traced to the teachings of the Buddha 2500 years ago, mindfulness practices are also found in most major wisdom traditions. Ancient mindfulness practices are being adapted to secular contexts—psychotherapy, education, and work environments—in response to the numerous clinically standardized applications of mindfulness and meditation practices (Burke 2010; Chiesa and Serretti 2009, 2011; Fjorback *et al.* 2011; Hussain and Bhushan 2010; Keng, Smoski, and Robins 2011; Shennan, Payne, and Fenlon 2011). As Thich Nhat Hanh (2012) states, "When you have enough energy of mindfulness, you can look deeply into any emotion and discover the true nature of that emotion, If you can do that, you will be able to transform the emotion (p.89)." Mindfulness practices can be learned within spiritual and secular settings, depending on what is right for each person (client and therapist).

We begin this chapter with an introduction to mindfulness in its essence—outside of any religious or spiritual context. Next, we give a brief overview of its spiritual roots, historical influences in the field of psychology and contemporary culture that have led to the application of mindfulness approaches in psychotherapy, followed by a discussion of the relationship of mindfulness to the expressive arts therapies.

The Essence of Mindfulness

We would like to introduce the essence of mindfulness using an image and metaphor. Imagine a storm. Take a moment to notice the storm depicted in Figure 1.1.

What do you notice? There is a swirling that can include high winds, rain, and sleet. In the center there is a place in all storms that is called the "eye" of the storm. The qualities of the eye of a storm are calm, peaceful, and clear. The practice of mindful awareness involves taking time to access the "eye"—the part of us that can observe the storm—as it is. Mindfulness practices help us to find a center (eye or "I") within ourselves to bear witness to the storm of thoughts, feelings, sensations, and all aspects of our experience, with acceptance.

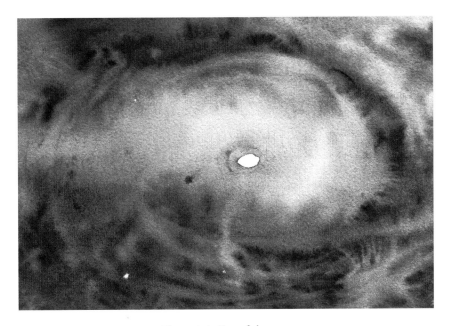

Figure 1.1: Eye of the storm

Two Wings of a Bird: Experiencing and Witnessing

Mindfulness practice can also be compared to two wings of a bird (Spring Hill 1983). One wing symbolizes our experience; the other represents our ability to witness and observe our experience. If we only have our experience, we can get lost in the storm. If we are only in touch with the witness aspect of ourselves, then we can be detached and disconnected from the aliveness within our experience—whether it is joyful, scary, fun, and so forth. As birds need both wings in order to fly, so too do we. Mindfulness practices and the expressive arts teach us how to become aware of the inner witness while noticing and sensing our experience at the same time.

Spiritual Roots and Applications of Mindfulness

Although it is beyond the scope of this book to provide an in-depth review of the spiritual roots of mindfulness, we would briefly like to include a beginning overview of its roots in Buddhism, Hinduism, Christianity, Judaism, and Islam (acknowledging there are other traditions as well). Awareness of mindfulness practices in different traditions can offer clients and therapists culturally sensitive options for those interested in learning within their cultural or religious roots.

Buddhism

As previously mentioned, the roots of mindfulness are most often attributed to the Buddha's teachings, approximately 2500 years ago. The Buddha's discourses describe an Eightfold Path for reducing suffering and living with greater happiness and peacefulness. The teachings, or *Dharma*, is "not a set of doctrines demanding belief but is a body of principles and practices that sustain human beings in their quest for happiness and spiritual freedom" (Bhikku 2011, p.20). The eight aspects include: (1) right view, (2) right intention, (3) right speech, (4) right action, (5) right livelihood, (6) right effort, (7) right mindfulness, and (8) right concentration. Thich Nhat Hanh (1975, 1976) describes the seventh aspect in the Buddha's Sutra of Mindfulness:

> When walking, the practitioner must be conscious that [s]he is walking. When sitting, the practitioner must be conscious that [s]he is sitting. When lying down the practitioner must be conscious that [s]he is lying down... No matter what position the body is in, the practitioner must be conscious of that position. Practicing thus, the practitioner lives in direct and constant mindfulness of the body... (p.7)

As can be seen from this quote, mindfulness is awareness. The Buddha describes *four foundations of mindfulness*—contemplation of the body, feelings, states of mind, and phenomena. Mindful breathing is a fundamental practice that serves as an anchor to notice the continuous arising and passing of thoughts, feelings, sensations, and phenomena. Mindfulness practices help to access an inner witness and a more spacious aspect of ourselves to examine the true nature of our experience; to dis-identify with feelings, thoughts, and sensations that are within our experience but not who we really are; understand that everything in life is constantly changing (impermanent); and to gain insight and compassion.

Buddhist mindfulness practices include formal practices—sitting meditation, walking meditation, body scan, eating meditation, and meditations on lovingkindness (bringing gentleness and compassion towards oneself and others)—as well as informal practices carried into daily life, such as practicing mindful breathing while doing the dishes, stopping at a red light, or in response to your cell phone ringing. Within Buddhism, mindfulness is taught through a variety of approaches, including Vipassana (Hart 1987), Insight Meditation (Goldstein 1993, 2007; Kornfield 2009; Salzberg 2011), Tibetan (Chodron 2013; Tenzin Gyatso 1995) and Zen (Hanh 1975, 1976, 1991).

Hinduism

Hinduism predates Buddhism and includes many practices for cultivating mindfulness. One basic approach to meditation consists of repeating a mantra—a sacred word, name, or sound. The practitioner silently repeats the mantra coordinating it with the in-breath and the out-breath—and notices thoughts, feelings, sensations, and occurrences in the environment—allowing them to pass by like the clouds in the sky. During this process of meditation, the steadiness and vibration of the mantra help one to access the inner witness (saksin)—who non-judgmentally notices the coming and going of inner and outer experiences. The witness helps the practitioner to observe and dis-identify with feelings, thoughts, and sensations that can lead to an experience of oneness with Consciousness, Self, or God (Anantananda 1996; Shantananda 2003).

Christianity

Mindfulness is applied in Christian traditions through contemplative prayer and meditation. Meninger, Pennington, and Keating (Keating 2009; Pennington 1982) developed the Centering Prayer that is based on practices by the Desert Fathers and Mothers from the fourth and fifth centuries and inspiration from Thomas Merton (1960, 1961). In Centering Prayer, the practitioner chooses a word, phrase, or sacred symbol that gives consent to God within, followed by closing the eyes and sitting quietly. In contrast to continuous repetition of a mantra, the sacred word or symbol is only focused on when the practitioner notices getting carried away into thoughts, feelings, and other distractions. Father Keating describes treating the thoughts and distractions with a "smile, friendliness, or jolliness" (Keating 2008). Blanton (2011) compares the Centering Prayer with mindfulness and discusses its application to psychotherapy. Symington and Symington (2012) present a Christian model of mindfulness based on three pillars—presence of mind, acceptance, and internal observation. A crucial aspect of Christian mindfulness is experiencing the presence of God.

Judaism

Although Jewish contemplative practice dates back thousands of years, meditation practices have "often been hidden in the oral tradition passed directly from teacher to student, or in Kabbalistic writings that are difficult to decipher" (Cooper 2000, p.6). Jewish meditation is understood to be the ability to master one's thinking, or the flow of consciousness which is seen as residing in the soul, guided by *kavanah* (intention) (Kaplan 1995). In recent years, Jewish meditation and mindfulness practices have become more accessible and are being introduced into many synagogues and practice centers (Cooper 2000; Kaplan 1995; Roth 2009; Schacter-Shalomi 2011, 2012; Slater 2004).

Rabbi Zalman Schacter-Shalomi (2011, 2012), founder of Jewish Renewal, studied various Eastern meditation traditions and describes how some forms of Jewish meditation are similar to Buddhist mindfulness practices except that the intention— *kavannah*—of Jewish meditation is the awareness of God's presence: "…when thoughts and feelings arise in your meditation, you can release them to God" (p.45). Rabbi Schacter-Shalomi (2013) describes this further:

> When something arises, to also make a window, as it were, to let God in. You would do everything the same way but you would open a window and say, "God look into this consciousness with me." It becomes a prayer.

Islam

The mystical branch of Islam is Sufism. The poet saint Rumi, born in 1207, founded the Mevlevi Order of Sufism, and is often quoted to inspire states of awareness, mindfulness, compassion, and the divine. Mirdal (2010) describes similarities between mindfulness and Sufism—"acceptance and acknowledgment of positive and negative experiences, unlearning old habits and looking at the world with new eyes" (p.1206), breathing and walking meditation (different from Buddhist methods), intentions, and cultivating insight and compassion. In addition, Mirdal discusses the significance of integrating Sufism and Rumi's philosophy and poetry with mindfulness-based approaches to psychotherapy as a way of providing a culturally sensitive approach for clients with a Muslim background.

As can be seen, mindfulness has deep roots in religious and spiritual traditions. As mindfulness continues to be taught and practiced in secular applications, it is important to remember that it comes from a lineage of ancient wisdom traditions.

Mindfulness in Psychotherapy

Mindfulness in theory and practice is increasingly being adopted by Western psychology. Historical influences leading to the current development of mindfulness in psychotherapy today can be found in psychoanalysis; the introduction of Buddhism and other meditation traditions to the West; the development of humanistic, transpersonal, and contemplative approaches to psychotherapy; and behavioral medicine.

Historical Roots of Mindfulness in Psychotherapy

PSYCHOANALYSIS

Beginning with Freud, *attention* has been an essential aspect in the practice of psychoanalysis (Mace 2007). In Freud's (1912) "Recommendations to Physicians Practicing Psychoanalysis," he describes the importance of attention:

> The technique, however, is a simple one… It simply consists in not directing one's notice to anything in particular and in maintaining the same "evenly-suspended attention (as I have called it) in the face of all that one hears." (p.110)

This quality of attention requires an openness to the present moment and is similar to Vipassana's bare attention or open awareness. Freud cautions that if one does not pay attention in this way, then the analyst is at risk of "never finding anything but what he already knows" (Freud 1912, p.111). This is similar to the benefits of mindfulness and meditation to go beyond preconceived notions, beliefs, and feelings. Wilfred Bion, (considered the greatest psychoanalytic thinker after Freud) also wrote about the significance of attention. Bion (2007) maintained that to accurately observe people, it was necessary for the analyst to attend to and notice thoughts as well as feelings— and, at the same time, to put one's own feelings and thoughts aside.

Neo-Freudian Karen Horney developed a strong interest in Zen Buddhism, forming close connections with D.T. Suzuki (Zen scholar) and Dr. Akihisa Kondo, a Japanese psychiatrist. Suzuki led Zen study groups, including meditation and Koan study at the American Institute of Psychoanalysis—and Horney and Kondo collaborated on integrating Zen with Horney's concept of the real self (Morvay 1999). Horney also traveled to Japan to learn about Zen and Japanese culture. One of Horney's final lectures highlights her knowledge of Eastern influences and the integration of Zen in her work:

The attention should be wholehearted... I think it is rather difficult to attain... This is a faculty for which the Orientals have a much deeper feeling than we do. Also, they have a much better training in it than we. We, as a rule, are not trained in concentrating per se. They must so concentrate in their exercises, powers, breathing, meditation, and Yoga. (Ingram 1987, p.18)

Horney also saw the impact of the therapist's quality of attention (awareness) on the client's awareness (similar to the impact of the Zen teacher's state on the student (Ingram 1987).

Erich Fromm also formed a close connection with D.T. Suzuki and in 1957 invited him to present at a week-long seminar on psychoanalysis and Zen at the Mexican Psychoanalytic Society, where Fromm also presented a paper, "Psychoanalysis and Zen." Fromm and Suzuki's papers are published in *Psychoanalysis and Zen Buddhism* (Fromm, Suzuki, and De Martino 1970). Fromm asserted that "both Zen and psychoanalysis sought to achieve the same ends: insight into one's nature, freedom, happiness, love, sanity, and the liberation of thwarted energy" (Friedman 2013, p.167).

INFLUENCE OF BUDDHISM AND MEDITATION IN THE WEST

The interest in Zen and other Buddhist influences in the West (especially the United States) can also be traced to World War II. After the war, American psychiatrists returned from Japan having been exposed to new ideas, Japanese culture, and Morita Therapy—a form of psychotherapy based on Zen Buddhism, developed by Shoma Morita (Dryden and Still 2006; Morita 1998). Morita's approach included accepting and experiencing symptoms rather than the traditional approach of actively attacking them to reduce their impact.

With the increased ease of world travel, meditation masters from India, China, Tibet, Vietnam, and other countries came, bringing their teachings to the West (e.g. Thich Nhat Hanh, Maharishi Mahesh Yogi, Chögyam Trungpa, Shunryu Suzuki Roshi), while many seekers went to the East to study with meditation masters. Today, many of those who studied in Asia are leading mindfulness teachers (Kornfield 1993, 2009, 2011; Goldstein 1993, 2007; Hanh 1975, 1976, 1991, 2012; Salzberg 2011).

HUMANISTIC, TRANSPERSONAL, AND CONTEMPLATIVE PSYCHOTHERAPY

In the 1960s and 1970s, humanistic psychology brought a holistic approach to the field. Influenced by Eastern ideas, this approach emphasized a non-judgmental acceptance and awareness of symptoms. It offered an "alternative to the reductionism of either psychoanalysis or behavior therapies" (Dryden and Still 2006, p.9). Carl Rogers (1951, 1961) emphasized *unconditional positive regard*; Perls (1992) focused on the here and now; and existential psychotherapists concentrated on "being" and presence (Bugental 1978; May 1994; Yalom 1980). Transpersonal psychotherapy developed and integrated spirituality with psychotherapy (Walsh and Vaughn 1981; Wilber 2001) and contemplative psychotherapy integrated Buddhist and other contemplative practices with psychotherapy (Wegela 1994). The interconnections between spirituality and psychological well-being were also being researched and observed (Kass 1995, 2007; Kass and Lennox 2005).

BEHAVIORAL MEDICINE

In the 1970s, Herbert Benson (1975) wrote a groundbreaking book, *The Relaxation Response* based on meditative methods that demonstrated the ability of the mind to reduce stress—thereby promoting relaxation and healing. After researching transcendental meditators and advanced meditators (Tibetan monks) Benson found that when people added something they had faith in (e.g. religious or spiritual word, phrase, image), they were able to "create other internal environments that can help people reach enhanced states of health and well-being" (Benson 1984, p.5).

Later, Jon Kabat-Zinn (1990) introduced *Full Catastrophe Living*, describing the eight-week Mindfulness-Based Stress Reduction (MBSR) method that he had developed. Kabat-Zinn's MBSR revolutionized the secular application of mindfulness to health and well-being in psychotherapy and other fields. During the same period of time as Kabat-Zinn's work, Langer (1991, 2000a, 2000b) was writing about mindfulness from a Western experimental psychology background.

Mindfulness and Psychotherapy Today

As a result of Kabat-Zinn's structured eight-week MBSR program and the subsequent 28 years of controlled and replicable outcome studies (Center for Mindfulness in Medicine, Health Care, and Society 2013; Dryden and Still 2006), mindfulness meditation is flourishing. In addition, by adapting traditional mindfulness meditation to a set of skills that can be taught independently of any religious belief system, mindfulness has become accessible and prevalent in Western psychotherapy (Baer 2006). Following is a brief overview of MBSR and other mindfulness-based approaches in psychotherapy.

MINDFULNESS-BASED STRESS REDUCTION (MBSR)

Kabat-Zinn's (1982) early research in MBSR began with people suffering chronic pain; continued research is demonstrating its positive results to decrease pain, depression, and anxiety—and improve quality of life and health in a wide range of health and clinical issues. The MBSR program includes mindfulness meditation training in a group setting that takes place over eight weeks, with weekly sessions lasting two and a half to three hours. The training includes both formal (body scan, sitting meditation, walking meditation, gentle yoga) and informal mindfulness practices done throughout the day that encourage mindfulness as a way of life. This model also includes homework, a didactic element, sharing, and a lovingkindness meditation.

MINDFULNESS-BASED COGNITIVE THERAPY (MBCT)

Mindfulness-Based Cognitive Therapy (MBCT) developed out of MBSR in the late 1990s to specifically address the prevention of relapse in depression (Segal, Williams and Teasdale 2013). With the help of Kabat-Zinn, a structured approach to MBCT was developed to integrate MBSR and cognitive-behavioral therapy (CBT). MBCT is similar in format to MBSR; however, the didactic material is focused more on understanding depression rather than on stress. MBCT helped to expand MBSR as an evidence-based practice within clinical psychology (Dryden and Still 2006).

DIALECTICAL BEHAVIORAL THERAPY (DBT)

Dialectical behavioral therapy (DBT), developed by Marsha Linehan (1993a, 1993b), incorporates mindfulness as a learned skill along with interpersonal effectiveness, emotion regulation, and distress tolerance. Clients learn about the Wise Mind, Reasonable Mind, and Emotional Mind. Although DBT was originally developed specifically as a treatment method for borderline personality disorder, it is now applied to other treatment issues, including eating disorders, trauma, substance abuse, depression and family (Dimeff and Koerner 2007).

ACCEPTANCE AND COMMITMENT THERAPY (ACT)

Acceptance and commitment therapy (ACT), developed by Steven Hayes, Kirk Strosahl, and Kelly Wilson (1999), focuses on acceptance and mindfulness strategies in conjunction with a commitment to specific goals and values, to encourage psychological flexibility. ACT has its roots in *functional contextualism* and is based on *relational frame theory* (RFT). ACT differs from CBT in that rather than trying to teach people to better control their thoughts, feelings, sensations, and memories, ACT teaches them to just notice, accept, and welcome both positive and negative events or feelings (Hayes *et al.* 1999). The emphasis of ACT is on ongoing present-moment awareness, valued directions and committed action. This notion of valued direction is key in ACT and describes the process of becoming aware of what is important to the individual, understanding the underlying value, and choosing to live in alignment with this value (committed action).

ADDITIONAL MINDFULNESS APPROACHES

Variations of MBSR have evolved to offer programs to different targeted needs, such as mindfulness-based relapse prevention (MBRP) for addictive behavior (Bowen, Chawla, and Marlatt 2010), mindfulness-based eating awareness (Kristeller, Baer, and Quillian-Wolever 2006), mindfulness-based relationship enhancement (Carson *et al.* 2004), and Mindfulness-Based Art Therapy (Monti *et al.* 2006).

The phrases *mindfulness-informed therapy* and *mindfulness-based therapy* are being used to classify specific approaches. According to Shapiro and Carlson (2009), mindfulness-informed therapy draws on ideas from Buddhist and Western psychology, mindfulness literature, and the personal mindfulness practice of the therapist. Mindfulness-based therapy implies therapies in which mindfulness meditation practices are explicitly taught as a key ingredient in the treatment. It is important to note that the phrase "mindfulness-based approaches" in this book (Part IV) has a broader application and refers to approaches that cultivate mindful awareness.

Mindfulness and the Arts Therapies

The roots of mindfulness and the arts therapies can also be traced back through the ages to the use of the arts in ritual to enhance spiritual and religious practices, and promote healing and transformation. Since the remaining chapters provide extensive literature on witnessing, mindfulness, and the arts therapies, we prefer not to be repetitive here. Instead, we will discuss how mindfulness in the arts therapies can be looked at from two perspectives: (1) the processes inherent within the arts that cultivate mindful awareness and engagement in the present moment, and (2) the application of mindfulness practices to the arts therapies.

Each art form offers opportunities to both access an inner witness and to be completely absorbed into present-moment experience. For example, artists engaging in the process of art-making can be absorbed into a state of *flow* (Csikszentmihalyi 1990). There is a sense of being immersed in the process, a quieting of the mind, an experience of oneness with the artistic experience engaged in the present moment, and an absence of linear time. At some point, the artist steps away from the painting, sculpture, or other art form to observe it. Stepping back engages an inner witness who looks at the work of art to sense its aesthetic balance—to decide what is needed— colors, shapes, and so forth.

This process of being both engaged in the experience and accessing an inner witness is present in all of the arts. For example, a professional dancer describes her experience in preparing for a performance:

> When practicing, I become aware of how the movement feels on the inside, in my body, but at the same time I have to be aware of how it appears on the outside, to the audience. I am in touch with my own experience of the dance as well as a part that witnesses myself in the studio mirror—observing how my dance experience appears. The more I bring mindfulness into rehearsal, the more prepared I am to accomplish what every dancer's goal is in performance—to quiet my mind and allow my body to take over—to be totally present in the experience. (Rappaport 2013).

This inherent ability to simultaneously be within the experience and outside of it can be seen in psychodrama, drama therapy, writing, and music. In psychodrama, the protagonist takes on different roles and speaks as different parts of self. For example, Sarah, a client in her forties, felt immobilized to make a change in a romantic relationship that repeatedly caused her pain. The therapist invited Sarah to put the "immobilized" part of herself in an "empty chair." Sarah took on the role of the immobilized aspect— slumping in the chair, feeling heavy. Speaking as the immobilized part, she said, "I'm heavy. I just can't do anything. I know this relationship isn't good for me but I have no energy, no oomph." Next, the therapist invited Sarah to step away from playing the part in the empty chair and to stand aside and observe that part in the empty chair. To reflect this part, the therapist role-played the immobilized part, just as Sarah had played it. Now Sarah could observe the immobilized part and have an experiential sense of it. Sarah spoke up: "C'mon! You're wasting yourself! The relationship is zapping all of your energy and good feelings. You deserve more than that!" The opportunity to stand outside of the immobilized place within and access a calmer, more centered aspect of herself, enabled Sarah to shift her perspective to an embodied knowing.

Writers also engage in practices of being in the experience and witnessing it. Writers capture what has meaning and allow words to flow or be crafted on a page. After, the writer steps back and can see, read, and hear the poem or writing.

As will be seen in the following chapters, the arts intrinsically provide access to two wings of the bird—experience and witness. The addition of mindfulness practices and mindfulness-based approaches bring complementary dimensions for deepening awareness and cultivating qualities of self-acceptance, self-compassion, and compassion toward others.

We would like to end this chapter with a Zen story about two frogs, as it contains an important message.

Two Frogs Story

Last summer, on an extremely hot day, there were two frogs in the backfield. They were thirsty and noticed a large bucket full of milk. Did you know frogs love milk? So, they hopped into the bucket of milk and began to drink. It was heaven! They drank down a whole lot of it.

After a while, the bigger frog, the more anxious and pessimistic of the two said, "Hey, wait a minute. We're in trouble. How are we going to get out of here? There's no way to jump out. We're going to drown."

The little frog said, "We'll figure it out. Just keep swimming." So they did. Soon the bigger frog said in a panicky voice, "There is no way out of here. We're doomed." The little frog said, "We'll think of something. Keep swimming." Finally the bigger frog said, "I can't take it anymore. I'm giving up." He stopped swimming and then he went—glub glub glub. The little frog kept swimming—around in a circle. As he swam and swam, he noticed that it became more difficult to swim. There was more and more resistance. The milk got thicker and thicker until…it turned into butter…and he perched his little feet on the butter and hopped out of the bucket! (Friedman 1987, pp.27–28)

May this story serve as a reminder that although we can separate mindfulness from its religious or spiritual contexts and apply it secularly, something profound occurs with these simple yet powerful transformative practices. This is why it is essential to receive proper training in mindfulness if you wish to integrate these practices with the arts therapies.

References

Anantananda, S. (1996) *What's on My Mind: Becoming Inspired with New Perception.* New York: SYDA Foundation.

Baer, R.A. (2006) *Mindfulness-Based Treatment Approaches: Clinician's Guide to Evidence Base and Applications.* Burlington, MA: Academic Press.

Benson, H. with Klipper, M.Z. (1975) *The Relaxation Response.* New York: Quill, Harper Collins Publishers.

Benson, H. (1984) *Beyond the Relaxation Response.* New York: Penguin Group.

Bhikku, B (2011) "What does mindfulness really mean? A canonical perspective." *Contemporary Buddhism 12*, 1, 19–39.

Bion, W (2007) (First published 1970) *Attention and Interpretation.* London: Karnac Books.

Blanton, P.G. (2011) "The other mindful practice: Centering prayer and psychotherapy." *Pastoral Psychology 60*, 1, 135–137.

Bowen, S., Chawla, N., and Marlatt, G.A. (2010) *Mindfulness-Based Relapse Prevention for Addictive Behaviors: A Clinician's Guide.* New York: Guilford Press.

Bugental, J.F.T. (1978) *Psychotherapy and Process: The Fundamentals of an Existential-Humanistic Approach.* Blacklick, OH: McGraw Hill.

Burke, C. (2010) "Mindfulness-based approaches with children and adolescents: A preliminary review of current research in an emergent field." *Journal of Child and Family Studies 19*, 2, 133–144.

Carson, J.W., Carson, K.M., Gil, K.M., and Baucom, D.H. (2004) "Mindfulness-based relationship enhancement." *Behavior Therapy 35*, 471–494.

Center for Mindfulness in Medicine, Health Care, and Society (2013) University of Massachusetts Medical Center. Available at www.umassed.edu/content.aspx?id=42426, retrieved March 5, 2013.

Chiesa, A. and Serretti, A. (2009) "Mindfulness-Based Stress Reduction for stress management in healthy people: A review and meta-analysis." *The Journal of Alternative and Complementary Medicine 15*, 5, 593–600.

Chiesa, A. and Serretti, A. (2011) "Mindfulness-based interventions for chronic pain: A systematic review of evidence." *The Journal of Alternative and Complementary Medicine 17*, 1, 83–93.

Chodron, P. (2013) *How to Meditate: A Practical Guide to Making Friends with Your Mind.* Boulder, CO: Sounds True, Inc.

Cooper, D.A., Rabbi (2000) *The Handbook of Jewish Meditation Practices: A Guide for Enriching the Sabbath and Other Days of Your Life.* Woodstock, VT: Jewish Lights Publishing.

Csikszentmihalyi, M. (1990) *Flow: The Psychology of Optimal Experience.* New York: Harper Perennial Publishers.

Dimeff, L. and Koerner, K. (2007) *Dialectical Behavior Therapy in Clinical Practice: Applications Across Disorders.* New York: Guilford Press.

Dryden, W. and Still, A. (2006) "Historical aspects of mindfulness and self-acceptance in psychotherapy." *Journal of Rational-Emotive and Cognitive-Behavioural Therapy 24*, 1, 3–28.

Fjorback, L.O., Arendt, M., Ornbol, E., Fink, P., and Walach, H. (2011) "Mindfulness-Based Stress Reduction and Mindfulness-Based Cognitive Therapy: A systematic review of randomized controlled trials." *Acta Psychiatrica Scandinavica 124*, 2, 102–119.

Freud, S. (1912) "Recommendations to Physicians Practicing Psychoanalysis." In *The Standard Edition of the Complete Psychological Works of Sigmund Freud, Vol. XII (1911–1913): The Case of Schreber, Papers on Technique and Other Works.* (Translated by J. Strachey.)

Friedman, L. (2013) *The Lives of Erich Fromm: Love's Prophet.* New York, NY: Columbia University Press.

Friedman, N. (1987) *You Cannot Stay on the Summit Forever: Talks and Stories from the Opening the Heart Workshop.* Ashby, MA: Spring Hill Press.

Fromm, E., Suzuki, D.T. and De Martino, R. (1970) *Zen Buddhism and Psychoanalysis.* New York: Harper and Row Publishing.

Goldstein, J. (1993) *Insight Meditation: The Practice of Freedom.* Boston, MA: Shambhala Publications.

Goldstein, J. (2007) *A Heart Fill of Peace.* Somerville, MA: Wisdom Publications.

Hanh, T.N. (1975, 1976) *The Miracle of Mindfulness: A Manual on Meditation.* Boston, MA: Beacon Press.

Hanh, T.N. (1991) *Peace is Every Step: The Path of Mindfulness in Everyday Life.* New York, NY: Bantam Books.

Hanh, T.N. (2012) *Fear: Essential Wisdom for Getting Through the Storm.* New York: Harper One, Harper Collins Publishers.

Hart, W. (1987) *The Art of Living: Vipassana Meditation As Taught By S.N. Goenka.* New York: Harper Collins.

Hayes, S.C., Strosahl, K., and Wilson, K.G. (1999) *Acceptance and Commitment Therapy.* New York: Guilford Press.

Hussain, D. and Bhushan, B, (2010) "Psychology of meditation and health: Present status and future directions." *International Journal of Psychology and Psychological Theory 10*, 3, 439–451.

Ingram, D.H. (ed.) (1987) *Karen Horney Final Lectures.* New York: W.W. Norton and Company.

Kabat-Zinn, J. (1982) "An outpatient program in behavioural medicine for chronic pain patients based on the practice of mindfulness meditation: Theoretical considerations and preliminary results." *General Hospital Psychiatry 4*, 33–47.

Kabat-Zinn, J. (1990) *Full Catastrophe Living: Using the Wisdom of Your Body and Mind to Face Stress, Pain, and Illness.* New York: Delacorte Press.

Kabat-Zinn, J. (1994) *Wherever You Go, There You Are: Mindfulness Meditation in Everyday Life.* New York: Hyperion.

Kaplan, A. (1995) *Jewish Meditation: A Practical Guide.* New York: Schoken Books.

Kass, J. (1995) "Contributions of Religious Experience to Psychological and Physical Well-Being: Research Evidence and an Explanatory Model." In L. VandeCreek (ed.) *Spiritual Needs and Pastoral Services: Readings in Research.* Decatur, GA: Journal of Pastoral Care Publications.

Kass, J. (2007) "Spiritual maturation: A developmental resource for resilience, well-being, and peace." *Journal of Pedagogy, Pluralism, and Practice 12* (Summer), 56–64.

Kass, J. and Lennox, S. (2005) "Emerging Models of Spiritual Development: A Foundation for Mature, Moral, and Health-Promoting Behavior." In W.R. Miller and H. Delaney (eds) *Judeo-Christian Perspectives on Psychology: Human Nature, Motivation, and Change.* Washington, DC: American Psychological Association.

Keating, Father (2008) "Thomas Keating Centering Prayer Guidelines Introduction." Available at www.youtube.com, accessed February 2, 2013.

Keating, Father (2009) *Intimacy with God: An Introduction to Centering Prayer.* New York: The Crossroad Publishing Company.

Keng, S., Smoski, M.J., and Robins, C. (2011) "Effects of mindfulness on psychological health: A review of empirical studies." *Clinical Psychology Review 31*, 6, 1041–1056.

Kornfield, J. (1993) *A Path with Heart: A Guide Through the Perils and Promises of Spiritual Life.* New York: Bantam Books.

Kornfield, J. (2009) *The Wise Heart: A Guide to the Universal Teachings of Buddhist Psychology.* New York: Bantam Books.

Kornfield, J. (2011) *Bringing Home the Dharma: Awakening Right Where You Are.* Boston, MA: Shambhala Publications.

Kristeller, J., Baer, R., and Quillian-Wolever, R. (2006) "Mindfulness-Based Approaches to Eating Disorders." In R.A. Baer (ed.) *Mindfulness-Based Treatment Approaches: Clinician's Guide to Evidence Base and Applications.* London: Academic Press, Elsevier.

Langer, E.J. (1991) *Mindfulness: Choice and Control in Everyday Life.* London: Harvill.

Langer, E. (2000a) "The construct of mindfulness." *Journal of Social Issues 56*, 1, 1–9.

Langer, E. (2000b) "Mindful learning." *Current Directions in Psychological Science 9*, 6, 220–223.

Linehan, M.M. (1993a) C*ognitive-Behavioral Treatment of Borderline personality disorder.* New York: Guilford Press.

Linehan, M.M. (1993b) *Skills Training Manual for Treating Borderline personality disorder.* New York: Guilford Press.

Mace, C. (2007) "Mindfulness in psychotherapy: An introduction." *Advances in Psychiatric Treatment 13*, 147–154.

May, R. (1994) (First published 1986) *The Discovery of Being: Writings in Existential Psychology.* New York: W.W. Norton and Company.

Merton, T. (1960) *The Wisdom of the Desert: Sayings from the Desert Fathers of the Fourth Century.* Boston, and London: Shambhala.

Merton, T. (1961) *New Seeds of Contemplation.* New York: New Directions Books.

Mirdal, G.M. (2010) "Mevlana Jalal-ad-Din Rumi and Mindfulness." *Journal of Religious Health 51*, 1202–1215 DOI: 10.1007/s10943-010-9430-z, published online November 25, 2010.

Monti, D., Peterson, C., Shakin Kunkel, E., Hauck, W.W., *et al.* (2006) "A randomized, controlled trial of mindfulness-based art therapy (MBAT) for women with cancer." *Psycho-Oncology 15*, 5, 363–373.

Morita, S. (1998) *Morita Therapy and the True Nature of Anxiety-Based Disorders (Shinkeishitsu).* Translated by Akihisa Kondo. Le Vine, P. (ed.) Albany, NY: State University of Albany Press.

Morvay, Z. (1999) "Horney, Zen, and the real self: Theoretical and historical connections." *American Journal of Psychoanalysis 59*, 1, 25–35.

Penningon, M.B. (1982) *Centering Prayer: Renewing an Ancient Christian Prayer Form.* New York: Image Books, Doubleday.

Perls, F. (1992) (First published 1969) *Gestalt Therapy Verbatim.* Gouldsboro, ME: The Gestalt Journal Press.

Rappaport, Z.A. (2013) Personal communication.

Rogers, C. (1951) *Client-Centered Therapy: Its Current Practice, Implications, and Theory.* London: Constable and Robinson Ltd.

Rogers, C. (1961) *On Becoming a Person: A Therapist's View of Psychotherapy.* NewYork: Houghton Mifflin Company.

Roth, J. Rabbi (2009) *Jewish Meditation Practices for Everyday Life: Awakening Your Heart, Connecting with God.* Woodstock, VT: Jewish Lights Publishing.

Salzberg, S. (2011) *Real Happiness: The Power of Meditation.* New York, NY: Workman Publishing Company, Inc.

Schacter-Shalomi, Z. Rabbi (2011) *The Gates of Prayer: Twelve Talks of Davvenology.* Boulder, CO: Albion-Anadalus, Inc.

Schacter-Shalomi, Z. Rabbi (2012) *First Steps to a New Jewish Spirit: Reb Zalmans's Guide to Capturing the Intimacy and Ecstacy in Your Relationship with God.* Woodstock, VT: Jewish Lights Publishing.

Schacter-Shalomi, Z. Rabbi (2013) Personal communication.

Segal, Z., Williams, J.M.G., and Teasdale, J. (2013) *Mindfulness-Based Cognitive Therapy for Depression: A New Approach to Preventing Relapse.* New York: Guilford Press.

Shantananda, S. (2003) *The Splendor of Recognition.* New York: SYDA Foundation.

Shapiro, S.L. (2009) "The integration of mindfulness and psychology." *Journal of Clinical Psychology 65,* 6, 555–560.

Shapiro, S.L. and Carlson, L.E. (2009) *The Arts and Science of Mindfulness: Integrating Mindfulness: into Psychology and the Helping Professions.* Wahington, DC: American Psychological Association.

Shapiro, S.L. and Carlson, L.E. (2009) "How is mindfulness helpful? Mechanisms of action." Washington, DC: American Psychological Association. DOI: 10.1037/11885-007. Available at http://dx.doi.org/10.1037/11885-007, accessed April 30, 2013.

Shennan, C., Payne, S., and Fenlon, C. (2011) "What is the evidence for the use of mindfulness in cancer care? A review." *Psycho-Oncology 20,* 7, 681–697.

Slater, J.P. (2004) *Mindful Jewish Living: Compassionate Practice.* New York: Aviv Press.

Spring Hill (1983) Personal communication.

Symington, S.H. and Symington, M. (2012) "A Christian model of mindfulness: Using mindfulness principles to support psychological well-being, value-based behaviour, and the Christian Spiritual Journey." *Journal of Psychology and Christianity 31,* 1, 71–77.

Teasdale, Z.V., Williams, J.M.G., and Teasdale, J.D. (2013) *Mindfulness-Based Therapy for Depression.* (2nd Edition) New York: Guilford Press.

Tenzin Gyatso, the Dalai Lama (1995) *The World of Tibetan Buddhism: An Overview of Its Philosophy and Practice.* (Translated by Geshe Thupten Jinpa.) Somerville, MA: Wisdom Publications.

Walsh, R. and Vaughn, F. (eds) (1981) *Beyond Ego: Transpersonal Dimensions in Psychology.* Los Angeles, CA: Jeremy P. Tarcher Inc.

Wegela, K.K. (1994) "Contemplative psychotherapy: A path of uncovering brilliant sanity." *Journal of Contemplative Psychotherapy 9,* 27–52.

Wilber, K. (2001) (First published in 1979) *No Boundary: Eastern and Western Approaches to Personal Growth.* Boston, MA: Shambhala Publications.

Yalom, I. (1980) *Existential Psychotherapy.* New York: Basic Books.

PART II

Cultivating Mindful Awareness and Presence through the Expressive Arts

Chapter 2

The Role of Witnessing and Immersion in the Moment of Arts Therapy Experience

Shaun McNiff

Opening to the Present in a New Way

The making of art and then perceiving those expressions with others has always been the basis of what I do within the arts therapies—and I appreciate the invitation to write about this work in relation to contemplative traditions. In this chapter I discuss how my experience with the witnessing consciousness may contribute to advancing mindfulness in the arts therapies.[1]

In my group studio practice, witnessing is a process that occurs primarily through the conscious reflection on what is happening in the present moment. I describe this as witnessing consciousness because it is both a physical act involving the body and senses and a mental state, a form of what we might call mindful perception and concentration.

The guiding philosophy of my work is that the depths of the world are on the surface of our experience, generally unseen and unappreciated. The arts offer an effective way of putting these principles to work in furthering healing through mindful perception. I view the act of witnessing by other group members, therapists, and the self as an integral part of the overall art experience—taking place either after a painting, poem, dance, or other artistic expression is created, or during the process of creative expression.

As I will describe, witnessing requires empathy, compassion, and creative perception—and it is much more than observation in the usual sense. As with meditation, it is an activity that requires practice and discipline. The witnessing of the self in action is arguably an ideal state and something toward which we strive when pursuing both in-depth art and healing experiences.

Formative Processes

I entered the field of the arts therapies serendipitously, with no formal background in psychology, and in retrospect this may have been my greatest asset in researching the process of art and healing in new and empirical ways. I was an aspiring painter and my college training focused on the humanities. I had the opportunity to attend small classes with two authorities on world religions, Buddhism, shamanism, and C.G. Jung—Thomas Berry (1989, 1999) and Ewert Cousins (1971). I gravitated toward

Buddhist and Zen studies largely because the aesthetic appreciation of the present moment had such a profound effect on transforming my own existential angst. This is what I knew about human experience and healing as a young person starting to work in the arts therapies—and even though these principles were then considered marginal within the mental health world, I observed their pragmatic relevance to every aspect of expressive arts therapy.

When beginning graduate studies in the psychology of art, I was fortuitously mentored by Rudolf Arnheim (1904–2007). He reinforced my inclination to become *aware* of the sensory and perceptual aspects of the most immediate actions in the art studio and how they stimulate corresponding effects within our more comprehensive experience. After publishing his classic *Art and Visual Perception* (1954), Arnheim underwent a personal transformation during a 1959 Fulbright residency in Japan. He integrated his background in Gestalt psychology with contemplative practice and haiku writing (Arnheim 1989). I learned how examinations of the past can be helpful in some ways, and limiting in others. Too much focus on previous events can restrict the possibilities of the present and our ability to appreciate and engage what is before us right now.

In the first years of my expressive arts therapy practice, I gravitated toward group psychotherapy and the therapeutic community model as developed by Maxwell Jones (1968) and the present-centered methods of Carl Rogers. In particular, I appreciated the problem-solving ability that happens within the group process if leaders provide support and safety and allow participants to find their way through complex entanglements.

Early Work—Arts in Therapy

When I began using the arts in therapy in 1970, I instinctively focused on how art-making and reflecting on the resulting expressions can be a way of becoming more aware of our experience in the present moment. The approach emerged in response to the needs of chronic adult psychiatric patients who were generally withdrawn, perceptually fragmented, unmotivated, and largely invisible to themselves and others. I observed how valuable it was for everyone involved, including the staff, to concentrate on the immediate process of aesthetic perception.

I encouraged people to contemplate the physical qualities of art objects, to look closely at them and then describe their perceptions. Rather than the usual emphasis—asking people what an artwork "means"—I asked, "What do you see when you look at the picture? What colors and forms attract your attention? Are there details and other qualities that you see for the first time or in a new way?"

I discovered that a systematic approach to the act of looking furthered awareness. These methods were expanded to listening to music and vocal expressions, dance and movement, drama, and poetry. Ultimately, I realized that the same kind of quality attention could be focused on the basic actions of the hand moving while it drew, painted, or constructed objects. We also used video as a reflective tool to further new perceptions of the self and others, as early as the mid-1970s (McNiff and Cook 1975).

As I experimented with these methods, I saw how conscious reflection became a partner and co-participant rather than an inhibiting factor. This way of perceiving increases one's appreciation of visual experience and offers an alternative to the tendency of psychological interpretations to quickly attribute a meaning that essentially replaces the generative presence of an artistic image. Even finished art objects continue moving and changing in relation to the attention we give them. This orientation to flux and the transformation of things through consciousness is close to the worldviews of the contemplative traditions.

A Current View of How Art Heals

When asked how my methods have changed, perhaps matured over the years, I say that they have become increasingly simplified in response to ongoing validation of the process of perceptual witnessing—which I apply to all of the arts and imaginal dialogue (McNiff 1992). In addition, I increasingly appreciate the energetic basis of arts therapy practice and how its ability to further the circulation of creative energy and imagination corresponds to Asia's traditional focus on *chi* as a kinetic healing force that treats and transforms the blocked energy manifested as symptoms.

In *chi* I found an archetypal basis for understanding the healing effects of artistic activities. I consistently experienced how art-making involves an autonomous intelligence that finds its way through the inevitable entanglements, setbacks, and struggles that cannot be separated from a serious commitment to it. I learned to trust this process and how it will always take us where we need to go—if we can stay with it and the challenges it reliably presents (McNiff 1998).

In my experience, art healing is not a "fix" that occurs through some kind of analytic process; a view that misses the basic, energetic mechanics of how problems form in the body–mind. The deeper, more complicated, and persistent difficulties are understood, accepted, and transformed when artistic practices engage these forces and give them a different place in our lives. The discipline involved in this approach entails relaxation, attentiveness, and opening to what is moving through the situation at hand. Within the context of art-making, a more complete immersion in the process through witnessing enhances this energy circulation.

As a therapist and leader, I am concerned with how the overall environment supports and enhances expression though safety, inspiration, and focused attention. The creative process is the healing agent, and my role involves its cultivation and helping others participate as fully as possible. Art heals by transforming difficulties into creative expressions if we can open ourselves to these processes. Witnessing is an integral part of the process where mindful attentiveness to the present moment and the outcomes of actions complement art-making.

Creative Space and the Role of Witnessing

An orientation to the circulation and augmentation of artistic energy has resulted in my concentration on environmental factors and making what I call the creative space (McNiff 2009)—which becomes a primary agent of healing and change. Creative space is determined by the quality of attention we give to one another, the support and safety that encourages experimentation and risk-taking, and the ways in which we genuinely witness the unique and authentic qualities of artistic expressions, without judgment. In keeping with the principles of mindfulness, creative space is transitory and never fixed. It needs to be made anew in each meeting (McNiff in press) and throughout the various phases of each session—like the breath that is continuously lost and regained.

Although the creative space is influenced by an environment's physical features (both the positive and negative qualities of buildings and rooms—light, structural design, aesthetic atmosphere, and so forth), in my view it has much more to do with the effects of the witnessing consciousness. Those of us working in the arts therapies typically operate within limited physical settings, so the ability to transform unlikely situations into creative space through mindfulness is a core element of arts therapy practice (McNiff 2003). As a largely invisible but a distinctly felt presence, creative space is egalitarian and influences everyone involved. It is an atmospheric and nonlinear presence that affects people at various levels of functioning, wherever we happen to be in our lives.

The way that contemplative traditions view change as an accumulation of small acts is also in accord with my longitudinal experience of more than 40 years of sustained arts therapy practice and research. I increasingly realize how the micro-actions of artistic processes as well as the witnessing of them are the most reliable base for enhancing experience and change (McNiff 2011, 2012). Small creative acts, as with Thich Nhat Hanh's *Peace is Every Step* (1992), may spread to other aspects of personal life, and in some situations can stimulate a larger contagion in social experience, as demonstrated by the worldwide expansion of the arts therapy community.

Art Process and Mindful Awareness

My decades of experience with the arts in therapy have given me the confidence, perhaps the audacity, to emphasize the most elemental items of experience as the basis of practice. This concentration on simplicity in no ways avoids the complexity of the individual psyche and its endlessly variable manifestations in art, which is enhanced by working with a variety of media and open methods—in contrast to approaches that exert more influence over content and ways of using materials.

Movement and Expression

In every situation of practice across the broad spectrum of human experience and age groups, I encourage movement as the basis of all expression (McNiff 2009), and this can be likened to concentration on the breath in sitting meditation. I say to participants in my studios, "If you can move, you can paint. Try not to be concerned with pre-existing pictures in your mind. They tend to be difficult, even impossible to represent by the most experienced artists. Concentrate on the unique features of how you move the brush or how the paint moves you—how you respond to its qualities." The same principles apply to dance and other art forms.

As we begin to move in the most elemental ways with art forms, expression emanates. The breath also influences movement with natural pauses and shifts, especially the voice.

Repetition

Repetition is encouraged in every art form as a way of relaxing, letting go, and concentrating on what we are presently doing rather than thinking about what will come next. For example, in painting and drawing, I encourage the repetition of simple marks and gestures that reliably give every person capable of holding a brush and moving the opportunity to make something significant: "Just start moving—and keep at it. Trust the movement to build and shape a composition. It always works if you can sustain the gestures and let them find their way with your assistance. Relax the controls and give more attention to watching what is happening. If you can become fascinated with the most basic movements, they will take on a new purpose and meaning. You need to give them the power to shape the composition and your consciousness. If you become resistant or bored, welcome these emotions as absolutely natural features of the process. Engage them as partners and as signs that you are getting closer to letting go and becoming more immersed in what you are doing."

Embracing the Shadow

What we call the shadow aspects of the psyche—the flip side of our beliefs, the imperfect and unrefined aspects of ourselves that we try not reveal—are also readily available just at or near the surface. I found that the frightening things that happen within our art and our dreams are intimates of our psyches that do not intend harm. They may, however, provoke fear and terror in order to get our attention and stimulate change. These shadow elements are partners and helpers, and we can learn to create with them. We simply need to accept them, pay attention to their expressions, and be more mindful of the roles they play in helping us. In this respect, art deepens and perhaps even expands conventional mindfulness practices through the witnessing consciousness.

Present Moment

The notion that depth and meaning lie somewhere other than the present moment not only prevents discovery but guards against it, keeping us attached to preconceptions and the whole constellation of mental preoccupations that we carry around rather than allowing us to step up to creative action. I encourage people to understand how depth is on the surface. It is in front of us waiting to be appreciated. Deep down is right now, unseen. As the dance therapist Norma Canner used to say to people on the fence, with a warm smile, "Come on, come on; give it a try."

Therapist as Witness

In recent years I have become ever more convinced that the defining quality of the arts in therapy is the presence of a therapist who furthers the process of witnessing by others in both individual and group settings. Contemplative art-making and healing can be practiced by people working alone, as I describe in *Art Heals* (2004), however, therapy involves the presence of another person who helps to establish and hold creative space largely through silent and contemplative witnessing. Of course, arts therapy can be full of talk and fun, and even sassy and confronting, but the truly unique element is the holding of a safe place where another person can express, explore, and understand the depths of the present moment and their relationship to the complex of the psyche—while the therapist bears witness and models this process for individuals and groups.

Therapists in training tend to find it challenging to silently observe basic actions because they are so conditioned to think about the acquisition of psychological techniques, which is sometimes at odds with witnessing. The current language of therapy describes virtually all therapeutic actions as "interventions," a word that denotes intentionally coming between two things, inserting oneself or something into a situation. The term was originally used in counseling, appropriately I believe, in relation to necessary steps taken, sometimes against a person's will, to deal with life-threatening behaviors. This specific meaning is lost and confused when it is applied indiscriminately to just about everything therapists do—not to mention what it says about the current language of the profession.

My approach to relationship in therapy calls for a more subtle course whenever possible. I am not advocating inaction or a complete use of what has been called "non-directive" practice. Of course, I will step into a situation when necessary, suggesting a change of course or mediating in some way. However, my overall goal is to help others by supporting and sometimes guiding the creative process, which like a force of nature does its most transformative work outside the scope of plans. D.W. Winnicott affirmed the importance of people finding their own way through the creative process when describing how he sometimes ruined a therapeutic experience by inserting himself or offering an interpretation (1971, p.51).

In training, I encourage learning how to actively give quality attention. When people commit themselves to this, they are generally taken aback by the emotional impact of being witnessed and observing another. The latter brings us to the depths of existential consciousness, and the former provides the opportunity to engage many shadow aspects of self and past impediments. The dynamics take us to the core of most psychological conditions in need of repair. I have thus made learning how to witness and be witnessed a core element of the work I do with the arts and healing. In addition to the connections to psychotherapy, it goes to the core of aesthetic and contemplative experience.

Studio and Training Applications

Witnessing in All Aspects of the Arts Therapy Experience

In my studio and training sessions, I make rhythmic music to further creative space and relaxation, encouraging people to connect to the movement basis of expression in the body. After a period of art-making, we respond to art objects through movement expression, imaginal dialogue, poetry, vocal improvisation, and performance, with individual partners or the group as a whole acting as witnesses.

Witnessing within my studio sessions is more than looking and watching. It is a disciplined, sensitive, and closely attentive process of observation that is informed by empathy and an overriding concern for the person and the actions being viewed in a physical context. It is an embodied presence that can be compared to the felt sense (Rappaport 2009, pp.28–29; Gendlin 1981). Witnessing is thus active rather than passive. Even when the witness is completely silent and still, it conveys interpersonal energy through support, protection, and an intentional process of infusing the immediate environment with a sense of significance.

In my practice I strive to approach what is happening before me as the most important thing in my life at that particular moment, feeling a sense of responsibility and a desire for quality witnessing. If I am distracted or thinking about something else, the empathy between the person making art and the witness is broken. When the witness is attuned (Kossak 2009) to the expressions and overall presence of the other person, there is a sense of entrainment that involves mind and body.

In my studio groups, everyone becomes involved with the different aspects of the witnessing process—witnessing others, being witnessed by others, and witnessing oneself. Rather than being the only witness, the therapist or group leader models the process. We witness others as they respond to art works in various forms, in performance art, and in the process of making art—a most elemental experience that I have only recently practiced in a systematic way, and one that has the most distinct similarities to contemplative dynamics.

RESPONDING TO IMAGES

In my groups I will often ask people to respond to their paintings or other visual art expressions through movement: "I tend to get a much clearer sense of your relationship to your art object and its expression, when you interpret it through movement rather than words." I ask the person to give a movement interpretation for approximately two minutes. We then hold the last gesture or a comfortable still position for 20–30 seconds, followed by an extended pause for another 10–20 seconds. Then, a person chosen by the artist at the start of the work offers a movement response to the painting following the same sequence of actions. The response is intended as a validation of what the artist just shared, and it imagines the expression further, as C.G. Jung would say, and supports the group experience.

Participants describe how the physical and bodily aspects of moving and witnessing enable things to happen quickly and deeply in a way that they have not found possible with words. They describe how there is a visceral effect that has a more lasting impact and that maintains a vivid place in memory. They affirm the importance of simplicity, a soft hand on the controls and plans, the value and support of clear and reliable structure in relation to the overall process, and the way witnesses validate what they do and the risks they take.

Pause
The pause time is always of great meaning. It gives people an opportunity to remember, reflect, and connect to what just happened—essentially, to be mindful in the present moment. I use these pauses in all phases of my practice, and people are taken aback by how important they become. The refrain "take a pause" has for some become a defining slogan for the work. This simple action is new for most people. We are all busy moving to the next thing in every aspect of our lives, and so the pause tends to offer a distinctly different way of being. Interestingly enough, making the space for pauses tends to further efficient time management. It slows everything down so that important things can emerge and be experienced.

Support of Witness
The presence and support of witnesses is experienced through facial and bodily expressions, but perhaps mostly through the silent feel of the space, reinforced and heightened by discussion after the process. We give timeframes for conscious witnessing—distinct periods with a clear beginning and end—because it is a disciplined process of holding the space for another person's creative exploration. Pauses and concentration on breath further slow down and help to let go of extraneous thoughts, fears, and other impediments to being present.

PERFORMANCE ART

My first formal experiments with the function of the witness happened when I began to incorporate performance art into my studio groups in the late 1970s. We adapted performance as developed in the visual art tradition in the mid-twentieth century whereby the artist's presentation of the body and physical actions is the primary focus of the artistic piece (McNiff 2009). As people performed for 8–12 minutes, the rest of the group watched in silence. At the completion of the piece we pause—and then witnesses offer responses to the performances. I used the term witness, aware of its place in authentic movement (Pallaro 1992), to describe the role of group members. People are invariably surprised at how their time awareness tends to disappear, for both performers and witnesses, especially for the former as they let go and become immersed in what they are doing.

I ask people to express what they experienced and felt during the enactment, in keeping with my earlier methods of articulating visual and perceptual awareness. In addition to verbal statements, witnesses can respond artistically with movement, voice, or poetic statements. They cannot ask performers questions because this interrupts the flow of the witnessing and responding process. After hearing from five to seven people, the performers describe what they experienced. The whole can be described as a discipline of mindful witnessing of the creative process for both audience members and artists, realizing how it is more challenging to do the latter.

As I experimented with performance, it soon became apparent how vital the function of witnessing is in terms of making creative space, channeling energy through attention, supporting performers, and lending a certain sanctity or ritual quality to what is taking place. My appreciation of the role of witnesses culminated when a woman in one of my early groups authoritatively expressed the obvious fact that the role of the witness is active, disciplined, and as important as what the performers do.

WITNESSING ART-MAKING

Participants giving performances repeatedly say that the presence and support of witnesses establishes an environment that enables them to do things that they could not do alone. Even when working with just one other person, they describe how something distinct happens through the partnership. There is a reciprocal energy created from the currents of doing and watching and holding the therapeutic space for another person. Students and participants in my studios made me aware of the primacy of witnessing in the work I was doing, and in turn I began using it in a more conscious way.

In recent years I have expanded the conscious process of witnessing in both my studios and training groups for therapists. In some ways, I backed into the process as a way to get risk-averse visual art therapy students to engage performance and the body. Because some were reluctant to embrace the challenges of open-ended performance art, I asked them to simply make a gesture with a particular visual art material (painting, drawing, molding, dripping, tearing, and folding) and to keep repeating it for a sustained period of time. I then applied the method to the process of one person witnessing another while making art for 6–12-minute frames, depending on the time available.

As always, the most elemental structures liberate expression and the drama of hands moving with paint, cutting and ripping paper, or molding clay become mesmerizing events when witnessed by others. It feels like a combination of drama, ritual, scientific observation, and contemplative prayer.

The reluctant students experienced an epiphany about essential bodily expression and witnessing, no doubt intensified by their initial doubts and resistance. The challenges to participation affirmed my adage "The simpler the deeper." Making the most elemental gestures became an object of fascination. I also appreciated how this shift to witnessing the basic acts of visual art made me more aware of overlooked gestures happening within the present moment. I realize how important it is to practice witnessing others and being witnessed while making art in silence—and how this is an essential element of art therapy that is given so little attention in training, as I will discuss in the following pages. I was impressed by the results and the overwhelmingly positive response to the process of giving attention to perceptual experience, and realized that my most recent explorations with art and healing are returning to the first things that I did as an expressive arts therapist more than 40 years before.

Exploring the Challenges of Practice

Once it became clear that mindful witnessing had great potential in arts therapy practice, we began to explore the intricacies and challenges of the discipline. Although there are no absolute principles relating to comfort and discomfort in the process of witnessing others or being witnessed, most people's fears are activated more by the latter. If this is a pervasive rule, then we need to look much more deeply at the implications for therapeutic practice and how the problem presents an opportunity for engagement.

Where most find it more difficult to be watched than to witness others, many feel uncomfortable at first in witnessing another. Watching at close range is an intimate act that can be very difficult for those unaccustomed to silent presence with another person. We find that the best way of becoming more comfortable with these new roles is to experience both sides of the process. Learning how to be witnessed can help us be more effective witnesses, and vice versa.

Boredom often appears as an obstacle in my groups. We have determined that it relates to an inability to see the significance of another person's gesture. Boredom can be the gate to a more complete and selfless immersion in the process of observation— learning how to see in a deeper way, looking psychologically, as Jung would say, or with a more refined aesthetic sensibility. Rather than attributing responsibility for boredom to the artist being observed, we see it as something to be addressed within ourselves. Anxiety appears in both aspects of the witnessing dynamic. A student described how accepting it helped her become aware of emotions evoked by the most rudimentary aspects of being with another person. She began to practice patience and the giving of closer attention, all of which brought comfort and the realization that her emotions significantly affected what she was able to observe.

When students eager for explanations and information ask how to apply these principles to various clinical situations, I underscore how the applications are infinitely variable in relation to the particulars of a context. I ask that they try to return to what they are doing in the present moment rather than leave it. A student who challenged me on this point said in response, "Something in me clicked when my attention was redirected back to the here and now. I had lost touch with these essential aspects."

An artist in one of my studio sessions was perplexed by the question of "what to do next" with her painting. She asked me if there is a way to ask the painting what it wants her to do. Sensing that she wanted some kind of technical answer from me, I said, "In my experience as a painter all I can do is respond to the particular moment of decision, for better or worse, and know that if I make a mistake it can help guide me."

I supported her desire to have a conversation with her picture, because in my practice imaginal dialogue serves as a form of mindful reflection through both visual perception and poetic speech (McNiff 1992). When she engaged the picture in dialogue, it affirmed how it could not tell her what to do. She had to trust her aesthetic reactions about what was needed and how to proceed.

I observed that through the process of grappling with the question, she was able to access her own answer, or better yet, response. The artist makes instinctive acts in response to a felt sense of quality in a particular situation, in contrast to decisions informed by categorical principles or data originating from a place other than the present moment. Experience and training certainly inform our decisions, but they are always trumped by assessments of the present context.

People asked to make art while being witnessed are often unsure of themselves, fearful, concerned with the views of others, feeling the need to entertain, and so are prone to be preoccupied with thoughts, feelings, and bodily states that potentially interfere with a complete immersion in and surrender to the present moment. This is a fairly common condition and shadow aspect for people in general. The artistic process combined with witnessing helps us become more aware of these conditions and to live more effectively with them. Mindfulness is often most effective when it holds a light to the darkness and places we are reluctant to engage. Partnership with art-making will guarantee that areas of fear, feelings of incompetence, perfectionism, being less capable than others, and harsh inner critics will not be overlooked.

Benefits of Witnessing

In my group studios, participants discuss the effects of witnessing after doing the work with their partners and then with the whole group. They describe unexpected outcomes—how what appeared to be the most ordinary actions became fascinating and new when closely contemplated. They say: "I take these things for granted"; "I never give this kind of attention to another person's actions"; "I resisted at first because I thought it was meaningless and trivial but as I stayed with it, everything changed and a new appreciation presented itself to me."

Many find it distinctly *weird* to silently watch each other. This is perhaps logical, because it is so different from our usual ways of being together. Weird is a feeling that indicates opening to the new. In witnessing others, we practice moving beyond self-consciousness to empathy and feeling the artistic actions of another person as though we are doing them ourselves. As empathy develops into compassion for others and their actions, we can begin to apply it to the process of witnessing ourselves as we act—a mode of consciousness encouraged by classical meditation practice (Franklin 1999).

I encourage people who are hard on themselves but empathetic to others to try to apply the latter consciousness to witnessing their own actions. The acts and gestures of the artist, the materials of expression, the physical context, the sensations in the body and the thoughts in the mind thus become "others" who are treated with support and careful attention. Shifting to this "other" focus in relation to the process of making art and reflecting on creative expression can help us be more compassionate, curious, attuned, accepting, relaxed, imaginative, and open. Inevitably, these states of relaxation and heightened attention further the quality and authenticity of expression. We become more concerned with doing what we are doing as completely and mindfully as we can, and less concerned with judging and relating to things beyond the immediate context.

As I have noted, with our own art or images, we are in many ways captured by preconceptions. Perhaps the process of being a witness in a more holistic way to our personal artistic expressions—seeing them as related to us yet separate and independent entities and establishing empathy with them—can further our ability to make the most familiar things mysterious and new. Witnessing others with compassion and openness can help us learn to do the same to ourselves.

Conclusion

While I am still committed to the classic vein of art healing—as based on the physical process of creating and then interacting with our own work—I am increasingly curious about the extent to which witnessing others can both support the artist's expression and give many therapeutic benefits to the witness. Acting as a witness to the expressions of another not only generates significant bodily, mental, and spiritual effects, but the person making the art can experience satisfaction in providing these resources to others. In this respect, the arts therapy context is profoundly reciprocal with respect to the medicines of giving and receiving.

The physical nature of the work in the presence of others is the basis for these dynamics, and the focus on mutual mindfulness offers something new and different. It engages what happens between people, but also between individual artists and their materials, actions, art objects, and the space within which they work. The context of art healing is thus "in the world" as much as "in the person," and the process of creating and witnessing serves both.

Notes

1   My colleague Pat Buoye Allen (2005) similarly grounds her practice on witnessing in the present moment.

References

Allen, P.B. (2005) *Art Is a Spiritual Path*. Boston, MA: Shambhala Publications.

Arnheim, R. (1954) *Art and Visual Perception: A Psychology of the Creative Eye*. Berkeley and Los Angeles, CA: University of California Press.

Arnheim, R. (1989) *Parables of Sun and Light: Observations on Psychology, the Arts, and the Rest*. Berkeley and Los Angeles, CA: University of California Press.

Berry, T. (1989) *Buddhism*. New York: Columbia University Press.

Berry, T. (1999) *The Great Work: Our Way into the Future*. New York: Random House.

Cousins, E. (1971) *Process Theology: Basic Writings*. New York: Newman Press.

Franklin, M. (1999) "Becoming a student of oneself: Activating the witness in meditation and supervision." *American Journal of Art Therapy 38*, 1, 2–13.

Gendlin, E.T. (1981) *Focusing*. New York: Bantam.

Hanh, T.N. (1992) *Peace is Every Step: The Path of Mindfulness in Everyday Life*. New York: Bantam.

Jones, M. (1968) *Beyond the Therapeutic Community: Social Learning and Social Psychiatry*. New Haven, CT: Yale University Press.

Kossak, M. (2009) "Therapeutic attunement: A transpersonal view of expressive arts therapy." *The Arts in Psychotherapy 36*, 1, 13–18.

McNiff, S. (1992) *Art as Medicine: Creating a Therapy of the Imagination*. Boston, MA: Shambhala Publications.

McNiff, S. (1998) *Trust the Process: An Artist's Guide to Letting Go*. Boston, MA: Shambhala Publications.

McNiff, S. (2003) *Creating with Others: The Practice of Imagination in Art, Life and the Workplace*. Boston, MA: Shambhala Publications.

McNiff, S. (2004) *Art Heals: How Creativity Cures the Soul*. Boston, MA: Shambhala Publications.

McNiff, S. (2009) *Integrating the Arts in Therapy: History, Theory, and Practice.* Springfield, IL: Charles C. Thomas.

McNiff, S. (2011) "From the Studio to the World: How Expressive Arts Therapy can Help Further Social Change." In E. Levine and S.K. Levine (eds) *Art in Action: Expressive Arts and Social Change.* London: Jessica Kingsley Publishers.

McNiff, S. (2012) "Art and Change: A Process of Creative Contagion." In S. Schwartz, V. Marcow Speiser, M. Kossak, and P. Speiser (eds) *Arts and Social Change: The Lesley University Experience in Israel.* Netanya: The Arts Institute Project in Israel Press and the Academic College of Social Sciences and Arts Press.

McNiff, S. (in press) "Creative Space in Organizational Learning and Leadership: 21st century Shapeshifting." In P. Meusburger, A. Berthoin Antal and E. Wunder (eds) *Organizational Learning, Knowledge and Space, Volume 6 of the series, Knowledge and Space.* Heidelberg and New York: Springer.

McNiff, S. and Cook, C. (1975) "Video art therapy." *Art Psychotherapy 2*, 1, 55–63.

Pallaro, P. (ed.) (1992) *Authentic movement: Essays by Mary Starks Whitehouse, Janet Adler and Joan Chodorow.* London: Jessica Kingsley Publishers.

Rappaport, L. (2009) *Focusing-Oriented Art Therapy: Accessing the Body's Wisdom and Creative Intelligence.* London: Jessica Kingsley Publishers.

Winnicott, D.W. (1971) *Playing and Reality.* New York: Routledge.

Chapter 3

Intention and Witness

Tools for Mindfulness in Art and Writing

Pat B. Allen

This chapter introduces the Open Studio Process (OSP)—a studio-based art and writing method of inquiry that uses *intention* and *witnessing* as fundamental mindfulness tools. This way of working grew out of the author's personal art practice (Allen 1995) and was refined and further developed in collaboration with others at the Open Studio Project, a community studio founded in 1995 in Chicago, Illinois by the author along with Dayna Block and Deborah Gadiel. The Open Studio Project served initially as a practice and research site and subsequently has developed into a non-profit community studio offering opportunities to individuals and groups of all ages to engage in art-making and writing. At the present site in Evanston, Illinois, the Open Studio Project maintains a gallery as well as a studio where programs take place. A training program is offered for individuals who wish to become OSP facilitators (see www.openstudioproject.org).

Background of Creation of the Open Studio Process

As a college student fleeing a Catholic girlhood, I was a failure at meditation. I tried my best at the Zen Center in Cambridge, MA, but sitting meditation only intensified the pressure against the walls I had built around my heart to separate me from the wounds of early loss, not that I would have had words for this at that time. I felt completely alien to the robed figures gliding by in apparent peaceful self-possession. Staying very busy had worked to keep the chaos at bay so far in my life. The cushion seemed a flimsy bulwark to my own anxious mind and the calm austerity of the zendo did not feel like a safe space. Neither did art school, where I spent most of my time, seem safe. There were so many possibilities in the early 1970s when the classical art curriculum had been overthrown in favor of each person doing his or her own thing. What was missing was any guidance toward a discipline or practice to create a safe container for what terrors might emerge in the freedom of artistic experimentation that had become the norm.

Eventually I discovered Carl Jung's analytic psychology, especially his technique of active imagination (Jung and Chodorow 1997). I took heart from the often strange images that had appeared to Jung and I learned to befriend my inner turmoil via images, see its origins, and watch it gradually subside and transform as I came to understand the stories I was living or trying to escape. By focusing on stillness, breathing, awareness of bodily sensation, and then inviting the felt sense (Gendlin 1978) to take form in an image created on the page, I was able to devise a practice that integrated my creative drive with my search for meaning and self-understanding. Art-making originating in the acceptance and exploration of sensations as they arise in the body constitutes an essential mindfulness practice that also granted me a sense of safety and autonomy that I had not often felt before. The continuing presence of the images served to confirm my awareness of what I had discovered and allowed me to recover a sense of mindful connection to my deepest self and to share that with others.

In 1995, after more than 20 years of practice and teaching as an artist and art therapist, I began a dialogue with two former students, Dayna Block and Deborah Gadiel, about a new way of working that became the Open Studio Project. We created a space dedicated to art as inquiry and set about to understand how to provide access to the creative process to others while remaining actively engaged as artists ourselves alongside those we served. Through empirical practice and study we created ways of working that allowed for a balance between safety and challenge, freedom and discipline. The method that emerged is known as the Open Studio Process and has been successfully taught to hundreds of people as an art and writing practice with deep roots in the traditions of mindfulness.

Theoretical Framework

The Nature of the Open Studio Process

The Open Studio Process is a spiritual technology with two core elements—*intention* and *witness*—which contribute mindfulness to the art experience (Allen 2005). While many use the OSP as a personal practice, it is most often introduced as a six-week program that provides drawing, painting, and a simple sculpture technique using aluminum foil and masking tape (Seiden 2001). A review of all images and writings done over the six-week period takes place in the final session of the series. Similar to the practice of yoga and other forms of mindfulness meditation, the OSP six-session format is often partaken in an ongoing fashion by participants, some coming weekly for many years. The OSP is also offered in workshop settings and in university curricula.

Ideally the OSP is offered in a studio setting where materials are visible and accessible to participants. A sense of sacred space is accomplished through the mindful use of music, careful attention to a calm and respectful atmosphere, and the use of sound cues such as chimes, bells, and singing bowls to mark the different segments of the process and provide non-verbal time checks for participants. Each one-and-a-half-hour session is predictably divided into segments: a short time to enter the process through attaining stillness and creating a personal intention, followed by art-making, and sharing through witness writing and reading. An experienced facilitator ensures that this clear format provides the necessary safety that allows each participant, including the facilitator, to enter the creative process as deeply as he or she is able in the moment. The structure in its simplicity, much as a meditation space, can hold individuals of differing needs and capacities, as it simultaneously provides both a shared experience and a deeply individual experience.

Before making a single mark, an *intention* is created by the artist to guide her work. The facilitator invites those present to begin by first becoming still, allowing distracting thoughts to quiet. One may focus on the breath, meditate, or free write until an intention takes shape. The intention is written in a journal in simple, clear language defining, requesting, and also setting the boundaries of the art experience one seeks. Beginners may make an intention such as "I enjoy making art" or "I relax and get in touch with myself." More experienced practitioners may ask for guidance around a personal issue or life circumstance. The facilitator, who is responsible for holding the space, makes both a personal intention as well as an intention for the work as a facilitator. A facilitator's intention may be something like: "I hold the space with ease and integrity to ensure the optimal experience for all present." Over time intentions grow out of the relationship each artist has with their images. Intention is a way to ground and settle and prepare to receive the image, which is the medium through which we communicate with the deep knowing that resides within us. Once we begin to make art, we set the intention aside.

In a typical six-week session of the OSP, one material is introduced during each of the first three weeks. Subsequently participants choose what they like to use. The facilitator issues only one directive: the suggestion to follow one's pleasure. Typically the shared calm energy in the room carries along the reticent and the unsure who quickly relax into the space and enjoy the experience. We strive to simply notice what comes up and let it go, allowing the image to emerge rather than attempting a predetermined outcome. Returning to the breath and to pleasure are recommended if one gets "stuck." Participants are also invited to look around the room at images that have been made by others or those in progress in the moment for inspiration. This practice of *referencing*—quoting or appropriating elements from other sources—is permissioned and defined as something all artists do. The facilitator functions as a role model and co-participant, in addition to keeping track of the music, timing, and flow of the session, engaging fully in the creative process as well.

After a period of engagement with materials, a time frame set either by the individual if working alone or by the facilitator in a group session, an image emerges. The next step in the Open Studio Process is the practice of *witness*: the state of being present to our images in compassion, without voicing judgments. The facilitator announces that the time for making art is drawing to a close and suggests that each participant come to a comfortable stopping place, tacitly acknowledging that the image may not be "finished." Like intention, witness requires stillness to create space for the image to speak to us and reveal its message. The witness segment of the process begins with a return to the moment, to self-awareness, to our body, to the chair in which we sit, to the particular image before us, all aspects that often seem to dissolve during art-making as we follow the pleasure of using materials and enter the flow that is the creative process. The facilitator says: "Return to your breath and to awareness of this time and space. Just notice what you see and experience as you regard your image. Pay attention to any feelings, thoughts, judgments, or stories and any other sensations or perceptions that arise, for example: 'I'm hungry,' 'It's too hot in here,' 'I don't feel like writing.'"

Writing comes next. In the same journal one writes down whatever comes up. Here judgments are welcome, along with any other perceptions of the space or materials, any reactions, any stories, and finally re-reading the intention and considering it in relation to the image. Sometimes a dialogue ensues with the image; that too is written down. The writing period is gently called to a close by the facilitator. In a group session each person is then invited, but not required, to read aloud both the intention and the witness.

Another important element of the Open Studio Process comes into play here: *No comment*—the one inviolate rule of the OSP. One may read all or part of one's writings but no other comments or explanations are spoken, no questions are asked. Those listening, if in a group session, also refrain from making any comments. Once each person who wishes to has read, the formal part of the session is finished. The facilitator rings a chime or bell to signal the close and invites all present to allow anything they heard or felt to sink into consciousness as they absorb the sound. Now a few minutes of general discussion, observations, questions about the process, comments about the experience are welcome. The facilitator gently enforces the *No comment* rule if a participant begins to talk directly about an image. This rule and other important aspects of the Open Studio Process will be explained in the example of using the OSP with a group of adolescents included in this chapter.

Open Studio Process and its Relationship to Mindfulness

INTENTION AND MINDFULNESS

Since the 1980s mindfulness research has been conducted in numerous empirical studies particularly in the area of stress reduction (Kabat-Zinn *et al.* 1992), oncology (Massion *et al.* 1995; Saxe *et al.* 2001), and chronic pain (Kabat-Zinn, Lipworth, and Bumey 1985; Kabat-Zinn, *et al.* 1986). Jon Kabat-Zinn (1982; Kabat-Zin, *et al.* 1992) among others, through the development of Mindfulness-Based Stress Reduction (MBSR), and consequent research on MBSR as a complementary medicine, is responsible for making mindfulness meditation known in the mainstream. It is now available to vast numbers of people who might never come into contact with it through spiritual seeking. More recently research that examines the mechanisms of mindfulness by defining its constituent parts have moved away from attempts to prove efficacy and instead focused on the question of defining central constructs. Shapiro *et al.* (2006) have identified several characteristics of mindfulness that are constituent parts as well of the Open Studio Process. They identify three characteristic mechanisms of mindfulness meditation—intention, attention, and attitude. These authors note that intention is a critical part of mindfulness meditation that was culled from the practice to make it more neutral in Western medical arenas. There is always an implicit intention in Buddhist meditation practice, such as enlightenment or compassion for all beings. Without this larger intention, meditation can serve the function of self-regulation, as breathing mindfully will reduce anxiety and agitation, but the practice may never reveal its full potential for transcendence and transformation. Shapiro's study in 1992 (cited by Shapiro *et al.* 2006) found "as meditators continue to practice, their intentions shift along a continuum from self-regulation to self-exploration, and finally to self-liberation" (p.376).

Similarly, our experience with the Open Studio Process has taught us that the intention is a co-evolving function along with our consciousness. Intention is a statement of *why* we are practicing, what we are aiming for. Over time we become more aware of our internal contradictions. Intention cannot manifest if it is in conflict with underlying unconscious beliefs. Therefore, one must follow the thread of intention that seems not to manifest to gain awareness and allow self-limiting beliefs to shift and change. This is accomplished through the review of one's intention during the witness part of each session of the OSP as well as in the final review occurring at the end of each six-week session. We learned that intention is an exquisitely calibrated tool that requires clarity, discernment and especially mindfulness as we learn what it is we really seek. Each individual is responsible for their own deepening awareness. Neither the facilitator nor other participants point out perceived contradictions in one another's witness writings. This is a critical difference between Open Studio Process and psychotherapy. Our role for each other is predicated on compassion and acceptance, trusting that change is an ever-present reality evolving at a pace and depth appropriate for each participant. If we feel reactive to another, that is information to invite into our own practice, gratefully accepted as a possible mirror of our own issues, reflecting a basic mindfulness tenet.

WITNESS AND MINDFULNESS

Witness, in the context of mindfulness, refers to paying attention to the contents of one's own mind and one's art. We pay attention as well to our relationship to others and their creative expressions letting go of the need to alter or explain that which we witness.

Witness writing is an element of the Open Studio Process in which participants are invited to simply notice and record their experience inclusively, without editing or explaining. It is not necessary for others to understand what we write. Often the words come in highly poetic forms, almost a sort of personal code that speaks to all present on a sub-cognitive level. Witness writing is the means by which we traverse the liminal space between the experience of merger with images and materials that occur in art-making and the re-emergence and integration of the experience into the flow of our lives. Art-making takes us into the place of all possibilities but eventually a particular image shows up; now we must get to know it, engage in dialogue, discern its meaning to us. Heart, head, and hand all converge in witness writing as the means of this engagement.

Witness consciousness, which is something larger than our individual energy, occurs when a group works together in the Open Studio Process. Our mutual sitting, being present with an attitude of non-judgment, paying attention without comment creates a spaciousness that allows the speaker to hear their own words as coming from a deep self without interference. We learn that each of us holds only a facet of the truth and we are all required for a larger knowing. *Witnessing* is a key element in creating a collective space that is safe and allows multiple truths to unfold—being held without a push toward consistency or uniformity.

The practice of listening without speaking, of noticing our own internal responses to others but taking them as our own medicine (McNiff 1992) rather than sharing them, deepens our mindfulness. As we practice *compassionate disinterest* in witnessing what we hear, we are actually the manifestation of divine acceptance in that moment. We are the calm awareness of body, mind, and spirit that breathes in and breathes out, that point to which the traditional meditation practitioners return to over and over again in their practice. We pay attention to ourselves and to each other, to the space and to the images, without desire, without expectation. Shapiro *et al.* (2006) say:

> In the context of mindfulness practice, paying attention involves observing the operations of one's moment-to-moment, internal and external experience. This is what Husserl refers to as a "return to things themselves," that is, suspending all the ways of interpreting experience and attending to experience itself, as it presents itself in the here and now. In this way, one learns to attend to the contents of consciousness, moment by moment. Attention has been suggested in the field of psychology as critical to the healing process. (p.376)

The notebook in which participants write becomes a record of a personal wisdom journey that can be returned to again and again. For some participants, such as the adolescents described in the following example, the collaging of the cover of a notebook can be substituted for drawing as the first task of the OSP six-week series and serves as both an introduction to the process and a way to set an intention for the entire course. Choosing magazine images can be a benign way to begin the art-making journey and a way of "making special" (Dissanayake 1992) and setting apart an ordinary object associated with school for a special experience and preparing it to hold much more than class notes.

Clinical Application

Open Studio Process with Adolescent Boys

Gunaratana (2011) makes the following suggestion:

> We should consider the person who shows us our shortcomings as one who excavates a hidden treasure of which we were unaware, since it is by knowing the existence of our deficiencies that we can improve ourselves. (p.42)

After working for a number of years primarily in a community studio setting where participants were self-selecting adults eager for an experience of heightened self-awareness and delighted to be engaged in art-making, as well as teaching university students interested in art therapy and creativity, I was asked to provide a program for adolescents who had been expelled from our local public school. The students would receive academic credit for participation toward their graduation from high school. Would the OSP translate to this group under these circumstances? Would the students be willing to work within the structure of the OSP? Did teenagers care about being mindful? A critical element of the efficacy of the Open Studio Process is that participation cannot be coerced and that the intention must be genuine.

I explained to the students that this class would be somewhat different from what they were used to. They would have complete freedom to create images that pleased them. They would learn only what they chose to learn. The only caveat was that they must write an intention that was true for them in the moment—not one written to please me or any other imagined authority. They must write an intention and later a witness but they need not read it aloud and if they did not, I would not read it either. They must refrain from making any comments aloud about their own images, as well as the images created by others. I would participate alongside them. The studio was a far more interesting space than the suite of drab offices the school had rented to house the alternative school program so the students were game to try it out.

Early intentions predictably included wording such as "I get through this so I can leave and get high," or "I do what I have to do to get my credit." Images included gang symbols, words from rap songs and crudely rendered male and female sex organs. I had no trouble maintaining my compassionate disinterest in what the boys produced since they did follow the simple rules.

We simply followed the process. I read my intention and witness writing aloud and made no comments on words or images created by the students in the studio. Some students read their witness; some did not. All art was kept in a flat file along with witness notebooks. It quickly became clear to them that I would indeed follow the rules as described and wasn't shocked or disapproving of what was created. My interest was as a fellow artist. If asked, I provided tools and materials to accomplish what the student sought to express but did not suggest or interfere with the content. Interestingly, the dictionary became a well-used tool as students sought to find the right word and correct spelling for their witness writing, although correct spelling was not a requirement.

As part of the process, music was usually played on CDs in the studio as a way to add to the relaxed ambience. Since it was my studio, I was the arbiter of musical choice. My music of choice for the OSP is usually some variation of wordless world music with percussion that provides a light entrainment for most Western adults and interrupts the thinking mind and adds to the sense of relaxation. As the students felt more comfortable, they began to complain about the "lame" music I played. Typically, participants are encouraged to simply take any element of the experience, positive or negative, into their witness writing. This practice of witnessing allows for the experience of noticing and following one's mind in a low-stakes form of discomfort, noticing what happens when one is simply mindful, without requiring or receiving immediate attention or relief. I modeled this behavior by including at times in my witness writing expressions of my frustration or displeasure; for example, with the clanging sound of the air conditioning unit that threatened to drown out the music at times.

However, with these teenagers, I saw an additional opportunity. I offered them the option of volunteering to choose the music each week, bringing music of their own to play during the art-making time. The following week Kevin brought several CDs and took charge of the music. The first one he played was a rap song full of misogynistic images and language. As I listened to lyrics that I found vile, insulting, and disturbing, I stood before a large piece of watercolor paper affixed to the wall. I chose red and black paint and began to make marks on the page (Figure 3.1).

I noticed my thoughts: "What was I thinking? This is my studio, my sanctuary, how dare Kevin bring this awful stuff into my space? I don't need to listen to this; I should march over and turn it off right now." I felt anger; I felt betrayed; I felt stupid; what did I expect him to bring, Beethoven?

Still, I kept painting, watching my mind. How quickly I considered exerting my power, how easily I gave up my value of "equal artists" in the studio. The students painted as well. I painted how I felt—sharp forms, red and black overlapping in controlled rage. When the track finished, Kevin changed the CD. Now the lyrics of Tupac Shakur's anthem to his mother, "Dear Mama," poured forth. This beautiful song holds the complexity and impossible opposites of the artist's life—Tupac's acceptance of his reality and his mother's, described as both a "crack fiend and a Black queen." By the end of the first verse I was moved to tears and relieved that our painting papers were hung on the wall and my emotions weren't completely visible.

Figure 3.1: Anger (tempera paint on paper 21" × 26")

We continued to paint. I was being given the opportunity to allow my judgments to arise and fall away as the Open Studio Process demands and was grateful that I had the paint and paper to hold my impulses and to give my feelings form. As the music ended we sat down to our witness writing. I was ready to pour my experience into words. I did not hold back. I wrote how angry I was, how unsure of whether listening to the first song would forever destroy my willingness to have the teens in my studio; why should I put up with this degrading song? I wrote about how I was personally insulted and I was insulted on behalf of all women—didn't these boys have mothers and sisters? And I wrote of how moved I was by Tupac's lyrics, his ability to hold such contradictory feelings, his honest anger, his loss, his disappointment—and his understanding, and finally, his real and abiding love. I wrote about how that ability to hold extreme opposites was the thing I loved about art and that I hoped the boys would learn. I wrote about my gratitude to Kevin and my admiration of the risk he took to bring in this music. Then I read my words out loud to the boys. There was wide-eyed silence when I finished. Peter, another student, said, "You really felt Tupac."

I cannot imagine another format that would have allowed us, a white, middle-aged art therapist and a group of teenage boys, to have shared the space together with all the contradictions of our different realities held simultaneously in deep truthfulness. Painting absorbed and held my emotional distress sufficiently that I could remain present and mindful. I received enough pleasure in mixing and applying the paint to tolerate the discomfort of hearing the first song's lyrics without resorting to exerting my authority to end my discomfort. The colors, movement, and painting process enabled me to express the honest and raw emotion, while silently and mindfully observing my judgments, thoughts, and reactions. My deepest beliefs about the power of creative work were challenged and affirmed.

Of course, I will never know entirely what effect this encounter had on each boy present but the artwork that was made in the studio in subsequent weeks was engaged and often fully formed, honest, and expressive of the boys' reality, as challenging as it was. We had a show of the work at the end of the semester, each art piece accompanied by a selection of witness writings. Parents, teachers, and administrators attended and had their negative interpretation of these students challenged. My painting hung with theirs and we witnessed the complexity of our relationships together. My *intention*, to be fully present in my truth as an artist and a human being while being witness to the same in these boys, was fulfilled. Intention and witness created spaciousness and freedom for the complexity of our shared reality to show up. It also enabled the meagre stories told about teenagers who did not fit the accepted behavioral norms in our community to expand and deepen.

Conclusion

My work with the boys showed me that I could enlarge my tolerance for difference, challenge my capacity for compassion, and fully rely on the creative process to support me. I deeply experienced the truth of these words of Thich Naht Hanh (2004):

> When you are angry, and you suffer, please go back and inspect very deeply the content, the nature of your perceptions. If you are capable of removing the wrong perception, peace and happiness will be restored in you, and you will be able to love the other person again. (p.145)

This method is accessible to anyone—it can be taught to clients as an adjunct to therapy or as an aftercare intervention; it can be used as a form of self-care and self-supervision for therapists; and it can serve as a form of mindful arts practice or inquiry into any subject matter for anyone.

These claims for the Open Studio Process (Allen 2001, 2005) may sound excessive unless we remember that the images that spontaneously emerge in engaged art-making form a bridge between inner and outer, between conscious and unconscious, and between self, others, and the world. When mediated with the additional tools of intention and witness, images arise that enlarge our mindful ability to guide the process and can be enlisted to manage the potential missteps of the therapist. The combination of an action-oriented approach using art and writing combined with close observation of self and others yields a unique mindfulness practice that has many applications.

Long-term meditators who experience the OSP have reported that they understand mindfulness in a much more profound way, having the actions of art and writing to render intention and witness visible as part of their practice. Many of us Westerners need an action-oriented approach to mindfulness that is more compatible with our culturally conditioned way of living. This approach to art and writing aids our balancing of head and heart, body, soul, and spirit by integrating awareness with an active practice that, through images, also leaves traces for us to contemplate as our ability to be mindful grows over time.

References

Allen, P. (1995) *Art is a Way of Knowing.* Boston, MA: Shambhala Publications.
Allen, P. (2001) "Art Making as a Spiritual Path: The Open Studio Process as a Way to Practice Art Therapy." In J. Rubin (ed.) *Approaches to Art Therapy: Theory and Technique* (2nd edition). Philadelphia, PA: Brunner-Routledge.
Allen, P. (2005) *Art is a Spiritual Path.* Boston, MA: Shambhala Publications.
Dissanayake, E. (1992) *Homo Aestheticus.* New York: Free Press.
Gendlin, E. (1978) *Focusing.* New York: Bantam Publications.
Gunaratana, Bhante (2011) *Mindfulness in Plain English.* Somerville, MA: Wisdom Publications.
Hanh, T. N. (2004) *Taming the Tiger Within.* New York: Penguin Publishing.
Jung, C.G. and Chodorow, J. (eds) (1997) *Jung on Active Imagination.* Princeton, NJ: Princeton University Press.
Kabat-Zinn, J. (1982) "An outpatient program in Behavioral Medicine for chronic pain patients on the practice of mindfulness meditation: Theoretical considerations and preliminary results." *General Hospital Psychiatry 4,* 1, 33–47.
Kabat-Zinn, J., Lipworth, L., and Burney, R. (1985) "The clinical use of mindfulness meditation for the self-regulation of chronic pain." *Journal of Behavioral Medicine 8,* 2, 163–190.
Kabat-Zinn, J., Lipworth, L., Burney, R. and Sellers, W (1986) "Four year follow-up of a meditation-based program for the self-regulation of chronic pain: Treatment outcomes and compliance." *Clinical Journal of Pain 2,* 159–173.
Kabat-Zinn, J., Massion, A.O., Kristeller, J., Peterson, L.G., *et al.* (1992) "Effectiveness of a meditation-based stress reduction program in the treatment of anxiety disorders." *American Journal of Psychiatry 149,* 7, 936–943.
Massion, A.O., Teas, J., Hebert, J.R., Wertheimer, M.D., and Kabat-Zinn, J. (1995) "Meditation, melatonin, and breast/prostrate cancer: Hypothesis and preliminary data." *Medical Hypotheses 44,* 39–46.
McNiff, S. (1992) *Art as Medicine.* Boston, MA: Shambhala Publications.

Saxe, G., Hebert, J., Carmody, J., Kabat-Zinn, J., *et al.* (2001) "Can diet, in conjunction with stress reduction, affect the rate of increase in prostate-specific antigen after biochemical recurrence of prostate cancer?" *Journal of Urology 166*, 6, 2202–7.

Seiden, D. (2001) *Mind over Matter: The Uses of Materials in Art, Education, and Therapy.* Chicago, IL: Magnolia Publications.

Shapiro, S., Carlson, L., Astin, J. and Freedman, B. (2006) "Mechanisms of mindfulness." *Journal of Clinical Psychology 62*, 3, 373–386.

PART III

Integrating Mindfulness with the Arts Therapies

Chapter 4

Mindfulness-Based Art Therapy
Applications for Healing with Cancer
Caroline Peterson

Mindfulness-Based Art Therapy (MBAT) integrates art therapy exercises with mindfulness skills training and educational curriculum elements from the Mindfulness-Based Stress Reduction (MBSR) Program developed by Jon Kabat-Zinn at the Stress Reduction Clinic, Center for Mindfulness (CFM), at the University of Massachusetts Medical Center. This chapter includes a brief overview of the development of MBAT, foundational theories that inform MBAT, a description of specific MBAT interventional exercises and an introduction to a recent MBAT program—Walkabout: Looking In, Looking Out, that I developed at the Joan Karnell Cancer Center at Pennsylvania Hospital/Penn Medicine. Walkabout includes integrating the outside environment, photography, and collage to cultivate mindfulness in daily life.

Development of Mindfulness-Based Art Therapy (MBAT)

By the mid-1990s, then an artist with a formal meditation practice, I discovered the work of Jon Kabat-Zinn (1994, 2009) and participated in an MBSR program sponsored by the CFM, later receiving advanced teacher training there. In 1998, I entered the Creative Arts in Therapies program at Hahnemann MCP University (now Drexel University), with the goal of integrating mindfulness into my intended work as an art therapist. As a derivative MBSR program (Kabat-Zinn 2009), I developed MBAT as a focus of clinical research in oncology beginning with my thesis research study (Peterson 2000) through 2010 at Thomas Jefferson University in Philadelphia. The integration of art therapy with the MBSR educational curriculum was an adaptation that created a delineated supportive group therapy (Peterson 2000), and is significant for being among the first interventions derived from the original MBSR program—in addition to Mindfulness-Based Cognitive Therapy (MBCT) (Williams *et al.* 2000) and Mindfulness-Based Eating Awareness Therapy (MB-EAT) (Kristeller and Hallett 1999).

Theoretical Framework

Natural Well-Being: Self-Regulation with Creativity

Mindfulness-based programs are wellness rather than illness focused, oriented to each person's innate capacity for well-being (Antonovsky 1996; Santorelli and Kabat-Zinn 2004). Perspectives that have influenced my thinking about integrating mindfulness with art therapy include John Dewey's (1980, 1934) reflections on the inherent naturalness and necessity of creative action as at the junction of consciousness and self-regulation (p.25), and Carl Rogers' (1954) view of creativity as inclusive of experiential openness, the relational value of feeling tone, and open-hearted playfulness. Rogers' elder colleague Abraham Maslow (1968) considered that creativity was self-actualizing and "seems to be sometimes synonymous with health itself" (p.145).

MBAT with Cancer

The diagnosis and treatment of cancer is associated with both physical and psychological distress (Carlson *et al.* 2004a; Carlson, Waller, and Mitchell 2012). Such distress may be experienced as normal to chronic hyper-arousal which can result in negative bias in attention and memory, behavioral inhibition, negative emotions, hyper-vigilance, and disruptive ruminative thinking (Britton 2005). Targeting stress-related variables is recommended care in cancer (Bultz and Carlson 2006).

MBAT gains strength with its two complementary modalities encouraging the activation of the body's rest and repair system—which is associated with balancing improvements in psycho-physiological self-regulation, increased attention, memory, and decision-making skills, positive emotional states, and improved immune functioning (Britton 2005). Such improvements in physical and mental well-being have been well documented for people with cancer receiving MBSR (Carlson *et al.* 2004b; Hoffman *et al.* 2012; Witek-Janusek, *et al.* 2008) and art therapy (Bar-Sela *et al.* 2007; Geue *et al.* 2010; Nainis *et al.* 2006; Svensk *et al.* 2009; Wood, Molassiotis, and Payne 2011) and with MBAT.

MBAT Research Study Outcomes with People with Cancer

In the MBAT pilot feasibility study, seven women with mixed cancer diagnoses were able to complete the eight-week program and showed clinical relevant improvements (Peterson 2000). As reported in Monti *et al.* (2006), a National Institutes of Health randomized clinical trial of MBAT with cancer patients showed significant reductions in psychological distress and increases in health-related quality of life post intervention for the experimental group. A later analysis of data showed comparable benefits for the control group who crossed over and received the program later in the study course (Peterson *et al.* 2008). Men with prostate cancer received benefit from the MBAT program with statistically significant reductions in psychological distress post intervention (Monti *et al.* 2007).

Clinical Application

MBAT Overview: Integrating Art Therapy Exercises with MBSR

With eight two-and-a-half-hour weekly sessions, the MBAT program follows a similar structure to the MBSR curriculum except that it integrates art therapy exercises as a way to teach and enhance mindfulness and has no additional all-day practice session.

In the spirit of an extended practice period, the seventh MBAT weekly session is retreat-oriented and equally timed for guided mindfulness practice and free art-making (Peterson 2000). In mindfulness practice, attention is brought to the awareness of body sensations, thoughts, and feeling tone. Mindfulness meditation forms in MBAT include awareness of breathing, body scan meditation, sitting meditations, gentle yoga practice, mindful eating, walking meditation, mindful awareness of the art materials, and creative expression as a meditative form. Lovingkindness meditation is a significant practice in mindfulness programs:

> In the coming week may you be safe and protected from harm, happy, peaceful and calm, and as healthy and strong as is possible for you. May you care for yourself with joy and have ease of well-being.

Given my work with people with life-threatening illness, I introduce this lovingkindness meditation earlier than it is taught in the MBSR curriculum. In beginning this way, participants have the experience of receiving these well wishes informally before offering it to themselves later in the program formally using the home practice meditation tape or CD (Peterson 2006). Following the MBSR curriculum (Kabat-Zinn 2009), daily homework is assigned for the use of guided meditation CDs and sequenced structured observational reporting related to mindfulness in daily life using program worksheets (pp.445–449).

MBAT Exercises

I developed the following exercises for the MBAT pilot study with women with cancer (Peterson 2000) and in my post-graduate clinical work on an inpatient addictions unit. They are not exclusive to medical art therapy and may be adapted to other groups and populations.

ORIENTING TO MINDFULNESS

The moment-to-moment processing in mindfulness is composed of intention, attention, and attitude (Shapiro *et al.* 2006, p.374). Themes of kindness and curiosity with program activities are supported with attitudes of non-judging, patience, beginner's mind, trust, non-striving, acceptance, and letting go/letting be (Kabat Zinn 2009, pp.33–40).

OFFERING INSTRUCTIONS

The practice of kindness in mindfulness is exemplified with the use of instructional language that supports participants' opening to possibilities rather than complying with directives automatically. Thus, verb forms are converted to nouns (gerunds) with the addition of -ing; for example, "keeping your effort playful," rather than "keep your effort playful" which may carry a more demanding tone.

SHARING, REFLECTING AND LISTENING

After the art process, participants share their images and engage in reflective dialogue. The reflection helps to deepen awareness within oneself, with others, learning mindfulness and experiencing the benefits of expressive therapy.

ART MATERIALS

These include pencils, colored pencils, marker paper, ink pens or markers, pastel paper, pastels, water-soluble crayons, watercolor pan sets and tempera paint, a range of paper types and sizes, colored construction paper, colored tissue paper, glue sticks, liquid paste, and a selection of brushes. Clay is made available in Session 7. Less abundant art supplies are fine.

Mindful Exploration of Art Materials (MEAM)

This art task, developed for the MBAT pilot study (Peterson 2000, pp.73–74), uses pairings of the wide variety of art media and papers available in the program to practice mindful attention to the awareness of the contact experience with each (Figure 4.1.).

Figure 4.1: Mindful exploration of art materials

MBAT Exercise

Each pair of art materials (newsprint/pencil; drawing paper/colored pencils, etc.) are presented for a three to five-minute exploration beginning with scribbling on paper approximately 4 x 6 inches. Participants are asked to report their awareness of body sensations, the arising of thoughts and the feeling experience of pleasant or unpleasant, verbally or in writing. As I introduce the art materials at a fairly rapid pace in a precise order, most structured (pencil) to least structured medium (watercolor/paint), I also model participation in this task at the table as I direct it.

In facilitating MEAM, the elements of each paired set are explored as objects that touch the sense gateways. Inquiry is the key to learning mindfulness. Examples of fostering mindful attention to awareness through MEAM include:

> Holding the paper, what is the experience of touch? Holding it to the light, what touches the eye? Bringing the pencil to your nose, what are you aware of as smell? Now that you have opened the box of colored pencils, what are you aware of in thoughts or feeling? As you are moving the ink brush color across the marker on the paper, what is the feeling in the body? What is the experience of sound touching the ear as the group works at the art table?

The next instructions I offer follow my intention for participants to open to engaging with the art materials, to support mindful presence and insight through the materials exploration:

> Remembering your hand knows what color to pick. If you haven't experienced pressing down hard or lightly, could you explore that experience, perhaps learning more about what this art material does? What thoughts or feelings are showing up with your picture content? What color(s) have you passed by? Could you invite one of them onto the page? (Peterson 2000; Peterson 2008)

These last questions are important to the MBSR curriculum. What do we turn away from out of preference, habit, or negative association. With this awareness, new possibilities arise—perhaps turning toward the rejected parts of our inner and outer experience.

Reflections

The invitation to scribble may be met with hesitation, sometimes rejected completely. In rejecting scribbling, drawing of known schema emerge as the default mode, generally appearing developmentally to be between seven to nine. In this context, associations to schools are often reported with the first the use of pencil and colored pencils. For some, there appears to be fear of breaking the art medium, as seen in light initial application, so encouragement is offered to explore what happens when you press down or bring more energy in; if a crayon or pencil point breaks, that's OK. Of course, the acceptance of what is experienced as broken is at the heart of this work (Santorelli 1999). The practical and reflective exploration through MEAM provides functional support for participants to learn mindful attention, to explore the art materials, art directives, and get to know the art therapist, while I gain an understanding of each participant as well.

Exploring the Mind/Body Relationship with Meditation

Expressive exercises before and after meditation practice were significant in the development of MBAT (Peterson 2000, p.110). Two-part directives of this type advance skillfulness in observing the mind and body and possible state change with practice (Peterson 2008; Peterson and Monti 2009, pp.180–181).

MBAT Exercise

At a reflective pace, I offer abbreviated instructions from my meditation practice CD, for bringing mindful attention to the body and mind using language along these lines (Peterson 2006):

> *Beginning, bringing attention to the full cycle of your breathing. Now bringing attention to the awareness of your feet on the ground slowly observing your body experience; noticing any sensations, perhaps tingling, pulsation, tension, or tightness, openness, coolness, or warmth; sensing in to any of these or other experiences. Now, bringing attention to the awareness of your head area, noting your mind experience; perhaps busy or slow, closed, open, agitated, calm, tense, or other experiences in your awareness.*

From these noticings, participants choose one of three cut-out circles (4, 5.5 and 7 inches in diameter) to represent the mind and one for the body, and are directed to place the circles on the paper; the size of each, the circle locations on the page, and their nearness or distance reflecting the mind–body relationship in the moment. Each circle may be traced with a color that feels appropriate. Following the MBSR curriculum for this session (Kabat-Zinn 2009), 30 to 45 minutes of guided gentle Hatha Yoga (pp.103–113) and/or body scan meditation (pp.92–93) follows this first exploration. Post meditation practice, the circle selection task and tracing is repeated, overlaid on the same page. I then ask participants, using any of the available art materials, to offer more information about their internal awareness within the circle shapes and if they wish outside the circle shapes (Figure 4.2).

Figure 4.2: Exploration of pre–post change

Reflections

I have noticed that premeditation, the mind and body circles are often at a distance on the page and often relationally off kilter, with one dominant in scale. Post meditation, the mind and body circles are often in contact as vertical or horizontal interlocking circles, or one within the other, the size differential mediated (Peterson 2008).

Bringing Attention to Pain and Care

With the body scan meditation, attention is directed to exploring the direct experience of pain. In MBAT, this is paired with an adaptive use of a well-conceived transformational art therapy task related to working with pain perceptions developed by Mari Marks Fleming and Carol Thayer Cox (1989).

MBAT Exercise

In adapting the Fleming and Cox task instructions (p.172) a body outline is drawn, MBAT participants are directed toward exploring "any physical, emotional or mental pain within the body boundary, using line shape and color" (Figure 4.3a). In both the original and adapted version, participants are then given the opportunity of moving these symbolic expressions of pain outside their body outline into the space of a new page as a next step (Figure 4.3b) and then invited to freely offer care using the art materials (Figure 4.3c):

> Stepping back, looking, with open-heartedness, at these expressions as a constellation, sensing in to your perceptions and awareness, addressing this constellation in any way you like with care using any of the art materials provided. (Peterson 2008)

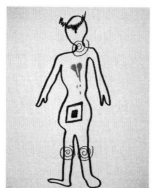 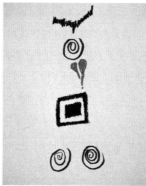 

Figure 4.3: (a) Pain inside body; (b) Pain outside body; (c) Offering care

Reflections

Care strategies from this exercise often express containment, expansion, and flow. Novel imaginary solutions emerge—a blue bird pulls strands from a cancerous tumor to build a nest elsewhere; practical solutions emerge, such as a bed and medicine. Often the symbolic expressions of care in the second picture points to previously unperceived inner resources. I ask participants to write a self-care prescription for themselves based on their final image.

Pleasant and Unpleasant Event Pictures

Key to skills training in mindfulness is the practice of bringing attention to the arising of pleasant or unpleasant feeling tone, or the movement toward or away from internal or external experience (Kabat-Zinn 2009, pp.142–143). These often automatic shifts are explored mindfully in relation to noting body sensations (loosening/constriction), thoughts and feeling tone (want/like/yes; don't want/don't like/no). Homework practice with these observations is assigned using MBSR weekly calendars between sessions (pp.445–449). Mid-program, as attention to these awarenesses becomes more attuned, there is an instructive lecture on the physiology of stress and relaxation (Britton 2005; Kabat-Zinn 2009, pp.235–273) which is enhanced through the image-based perspectives of the participants on the topic (Peterson 2000, pp.110–123).

MBAT Exercise

In this exercise I ask participants, using any of the available art materials, to work from their observational homework on the pleasant and unpleasant events calendars to create an image conveying the feeling of a pleasant and unpleasant event in any order (Figure 4.4a and b).

The resulting group pictures in each category are observed for common lines, shapes, colors, content, and feeling tone. These observations provide graphic representations for lecture content related to the physiology of stress and relaxation (Kabat-Zinn 2009, pp.235–273).

Figure 4.4: (a) Pleasant: resting by waterfall; (b) Unpleasant: broken relationship

Reflections

I reported on trends from this task at my first presentation of MBAT at a CFM research conference in 2004 (Peterson 2004). Unpleasant pictures often describe the feeling tone of a nervous system associated fight–flight arousal. Art includes themes and colors with—sadness, storminess, isolation, deprivation, body-size distortion, airborne expression, repeating marks, agitation, lack of color, red/black, explosions, obstacles, disconnection, minimal or maximal use of page space. Images for pleasant events often typically describe the feeling tone of a nervous system associated rest and repair activation. Images and themes include sunny, ground, green, grass, water, scenic natural world, peacefulness, freedom, flow, evocation of happiness, range of color, connection, people together, balanced use of page space (Peterson and Monti 2009, p.185).

Peterson Mindfulness Meditation Practice Experience

By the second half of the MBSR program, participants are able to say more about their meditation experience. With MBAT, I ask them to do so using images (Figure 4.5); the results support my understanding of participants' thinking about the practice of meditation and how they experience practice directly midway in the program (Peterson 2000, pp.128–129; Peterson and Monti 2009, p.187).

Figure 4.5: Riding the waves of thinking and feeling with an open heart

MBAT Exercise

I offer a selection of black and white copied collage images of persons sitting, including a few in meditative postures, with the following instructions:

Choosing an image that most represents/mirrors you in meditation, the image perhaps that you could agree, feels like me when I'm meditating, feels like my frame of mind when I'm meditating. Next, selecting the largest piece of paper you are comfortable with, gluing this image onto the page as a starting point for representing yourself in meditation. Now, reflecting on your experience of practice, your awareness of what has been showing up related to body sensations, thoughts and feeling tone, exploring these reflections using any of the available art materials.

Reflections

Common images depict people in the comfort of nature; a range of energies— peaceful, rapid; contradictions were expressed—some beautifully balancing steadiness with the flow of events and experience. These explorations foster verbal inquiry around the cultivation of an awakened and accepting presence, with both the arising of ease and discomfort. The art also supported a deeper articulation of the challenges in both practice and life. A number of participants placed their collage image at the top or top corner of the page, adding a second image of themselves, as if they were symbolizing both their experiencing self and observing self in relation to each other. Reflecting now, my sense is that these images may have been quite exquisite representations of integrated learning within the curriculum.

Feeling Vocabulary of the Body

Themes related to the awareness of feeling stuck and the cultivation of openness to possibilities advance learning in the curriculum (Kabat-Zinn 2009, pp.248–273). This exercise broadens participants' understanding of the range of normal human emotions and how the body reacts and responds to feeling experience.

MBAT Exercise

Using a standard feeling vocabulary list (Figure 4.6a), I ask participants to identify two kinds of feeling states (Peterson 2008): the first four to six that may be "habits perhaps that feel sticky for you. Perhaps places that you can end up hanging out in that are discomforting, discouraging, perhaps a pattern related to reactivity to experience." Next, identifying four to six feelings "that you would like to cultivate, emotional states you would like more contact with." After, a large sheet of paper is folded vertically and horizontally to impress a grid of two rows of four to six blocks. Chosen feelings are written at the top of each block (Figure 4.6b). Participants are asked to use line, shape, and color to explore the energetic experience for the identified feelings by making a mark or series of marks which are described as "like a hieroglyphic." To complete this exercise, a second large piece of paper is offered and participants are asked to draw a body boundary where they may locate these feelings hieroglyphics (Figure 4.6c).

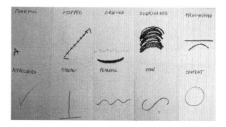

FEELING VOCABULARY LIST				
Warm	Gutsy	Spunky	Defeated	Del
Calm	Suspect	Important	Masculine	Disc
Fearful	Needed	Unneeded	Free	No
Cared For	Protected	Secure	Hopeless	Ligh
Lost	Inadequate	Feminine	Disgusted	Use
Rewarded	Appreciated	Unrewarded	Heard	Jun
Stopped	Cornered	Risky	Anxious	Put
Inferior	Childish	Indifferent	Seen	Gu
Ignored	Unseen	Buoyant	Icy	Co
Safe	Helpless	Useless	Giddy	Wo
Childlike	Sunny	Timid	Loved	Bol
Unnoticed	Overloaded	Humiliated	Withdrawn	Ser
Grieved	Poor Me	Avoided	Relieved	Clc
Refreshed	Strong	Happy	Enduring	Sac
Lonely	Desperate	Powerful	Tough	Co
Pitiful	Bright	Let Down	Babied	Spl
Healthy	Despondent	Close	Stepped On	We
Alone	Calm	Quiet	Left Out	Em
Foolish	Ashamed	Cold	Jittery	Hol
Rejected	Trapped	Dejected	Funny	De
Shy	Gloomy	Vulnerable	Open	Sat
Tender	Joyous	Peaceful	Captivated	Fra
Wounded	Hurt	Martyred	Impish	
Positive	Complete	Fulfilled	Clumsy	
Longing	Heavy	Nervous	Content	
Crushed	Alarmed	Frightened	Unhappy	
Brave	Grounded	Carefree	Whole	
Needy	Frustrated	Afraid	Unwanted	

Figure 4.6: (a) Feeling vocabulary list; (b) Feeling states;
(c) Feeling states in body boundary

Processing begins with the grid sheet's two horizontal rows of sticky and beneficial feeling hieroglyphics and then moves to the feeling experience in the body.

Reflections

In my experience, artistic expressions across the two sets often point to relational inversions—from contracted forms (discomforted, unpleasant, rigid) to forms that open (comforting, pleasant, flowing). These gestural forms often reflect bodily modes or postures and offer possibilities for working physically with sticky emotions. For example, I may ask, "Could you explore this (alternative) posture or form in your body as you are experiencing discomforting feelings?" Insights into the mind–body relationship are often enhanced with mapping this feeling-scape of forms within a body outline.

Healing Place

In the last MBAT session there is a change from the traditional mindfulness curriculum with a guided imagery activity toward a safe place in which to sit with awareness of breathing. This exercise, developed for the MBAT pilot study (Peterson 2000), resulted from a personal interview with Paola Luzzatto at Memorial Sloan Kettering early in 2000, in which she shared an art task *The Hidden Seed*, that she developed for her program (Luzzatto and Gabriel 2000, p.286). Luzzato asks participants to draw a barren place and then show something growing there.

MBAT Exercise

This guided imagery begins with "walking around the corner from your home, only to encounter an unfamiliar barren landscape, a lifeless moonscape without a horizon line." Guidance continues as participants are directed to evoke their mindfulness skills and find their way toward a healing place, "being with the breath, one step at a time, sensing in to available light or air, smell or sound that may be nearby that would be comforting to you." Guidance here focuses on attunement to body-centered awareness and inner experiences of relational safety as a healing pathway. Different from mindfulness training, this guided imagery experiential is intended to support the re-collection of comforting preferences, time of day, season, weather, and landscape, to evoke a personally meaningful symbolic environment in which to rest in with nourishing breaths. I close this experiential with a lovingkindness practice. Participants are invited to explore and further develop any images or sensations that emerged using the art materials of their choice (Figure 4.7) (Peterson and Monti 2009, p.193).

Figure 4.7: Floating in a protected moonlit pool

Reflections

Images that result from this exercise often have natural environments with supports and shelters outside logical construction. For example, a bean field goes right to the beach and a favorite upholstered couch sits at the water's edge as a natural element. Additionally, images may be ethereal or abstract with a sense of figurative movement into an open space, conveyed as a space between—earth and sky, color fields, or within circular forms. This exercise with a focus on safety and healing fittingly ends the eight-week program.

Summary of Standardized MBAT Program

I have noticed that as a result of the standardized MBAT program, the overall arc of observed change in participants' art productions is toward a more illuminated and connected narrative, outside the box of cancer, indicative of a more inclusive identity closer to wholeness. This is affirmed by others working in oncology with art therapy (Reynolds and Prior 2006) and mindfulness (Weitz, Fisher, and Lachman 2012). I still hold this culminating observation with wonder and deep satisfaction, particularly as it mirrors the clinically significant post-intervention improvements evidenced by participants in the MBAT randomized clinical trial (Monti *et al.* 2006; Peterson 2008; Peterson *et al.* 2008).

Walkabout: A New MBAT Intervention

Within cancer distress as with much illness, there is a profound separation from the individual's known world, known freedom, and frequently severed relationship with the natural world. I have noticed consistent images in MBAT, in which healing emerges as remembrance of a connection with a wider world—a more natural world where the sun expressively dawns. To further develop Mindfulness-Based Art Therapy, I sought and received a position at the Joan Karnell Cancer Center at Pennsylvania Hospital/ Penn Medicine that has the most extensive supportive care service in Philadelphia for persons with cancer.

Walkabout: Looking In, Looking Out

Walkabout combines an introduction to formal mindfulness practices with a focus on informal practices, including mindful walking about—outside and away from the hospital/clinical setting—with the use of digital photography to explore mindful attention. Participants are asked to take pictures recording their awareness of what touches the sense gateways, both what they find pleasant and unpleasant. They then choose eight to ten images from each outing to print, which are then used for collage-making. As in mindfulness-based interventions, the attitudinal foundations of mindfulness practice—openness to experience and inquiry born of curiosity—are encouraged. Originally developed for young adults with sarcoma, Walkabout is an eight-session program of two and a half hours in length and is now open to adults in active or post-treatment for cancer and care partners.

Walkabout to Art-Making

The first walkabout is from the front door of the cancer center across the street into historic Washington Square Park, a green space with lawns, magnificent large trees, benches, and seasonal fountain. The park is a historic burial ground for George Washington's revolutionary army, graced with a significant monument in recognition of their valor and sacrifice. In *walking about*, there is a structured framework for being present to unfolding experience—the seeing contact, for example, with the monument to the revolutionary war dead; the felt pull toward the monument's eternal flame; the contact with the image captured on the small camera display.

At the art table, the process of opening to experience in the present moment continues with the now printed photo, further explored, transformed, or altered, joined with other images or art media in collage. Many participants are pulled to the feeling experience of the monument's eternal flame as recognition of human mortality. Kerrey, a middle-aged Walkabout participant, post-chemotherapy and awaiting cancer surgery for metastatic disease to her liver, created a collage titled *Eternal Nourishment* (Figure 4.8).

Kerrey shared:

> I love to cook, so when I saw the flame in the park, I thought about all of the good day-to-day things that fire produces, especially nourishing food as I battle cancer. And I was also struck by the fact that the flame is eternal, living on long after we do, standing as a reminder of those who came before us, and "fought the good fight," whether it was cancer, or war. I also put a muted "sun" in the picture, as a reminder of how many days you don't see the sun when you're sick, yet it is also eternal, whether we see it or not. I felt hopeful when I finished the piece, feeling that, no matter what, life continues. (Peterson 2012)

Figure 4.8: Eternal Nourishment

Kerrey was able to create an interactive image narrative in nine collages that allowed her to be with her cancer experience outside of thinking, and deeply inside her own generative creativity. Common in mindfulness-based expressive therapy (MBET), without direct solicitation, what is difficult or challenging emerges; the possibility of death with cancer is constructed with collage, expressively, symbolically, and with acceptance. Working this way in Walkabout, being human in the larger world outside of cancer, opens participants to a greater freedom to play with the shared relational puzzle of living—that of being both human and mortal.

Conclusion

Mindfulness has become a focus of therapists internationally and MBET is growing naturally with it. The dance between mindfulness practices and expressive therapies is exceptionally promising as a path for healing, fostering the evolution of coping skills born of embodied presence, authentic meaning-making, and intentional action.

Integrating mindfulness into clinical practice requires a deep reservoir of meditation practice marked in hours toward years practicing meditation. The fulfillment of the promise of MBET will not be well advanced if we ask our clients to do, practice mindfulness and create expressively, what we may not do or know from our own deep experience. I offer the Mindfulness-Based Art Therapy approaches I have developed here in the spirit of such an ethical and heartfelt commitment to practice. Thank you and be well.

Acknowledgements

An acknowledging bow of gratitude to my mentors: art therapist Paola Luzzatto (1998; Luzzatto and Gabriel 2000) who integrated mindfulness in her work with cancer patients; Elena Rosenbaum (2007), a senior CFM teacher who used art-making in her own battle with cancer; art therapist and researcher Linda Chapman (Chapman *et al.* 2001) for her inspiring work and intelligent advice; art therapy program directors Karen Clark-Shock and Nancy Gerber, keen thesis advisers. At the CFM, Jon Kabat-Zinn, Melissa Blacker, Florence Meleo-Myer, and Saki Santorelli (1999) whose caring welcome and ongoing encouragement has been an enduring gift in my life and work. At Thomas Jefferson University, gratitude to my MBAT research colleagues, Daniel A. Monti, MD, Principal Investigator and Co-Inverstigators Elisabeth S. Kunkel, MD, and George C. Brainard, Ph.D. And importantly, Michael Bergren who has kept the home fires nourishing.

References

Antonovsky, A. (1996) "The salutogenic model as a theory to guide health promotion." *Health Promotion International 11*, 1, 11–18.

Bar-Sela, G., Atid, L., Danos, S., Gabay, N., and Epelbaum, R. (2007) "Art therapy improved depression and influenced fatigue levels in cancer patients on chemotherapy." *Psycho-Oncology 16*, 11, 980–984.

Britton, W.B. (2005) "The physiology of stress and depression and reversal by meditative techniques." Integrating Mindfulness-Based Interventions into Medicine, Health Care, and Society. Fourth Annual Conference for Clinicians, Researchers and Educators. Worcester, MA: Center for Mindfulness, University of Massachusetts Medical School.

Bultz, B.D. and Carlson, L.E. (2006) "Emotional distress: the sixth vital sign—future directions in cancer care." *Psycho-Oncology 15*, 2, 93–95.

Carlson, L.E., Angen, M., Cullum, J., Goodey, E., *et al.* (2004a) "High levels of untreated distress and fatigue in cancer patients." *British Journal of Cancer 90*, 12, 2297–2304.

Carlson, L.E., Speca, M., Patel, K.D., and Goodey, E. (2004b) "Mindfulness-Based Stress Reduction in relation to quality of life, mood, symptoms of stress and levels of cortisol, dehydroepiandrosterone sulfate (DHEAS) and melatonin in breast and prostate cancer outpatients." *Psychoneuroendocrinology 29*, 4, 448–474.

Carlson, L.E., Waller, A., and Mitchell, A.J. (2012) "Screening for distress and unmet needs in patients with cancer: Review and recommendations." *Journal of Clinical Oncology 30*, 11, 1160–1177.

Chapman, L., Morabito, D., Ladakakos, C., Schreier, H., and Knudson, M. (2001) "The effectiveness of an art therapy intervention in reducing post-traumatic stress disorder (PTSD) symptoms in pediatric trauma patients." *Art Therapy: Journal of the American Art Therapy Association 18*, 2, 100–104.

Dewey, J. (1980, 1934) *Art as Experience.* New York: Minton, Balch and Company.

Fleming, M.M. and Cox, C.T. (1989) "Engaging the Somatic Patient in Healing through Art." In H. Wadeson, J. Durkin, and D. Perach (eds) *Advances in Art Therapy.* New York: John Wiley and Sons.

Geue, K., Goetze, H., Buttstaedt, M., Kleinert, E., Richter, D., and Singer, S. (2010) "An overview of art therapy interventions for cancer patients and the results of research." *Complementary Therapies in Medicine 18*, 3–4, 160–170.

Hoffman, C.J., Ersser, S.J., Hopkinson, J.B., Nicholls, P.G., Harrington, J.E., and Thomas, P.W. (2012) "Effectiveness of Mindfulness-Based Stress Reduction in mood, breast- and endocrine-related quality of life, and well-being in stage 0 to III breast cancer: A randomized, controlled trial." *Journal of Clinical Oncology 30*, 12, 1335–1342.

Kabat-Zinn, J. (1994) *Wherever You Go, There You Are: Mindfulness Meditation in Everyday Life.* New York: Hyperion.

Kabat-Zinn, J. (2009) (First published 1990) *Full Catastrophe Living: Using the Wisdom of Your Body and Mind to Face Stress, Pain and Illness: The Program of the Stress Reduction Clinic at the University of Massachusetts Medical Center.* New York: Delta Trade Paperbacks.

Kristeller, J.L. and Hallett, B. (1999) "Effects of a meditation-based intervention in the treatment of binge eating." *Journal of Health Psychology 4*, 3, 357–363.

Luzzatto, P. (1998) "From psychiatry to psycho-oncology: Personal reflections on the use of art therapy with cancer patients." In M. Pratt and M.J.M. Wood (eds) *Art Therapy in Palliative Care: The Creative Response.* London: Routledge.

Luzzatto, P. and Gabriel, B. (2000) "The creative journey: A model for short-term group art therapy with posttreatment cancer patients." *Art Therapy: Journal of the American Art Therapy Association 17*, 4, 265–269.

Maslow, A. (1968) *Toward a Psychology of Being* (Second edition). Toronto: Van Nostrand.

Monti, D.A., Gomella, L., Peterson, C., and Kunkel, E. (2007) *Preliminary Results from a Novel Psychosocial Intervention for Men with Prostate Cancer.* Orlando, FL: American Society for Clinical Oncology Prostate Cancer Symposium.

Monti, D., Peterson, C., Shakin Kunkel, E., Hauck, W.W., *et al.* (2006) "A randomized, controlled trial of mindfulness-based art Therapy (MBAT) for women with cancer." *Psycho-Oncology 15*, 5, 363–373.

Nainis, N., Paice, J.A., Ratner, J., Wirth, J.H., Lai. J., and Shott, S. (2006) "Relieving symptoms in cancer: Innovative use of art therapy." *Journal of Pain Symptom Management 31*, 2, 162–169.

Peterson, C. (2000) *A National Institutes of Health R-21 Grant Application with Discussion: Mindfulness-Based Art Therapy for Cancer Patients.* Philadelphia, PA: MCP Hahnemann University, School of Health Professions, Department of Mental Health Sciences.

Peterson, C. (2004) "Development, innovations and outcomes: Mindfulness-Based Art Therapy for cancer patients." Worcester, MA: Integrating Mindfulness-Based Interventions into Medicine, Health Care, and Society. Third Annual Conference for Clinicians, Researchers and Educators.

Peterson, C. (2006) Mindfulness-Meditation Practice Recording.

Peterson, C. (2008) "Mindfulness and creativity: Expanding opportunities for learning and self-regulation within the MBSR curriculum." Workshop given at the Sixth Annual Conference for Clinicians,

Researchers and Educators, University of Massachusetts. Integrating Mindfulness-Based Approaches and Interventions into Medicine, Health Care and Society.

Peterson, C. (2012) Personal communication.

Peterson, C. and Monti, D. (2009) *Mindfulness-Based Art Therapy: An Intervention Manual*. Philadelphia, PA: Thomas Jefferson University. Unpublished manuscript.

Peterson, C., Moss, A., Leiby, B., Pequignot, E., and Monti, D.A. (2008) "A whole person perspective on outcomes of a clinical trial of a mindfulness-based intervention for women with cancer." Worcester, MA: Integrating Mindfulness-Based Interventions into Medicine, Health Care, and Society. Sixth Annual Conference for Clinicians, Researchers and Educators, University of Massachusetts.

Reynolds, F. and Prior, S. (2006) "The role of art-making in identity maintenance: Case studies of people living with cancer." *European Journal of Cancer Care 15*, 4, 333–341.

Rogers, C.R. (1954) "Toward a theory of creativity." *ETC: A Review of General Semantics 11*, 4, 350–358.

Rosenbaum, E. (2007) *Here for Now: Living Well with Cancer through Mindfulness*. Hardwick, MA: Satya House Publications.

Santorelli, S.F. (1999) *Heal Thyself: Lessons on Mindfulness in Medicine*. New York: Bell Tower.

Santorelli, S.F. and Kabat-Zinn, J. (2004) *Mindfulness-Based Stress Reduction Professional Training: Mindfulness-Based Stress Reduction Curriculum Guide and Supporting Materials*. Worcester, MA: University of Massachusetts Medical School.

Shapiro, A., Carlson, L., Astin, J., and Freedman, B. (2006) "Mechanisms of mindfulness." *Journal of Consulting Psychology 62*, 3, 373–386.

Svensk, A.-C., Öster, I., Thyme, K.E., Magnusson, E., *et al.* (2009) "Art therapy improves experienced quality of life among women undergoing treatment for breast cancer: A randomized controlled study." *European Journal of Cancer Care 18*, 1, 69–77.

Weitz, M.V., Fisher, K., and Lachman, V.D. (2012) "The journey of women with breast cancer who engage in Mindfulness-Based Stress Reduction." *Holistic Nursing Practice 26*, 1, 22–29.

Williams, J.M., Teasdale, J.D., Segal, Z.V., and Soulsby, J. (2000) "Mindfulness-Based Cognitive Therapy reduces overgeneral autobiographical memory in formerly depressed patients." *Journal of Abnormal Psychology 109*, 1, 150–155.

Witek-Janusek, L., Albuquerque, K., Chroniak, K.R., Chroniak, C., Durazo-Arvizu, R., and Mathews, H.L. (2008) "Effect of a mindfulness based stress reduction on immune function, quality of life, and coping in women newly diagnosed with early stage breast cancer." *Brain Behavior and Immunity 22*, 6, 969–981.

Wood, M.J.M., Molassiotis, A., and Payne, S. (2011) "What research evidence is there for the use of art therapy in the management of symptoms in adults with cancer? A systematic review." *Psycho-Oncology 20*, 2, 135–145.

Chapter 5

Mind-Body Awareness in Art Therapy with Chronic Pain Syndrome

Jürgen Fritsche

The approach, described here, of including mindfulness in art therapy with people experiencing chronic pain syndrome (CPS) is inspired from the practices of Vipassana Meditation. This type of meditation trains the ability to develop and maintain mindfulness toward body sensations, as they accompany feelings, emotions, and mental processes. In Vipassana, as taught by S.N. Goenka (Hart 1991), meditators mindfully observe physical sensations in the body by systematically moving the focus of awareness throughout the whole body, without judgmental reaction to the experience.

I developed this approach for art therapy at a day clinic for CPS in Munich, Germany. A good way to term this approach is Mind-Body Awareness in Art Therapy. The central method includes beginning with a body scan and non-judgmentally observing body sensations, followed by expressing one's experience visually through creative means. The creative product then serves as an object of reflection for the patient as they share their experience with the therapist and the group. Through the experience of Mind-Body Awareness, memories, future ideas, and personal insights may emerge. These can now be integrated into the therapeutic work.

This chapter includes a brief overview of Vipassana Meditation and references to Mindfulness-Based Stress Reduction (MBSR) (Kabat-Zinn 1990) and art therapy. In addition, an overview of the Mind-Body Awareness in Art Therapy process with patients with chronic pain is presented, followed by a case study of a woman with CPS over a 12-week period. As will be seen in this example, the combination of Mind-Body Awareness and creative expression leads the patient to become more subtly aware of the quality and context of her pain experience, to address underlying emotional issues, and to access inner resources that she had not yet been in touch with. As the patient learns to move beyond the limitations of her pain, she gains insight about herself, optimism for the future, and a sense of empowerment in everyday life.

Theoretical Framework

Vipassana Meditation

In Buddhist psychology the Pali term sati means "mindfulness," "(non-conceptual) awareness," or "bare attention" (Henepola Gunaratana 2002, p.140). Sati is a crucial quality in the practice of Vipassana Meditation (Gruber 1999, pp.38–39). Vipassana Meditation is based on the earliest Buddhist canons and is taught in Theravada Buddhism (Gombrich 2006) as part of various traditions (Gruber 1999, pp.15–16). In the West, Vipassana Meditation is often called Insight Meditation (Goldstein 1993; Kornfield and Goldstein 1987).

In Vipassana, as taught by S.N. Goenka (Hart 1991) the meditator develops mindfulness of the present moment—observing body sensations as they arise and pass away. Perceptions, emotions, even thoughts are all accompanied by sensations within the body (*vedana*), to which the (unconscious) mind immediately reacts. Even when the reaction seems to relate to an outer phenomenon (e.g. unpleasant sound) it actually relates to the unpleasant *sensation* that arises at the same time within the body (here: in the moment when the sound is perceived).

What seems like a reaction to "something outside" really becomes apparent as a reaction to body sensations. The mind continuously reacts with attachment, neutrality, or aversion to *vedana* (body sensation)—thus staying in a constant state of unrest. Peace of mind can only be attained when the reactive mode toward *vedana* is recognized and gradually dissolved through the practice of mindful and equanimous observation of *vedana*. The meditator eventually experiences that all phenomena are impersonal (*anata*) and ephemeral (*anicca*)—they do not belong to anybody and they are impermanent. Therefore, clinging or aversion to them cannot lead to satisfaction. The not-understanding of this and maintaining in the reactive mode leads to suffering (*dhukka*) (Goenka and Hart 2000).

Through the practice of Vipassana, the mind becomes increasingly equanimous and conscious of body sensations. This process causes deeper layers of reactive complexes (*sankharas*) to arise and manifest in physical sensations—like pain or pleasant feelings, often accompanied by emotions and thoughts. As these are mindfully and equanimously observed by the meditator, they dissolve naturally. With continued practice, the mind–body complex becomes gradually freed from conditioned patterns of clinging and aversion. The meditator experiences growing insight into inner processes and increased inner balance (Goenka and Hart 2000).

S.N. Goenka instructs the meditator to begin with Anapana Meditation: closing the eyes and observing the feeling of the incoming and outgoing breath as it passes over a small area underneath the nostrils (Hart 1991, pp.72–77). When a certain degree of concentration is established, the meditator enters Vipassana Meditation, now being able to perceive subtler sensations on this focused point of the body, independently from the breath-feeling. The meditator now shifts the sharpened awareness onto the top of the head and starts moving it systematically over and through the whole body. The meditator is asked to observe all sensations that can be felt with moment-to-moment awareness, without reacting to them by clinging or aversion. This is done either part by part, moving awareness through all parts of the body consecutively, or by moving through the whole body in a flow movement (Gruber 1999, pp.45–51).

Chronic Pain, Mind-Body Awareness, and Art Therapy

Recent studies demonstrate that chronic pain is closely linked with socio-psychological and emotional factors (Henningsen 2008, p.279). Chronic pain patients define their suffering at first mostly in terms of the somatic experience (Henningsen 2008, p.280), leaving out any socio-psychological or emotional context. Research from the University of Massachusetts Stress Reduction Clinic demonstrates that mindfulness-based exercises are especially effective for people who suffer from chronic pain (Kabat-Zinn 2011, pp.338–385). In this clinic Jon Kabat-Zinn uses the Body Scan, based on the Vipassana technique of body-observation, along with sitting and walking meditation in his approach to treating patients (Meribert, Michalak, and Heidenreich 2009, pp.141–191). An MBSR study using the Pain Rating Index (PRI) showed a clinically significant decrease in the experience of pain level and an increase of positive emotions as an effect of this program (Kabat-Zinn 2011, p.338).[1]

Art therapy can help to deepen observation of the pain experience and uncover its symbolic aspect (Dannecker 2008, p.288). Chronic pain seems to conceal unveiled messages from suffering or conflict, which in many cases have been suppressed for a very long time. Through the creative act, these messages can finally be expressed and worked with. Most patients with chronic pain report that the suffering from pain significantly decreases while they engage in the creative process of art therapy (Dannecker 2008, pp.288–289).

In sum, chronic pain includes both physical and psychological aspects. In order to address both the approach of Mind-Body Awareness in Art Therapy oscillates between *the physical experience* (awareness of the pain phenomenon) and *creative expression* (with the mental and emotional implications). Although this approach is inspired from meditative practice, the purpose is *not* to teach meditation to patients (Fleischman 1986, pp.13–14).

Mind-Body Awareness in Art Therapy Stages

Seven stages can be described in the Mind-Body Awareness in Art Therapy model— *Examination, Expression, Expansion, Energetic Release, Redirection, Recognition,* and *Relief* (see Box 5.1). These stages are reflected in the case study.

Box 5.1 Stages in Mind-Body Awareness in Art Therapy
  1. *Examination* of the physical experience with mindfulness to body sensations: focus on the problematic/painful area.
  2. *Expression*: transfer into a creative work.
  3. *Expansion*:
     (a) Widening the focus of mindfulness: what else is there?
     (b) Expanding the artwork: allowing more space for the expression.
     (c) Experience of widening inner space.
  4. *Energetic Release*: previously overlooked potential of energy becomes accessible. Physio-emotional blocks can be released—the activity level increases.
  5. *Redirection*: life energy can be directed toward creative and life-enhancing aspects.
  6. *Recognition*: feelings, emotions, memories, situational or biographical factors emerge to the level of consciousness. The emotional/biographical context of the pain experience can be recognized and subsequently be worked with.
  7. *Relief* from limitation by pain-dominance. Optimism, vital power, and self-esteem increase.

Clinical Application

Art Therapy at the Day Clinic for Pain

Art therapy is part of a multidisciplinary approach at the Day Clinic for Pain at the Munich Schwabing Hospital, Munich, Germany.[2] The program includes the collaboration of medical doctors, psychologists, physio-therapists, one Feldenkrais-therapist, one art therapist, nurses, and other clinical disciplines. This approach is based on the understanding that chronic pain is the result of a combination of bio-medical, psycho-emotional and socio-psychological factors and has to be addressed on those various levels (Pöhlmann *et al.* 2009, p.40). The therapeutic objective of working with CPS is to foster the reduction of the subjective pain experience, prevent further chronicity, and to increase quality of life.

ART THERAPY GROUP

The art therapy group consists of five to eight patients who meet once every week during their cycle of treatment, typically between 10 and 12 weeks. The session lasts 90 minutes.

THE ART THERAPY STUDIO

The studio complex consists of three connected rooms. One serves as a main studio for the whole group to work in and to have group discussions. The other rooms are used freely for individual creative activity. The multi-usable space allows maximum freedom in the creative process by offering different possibilities: patients can work on tables, easels, walls, on the floor, and three-dimensionally in the center of the studio.

OVERVIEW OF ART THERAPY SESSIONS

Beginning: Roundtable

Each session starts with a roundtable in which all patients are invited to share their current situation regarding their therapy and personal issues. This takes about 20 or 25 minutes.

Warm-up and Studio Work

The practical work, about 40 minutes, begins with a short warm-up exercise. This can be a Mind-Body Awareness exercise or a thematic impulse I give to initiate the creative activity. One example is "painting music." I put on a piece of "easy listening" instrumental music and invite the patients: "Listen and enjoy the music. Try to let the sound move through you and allow it to flow onto the paper by using paint brushes, sponges, scrapers—or directly applying the paint with your fingers. Be aware of your feelings and flow along with the sound." Soon a connection is made between listening to the music, engaging into the sensory dimension, and feeling an emotional response. This leads directly into the visual expression. The patients experience that being involved in a creative activity can be easy and natural, while the pain becomes less predominant during this activity.

After the warm-up, the patients are usually ready to work on their project for the day. I suggest a subject or give them a motivating clue they may use to keep on working individually. They can now freely experiment with technique and materials and develop personal ideas.

Introducing the Body as a Theme: The Body Image Picture

In one of the first sessions of art therapy with CPS patients, I often invite them to create a body image picture. After paying close attention to how their body feels in a Mind-Body Awareness exercise, I invite them to outline each other's body shape on a large sheet of paper by having a partner draw a line around their body and then filling in their own silhouette with paint and other material. With patients who cannot lie down on the paper or don't feel comfortable doing so, I offer pre-designed body outlines on scrapbook-size paper, which they can alter individually and fill in with watercolor, pastels, pencils, or ink pens (Figure 5.1).

In Figure 5.1, the patient added red within the figure to represent the pain. The second step in the process is to create the space on the outside of the body image. This body image picture serves as a visual manifestation of how patients *feel*—not only how they see themselves. For some it is a helpful "map" to identify the location and quality of perceptions, such as tension, pressure, or pain in their body.

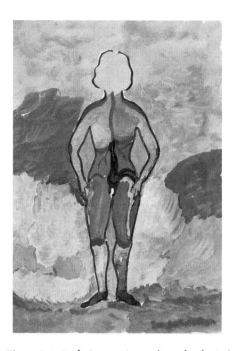

Figure 5.1: Body image picture (scrapbook size)

Sharing

At the end of the session, the artwork is viewed by the whole group with each patient sharing about their experience, problems, and/or insights. These reflections within the group help to realize problematic issues with regard to the pain experience, its meaning and history, as well as ideas for pain management. This part of the therapy session is sometimes quite emotional as patients start to gain personal insights about themselves and to open more intimately toward their fellow patients. Through the collective reflection, supported by the art therapist, patients gradually learn to recognize needs and conflicts and discover their own competence for further healing. The sharing lasts about 20 or 25 minutes. Five or ten minutes are usually reserved for cleaning up and storing the working materials back in place.

Case Study: Linda

Linda is a 63-year-old female patient with musculoskeletal pain syndrome, fibromyalgia, diffuse pain in her hip, lower spine, right arm and shoulder, upper left elbow, and pain of polyarthrotic origin in finger- and toe-joints.

Week 1: Getting Acquainted

Linda complains about severe stress, migraine headaches, and lack of drive in the morning. When I ask her to name an objective for her therapeutic development, she answers: "I want to regain power, stand up in life and become more agile and less tense and blocked in my movements." Linda appears to be a sophisticated lady with a neat and quite elegant appearance. Her posture is upright; her movements and gestures appear somewhat controlled and stiff. She is one of five patients who participate in this art therapy group.

In order to get acquainted I ask the group: "Please introduce yourselves with your first name by painting it on paper using writing, symbols, or just a favorite color, that represents you." The orderly but dynamic writing of her name "Linda" surrounded by flowers carries a decorative style and shows a certain expertise in working with watercolor. Linda tells the group how she chose the short version of her name herself, because the full name reminded her of difficult times in her childhood.

Week 2: Free Choice of Motive and Material
In her first free-style picture, Linda uses watercolor on paper and spontaneously creates a harmonious landscape with a blossoming tree. It seems that in this initial phase Linda chooses the harmonious motive to avoid encountering unpleasant feelings (Dannecker 2008, p.288). She talks about her love of nature and her interest in traveling, which she feels she cannot fully enjoy because of the limitation of the physical pain.

Week 3: Working with the Body Scan: Examination, Expression, Expansion
By now the group feels comfortable in the therapy situation. At this stage I start directing the emphasis on Mind-Body Awareness. I ask the group to sit comfortably on their chairs and resume an upright but relaxed position and—if possible—to close their eyes. I ask them to mindfully perceive their bodies' presence and direct their awareness to the incoming and outgoing breath for about two minutes: "When you observe the breath, as it comes in and as it goes out, some thoughts, feelings, or images might come up. Don´t be bothered by them, just notice them without judgment and then return to feeling the breath, as it comes in and as it goes out." Soon the patients become still and quite concentrated.

After a while, I start leading them into observing the body: "Now direct your attention to the feeling on the surface of your face. What do you feel as you move mindfully over your facial area? Your eyes, your nose, your lips… Now expand your awareness over the entire head, observing all physical sensations that you can feel." I then lead their awareness through their whole body, from the head to the shoulders and arms, through to their hands…neck…back…trunk…the lower area of the trunk where they feel the touching contact with the chair…thighs…knees…lower legs…and the feet where they can feel the contact with the ground.

After a few moments, I invite the group to continue exploring their body this time paying attention to sensations "in the painful areas" with curiosity and a welcoming attitude.[3] After a couple of minutes I invite the group members to slowly return from the experience, open their eyes and to look around to notice the outer world—colors, shapes, persons. The exercise ends with some stretching and gentle movements with the body, standing and shaking the arms and legs. This exercise takes about 10 or 20 minutes.

I hand out postcard-sized papers to the group and ask them: "Please make a spontaneous, quick sketch with watercolor, pencils or crayons to illustrate how the painful area feels." After two or three minutes I ask them to find (one or more) words, to name this experience and to write them down.

Linda designs a fire-like combination of watercolor strokes in red, orange, yellow and black on the sketch paper (Figure 5.2a). With a pencil she writes the words: "burning, drilling, stinging." She appears very interested and satisfied with this experience. As Linda explains the three words, she emphasizes that the sensations are grave and really painful.

Figure 5.2: (a) Burning, Drilling, Stinging I (10.5 x 15 cm);
(b) Burning, Drilling, Stinging II (50 x 70 cm)

After this I ask the group to develop a free creation as a continuation of their postcard sketch, preferably with another material and in a bigger size. Linda keeps painting with watercolors until the end of the session. The image of the "fire" remains, but it unfolds into larger dimensions, with expressive colorful brush-strokes in red, orange, pink, and black (Figure 5.2b).

At the end, Linda speaks with enthusiasm about the painting experience, emphasizing again the intensity and quality of the pain feeling by referring to the fiery colors and the words she has written down. She seems very satisfied to have found a valid expression for her pain experience.

In this session Linda was able to come into direct contact with her body sensations and *examine* the quality of the pain. The pencil words served as a label to pinpoint the experience and narrow it down to naming the somewhat diffuse experience.[4] As Linda came in contact with the actual pain-feeling, the quality of mindfulness served as the source for her creative expression, first reduced and focused in the sketch—and second enriched with imaginary quality in the enlarged picture (*expansion*).

Week 4: Pain Awareness and Surrounding Space/Vital Energy

In the next session, the group is guided through the Body Scan again. After directing their awareness to the pain area for some focused examination, I ask: "Now expand your awareness and look around the painful area. What else is there, around it?" At the end of the body scan, stretching, and gentle movement, I ask the members to create a three-dimensional object representing the painful experience and to create a background symbolizing the area around the pain. Linda assembles wire, deco-paper, screws, wall-pins, and tape to form a sculptural interpretation of the painful area mounted on paper. The result is similar to the image of her earlier watercolor picture but even more intense in its sculptural shape (Figure 5.3a). Linda enjoys this work. For the surrounding space she chooses acrylics to paint shades of blues and greens and later yellow and orange (Figure 5.3b).

 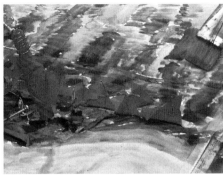

Figure 5.3: (a) 3D-representation of "pain"; (b) Adding surrounding space

Soon the space of the paper is all filled, but Linda is still eager to continue. "The space is not big enough," she explains. I suggest that she enlarge the background by mounting it on a larger piece of paper and continue the painting in all directions. The result is a 70 x 100-centimeter composition of energetic whirls and strokes in shades of bright blue and green, yellow, and orange, incorporating the wire structure expressively (Figure 5.4a). The other patients respond with great acclaim for the outcome.

This session deepened the *focal examination* of the pain experience and added another step of *expansion*. The whole composition gained more *space*. Linda's work shows a rich repertoire of dynamic strokes and intense colors. During this activity Linda was in vivid motion, thoroughly engaged with the painting process. Her movements seemed natural, fluent, and vital. Linda shares her experience: "Making this picture gave me power! Normally I block the pain experience away, but today I didn't." She continues excitedly: "I discovered a center of energy—close to the pain area—that I had never noticed before" (Figure 5.4b).

Figure 5.4: (a) Enlargement of the surrounding space; (b) Center of energy

Week 5: Emotions/Energetic Release

One week later, Linda looks worn out and exhausted. For the first time she really shares personal issues with the group. She talks about painful aspects of her life that have come to her mind in the recent days, among them very painful childhood memories: "I have never really confronted these memories." Later she states: "In that week I felt so much anger and sadness, that I hadn't been able to feel for years." Linda became aware of a pattern of avoiding communicating her feelings to others and taking more care of others' needs than her own.

Today Linda says, "I want to paint on a really big size." Together, we attach an oversize paper (1.5 by 2 meters upright) on the wall in the adjacent room because she wants to work separately from the group. Linda explores various experimental ways to apply color and create texture with paint rollers, scrapers, sponges, and broad paintbrushes (Figure 5.5). During the process, her whole body is in action, as she moves her arms in big strokes, out from the shoulders. Bending her hips and knees up and down, she fills the whole paper in continuous expressive movements. It seems as if her tensions and physical blocks have no relevance.

Figure 5.5: Linda painting

Afterwards, Linda seems relieved and more at ease. Linda shares that she had totally lost the feeling of time and no worries or pain had bothered her during the painting process. She experienced a flow experience as described by Csíkszentmihályi (1990; Rheinberg 2010).

Week 6: Expressing Anger

The next week Linda continues working on oversize paintings (Figure 5.6). The images are abstract, the style experimental, rhythmic and colorful. When she presents her work to the group she shares: "My pictures are actually no pictures. They are just paint on paper." Later she adds: "Working on the big pictures gave me the chance to express a lot of anger." These statements indicate that the act of expression seemed to be more significant to her than an imagery representation.

Figure 5.6: Working on oversize paintings

Week 7: The Oversize Landscape

Today Linda seems noticeably more relaxed—as if a weight has fallen away from her. She tells the group how she had gone through an intense emotional unrest. As I have done the previous two weeks I let Linda decide how she wants to continue with her work. Again she chooses to paint on oversize paper, separately from the group. Her picture shows a wide desert-like landscape with an arid-looking tree and bush in the foreground (Figure 5.7).

Figure 5.7: Oversize landscape

The style has become more quiet and melancholic than the week before. The bush without leaves crouches beside a tree, also leafless. The paint in the central part of the picture is flowing down due to its watery quality. To me the picture has a somewhat sad expression. Linda comments: "I love desert landscapes and wide space." I remember the biographical stories she talked about, having to do with a very rigid education, the missing of love and appreciation in her childhood and complex problems concerning a very important intimate relationship. I wonder whether the two arid plants in the dry landscape reflect this, but decide not to push her to comment any more on it. Linda seems very content.

Week 8: Black and White: The Open Door

The next week, Linda comes in with a surprise: "Since the last session, my tiredness and feeling down in the morning has suddenly disappeared." From now on Linda appears increasingly optimistic. Her physical pain is no longer her main focus in art therapy. Linda resumes her artwork with medium-size papers and returns to the main studio room, where she continues actively working in the group. Today she accepts my suggestion to paint in black and white. After the practical work she remarks how much she liked to use black—a color that she had previously avoided using in her pictures. Her picture reminds the group of an open door. Linda likes this interpretation.

Weeks 9–11: Optimism and Empowerment

The last two weeks (Linda misses one week) Linda continues working with a lot of enthusiasm using the techniques of experimental painting she had developed in the oversize pictures. In general she appears happy and noticeably more optimistic than some weeks before. Her movements and her interaction with others seem much softer, more flexible—less tense. Linda works on recognizing and naming her personal needs and limits as they are expressed in her pictures. She continues including emotional and biographical topics in the group discussions and directs her interest to the future. Linda's last picture shows the image of a shining oriental city somewhere in the south (Figure 5.8). She shares: "I want to just go to a beautiful place and take care of myself."

Figure 5.8: White city

Closure

At the end of the therapy cycle Linda shares: "I profited enormously from art therapy. When I experience pain, I can now balance it out better. I am much more positive! After I encountered all that anger, it felt like a miracle happened. Now I feel more inner space and power. From now on I will care more about myself than carrying responsibility for others."

I remember what Linda said the first day we met: "I want to regain power, stand up in life and become more agile and less tense and blocked in my movements." Linda has approached her goal substantially. Later that year, she decided to spend the following winter in Tunisia, pursuing her vision of the shiny city in the south.

Conclusion

Mind-Body Awareness in Art Therapy helps people with CPS to access their physical symptoms *directly*. When patients examine the felt *reality* of body sensations in the painful area, they can access underlying aspects deeper than through a theoretical reflection about their pain. It seemed that, when Linda expressed her body experience creatively, energy that was previously blocked within the pain resistance started to become free and flowed into her artwork. When this occurs, patients often feel an increase of vitality and joy and the dominance of the pain-suffering diminishes. When Linda expanded her focus of perception around the pain area to see what else was there, she felt the inspiration to expand the dimensions of her artwork as well. At the same time, she started feeling a widening of inner space (Franklin 1999, p.6).

In conjunction with the opening of the creative flow, ambivalent feelings and emotions linked to past memories often emerge as a natural side effect. These issues can furthermore be integrated into the therapeutic work. The pain loses part of its restricting force as the patient learns to accept and manage it better through mindful and creative observation. By strengthening the autonomy-enhancing properties (as can be seen in Linda's independent oversize artworks), patients start feeling more vital and optimistic. Stronger resilience and the increased energy level can catalyze power for everyday life and future perspectives.

Although this application of Mind-Body Awareness in Art Therapy is inspired by the practice of Vipassana Meditation, it is important to note that this refers solely to the aspect of directing mindfulness to body sensations. Vipassana does not encourage the act of expression—as art therapy does. Mindfulness is the common denominator.

Notes

1. A good survey about empiric studies of long-term effects of MBSR (before 2009) is presented by Michalak and Heidenreich (2009, pp.243–251).

2   The Day Clinic for Pain at the Munich Schwabing Hospital can be found on the internet at www. klinikum-muenchen.de/kliniken-zentren/schwabing/fachbereiche-ks/anaesthesiologie-operative-intensivmedizin-schmerztherapie/schmerztagesklinik-schwabing, accessed April 29, 2013.

3   This welcoming attitude is an important characteristic for openness to inner phenomena and creates "a safe inner holding atmosphere" as Laury Rappaport describes with regard to Focusing-Oriented Art Therapy (Rappaport 2009, pp.26–27).

4   In the Mahasi tradition of Vipassana labeling (or noting) serves to add a minimal mental concept to an experience, which is then left behind, followed by the next one (Gruber 1999, p.110).

References

Csíkszentmihályi, M. (1990) *Flow: The Psychology of Optimal Experience*. New York: Harper and Row.

Dannecker, K. (2008) "In tormentis pinxit Kunsttherapie mit Schmerzpatienten." In Ph. Martius, F. von Spreti, and P. Henningsen (eds) *Kunsttherapie bei psychosomatischen Störungen*. München: Elsevier.

Fleischman, P.R. (1986) "The Therapeutic Action of Vipassana." In *Samyutta Nikaya – An Anthology, Part III*. Kandy, Sri Lanka: Buddhist Publication Society.

Franklin, M. (1999) "Becoming a student of oneself: Activating the witness in meditation, art, and supervision." *American Journal of Art Therapy 38*, 1, 2–13.

Goenka, S.N. and Hart, W. (2000) *Discourse Summaries: Talks from a Ten-day Course in* Vipassana *Meditation*. Onalaska, WA: Pariatti Press.

Goldstein, J. (1993) *The Practice of Freedom*. Boston, MA: Shambhala Publications, Inc.

Gombrich, R.F. (2006) *Theravada Buddhism*. London: Routledge.

Gruber, H. (1999) *Kursbuch* Vipassana. Frankfurt: Fischer.

Hart, W. (1991) (First published 1987) *The Art of Living*. Singapore: Vipassana Publications.

Henepola Gunaratana, B. (2002) *Mindfulness in Plain English*. Somerville, MA: Wisdom Publications.

Henningsen, P. (2008) "Schrei, wenn du kannst – Schmerzen." In Ph. Martius, F. von Spreti, and P. Henningsen (eds) *Kunsttherapie bei psychosomatischen Störungen*. München: Elsevier.

Kabat-Zinn, J. (2011) *Gesund durch Meditation*. München: O.W. Barth. (English Edition: Kabat-Zinn, J. (1990) *Full Catastrophe Living*. New York: Delacourtes Press.)

Kornfield, J. and Goldstein, J. (1987) *Seeking the Heart of Wisdom: The Path of Insight Meditation*. Boston, MA: Shambhala Publications, Inc.

Meribert, P., Michalak, J., and Heidenreich, T. (2009) "Achtsamkeitsbasierte Stressreduction – Mindfulness-Based Stress Reduction (MBSR) nach Kabat-Zinn." In J. Michalak and T. Heidenreich (eds) (2009) *Achtsamkeit und Akzeptanz in der Psychotherapie. Ein Handbuch*. Tübingen: DGVT.

Pöhlmann, K., Tonhauser, T., Joraschky, P., and Arnold, B. (2009) "Die Multimodale Schmerztherapie Dachau (MSD). Daten zur Wirksamkeit eines Diagnose-unabhängigen multimodalen Therapieprogramms bei Rückenschmerzen und anderen Schmerzen." *Der Schmerz 23*, 1, 40–46. DOI: 10.1007/s00482-008-0727-8.

Rappaport, L. (2009) *Focusing-Oriented Art Therapy: Accessing the Body's Wisdom and Creative Intelligence*. London: Jessica Kingsley Publishers.

Rheinberg, F. (2010) "Intrinsic Motivation and Flow." In J. Heckhausen and H. Heckhausen (eds) *Motivation and Action*. New York: Cambridge University Press.

Chapter 6

Mindfulness and Dance/Movement Therapy for Treating Trauma

Jennifer Frank Tantia

Present awareness through mindfulness creates a foundation for embodiment, an enlivened sense of oneself in the world. Dance/movement therapy can facilitate the movement from mindfulness to embodiment by helping a client to kinesthetically engage with sensations, images, emotions and memories, leading to improved physical, mental and emotional well-being. However, for clients who have experienced ongoing trauma throughout their lifetime, the body is perceived as unsafe, and requires a more subtle approach to healing.

This chapter explains how mindfulness is used as a pathway toward embodiment, as it is applied in an inter-disciplinary somatic psychotherapy and dance/movement therapy session with a client, "Hanna," who had been sexually assaulted the previous year. That trauma triggered repressed memories of a lifetime of physical and sexual abuse, and the vignette illustrates how I help Hanna safely track her awareness from a dissociative state back into her body. By engaging in mindfulness, Hanna shifts from intellectualization to identification with herself and finally is able to express herself as an enlivened, embodied woman. Using creativity and imagination through images, body awareness and movement, Hanna emerges from a frozen dissociated state to an enlivened place of embodied action.

Theoretical Framework

Somatic Modes of Attention

Somatic Modes of Attention (Csordas 1993) is a theory from anthropology that delineates the ways in which people perceive themselves by differentiating between attention *to* and attention *with* the body. Attention *to* the body, for the purposes of this chapter, will be aligned with mindfulness—a gentle awareness to one's own physical, emotional and/or cognitive experience and a first step toward self-awareness in the present moment. Although this type of attention often appears to originate from outside of the self, it can be a safe place to start for those who have experienced trauma. Attention *with* the body will be expanded upon in this chapter as embodiment, or the spontaneous enlivened response to one's attention to their body, such as a spontaneous exhale, a smile or even a joyous movement.

To the healthy individual, mindfulness and embodiment might at first seem to be inseparable. For instance as you read this sentence, bring attention to your breath. The moment that you do that, it deepens—an enlivened response to the attention that you just gave it. The next thing you might notice is attention to your body's subtle sense of grounding or relaxation from the deeper breathing that just happened. This is a cyclical loop that naturally occurs in healthy individuals, and can be so quick and subtle that it feels as if it happens simultaneously.

However, for clients who have experienced complex trauma (exposure to multiple traumas or prolonged exposure to extreme levels of stress), there is a clear body/ mind split that might best be addressed as it is, prior to attempting an integration. Trauma is felt and held in the body; therefore, to avoid or "block out" feeling any part of the trauma, clients also avoid or "block" their embodied experience. Under these circumstances, even mindfulness applied as *attention to* the body can feel overwhelming and possibly retraumatizing. For work with these clients I suggest that mindfulness does not have to start with attention directly *to* the body, but may begin from outside of the body. In this chapter I introduce how mindfulness may be directed through three sequential *arenas of attention* that precede embodiment for working with traumatized clients: (1) attention to environment; (2) attention to body boundary; and (3) attention to sensation within the body. These three arenas are explored in the case example as they illustrate a gentle path that leads a client's dissociative state toward the integrated experience of embodied awareness.

MINDFULNESS: ATTENTION TO THE BODY

Mindfulness has been found to increase psychological well-being by increasing awareness of one's current experience (Brown and Ryan 2003). In healthy clients, the practice of bringing attention to their present experience usually produces a simultaneous feeling of relief and aliveness that is accompanied by the realization that one can "be" without having to "do" anything. This state of awareness helps one to know that there is a way to respond to experiences without feeling flooded or distanced from them.

Mindfulness has been successfully used to treat patients with psychogenic and dissociative disorders (Baslet and Hill 2011) and integrated into dance/movement therapy practice to treat clients with severe mental illness (Barton 2011), increase resilience in victims of torture (Harris 2007) and increase well-being in clients with medically unexplained symptoms (Payne 2009). Present awareness of thoughts, emotions and sensations can facilitate a client's awareness of what is happening in a current experience without feeling overwhelmed by it.

Mindfulness is also a cornerstone in the practice of somatic psychotherapy (Weiss 2009). When a client has trouble bringing attention within oneself, bringing attention to areas of the room can facilitate the client's sense of safety in the environment (Levine 1997). Once the room feels safe, a client may then begin to become aware of themself in the room. In terms of treating trauma, feeling safe enough to show up in the present moment is the beginning of mindful awareness.

Feeling safe enough to acknowledge oneself in the present moment offers an opportunity to bring attention to one's own body boundary. The body boundary that is created by the skin is the barrier of protection that separates the client's internal world from the external environment. This can be discovered by touching the back of one's own hand, or touching to explore the temperature of one's own face. When working with clients who have had trauma, arriving at this step may take a long time, and only after clients feel comfortable noticing and exploring their boundary should a therapist invite further exploration of the internal experience. Helping clients to explore their internal experience might mean bringing attention to their viscera, such as heartbeat or digestion. Attention to physical sensations such as these may feel less threatening than internal emotional awareness that may feel overwhelming and out of control, so a vacillation between the skin boundary and internal physical experience may be a large piece of the work. Once safety is established in the internal physical awareness, an exploration of connections between internal physical and internal emotional experience might be possible. For instance, "I feel my heart beating quickly, and it's telling me that I am very anxious" is an example of connecting the internal visceral with emotional experience from a mindful perspective.

EMBODIMENT: ATTENTION WITH THE BODY

Embodiment—the enlivened expressive response to awareness of one's present-moment experience—is the cornerstone of dance/movement therapy. Both mirroring and rhythmic variation are two fundamental techniques for cultivating embodiment in dance/movement therapy (Levy 2005; Sandel 1993). By mirroring a client's rhythm, posture and gesture, a dance/movement therapist can cultivate a healing relationship. Mirror neurons are the source of inter-subjective empathy (Gallese 2003) and are activated in movement (Sheets-Johnstone 2011) as applied in dance/movement therapy (Berrol 2006). A dance therapist can vary her rhythm while moving with a client to help identify or even change emotional states. For instance, slowing down a quick rhythm can deepen a client's embodied emotional experience providing potential for insight and change.

Just as mindfulness is not limited to *attention to* the body, embodiment is not limited to *attention with* the body. Although Csordas correlates *attention with* the body to physical exercise and dancing, in dance/movement therapy, *attention with* the body applies a much deeper meaning. From the subtlest movement of the breath to the grand movement of the limbs, *attention with* the body in dance/movement therapy is the active aliveness of feeling one's own presence. More than physical sensation alone, embodiment includes a gestalt of a client's total experience (Anderson 2002). Koch and Fuchs (2011) suggest that the mind does not direct the body, nor does the body act without consciousness, but there is an integrated experience. "The embodied self unifies phenomena of embodied cognition, perception, emotion and action" (p.277). In dance/movement therapy, embodiment is attention *with* the body and expressed through movement that emerges from within—a celebration of the true nature of oneself in the present moment. Embodiment brings mindfulness into a living form of expression.

Clinical Application

Working with Individuals with Dissociative Symptoms in Dance/Movement Therapy

When a new client begins dance/movement therapy sessions with me, I often hear the pressing desire, "I want to get back into my body." Ironically, the clients with the most pervasive traumas are those who want most to get into their bodies, yet simultaneously feel the most unsafe there. In particular, clients who have experienced complex trauma often present with medically unexplained symptoms (Payne 2009). Dissociation is abandonment *from* the body rather than an expression of it. Rothschild (2000) describes dissociation as "the mind's attempt to flee when flight is not possible" (p.66) and it becomes a part of a client's life long after the threat is gone. From a dance/movement therapy perspective, dissociation is a psychosomatic split of the mind from the body.

When treating clients with dissociation, the process of awareness *to* and *with* the body requires a particular approach. Dissociation is a cumulative effect of the "freeze response" that originated during a traumatic event (Rothschild 2000; Scaer 2005) and is characterized by intense rigidity and undetectable breathing within a client's body. The freeze response is often referred to as *frozen torso*—a metaphoric term that describes the physical appearance of simultaneous panic and resignation. Concurrent with a frozen torso, bodily dissociation is also characterized by a client's avoidance of internal experience (Price 2007). A lack of natural movement and disconnection from one's internal states provides a unique challenge for dance/movement therapists that necessitates a refined attention to the client's more subtle movements. Depth and rhythm of breath, posture and muscle tension, or a shift and direction of eye gaze are ways in which a dance/movement therapist can attune to a client's non-verbal experience when larger, intentionally expressive movement may be too overwhelming, or even retraumatizing.

Since direct attention to the body can increase the dissociative response, it is also important to resist the desire to "teach" a method for helping clients feel their body, but rather to notice where the client's attention is already focused. Attention away from one's body is often an indicator of avoiding internal experience. In many instances I have asked a client: "What are you aware of in your experience right now?"—expecting a response in reference to clients' awareness of their bodies. Instead, I heard replies that referred to areas of the room such as "the door," "the clock" or sometimes, "your shoes." By following clients' awareness that started from outside of their bodies, I've discovered a graduated approach to bringing them back to their bodies. The following describes three *arenas of attention* that delineate this subtle use of mindfulness as a gateway toward embodiment.

EXPANDING ATTENTION IN HEALING TRAUMA

Figure 6.1 illustrates three *arenas of attention:* attention to the environment (area surrounding the body outline), attention to body boundary (thick outline of the body), and attention to internal sensation (space inside the outline). By sequentially and separately bringing attention to these arenas, clients can find a safe way to navigate their experience from the outside in, eventually culminating in an opportunity for embodiment.

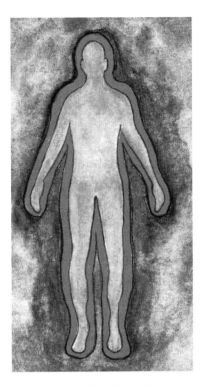

Figure 6.1: Arenas of Attention (digitally enhanced watercolor by Caitlyn Densing)

The first arena—attention to the environment—is an initial step in establishing a client's safety. In trauma healing, Levine (1997) calls this the "orienting response" (p.92). To address this, I ask clients to name aloud the things they see in the room. By orienting to the space surrounding them, clients may begin to find the capacity to judge the level of safety in the room without having to address their own body. By using vocal and auditory reinforcement, clients create a feedback loop to their sense of present awareness.

The second arena—attention to body boundary, sometimes called exteroception (Fogel 2009)—creates a defining sense of locating oneself in the environment and a safe invitation toward sensory awareness. "All of our senses—smell, vision, hearing, vestibular input, taste, touch, nociception (pain) and proprioception—contribute to the formation of these boundaries that eventually tell us where we as a perceptual whole [end], and the world begins" (The Foundation for Human Enrichment 2007, p.B2.32). Inviting attention to the body boundary might include suggestions, such as bringing clients' attention to contact with their chair, awareness of their skin through self-touch, or measuring the distance between their body and the door, the wall or even the therapist. This mindful practice of attention to one's body in the space creates another level of safety by helping clients to locate themselves as both separate and in relation to the environment.

Finally, the third arena—attention to one's internal experience or interoception—can help a client to recognize the way in which bodily sensations are correlated with emotions. Gendlin (1981) named this a felt sense (p.10), an embodied awareness of one's present internal experience. A foundation for somatic psychotherapy practices (Aposhyan 2004; Barratt 2010; Hartley 2004; Kurtz 2007), the felt sense is used successfully in trauma healing practices (Levine 1997; Ogden and Minton 2000). When a sense of safety and present experience accompanies mindful attention of one's internally felt sense, clients can begin to feel freed from a frozen state and even begin to express themselves in movement. *Attention to* the body as mindful interventions can foster the safety, self-awareness and self-efficacy that may then fortify *attention with* the body in movement, offering the possible experience of an integrated healthy aliveness.

Case Example: Thawing the Frozen Body

The following illustrates a vignette of "Hanna," a 34-year-old European female, suffering from moderate dissociation and bursts of rage. Hanna recently moved to the United States to marry her American fiancé. Strikingly beautiful, Hanna had thick black hair, flawless complexion and always dressed in designer clothes with tastefully expensive jewelry. An artist who used painting as her preferred medium, Hanna arrived at my office eager to understand her "out of control" emotions that had recently worsened. She also wanted to work somatically, stating, "Talking isn't helping anymore."

During our first session, Hanna told me how "chaotic" the past year had been, and that she was unsure about her decision to move to New York. I asked what other things had happened in her life that year, and along with her marriage, moving to a new country, and being unemployed for the past year, she also revealed that the previous summer she had been raped by two men after being given a date rape drug. She then added that she had been sexually assaulted by several men throughout her life. During our second session Hanna further revealed that she and her husband often engaged in physical altercations, but refused to speak about it.

Despite Hanna's beautiful exterior, her blunted affect and tense body immediately revealed her pain. Torso curled forward in a frozen position, she would sit with her thin legs crossed twice around each other; right knee over left, with her right foot twisting again around the back of her left ankle as if to double-lock her security. Her face jutted forward, intensifying her eye contact with very little blinking—a frozen deer in the headlights who wanted me to see only her face and disregard the rest of her presence. Her prolonged gaze seemed to dominate the sessions, and as I would gently hold her gaze, it was often evident that she had "left the room." If I reflected that she seemed to be "somewhere else," she would "snap back" to the present and change the subject by suddenly noticing a picture on the wall, or complimenting my outfit. She was unknowingly teaching me about her safe zone, the *arena of attention* outside of her body. Despite her desire to do "body things," Hanna was clearly not safe enough to go there.

Her posture remained hunched and "frozen" for about six weeks. In my own discomfort, I would sometimes ask: "Are you comfortable right now?" to which she would respond, "Yes, I'm OK," contradicting her frozen, unblinking body while my own internal alarm screamed loudly from the disconnection between her posture and her words. Hanna's posture reflected the immense fear and shame that she could not verbalize. Layers of clothing attempted to cover bruises over her ghostlike skin. She also negated her needs by not eating. In addition, Hanna reported harmful rituals such as biting herself and hitting her head against the wall when she became stressed—possible attempts to feel her body boundary.

Hanna minimized her feelings by telling me that crying was a waste of time and that it didn't change anything—a perspective she learned from childhood. She recounted being beaten with her father's belt for misdemeanors, such as not finishing a full hour of violin practice. She often disconnected from her experience by stating, "That was interesting," but without further insight. Whenever I asked Hanna what she felt in her body, she would pull back her chin and look down at her chest and arms as if expecting them to do something. It surprised me each time, but I began to realize that she might not have an internal sense of herself. Our initial work began by focusing on her sense of safety in the room.

Attention to the Environment

The first time I invited Hanna to notice what was happening in her experience, she offered an unusual response. When I suggested: "See if you can take a moment to check in with whatever you might be experiencing right now. See if you can just notice what's happening," she listed things in the room—"that picture" (pointing to the wall with her eyes)... "your chair" (clearly avoiding eye contact)…"the clock" (scanning her attention from the left side of the room to the right). Recognizing that her arena of awareness was in the environment outside of her body, I asked her to explore other aspects of the room that she found interesting. By bringing attention to her environment, Hanna could assess her safety in the present moment, and even though she might not have felt it, began the process of self-regulation.

After a few months Hanna began to identify feelings in her body symbolically as colors, shapes and textures, and would "point" to locations of her body to identify them—an indicator that her perspective was coming from outside her body. Sometimes Hanna would identify an emotion as if it occurred accidentally. At those moments, she would immediately shift in her seat as if shaking it off. She would then lean forward, crossed elbows resting on crossed knees and say, "That's very interesting," and change the subject. When I asked her what was interesting about her observation, she would return, "I don't know. It's just interesting." I learned that this was her way of telling me that she had had enough exploration for the moment.

One day Hanna identified a knot in her stomach that was "pulling in" toward her spine. Surprised at her own sensation, she immediately identified it as "disgusting," and tried to change the subject. This time instead of going with her resistance, I suggested that she gently pursue this new discovery: "Try to stay with this experience if you can. Just notice it; see if you can give yourself just enough distance from it to be curious about it, rather than feeling that you have to run away from it." She sat for a moment and soon associated "pulling in" and "disgusting" with the feeling that she has when she sees her parents. Hanna said, "I really don't like this. I want to get rid of it." Supporting her experience including her desire to "get outside" of her body, I invited her to physically reach with her hand and pretend to "take the knot out of her stomach" and set it outside of herself. With a smirk on her face she reached with one hand and, roughly grabbing the imaginary knot, tossed it out in front of her.

I asked her what it looked like, and as tears pooled in her eyes, she laughed. She told me that it was a gorilla in a cage, and called it a "stupid" image. I asked her what it was doing. She said, "He's lonely," and after a moment, "He wants to play." She then tossed something gently toward the gorilla. "There. I gave him a ball to play with." Silently attentive for a long time to the gorilla image, she then said with a slight smile, "He's hungry." I asked if she might give him some food. "He can have some bread," she said, and tossed imaginary bread toward her gorilla. Sitting quietly again she finally said, "He wants to sleep." When I asked if there was anything that she could give him to sleep more comfortably, she said, "He's fine." In dance/movement therapy, imagery sometimes precedes movement, especially in clients who are in a "freeze" state of dissociation. Hanna's propensity for imagery might have also been fortified by her work as a visual artist. In a creative psychodynamic way, Hanna was externalizing herself as a gorilla in order to justify caring for herself. By "acting out" the process of nurturing the gorilla, she enlivened her experience in the present moment. She embodied both her desire for being nourished as well as her desire to nourish herself. In this way, she was addressing basic homeostatic needs of eating, sleeping and play, as she *physically took action* to nourish the gorilla rather than just thinking about it.

After deep experiences such as these, Hanna would revert to her defenses stating, "That was interesting," without further insight. However, I realized that Hanna was describing an autonomic nervous system (ANS) regulation.[1] Play is an active sympathetic response in the nervous system, while eating and resting are down-regulated activities of the parasympathetic nervous system. Hanna was using symbolic imagery that described the way a healthy nervous system functions, rather than the freeze state in which both are activated simultaneously. By using the image of the gorilla, she was able to externalize compassion that she could not yet give to herself.

Attention to Body Boundary

One day Hanna came into the session and burst into tears. She said she felt afraid and was awake all night, and the only thing that felt "right" to her was to paint her whole body red. She said that the thought was crazy, but it really did feel "right." I invited her to draw it as an attempt to facilitate what seemed to be a self-soothing gesture. Instead, trumped by her own self-degradation, she said that drawing was childish. I asked if she could feel the red on the surface of her body and what the temperature might be. In somatic psychology, delineation of a body boundary by identification of one's own skin and in dance/movement therapy the awareness of one's body in proximity to another person often facilitates a separate sense of self—a shift toward autonomy from the symbiotic dyad of mother and infant. Hanna then identified areas of heat in her torso and cold from her elbows to fingers and knees to toes. She then called the "paint" comforting. I encouraged her to feel the comfort that her image/sensation had provided. She reported a feeling of calmness and could feel her presence inside the "red paint."

At a subsequent session, I offered an exercise to help Hanna strengthen the comfort of her body boundary. I asked her to gently touch the back of her left hand with her right fingertips, inviting her to oscillate between sensing what her right fingertips feel, and sensing what it felt like for her left hand to "be felt." Hanna spent a very long time doing this as I quietly witnessed. After a while she said, "I really like that. It's so gentle." About self-touch in dance/movement therapy, Chodorow (1999) suggests, "As the mover's hands shape themselves to the bulges and the hollows, the hard bones and the soft flesh, there is a profound sense of self-recognition—as if meeting oneself for the first time" (p.292). Hanna was beginning to locate herself through contact with her body.

Attention to Internal Experience

After several weeks, a "golden frog" replaced the "disgusting knot" and Hanna smiled awkwardly while describing the frog, as if having difficulty criticizing it, yet simultaneously delighted at its appearance. I surmised that Hanna's awareness of herself was facilitating a natural healing process. Although she had difficulty providing further description about her experience, she said that the she liked the golden frog and that it needed protection. As the golden frog reappeared in our sessions with quiet, comforting presence for several more months, something unexpected happened. One day while touching her stomach to address the frog, she suddenly remembered being a little girl imagining herself as a fairy princess. However, instead of a wand, the princess held a sword. Hanna immediately judged the image as silly, and berated herself for thinking such a childish thought "in therapy." She then took a breath and to my surprise continued her thought path, telling me how she used to fence. As she said this, she made a sweeping motion with her hand that created an arc in the air.

Surprised at the sudden movement, I chose to mirror her movement verbally rather than repeating her movement with my body. I learned early in our sessions that too much physical expression from me seemed to shut her down. I reflected: "I just noticed that when you said that, you kind of brightened a little bit, and I saw a strong sweeping motion with your arm, like a rainbow. Did you notice that, too?" As suspected, Hanna constricted in embarrassment, but then stated that she did notice her movement. She also seemed conflicted about her own spontaneity. I asked gently if she would like to investigate the gesture. She cautiously agreed.

Integrating Attention "To" and "With" the Body

I asked Hanna if she would repeat the action but this time slower. Slowing movement increases the mover's awareness of physical and emotional presence. She appeared confused about how to make a movement in the air even though she had just done it (a lack of ego awareness often accompanies a lack of proprioception). Since she was an artist who used paint as her medium, I asked if she could imagine painting the movement onto a wall. I also asked if I could join her, since by mirroring her movement, I could provide her with a visual connection with feeling her own movement while offering her my presence for support.

Shadowing her movement, I carefully followed her lead to support her autonomy as she created the stroke in the air. This time, her movement expanded into a large arc using her whole arm, akin to the defending action of drawing a foil, known as a "Parry" in fencing (Figure 6.2).

She gasped and started to laugh. Her eyes became wide, and she exclaimed, "How did that happen? It felt so good to do that! This is really weird. I can never tell anyone what we do here!" I asked, "What did you sense in your body when you did that?" She described a sudden rush of "incredible energy" through her body and that it felt good. She said she felt powerful and protective (an interesting word choice, indicating that she was identifying with "the protector" rather than victim). Hanna added that the arc that she drew was purple and it was exhilarating, but she didn't know why.

Figure 6.2: "Arc" "Parry" move in fencing

I asked if she wanted to try it a few more times to sense what it is like to command this type of feeling (following her "protector" identification); she smiled as she continued to "parry" her color (Figure 6.2). I offered different sized strokes as we moved together to help her expand her movement repertoire, but after a short time I slowly stopped my own movement as I noticed that she was working on her own.

Hanna's spontaneous movement of "drawing" the streak of purple, and "drawing" her sword was a spontaneous expression of self-efficacy in self-protection. Although she was just beginning to own her emotions through her felt sense, there was a leap of faith in her movement that connected the dainty princess, the adult artist and the adept fencer with the ability to protect rather than fall victim to circumstance.

This experience catalyzed Hanna's sense of embodied power and resilience. Following this session she was able to engage in further somatic work with me and eventually began to discharge the residual energy from her body caused by the rapes. Eventually we were able to address her emotions and connect her relationship with her husband to her childhood relationship with her father. In one session she cried, and when I verbally reflected it to her, she said through her tears, "Oh, it's OK. I understand now. Tears are a way to release emotion from the body."

Conclusion

As illustrated in this chapter, mindfulness can be used as a pathway to embodiment when clients are not ready to engage directly with their body. When Hanna became mindful of her environment, she was able to stay present and assess her level of safety in the room. Engaging her body boundary by touching her hand, she was able to perceive her physical existence and increase awareness of her presence. Finally, by being mindful of her internally felt sense, Hanna arrived at an enlivened sense of embodiment, and her creativity became a tool for self-efficacy. Identifying with the images produced by her "fairytale" relationships; the princess holding a sword, frogs and gorillas allowed Hanna to address and begin to integrate the split-off parts of herself. Finally, the spontaneous movement that emerged from within facilitated Hanna's ability to express herself in a "safe" way, an expression that had previously been suppressed and met with abusive repercussions. With mindfulness, Hanna was able to define a secure inner sense of herself that eventually led to empowerment through her "stroke" of enlivened embodiment.

Notes

1   ANS regulation is the reciprocity between two branches of activation: the sympathetic branch, which activates during increased physical arousal and activity, and the parasympathetic branch that activates during activities such as rest and digestion.

References

Anderson, R. (2002) "Embodied writing: Presencing the body in somatic research, Part I." *Somatics*, Autumn/Winter, 40–44.

Aposhyan, S. (2004) *Body–Mind Psychotherapy*. New York: W.W. Norton and Company.

Barratt, B.B. (2010) *The Emergence of Somatic Psychology and Bodymind Therapy: Critical Theory and Practice in Psychology and the Human Sciences*. London: Palgrave Macmillan.

Barton, E. (2011) "Movement and mindfulness: A formative evaluation of a dance/movement and yoga therapy program with participants experiencing severe mental illness." *American Journal of Dance Therapy 33*, 2, 157–181. DOI: 10.1007/s10465-011-9121-7.

Baslet, G. and Hill, J. (2011) "Case report: Brief mindfulness-based psychotherapeutic intervention during inpatient hospitalization in a patient with conversion and dissociation." *Clinical Case Studies 10*, 2, 95–109. DOI: 10.1177/1534650110396359.

Berrol, C. (2006) "Neuroscience meets dance/movement therapy: Mirror neurons, the therapeutic process and empathy." *The Arts in Psychotherapy 33*, 4, 302–315.

Brown, K.W. and Ryan, R.N. (2003) "The benefits of being present: Mindfulness and its role in psychological well-being." *Journal of Personality and Social Psychology 84*, 4, 822–848.

Chodorow, J. (1999) 'The Body as Symbol." In P. Patrizio (ed.) *Authentic movement: Essays by Mary Starks Whitehouse, Janet Adler and Joan Chodorow*. London: Jessica Kingsley Publishers.

Csordas, T. (1993) "Somatic modes of attention." *Cultural Anthropology 8*, 2, 135–156.

Fogel, A. (2009) *The Psychophysiology of Self-Awareness: Rediscovering the Lost Art of Body Sense.* New York: W.W. Norton.

Gallese, V. (2003) "The roots of empathy: the shared manifold hypothesis and the neural basis of intersubjectivity." *Psychopathology 36*, 4, 171–180. DOI: 10.1159/000072786.

Gendlin, E. (1981) *Focusing.* New York: Bantam.

Harris, D.A. (2007) "Dance/movement therapy approaches to fostering resilience and recovery among African adolescent torture survivors." *Torture 17*, 2, 134–155.

Hartley, L. (2004) *Somatic Psychology: Body, Mind and Meaning.* London: Whurr Publishers.

Koch, S. and Fuchs, T. (2011) "Embodied arts therapies." *The Arts in Psychotherapy 38*, 4, 276–280.

Kurtz, R. (2007) *Body-Centered Psychotherapy: The Hakomi Method.* Mendicino, CA: LifeRhythm.

Levine, P. (1997) *Waking the Tiger: Healing Trauma.* Berkeley, CA: North Atlantic Books.

Levy, F. (2005) *Dance/movement therapy: A Healing Art* (Second edition). Reston, VA: National Dance Association.

Ogden, P. and Minton, K. (2000) "Sensorimotor psychotherapy: one method for processing traumatic memory." *Traumatology 6*, 3, Article 3.

Payne, H. (2009) "Pilot study to evaluate Dance Movement Psychotherapy (the Body Mind Approach) in patients with medically unexplained symptoms: Participant and facilitator perceptions and a summary discussion." *Body Movement and Dance in Psychotherapy 4*, 2, 77–94.

Price, C. (2007) "Dissociation reduction in body therapy during sexual abuse recovery." *Complementary Therapy in Clinical Practice 13*, 2, 116–128.

Rothschild, B. (2000) *The Body Remembers: The Psychophysiology of Trauma and Trauma Treatment.* New York: Norton.

Sandel, S. (1993) "The Process of Empathic Reflection in Dance Therapy." In S. Sandel, S. Chaiklin, and A. Lohn (eds) *Foundations of Dance/movement therapy: The Life and Work of Marian Chace.* Columbia, MD: American Dance Therapy Association.

Scaer, R. (2005) *The Trauma Spectrum: Hidden Wounds and Human Resiliency.* New York: Norton.

Sheets-Johnstone, M. (2011) "Movement and mirror neurons: A challenging and choice conversation." *Phenomenology and the Cognitive Sciences.* First published online: December 1, 2011. DOI: 10.1007/s11097-011-9243-x.

The Foundation for Human Enrichment (2007) *Somiantic Experiencing: Healing Trauma.* Boulder, CO: The Foundation for Human Enrichment.

Weiss, H. (2009) "The use of mindfulness in psychodynamic and body oriented psychotherapy." *Body, Mind and Dance in Psychotherapy 4*, 1, 5–16.

Chapter 7

Mindfulness and Drama Therapy

Insight Improvisation and the Transformation of Anger

Joel Gluck

In combining drama therapy with mindfulness and meditation over the years, I have noticed a powerful complementarity between the two: meditation/mindfulness is inward-directed and contemplative, whereas drama therapy tends to be more outward-directed and expressive. As human beings, we need both of these qualities in our lives for balance as well as healthy development and learning. The combination of the two in therapy invites inner exploration and emotional expressiveness—vehicles for insight, catharsis, and change.

Mindfulness/meditation also complements the drama therapy work in that it provides a set of skills and approaches that can be taken into daily life, both as a practice in itself (meditation) and as an approach to living one's life (mindfulness). Skills learned and qualities developed in the practice of meditation—including concentration, openness, acceptance, and lovingkindness—contribute to the power of the drama therapy work, and the effectiveness of the therapy overall.

This chapter explores mindfulness and meditation in relation to drama therapy and psychodramatic approaches. It includes an examination of why mindfulness is a powerful addition to, and even intrinsic to, drama therapy; a survey of drama therapy approaches that acknowledge the importance of mindfulness, meditation, and Eastern philosophies; and an introduction to Insight Improvisation—a drama therapy approach that integrates mindfulness and meditation with drama therapy. A case example demonstrates the use of mindfulness with drama therapy in a client exhibiting uncontrolled anger.

Theoretical Framework

Mindfulness in the Field of Drama Therapy

Drama therapy has been defined as "the intentional use of drama and/or theater processes to achieve therapeutic goals" (National Association for Drama Therapy 2012). Much has been written about the history of and the many types of drama therapy—over two dozen commonly used approaches (Johnson and Emunah 2009)—most of them indebted to the work of Jacob Moreno, the creator of psychodrama (Blatner 2000).

Mindfulness as Intrinsic to Drama Therapy

In one sense, mindfulness—when broadly defined as "the quality or state of being conscious or aware of something" (Oxford Dictionaires Online 2013, para. 1)—is intrinsic to nearly all drama therapy methods. The client in drama therapy is fully engaged in the therapy process in the same ways an actor is fully engaged in a performance—mentally, physically, vocally, and emotionally. Professional actors are trained to be aware in every moment—of their senses, connection with other actors, voice, body, intention, and so forth. In a similar way, every moment of a drama therapy session can be an invitation to return to or be in the present moment, with awareness. This is particularly true, for example, in Developmental Transformations (Johnson 2009), a form of drama therapy in which the client improvises with the therapist—taking on new roles and playing out a series of transforming scenes—for the entire session. Improvising throughout the interaction, the client is compelled to remain aware and present, expressing their feelings and exploring memories and fantasies, not by talking about them but through the dramatic interplay unfolding in the present scene.

Integrating Mindfulness Practices with Drama Therapy

Some forms of drama therapy, however, explicitly reference and use mindfulness in its clinical sense: "a mental state achieved by focusing one's awareness on the present moment, while calmly acknowledging and accepting one's feelings, thoughts, and bodily sensations, used as a therapeutic technique" (Oxford Dictionaries Online 2013, para. 2). The Omega Transpersonal Drama Therapy approach (Linden 2009), for example, refers to the power of focusing the mind, specifically the ability to "master the discipline of becoming mindful of our thoughts" as a core principle (p.216). Satitherapy (Frýba 1989), a system developed by a Czech meditation teacher turned Buddhist monk, integrates different forms of mindfulness practice—such as Focusing and meditation—with psychodrama. Insight Improvisation (Gluck 2007) is based on the mindfulness principles of Theravadan Buddhist meditation teachings—known in the West as Insight Meditation.

Insight Improvisation: Drama Therapy Based in Mindfulness

The Development of Insight Improvisation

In the early 1990s, I was first exposed to the practice of meditation in a theater workshop offered by a teacher from Grotowski's Polish Laboratory Theater, and later, in programs offered by one of the original playwrights for the Open Theater, Jean-Claude van Itallie. Around that time, I was also studying Process-Oriented Psychology with Arnold Mindell, as well as Systems-Centered Therapy with Yvonne Agazarian, therapeutic approaches that encouraged deep listening to the body, senses, emotions, and inner imagery.

A few years later, in 1997, I began to practice meditation on a daily basis, and sat my first weeklong retreat at the Insight Meditation Society in Barre, Massachusetts. As an actor, I was experimenting intensively in my theater work with ways of improvising that were not about being clever or inventive but instead based on inner listening. I joined an authentic movement group, regularly practicing this form of spontaneous movement in which one listens deeply to the body and its impulses—while in the process learning to be a supportive and nonjudgmental witness for others.

From this rich stew of influences and pursuits, I began to develop exercises that had a common theme of being embodied and expressive, while at the same time based in mindful awareness. I taught my first program of this work—"Mindfulness and Choicelessness: Freedom in Performance"—in 1999. When my colleague Nat Warren-White introduced me to drama therapy around 2001, I realized that I had already begun to develop my own approach, and I continued to expand on it throughout my drama therapy studies, finally writing my Master's treatise (Gluck 2005b) on what I had begun to call Insight Improvisation—a name signifying the combination of Insight Meditation with improvised drama and psychotherapy.

PERFORMANCE MIND VERSUS BEING MIND

In an Insight Improvisation therapy session the client is not performing as an actor would. One of the first distinctions made in Insight Improvisation is between "Performance Mind" and "Being Mind" (Gluck 2005b, pp.59–62). Performance Mind is the somewhat tense state we may habitually find ourselves in when onstage and required to perform—the perceived demand to entertain, be clever, and to please the audience. Being Mind is a state of relaxation and awareness, in which one is present to the body, sensations, feelings, emotions, one's surroundings, other people, and so forth; inspired and informed by this awareness, one is spontaneously expressive and creative. All Insight Improvisation methods are designed to cultivate the state of Being Mind. Working with eyes closed, for example—an approach borrowed from authentic movement and applied in many Insight Improvisation exercises—helps the client break out of the tendency and pressure to perform.

ENTERING EMPTY

Another distinction in Insight Improvisation, related to Being Mind, is the concept of "entering empty" (Gluck 2005b, p.69). Unlike psychodrama, for example, in which the client is usually asked to share their issue before the director assists them in exploring it through a series of role-plays, in Insight Improvisation the client—after checking in and sharing—is invited to let go of their presenting problems and instead enter into meditation, movement, and improvisation empty—without preconceptions. In the same way that one typically does not enter meditation with an issue to work on (or do authentic movement using a prescribed topic or theme), in Insight Improvisation the client listens to their body, senses, thoughts, feelings, inner imagery, roles, and other sources, allowing the spontaneous and unexpected to happen. The result is often a solo improvisation of great depth and symbolism, accessing archetypal roles—and raising fundamental (sometimes existential) issues that relate to the client's presenting problems but are several levels below them and informing them. This is not to say that Insight Improvisation is more spontaneous than psychodrama or other methods— however, the moment-by-moment impulses the client follows in Insight Improvisation tend to be less informed by conscious decision-making, and more by the inexhaustible flow of inner and outer stimuli arising and passing away in each moment.

THREE KINDS OF MEDITATIVE AWARENESS

Insight Improvisation is based in three kinds of awareness taught in traditional Theravadan Buddhism—teachings that originated in India and spread throughout several countries of the region, among them Thailand, Burma, and Sri Lanka (Kornfield 2010). The three types of awareness are:

- *Mindfulness:* described above, and developed in *samadhi* (concentration) practices such as *anapanasati* (mindfulness of breathing) (Kornfield 2010, pp.303–306).

- *Choicelessness:* open awareness, encompassing all five senses as well as mind objects, developed in *vipassana* practice (known in the West as Insight Meditation) (Goldstein 2003).

- *Lovingkindness:* love and caring for oneself and for others, developed in *metta* practice—a form of concentration meditation that uses lovingkindness as its object (Salzberg 2002).

These types of awareness are practiced directly (e.g. as sitting meditations in which the therapist guides the client in *samadhi, vipassana,* and/or *metta*), but also inform each Insight Improvisation activity. For example, in order to practice psolodrama—an Insight Improvisation form that combines authentic movement and psychodrama—it is very helpful to be mindful, returning to the present moment (rather than lost in thought); to bring "choiceless" awareness—opening to the body, the senses, inner imagery, etc.; and to cultivate an attitude of lovingkindness, noticing, for example, the attitude of the inner witness (or inner critic), and choosing to consciously send love and support to oneself during the process, especially if one's confidence is flagging.

Insight Improvisation: Form and Therapeutic Process

BEGINNING

A therapist practicing Insight Improvisation with a client begins the process with talk therapy, learning about the client, their goals for therapy, and their background.

MEDITATION

As the process proceeds, and depending on the client need, the therapist can introduce simple forms of sitting meditation—e.g. *samadhi, vipassana, metta*—devoting time to them in the therapy session, as well as encouraging the client to practice them at home, and providing written guidelines (Appendix 1).

Many clients of Insight Improvisation either develop or strengthen their own daily practice of meditation, and by doing so reap the many benefits of mindfulness (discussed elsewhere in this book—see also Kornfield 2010, pp.13–14).

Active Exercises

Initially, the therapist introduces simple activities that build directly on meditative awareness and begin to use the body and voice. The therapist can draw on the more than 50 different experiential activities in the Insight Improvisation system (Gluck 2005b), ranging from simple active meditations, to contemplative theater exercises, to more advanced drama therapy forms.

Over time, clients become ready for experiential activities of greater sophistication and depth. Ultimately, clients become familiar with a standard progression of exercises, for which they no longer need guidance—the therapist serves primarily as witness and partner in reflection afterward. The exercises are as follows:

Authentic Movement

Authentic movement is a dance/movement therapy form originally developed by Mary Whitehouse (Pallaro 2000). The client moves with eyes closed, following what their body wants to do. Authentic movement naturally elicits a state of mindful awareness—which the therapist can support with guidance to notice sensations, emotions, inner imagery, memories, etc.

Shared Vipassana

Continuing their movement, the client—being aware of sensations, thoughts, feelings, and inner imagery—begins to "share" them by speaking aloud (Gluck 2007, p.193). The purpose and effect of the sharing is to further heighten the mover's mindful awareness and immersion in what is happening now. It is not a performance, and the mover does not need to make what they are experiencing clear to the therapist—if the therapist wishes to clarify something, they can do that in the sharing process that follows the progression.

Role Stream

The client, still moving with eyes closed, notices what role or character their movement or body position reminds them of (Gluck 2005a). They can embody that role, make sound, and let the role speak. At any time they can let the role go, returning to authentic movement or shared vipassana, and discover what new role their movement leads them to next. Roles that arise may be human, animal, inanimate, or purely imaginary. No matter what the role, speaking aloud is encouraged as it often deepens one's experience of the role—by speaking the character's thoughts aloud, the client is more able to enter the flow of the improvisation.

Scene Stream

Having discovered more than one role through their movement, the client allows those roles to interact, creating spontaneous dialogues, scenes, and stories—in which they play all the parts (Gluck 2011). As always, it is important that the client is not "performing" for the therapist/witness—instead, the scenes they are enacting are an exploration and expression of their own inner state.

Psolodrama

The client begins to notice what theme, conflict, or issue is arising in the present scene, and begins to "cook" it, heightening the conflict and/or discovering its meaning, through the use of the five psychodramatic roles: protagonist, auxiliary ego, double, director, and audience (Gluck 2011). A psolodrama can be comprised of any number of scenes; roles can be real (e.g. an actual or imagined scene of the client confronting his father) or imaginary/metaphorical (e.g. a young prince facing a giant in battle). Each step in the aforementioned progression, from authentic movement to psolodrama, is a mindful practice in itself—a meditation engaging all the faculties of the client.

Clinical Application
Case Study: Jake Working with Uncontrolled Anger

Jake, a 26-year-old airport worker, came to me because his tantrums and anger were interfering with his work and personal life. He drove a truck as part of his work, and three times a day or more he would have an outburst in his truck, pounding loudly on the walls or windshield with his fists, cracking the glass or damaging property on more than one occasion. Anything could set him off—another driver cutting him off, or simply running late. He also got into frequent fights with his girlfriend, and often had threatening interactions with others. Jake's self-description seemed to fit the *DSM-IV* criteria for Intermittent Explosive Disorder (American Psychiatric Association 2000, pp.663–667).

Jake had grown up in a tough household. When he was a boy, his father would come home from work and greet Jake by throwing him across the room and against a wall. His childhood was filled with screaming and hitting—verbal, physical, and emotional abuse from both his parents.

As a teen, Jake felt betrayed when his father left his mother for a younger woman, and then reneged on a promise to pay for Jake's college. Now that he had the airport job, Jake's mother repeatedly urged him to work hard so he might be promoted to manager some day. Jake kept wondering if this was what he really wanted—he was more interested in music and other pursuits.

Excerpts From the Therapy Process
Session 2

Jake observed that what triggered his anger were stressful situations and interactions, and he wondered how he could better cope with stress. In our second session, I introduced meditation and led him in a simple concentration on the breath (Appendix 1).

Although challenging for Jake, he was able to remain somewhat focused and notice the sensations of breathing. I gave him the homework assignment to begin meditating daily, as well as a book to read—Thich Nhat Hanh's (1992) *Peace is Every Step*, which discusses how to bring mindfulness into everyday life. As our sessions progressed, I introduced different types of meditation, which he began to incorporate into his daily practice. At his request, I also gave him written and audio instructions for meditation (Appendix 1).

I then introduced a simple exercise I call "couples therapy" or "family therapy"— inviting Jake to "bring in" either his partner or a family member of his choosing for a joint therapy session with me—with Jake playing both roles (I play myself, but in the role of a couple or family therapist). Jake chose his older sister, with whom he'd had a contentious relationship; they were currently not in contact. He began the role-play by apologizing to her, and within a minute he was crying. What unfolded was a very honest conversation between the two siblings, with Jake sharing his real feelings about her and about what they had been through as teens. When he played the role of his sister, she came across as tough, brutally honest, someone who had been deeply wounded by her father and felt betrayed by Jake—but willing to listen to him. In the end, they forgave one another.

Jake's feedback at the end of the session was very positive—he had tapped into feelings that were buried, that he didn't know were there at the outset. I suggested he reach out to his sister and have an actual conversation with her.

Session 6

Jake had been meditating regularly and reported—concerning his anger—"I'm better in the morning when I meditate now." He was enjoying Thich Nhat Hanh's book and was beginning to apply some of the lessons about mindfulness in his life, such as eating with awareness.

Meditation: After reviewing the concentration meditation on the breath, I introduced *vipassana* meditation: we visited each of the six sense doors—the five senses plus mind objects (thoughts)—and then opened to choiceless awareness, noticing what is entering through any of the sense doors, moment by moment, and cultivating mindfulness and acceptance in response (Appendix 1).

After the meditation, Jake said: "I'm usually tense, but right now I feel light as a feather. I saw myself as the stone going to the bottom of the pond," referring to an image I had used in a previous session. "It was a feeling of freedom—I felt good."

Authentic movement: Next, I introduced authentic movement as a bridging activity, a way to maintain the awareness of meditation while moving off the cushion into movement. I guided Jake step by step:

> Find a place in the room to begin, and a position you feel comfortable in. Take a moment in stillness to close your eyes and be aware of your breathing...your body... and how you feel right now. Become aware of movement in your body—your pulse, your breath, muscle movement—as well as any impulse to move. Begin to follow how your body wants to move right now, with your eyes still closed...

> At any time during this exercise, if you are moving rapidly or through the space, open your eyes slightly so that you do not collide with objects in the room. Allow your mind to be a witness as your body leads the movement. If you have a thought or clever idea about how you'd like to move, just let it go, and come back to noticing how the body wants to move, letting the body lead.

Jake closed his eyes and began to move, tentatively at first, but then began to relax his body, stretch out, and use the space.

Shared vipassana: Next, I introduced shared vipassana: I invited Jake to continue moving, but now to speak aloud what he was noticing—what was coming in through the six sense doors. He identified body sensations, sounds he was hearing, and thoughts he was having.

Role stream: Next, I added a new instruction: "As you continue to move, begin to notice what role or character this body position or movement reminds you of. Feel free to enter that role, that character. Once you enter it, you can move like that character, make sounds, and even speak aloud as that role."

Jake began to amplify his movement—he was already standing, but began to move around the room more, making fists and punching the air. He spoke: "I'm a boxer... I'm gonna tear this kid up..."

Then he slid to the floor, and spoke in a hissing voice: "I'm a snake … waiting for a mouse to come by… I sit in the grass… There it is…"

Suddenly Jake's hand shot out, and captured the "mouse." Jake sat up, paused, and said: "I'm a little boy…staring at the sky…tall yellow grass around me…I got a girl with me…I could sit out here forever…close with you…sun going down…like a dream. Don't leave…"

After a pause, Jake opened his eyes and looked at me. "That was my first real girlfriend, Jessica, freshman year of high school. I think about her every day. That was the last time I was happy."

At the end of the session, Jake acknowledged the work we had done: "I liked the new meditation we did (*vipassana*)—it keeps it fresh—I want to learn more. I was skeptical at first about the drama therapy. I was forcing at first. Then something magical happened—it was beautiful. Not judging it is key. I'm glad to have more understanding now of the whole Jessica thing."

Therapist reflection: Later, after the session, I reflected on how the role of the boxer seemed like Jake's dad, "tearing this kid up"; and how the snake felt like Jake himself, fairly peaceful until something set him off—for example, a mouse coming by—and then exploding with anger. These roles could be any of the men in Jake's family—Jake's father or his grandfather, who beat and kicked Jake's father and brothers horribly. Jake was then able to connect with a very different emotional state through the scene with his first girlfriend: outdoors, away from the oppressive atmosphere of his family, a time of being truly happy.

Session 7

Metta practice: The following session, I introduced Jake to a third form of meditation/ awareness, *metta*, or lovingkindness (Appendix 1). Traditionally, *metta* includes three parts: lovingkindness for oneself, for another, and for all beings. The idea of sending lovingkindness to himself felt alien to Jake; his self-image was one of not deserving love, but rather one of deserving abuse and self-punishment. We added *metta* to Jake's daily meditation practice.

As our sessions continued, the experiential work began to fall into a pattern—a short guided meditation, followed by authentic movement, shared vipassana, role stream, scene stream, and a psolodrama (described above) with the addition of coaching, when needed, from the therapist.

Session 8

In a psolodrama, Jake becomes himself as a boy, catching frogs by a river. His father appears for the first time as a role in our drama therapy work, warning Jake not to get too dirty. I encourage Jake to become his own "double"—a role expressing the boy's inner thoughts and feelings. Jake, as double, apologizes to his father for not being a better son, and forgives him: "You did the best you could. You're a good father. I'm not mad at you…" Jake becomes his father's double and apologizes for how he's treated Jake. Jake cries.

Once his tears have subsided, I invite Jake to let another part of the boy speak. Jake lets his anger pour out, cursing his father for all the suffering he put Jake, his mother, and his whole family through: "You really f—d me…I'd rather you hit me with a baseball bat 100 times in the face than that s—t… If you were anyone else I'd kick the s—t out of you!!!"

At the end of the session, Jake says: "I never felt anything like that. I cried twice. The drama therapy is opening up something for me." In our next session he adds: "I didn't know I was that mad at my dad—I've never said it to him."

Sessions 9–20
Over the course of the next 12 sessions, Jake's father appears as a role five more times. In each psolodrama, Jake is able to speak more and more of his truth to his father. In the final scene, after a verbal battle, they reconcile with a hug. Jake cries as he embraces his father:

Jake: I'm sorry... I missed you—I just wanted you to be proud of me. I feel so bad for you—you missed out on everybody. It could have been so good. I feel sorry.

Father: It's all right. I know. It's all right buddy...

Jake: I don't blame you, Dad, for doing what you wanted to do... I just want your support. Just be my dad.

Father: I'll always be your dad.

Two sessions later, Jake reported that he'd had an actual conversation with his father: "I was able to talk with my dad about what I'm doing in therapy—I've never spoken with him like that before."

Therapeutic Outcomes
Over the course of our work together, Jake was increasingly able to gain control of his anger, bringing greater awareness to his actions. The number of tantrums gradually reduced, although progress was sometimes uneven; often Jake would report that he had reverted to old habits.

Jake developed a daily practice of meditation, starting simply and adding to it over time. At its height, he was meditating three or more times per day, in the morning, the evening, and at least once in his truck—especially when he felt the urge for a tantrum.

Jake began to relate to people differently, including members of his family, who told Jake they found him easier to be around. At one point, midway through our work, Jake reported that he had shared with his mother that to save money he was thinking of either dropping music lessons or therapy. She said to him: "Whatever you do, don't stop the therapy—it's working."

Ultimately, after 15 months of our working together, Jake was able to reduce his number of tantrums from three or four explosions per day to one episode of anger *per month*. Today, more than two years after our last session, Jake continues to have improved control of his anger and continues to meditate.

Conclusion

Applying mindful awareness *in* the drama therapy—as Insight Improvisation and some other approaches do—helps clients achieve a relaxed presence while using their imagination and being expressive. The clients' work deepens as they are able to listen more carefully in their stillness (or movement) to the innermost messages of their body, emotions, and imagination—rather than surface thoughts.

I have observed clients take greater ownership of their process if the subject matter emerges organically from their own mindful self-awareness—such as, through the progression of meditation, authentic movement, shared vipassana, etc.—rather than having a particular topic or theme imposed beforehand. Similarly, having the therapist remain primarily in the role of witness—only adding coaching from outside when necessary—increases this sense of ownership, as well as a feeling that the material is emerging organically, naturally—that it was there all along, in fact.

I would love to see more drama therapists—and creative arts therapists in general—incorporating mindfulness in their work, and teaching meditation to clients. In a world that can at times feel overly dramatic, with stimulation coming from every direction, both we and our clients need opportunities to return to a place of stillness, centeredness, peace, and awareness—helping us create balance in our lives and in our work.

References

American Psychiatric Association (2000) *Diagnostic and Statistical Manual of Mental Disorders* (Fourth edition, text revision). Washington, DC: American Psychiatric Association.

Blatner, A. (2000) *Foundations of Psychodrama: History, Theory, and Practice* (Fourth edition). New York: Springer.

Frýba, M. (1989) *The Art of Happiness: Teachings of Buddhist Psychology.* (Translated by M.K. Kohn.) Boston, MA: Shambhala.

Gluck, J. (2005a) *The Role Stream.* Available at http://www.insightimprov.org/Resources_files/role_stream_autumn_2005.pdf, accessed on January 27, 2013.

Gluck, J. (2005b) *Insight Improvisation in Context: Antecedents in Meditation, Theater, and Therapy; Individual and Group Experience.* Master's treatise, Lesley University, Graduate School of Arts and Sciences. Available at http://www.insightimprov.org/Resources_files/ii_treatise_web.pdf. accessed on January 27, 2013.

Gluck, J. (2007) "Insight Improvisation: Integrating Meditation, Theater, and Drama Therapy." In A. Blatner and D.J. Wiener (eds) *Interactive and Improvisational Drama.* Lincoln, NE: iUniverse.

Gluck, J. (2011) *Psolodrama in Brief.* Available at www.insightimprov.org/Resources_files/psolodrama_in_brief.pdf, accessed on January 27, 2013.

Goldstein, J. (2003) *Insight Meditation: The Practice of Freedom.* Boston, MA: Shambhala.

Hanh, T.N. (1992) *Peace is Every Step: The Path of Mindfulness in Everyday Life.* New York: Bantam.

Johnson, D.R. (2009) "Developmental Transformations: Toward the Body as Presence." In D.R. Johnson and R. Emunah (eds) *Current Approaches in Drama Therapy.* Springfield, IL: Charles C. Thomas.

Johnson, D.R., and Emunah, R. (eds) (2009) *Current Approaches in Drama Therapy* (Second edition). Springfield, IL: Charles C. Thomas.

Kornfield, J. (2010) *Living Dharma: Teachings of Twelve Buddhist Masters* (Second edition). Boston, MA: Shambhala.

Linden, S. (2009) "Omega Transpersonal Approach to Drama Therapy." In D.R. Johnson and R. Emunah (eds) *Current Approaches in Drama Therapy.* Springfield, IL: Charles C. Thomas.

National Association for Drama Therapy (2012) *What is Drama Therapy?* Available at www.nadt.org/what-is-drama-therapy.html, accessed on May 2, 2013.

Oxford Dictionaries Online (2013) Definition of "Mindfulness." Available at http://oxforddictionaries.com/definition/mindfulness, accessed on January 27, 2013.

Pallaro, P. (ed.) (2000) *Authentic movement: Essays by Mary Starks Whitehouse, Janet Adler and Joan Chodorow* (Second edition). London: Jessica Kingsley Publishers.

Salzberg, S. (2002) *Lovingkindness: The Revolutionary Art of Happiness.* Boston, MA: Shambhala.

Chapter 8

Music, Imagery, and Mindfulness in Substance Dependency

Carolyn Van Dort and Denise Grocke

Music and imagery (MI) is a receptive form of music therapy where clients listen to music for a therapeutic purpose, such as mood regulation, relief from pain or anxiety, or personal growth (Grocke and Wigram 2007). MI also falls under the umbrella of guided imagery and music (Bonny 2002), which is practiced with individuals (Bruscia and Grocke 2002) and groups.

Group music, imagery, and mindfulness sessions are effective for people who are living with drug and alcohol addictions. Participants can learn affect regulation through mindfulness breathing enhanced by quiet gentle music selections and supportive focused imagery. When listening to music in a deeply relaxed or focused state of mind, images may come spontaneously to the listener's mind. These images may be visual associations with the music, or direct memories that the music evokes, or physiologic responses in which the listener feels a release of tension within the body. Mindful listening enhances the awareness of sound, and transfers to everyday life, in that it enables the listener to appreciate natural sounds in everyday life—becoming more aware in the present moment. In addition, music, listening, and mindfulness can lead to greater self-acceptance and insight.

This chapter includes a theoretical overview of music, imagery, and mindfulness followed by a ten-session example from a group with clients in an outpatient setting for drug and alcohol dependencies. It also includes a discussion of considerations in music selection and a resource for music (see Appendix 1).

Theoretical Framework

Music, Imagery, and Mindfulness

In the application of music, imagery, and mindfulness, awareness emerges from being attentive, in the present moment, to the qualities of carefully selected music. Music provides a focus for the experience of the client, in that melody and rhythm draw the person's attention inward, and changes in harmony, instrumentation, and dynamics maintain the listener's interest. The intention in music, imagery and mindfulness is to be aware of the responses to music, but not to be overwhelmed by them. Thich Nhat Hanh (1975, 1976) writes, "to take hold of your mind, you must practice mindfulness of the mind. You must know how to observe and recognize the presence of every feeling and thought which arises in you" (p.37). The music provides a listening experience within which the client can become aware of feelings and other perceptions in a manner that promotes understanding and insight.

Both music and imagery align well with mindfulness practice. As in mindfulness, the intention in music and imagery is to develop the understanding of the witness or observer—that part of oneself that notices, is aware, and observes the responses to music, as well as integrating these responses into the context of the person's life. Inviting the client to become aware of their breath can activate the observer part of self—which serves as helpers, anchors, or tools to support the client in an imagery experience, and to contain the experience for the client (Körlin 2007–2008). Awareness of the breath is also particularly important when working with clients who are living with addictive behaviors and/or recovery from trauma and abuse (Blake 1994; Blake and Bishop 1994; Skaggs 1997).

In groups, therapists can facilitate discussions in order to set a theme for the music and imagery experience. Kabat-Zinn (2005, p.105) refers to deliberate mindfulness as that which is cultivated intentionally, as in setting a focus, or a theme for the group. Effortless mindfulness is that which spontaneously arises as the clients become more practiced in the MI process.

In mindfulness, the objects of the mind are grouped into five aggregates:

1. bodily and physical forms

2. feelings

3. perceptions

4. mental functioning

5. consciousness.

(Hanh 1975, 1976, p.46)

In music, imagery, and mindfulness, the imagery experience may comprise one or more of these aggregates. For example, in response to carefully chosen music, a client may have body sensations of lightness, and heaviness, or of expanding. The senses are important, and responses may include visual imagery, sound, taste, smell, and/or touch; these are recognized through the interaction between the senses and the mind. The music also evokes feeling states, and when imagery is present these may heighten perceptions of colour, shape, and form, that may be experienced aesthetically or symbolically. For example, a tree may be experienced in color and shape, or it may be perceived as a tree of life (Grocke 2009).

The music itself contains the blueprint of the five aggregates, in that it:

1. has discernible form and structure

2. conveys feelings through its composed form

3. enhances perceptions

4. is an organized, non-verbal language open to interpretation by the listener

5. is a complete whole, heard in the present moment.

(Bonny 2002; Grocke and Wigram 2007)

In music and imagery, Goldberg (2002) states that, "[the] Self is both a centering, organizing principle and a part of all states of consciousness that knows what it needs and seeks and finds it through its own personal hierarchy" (p.369). The Self can spiral through all different levels of consciousness in the process of understanding and integration of these separate entities. The presence of the witness, the observer, or the distal self, gains reflective distance and can lead to dis-identification from the ego and self-concepts (Goldberg 2002, p.369).

Selecting Music for Mindfulness

The most effective music for mindfulness has certain characteristics, including a steady pulse, quiet mood, and predictability, with little dynamic change, as the purpose of the music is to enhance mindful awareness of the body, or the focus for the session. The melodic line should be predictable, with a rounded shape, and small range of intervals (often in step-wise progression). The phrases of the melody may match the intake and exhale of breath. The harmonic structure is typically tonal and consonant, with a predictable sequence of chords, or suspended harmonies that resolve. Instrumentation is likely to include strings and woodwinds, and exclude brass and percussion. Repetition is a key feature of music that enhances mindfulness, so that the mindful brain is not stimulated by new sounds and patterns that require processing. The over-riding aspect of suitable music is that is it predictable in melodic, rhythmic, and harmonic features (Grocke and Wigram 2007).

Clinical Application

Music, Imagery, and Mindfulness in an Outpatient Group at a Drug and Alcohol Rehabilitation Facility

The music, imagery, and mindfulness group was held every two weeks for ten weeks with people in an outpatient drug and alcohol rehabilitation facility. Prior to each session, the therapist discussed possible themes with staff. The principles of mindfulness were facilitated by staff in other groups offered to the outpatients, so the mindfulness practice was familiar to the group participants. Themes focused on self-awareness, personal value systems, and an acceptance of the innate wisdom in being an authentic person.

Group Structure

Each session lasted approximately 90 minutes, and comprised seven parts:

1. Sitting in a circle, participants discussed possible themes or focus images for the music and imagery segment (20 minutes).

2. Members lay down on mats on the floor with eyes closed.

3. The therapist led the group in a mindfulness relaxation induction exercise bridging the theme/image with the music (see Box 8.1).

4. The group silently listened to the music in a relaxed state allowing imagery responses to come to their minds.

5. At the end of the music, the therapist brought the group back to an alert state, with eyes open and sitting upright: "The music has come to an end… allow any images to come to a close…(a period of two or three minutes of silence)…now bring your awareness to the room, and to your body as you lie on the mat…(a period of silence)…begin to move your fingers…toes… gradually awakening your body…and when you are ready come to a sitting-up position."

6. Group members were encouraged to either create a drawing, using a circle in the center of the page as a reference point (mandala), or to write about their experience, without criticism or judgment.

7. Members shared their imagery experience.

Box 8.1 Mindfulness relaxation induction with theme/image

Become aware of your breathing, noticing the breath as it enters the nose, the rise and fall of your chest, and the breath leaving through nose or mouth. Be aware that the breath is cool as it is taken in, and warm as it leaves the body… Become aware of the rhythm of your breathing. Sometimes the "in" breath is longer than the "out" breath. Simply follow the breath, and notice the difference…

Be aware of the movement between finishing the "in" breath and starting the "out" breath. Notice the movement between finishing the "out" breath and starting another 'in' breath… Follow the breath into your chest area…be aware of your chest area, noticing what is there, noticing what you can feel in your chest, noticing your breath as it comes into your chest and leaves your chest… With your next "out" breath let go your awareness of your chest area, and become aware of your shoulders…noticing what is there, noticing what you can feel in your shoulders. Now imagine you can breathe into your shoulders… (Continue with this pattern moving through the different parts of the body—the arms, hands, fingers, neck, face, head, abdomen, hips, buttocks, legs, feet, and toes. It is important to keep using the same words for the relaxation and not introduce different concepts, as this will cause confusion.)

(Introduce image or theme.) Now become aware of the focus image or theme (see sessions below). Allow it to take shape in whatever way is right for you—allow the music to be with you as you explore this image.

Ten-Week Group Format

SESSION 1

*   Discussion: Daydreaming was discussed and led into an understanding of music, imagery, and mindfulness. Daydreaming is often about wishing to escape the present moment, to be somewhere else, a way of being where life's roles fall away and the person can be him or herself. A description of the music and imagery process was presented and how it supported mindfulness practice.

- Mindfulness relaxation induction (see Box 8.1).

- Focus image: Being in nature with water.

- Music: Tchaikovsky: *Andante Cantabile* op. 11. This music, written for string orchestra, has even melodic phrases with a variation in sound texture in the middle section.

- Sharing: Most of the group had images of "being near water"; "walking along the seashore," "on a pier," "fishing on a river." Others had images of being "close to nature." All the participants were aware of unwanted thoughts and images intruding into their experience yet they maintained their imagery awareness. Eve was aware she did not like "stillness." Vera was content with "being near the sea" until the waves began breaking on the sand, and she "felt uncomfortable." Everyone commented on the "wordless experience."

- Mindfulness: Being attentive to this focus image gave the participants an opportunity to reflect on, and experience, an enjoyable activity as well as acknowledging their control over unwanted intruding thoughts.

Session 2

- Discussion: Some of the participants described managing well in the busyness of their lives. George shared: "Life takes me along with it. It feels better to be busy, to be doing things." Most of the participants agreed; it was not comfortable to slow down and relax. The group was asked, "How would you describe your mind?" They shared: "scattered"; "leaping from one thought to another"; "there are holes in my mind affecting my memory and concentration"; "my mind is always going on and on." The group chose the focus image of "the breath."

- Mindfulness relaxation induction.

- Focus image: The breath.

- Music: Vaughan-Williams: *Rhosymedre*. The melodic phrases in this piece support an even intake and exhaling of the breath. The cello sound resonates within the body, offering the participants an opportunity to let go of their awareness of the mind and its dominance and breathe into the body.

- Sharing: Eve focused on her breathing but she was aware the "music evoked some memories." George was aware of "breathing only in the top part" of his body. Others were aware of visual images occurring with the music.

- Mindfulness: Each person focused either on breathing, or on the body or on images and memories. They described not fusing with their memories or images. Each person could *remember* and *relate their experience* quite clearly afterwards.

Session 3

- Discussion: The therapist brought various symbols—figurines, animals, semi-precious stones, rocks, shells, seeds, miniature toys, and so forth—and placed them randomly on a table. The discussion focused on the meaning of symbols—that they are imbued with values that have personal meanings and understandings. The participants were invited to choose a symbol and describe it using the first person. Vera chose a piece of rough amethyst— "I am smooth and solid with rough edges." George selected a dog—"I am faithful and loyal." Michael chose a moneybox—"I am like the moneybox… always giving out, and now I am empty." Being able to project onto the symbol helped the members have a degree of objectivity in describing an aspect of themselves.

- Mindfulness relaxation induction.

- Focus: Self-understanding.

- Music: Massenet: *The Last Sleep*. This music has even phrases suitable for supporting the breath, contrasting with shorter phrases in the middle section.

- Sharing: Vera, who chose the amethyst, was aware of "feeling false—I am not sure what purpose I serve." George experienced being in a lost dog's home looking for a lost dog. Was he aware that his "faithful and loyal" aspects were temporarily lost? Michael was aware the moneybox had "virtues and values" that he hadn't noticed—"It has withstood storms and snow and has strength in adversity. It is much more than it first appeared." Sally had chosen a diary for her symbol—"I am organized, there is a place for appointments and it is the right size." In her experience she became aware of the diary as "a sacred scripture book," an "opening" into someone's life. Eve had chosen her own ring as her symbol—"I am a black diamond, surrounded by diamonds. There are black depths to me." In her experience she remembered her grandmother who had given her the ring. She reflected—"There are some painful memories from childhood and I wonder what Grandma would say."

- Mindfulness: These experiences held a mixture of pleasant and unpleasant images. The participants were non-judgmental of their experiences accepting they were left with some unanswered questions.

Session 4

- Discussion: The participants were asked to share a positive comment said to them by a significant other. Sally recalled her brother saying she was a "strong person." George recalled his mother saying he was "reliable—you are my rock." Michael was aware of a "softness" within, an aspect he kept hidden. Vera's work colleagues told her, "We can count on you." Eve was experiencing a relationship break-up. She was "overwhelmed by her feelings" and fusing with perceived negativity about herself. Accepting that all people have assets and vulnerabilities of character, and are not perfect, became the focus for the session.

- Focus: Self-understanding.

- Mindfulness relaxation induction.

- Music: Elgar: *Serenade for Strings,* Larghetto. The music has smooth even-lengthed phrases and no tension in the harmony.

- Sharing: Sally was aware the music helped her "not to fuse" with her negative feelings. She became aware of the "need to nurture" herself, so that she could nurture relationships in her life. George was aware he was a "dependable and reliable" workmate. Michael was aware he could "allow this inner softening"; he could let the "macho" masculine image go and learn to "express emotions" appropriately. Vera was aware that even in her worst times she is "reliable." She had come close to drinking recently and was stuck in a sense of self-pity—"The flow of the music moved me through this awareness and took it out of my head allowing me to view it objectively." Eve experienced a "blackness," however she was aware of calm and surrender toward the end of the music. She did not "fuse" with the blackness.

- Mindfulness: Members were able to be more accepting of their vulnerabilities and to embrace their strengths.

Session 5

- Discussion: Family values were very important to the participants. Each spoke of the "love, support, and close connections" they had with family members, partners, and friends. The participants were not able to decide on a specific focus image. This is not unusual. As participants become familiar with this music and imagery process they are able to trust that the music will evoke an awareness of something significant in relation to the discussion—in this case family values.

- Mindfulness relaxation induction: Just before the music began the participants were asked to imagine a ball of light resting in their hands, which would open to reveal a gift for them.

- Music: Dvorak: *Czech Suite*, Romance. The bright solo flute heard at the beginning supports the image of a ball of light.

- Sharing: George had an image of his family of three generations all "bathed in the glow of the light." Vera had an image of "the light holding her soul—the music touches what is already there and holds it for all to see." Eve had a sense of the light "shining on the beauty of music, art and poetry." She remembered her childhood when creative arts were very special for her. There was a sense of "loss" as she realized her dreams of being a writer had not been fulfilled— "Tread softly or you'll tread on my dreams." Michael was aware of "streams of butterflies and love" flowing out from the ball. He was aware of an "inner goodness" and how this impacted on his relationship with his children. Sally felt a "sense of disappointment—I'm a young person in an old person's body." She "valued all her experiences" within the group, yet had a sense of two steps forward and one step backwards.

- Mindfulness: These responses are examples of effortless mindfulness— experiences that spontaneously arise. In this case their response to the suggestion that the ball of light open up with a gift inside.

The next four sessions focused on looking beyond the ego, beyond the person.

SESSION 6

- Discussion: An awareness of time was the focus for this session. The topics included: linear or clock time; multi-dimensional time which contains memories and experiences; and timelessness as in the vastness of the universe and eternity. Comments from this discussion included "lost time"; "wishing time away"; "counting time"; "negotiating time"; "good times"; "not-so-good times."

- Focus image: Any aspect of time that was of interest.

- Mindfulness relaxation induction.

- Music: Vaughan-Williams: *Serenade to Music*. This music has a gentle holding structure. The interweaving of instrumental sounds invites depths of meaning experienced in a moment of time.

- Sharing: George recalled a "peaceful happy time" when he and his wife planned things together. He realized he could be like that again. Vera said she was "looking forward to time" for herself. She "negotiates" with time, "wishing she could turn back time" and now to "make time" work for her. Michael was aware of "turning back time" and his grief over "wasted time." Sally was aware of Greenwich Mean Time placing an emphasis on the "mean." She experienced "time lapses" and was anxious about that. Eve was aware of "time being seasonal" for her and she had survived. She was aware of "flying freely" like a bird, "feeling" the wind.

- Mindfulness: The qualities of the present moment in relation to the past, present, and future.

SESSION 7

- Discussion: Spirituality, or what gives meaning to life. The participants acknowledged that any form of self-discovery leads to an awareness of an "expanding consciousness," including a sense of spirituality. Comments included being "open to spiritual awareness," spirituality cannot be "enforced" from an outside influence, and it is "felt, experienced and understood as an internalized process." They summarized spirituality as: further horizons—a sense of infinity; deepening in the understanding of a soul, and that spirituality is what gives meaning to life.

- Mindfulness relaxation induction.

- Focus image: The image of a fern frond; looking closely at the leaves and the spaces within (this focus image was decided by the therapist to suggest a depth of the infinite).

- Music: Grieg: *Last Spring*. This music has a slow reflective melodic line, with even-lengthed phrases shaped with gentle dynamic swells (getting louder, then softer) together with supportive harmony.

- Sharing: George reflected, "What happens after death? There must be a place beyond, a place for your soul." Eve experienced warm feelings—"The music had sighs and warmth. I was comfortable with the experience, it was something I had not felt for a while." Sally felt sad but safe. "I'm sad that I stopped being me," she said. "There is a reality deep inside me. I can't be anything other than being me." Michael was aware of a close view of the soil and the recycling process of leaves and branches. "Then I had a sense of letting go, feeling at peace and moving out into the realms of space." Vera resisted being aware of anything spiritual but was prepared to hold that awareness for the duration of the experience.

SESSION 8

- Discussion: Is self-worth to be found in doing or being? If self-worth is based on doing and achieving, then the ego, or self, tightens up; anxiety and suffering emerge. From the perspective of Taoism, the doing is to be effortless, unconditional, creative, and free. Buddhism holds that action coming from selflessness is spontaneous, useful, and generous. The negative aspects of doing were described by the participants as being "like the ripples on a lake."

- Focus image: The impact of the ripples caused by *doing*.

- Mindfulness relaxation induction.

- Music: Liadov: *The Enchanted Lake*. The start of this music conveys a sense of movement in the low tones of the string instruments (cellos and double basses) that create a musical metaphor of something disturbing calm water and the ripples from that disturbance moving outwards.

- Discussion: Michael was aware of the serene beauty of a lake. He noticed the effects of "storm damage, land-slides" and "erosion" that had "disrupted" this serenity, yet added to its presence. "It's jaggedly beautiful," he said. George was aware of swans and ducks swimming on a lake as he walked beside it. He was aware of a snake in the water "frightening" him. He shared, "The lake did test my heart and soul." Vera was aware of a tranquil pond—"The ripples are caused by my presence. They distort the image of the pond and they don't stop." Sally was aware that the ripples appearing on her calm lake were not just on the surface—"The whole lake is disturbed, the impact goes very deep." Eve did not share her experience, as is permitted in a mindfulness approach.

SESSION 9

- Discussion: The group discussed the value of inner wisdom. They agreed that "life is a complex weave" of personal and social history. Is it possible to accept these complexities; to recognize imperfections, flaws, and excesses as part of being a person? What can be "let go" as it no longer serves a useful purpose?

- Focus image: An image of oneself carrying a backpack. How heavy is this backpack? What is carried in it and how does it affect the way one walks?

- Mindfulness relaxation induction.

- Music: Albinoni: *Adagio*. This music has a slow solid pulse, which suggests a gentle walking speed. There are spaces when the pulse stops, allowing for reflection, before continuing.

- Sharing: Vera was aware of walking through stages of her life feeling "small, insignificant and wishing it was different. Drinking gave me confidence. I am getting to the point where I can throw my backpack over a cliff." Sally was aware that she was carrying several backpacks. They didn't all belong to her. She had to return these to their owners before she could even look inside her own. Eve struggled with this experience. She recalled the music was played in a film set in World War I. She was caught up in emotional turmoil; she felt "gutted and mown" down like the soldiers in the film. She jettisoned some of her emotional backpack in a cathartic verbal outburst about "injustice," the "devastation of war" and "man's inhumanity to man." Michael experienced his backpack as "full and heavy." He "struggled" to walk, the path was "crumbling," the "weight pulling him down." He stopped several times to empty it but there was "nothing" there. He was aware of a monk outside a temple who said, "It's not the place you seek, it's the journey you take." George wrote about his experience:

As people do
Whilst walking down the city street
My mind begins to wander as it takes in
The sights and sounds of life in all its wonder
The panting preacher on the town hall corner
The homeless man selling the local paper
People rushing, people talking, people living life
As people do

I am now walking in my local suburb
Which to all is a place to call home
To some a place to respect and cherish, to call a loving home
To others just a bloody box
That they don't respect and don't give a toss
Just people living life
As people do

I am walking on my own for just a few minutes
Taking in the local area, and all the great things in it
But most of all I'm within myself and at peace
Thinking of my grandkids, my family and my sanity
There but for the grace of God go I
As people do.

SESSION 10

This session was a review of the series, and did not include an MI experience. The participants reflected on the series. Vera spoke of an unveiling of herself: "There is a deeper me with more substance. I feel I can be the person I should have been. I'm in the process of becoming." Michael experienced the series as "fulfilling, being a part of something greater than just me, there is a richness there that I am just beginning to be aware of." Eve realized that art, poetry, and music hold a deep connection for her. She felt she could slowly bring them back into her life valuing the emotional expression they contain. Sally was aware of the deep bond with the other participants. "Their presence and experiences helped me to see beyond myself. I am a person worth knowing," she said. George wrote about his experience:

The Flow
I had the flow so long ago, the timing and the beat
But as time went on, I lost my soul, my love, my life, my feet.
And now I feel the rhythm's back, the harmonies, the ebb and flow,
The coming together of music and life
The wisdom of the teachings and the unfolding of life.

Conclusion

In these ten sessions the participants explored a group music and imagery process from a mindfulness perspective. As Thich Nhat Hanh (1975, 1976) writes, "You must know how to observe and recognize the presence of every feeling and thought which arises in you" (p.37). Music, predominantly of the Western classical tradition, contains melodies crafted with elegance and grace and heard deeply. For example in Session 5 Eve was aware of the light shining on the beauty of music, art, and poetry; Vera was aware of the music touching and holding her soul; and George was aware of his family bathed in the light.

The underlying pulse or rhythm of the music is crucial to a sense of movement in imagery experiences, such as slow walking, or cradling something precious. For example, Vera experienced walking along the beach in Session 1, and in Session 9 all the participants experienced walking. In Session 7, Eve was aware of the "sighs and warmth" experienced in the music and George was aware of a "place for his soul."

From a mindfulness perspective the participants were open to this new experience of music and imagery. They commented on the music as guiding and supporting their experience. While puzzled sometimes about their experiences, they acknowledged that these felt familiar and could be placed in the context of their lives, for example, in Session 3 Eve described the "black depths" within her. She struggled during some of the sessions but came to the realization that she had lost something of value—the creative arts. In Session 9 she reacted strongly to her associations with the music, but was able to process these reactions in a safe environment. Michael's experiences showed a new understanding of himself as a person. He accepted his experiences with deep insight. George reconnected with his creative writing giving him a renewed confidence. Sally and Vera also became aware of deeper and more personal qualities that were respected within the group.

These are rich, emotional, and personal experiences that have been a privilege to facilitate, and certainly demonstrate mindful awareness within the music and imagery process.

References

Blake, R. (1994) "Vietnam veterans with Post-Traumatic Stress Disorder: Findings from a music and imagery project." *Journal of the Association for Music and Imagery 3*, 5–17.

Blake, R. and Bishop, S. (1994) "The Bonny Method of Guided Imagery and Music (GIM) in the treatment of Post-Traumatic Stress Disorder (PTSD) with adults in the psychiatric setting." *Music Therapy Perspectives 12*, 2, 125–129.

Bonny, H. (2002) *Music and Consciousness*. Gilsum, NH: Barcelona Publishers.

Bruscia, K. and Grocke, D. (eds) (2002) *Guided Imagery and Music: The Bonny Method and Beyond*. Gilsum, NH: Barcelona Publishers.

Goldberg, F. (2002) "A Holographic Field Theory Model of the Bonny Method of Guided Imagery and Music." In K.E. Bruscia and D.E. Grocke (eds) *Guided Imagery and Music: The Bonny Method and Beyond*. Gilsum, NH: Barcelona Publishers.

Grocke, D. (2009) "Guided Imagery and Music (the Bonny Method) as psychotherapy." *Psychotherapy in Australia 15*, 3, 64–71.

Grocke, D. and Wigram, T. (2007) *Receptive Methods in Music Therapy*. London: Jessica Kingsley Publishers.

Hanh, T.N. (1975, 1976) *The Miracle of Mindfulness: A Manual on Meditation*. Boston, MA: Beacon Press.

Kabat-Zinn, J. (2005) *Coming To Our Senses*. New York: Hyperion.

Körlin, D. (2007–2008) "Music breathing: Breath control and modulation of the Bonny Method of Guided Imagery and Music (BMGIM): Theory, method, and consecutive cases." *Journal of the Association for Music and Imagery 11*, 79–109.

Skaggs, R. (1997) *Finishing Strong: Treating Chemical Addictions with Music and Imagery*. St Louis, MO: MMB Music.

Chapter 9

Poetry Therapy, Creativity and the Practice of Mindfulness

John Fox

By making us stop for a moment, poetry gives us an opportunity to think about ourselves as human beings on this planet and what we mean to each other.

Rita Dove (Moyers 1995, p.112)

In this chapter I explore how poetry and poem-making improve and deepen the practice of mindfulness and how mindfulness is essential to the best practice of poetry therapy. By poetry I mean making use of poems already written (Mazza 1999). Poems, when intentionally chosen for particular needs and populations of people, can act as catalysts, prompts, touchstones, affirmations to the healing journey. By *poem-making* (Fox 1995) I mean the expressive, creative act by a person who writes their own poem in response to that catalyst—or in response to any other inner or outer catalyst, inspiration or stimulus. It is not writing done for critique and evaluation or for the purpose of creating a finished product for publication.

Through the practice of mindfulness, a poetry therapist holds in balance both unimpeded process and the development of awareness and insight. That *sense of balance* helps to weave a sacred and safe container with threads of reflection, discernment and loving consideration.

When I use the word "mindfulness" I don't offer a single definition. There are a range of workable and meaningful definitions (Didonna 2009). The varied *emphases* of these definitions and how they apply with particular accuracy to the practice of whole person poetry therapy is a significant part of my focus in this chapter.

I write about how applications of poetry and poem-making stretch and connect between *therapeutic* and *transformative* ways of healing. I see these healing actions (Shieman 1985) of the therapeutic and transformative as occurring on a continuum. By *therapeutic* I mean how poetry therapy can be used to:

- acknowledge and name hurt, by simply speaking truth

- ameliorate suffering; encourage the release of trauma and pain

- support a person to make healthy connections with self, other, community and the natural world.

- increase self-awareness and self-care; bolster resilience and trust.

Allen Ginsberg (in Carter 2001) affirms this: "The only thing that can save the world is the reclaiming of the awareness of the world. That is what poetry does" (p.273).

By *transformative*, I mean how this expressive modality can help a person and group of people to:

- open to being a whole person regardless of condition, primarily by awakening soulfulness in the human voice and reclaiming a deep sense of essence and authenticity

- make life choices that nourish inner growth and expand consciousness; explore meaning and ask existential questions about death and identity

- open to a spiritual dimension to life.

The poetry therapist is trained to help a person or a group of people work with their writing so that it can serve them in their search for meaning. We believe that poetry provides us with another way to relate (in a spirit and practice of mindfulness) to emotional distress, trauma, physical illness, suffering and our will toward well-being (Fox 1997).

The magic of words offers a person a pathway to enter a new and creative viewpoint. It opens us up channels of insight that connect us to something we don't know rationally but something we inherently recognize, feel and understand.

To a person dealing with suffering, with grief, and, to a practitioner attending to that client or patient, to apprehend together this moment of recognition on the part of the person can initiate an empathic resonance between client and therapist, patient and physician, fostering a healing environment that can make all the difference in their relationship.

Theoretical Framework

Mindfulness and Poetry Therapy

I am applying both of these—poetry and mindfulness—to explore how the expressive art of poetry is a tool for deep therapeutic work and a catalyst for transformation. Two varied ways for us to consider mindfulness are expressed in the following quotes: "Bringing one's complete attention to the present experience on a moment-to-moment basis" (Marlatt and Kristeller 1999, p.68) and "A good definition of mindfulness is cultivating a certain kind of intimacy with the core of our being" (Kabat-Zinn 2005, 9:27).

These two definitions focus on:

- intimacy and attention

- present experience and being present

- bare attention and compassionate presence.

These bring together the inward and outward aspects of mindfulness. Here are two ways to think about what poetry as healer means:

Poetry is indeed a force, an act of human magic, which alters the way we see our lives and so changes us. (Morrison 1978, p.97)

...only metaphor can be both precisely concrete and richly suggestive, both utterly mundane and mysterious at the same time. (Behn and Twichell 1992, p.49)

Morrison speaks to the overall potential of poetry to initiate therapeutic and transformative change. At its roots, there is magic and energetic power in poetry. There are strongly felt transpersonal qualities in poetry. Broughton (cited by Behn and Twichell 1992) describes how metaphor joins the mundane and mysterious. Metaphor acts simultaneously as a useful tool and as an active agent of transformation.

How the Tools of Poetry Empower Self-Expression

Even though we are not concerned with rules and critiques in expressive arts practice, the very making of a poem introduces a kind of craft. By craft I mean the act—the direct action—of giving shape to a unique expression of a person's own way of making. The word "poetry" in Greek is "*poesis*" and it means "to make."

There are certain basics in a practitioner's poetic "tool box," that are useful to become familiar with. A person can learn how to apply these tools as they engage in the art of poem-making for healing and growth.

Primary materials for poem-making include:

- simile

- metaphor

- image

- line breaks

- word choice.

A poetry therapist will offer examples of these elements. These examples serve to inform a client or patient without turning the experience into what they remember in English class. I like to present these elements as something to "mess around" with. It is not necessary to rigorously learn these tools. I have found people will, through the process of writing, naturally discover what these basic and essential elements of poetry are and how they work. We also learn from one another when working in a group and looking at one another's poems.

The key is this—poetic elements empower a person. Poetic elements connect with and feed the creative spark within. Like the discovery of fire or creating a wheel, the use of metaphor is empowering. As profoundly as wheel and fire did, metaphor transforms human experience.

Because creative expression emphasizes personal agency rather than seeking answers outwardly from the expertise of the therapist, it strengthens a collaborative therapeutic relationship. Self-discovery, as part of a creative process, can imbue a person with a feeling of surprise (fire) and of movement (wheel). Surprise and movement are like giving a spark and breath to our inner life. This emphasis on self-empowerment is a unique capacity offered by the creative/expressive arts.

Permission and Playfulness: Making Room for the Child's Voice

Especially in the initial creation of a poem, we want a person to allow for nonjudgmental openness, so that whatever wants to be expressed can make its way onto the page unimpeded. To promote this, a poetry therapist holds a space for experimentation and encourages a trust in the flow of image, word and feeling.

The quality of "mindfulness" for holding "sacred space" is not by paying austere attention to only the present moment. I'm interested in allowing a person to ramble and ruminate, to trust whatever comes, to allow memories to emerge and vivid sense experiences from the past to come forward. I do my best to get out of the way.

I welcome fresh perception. Welcome? For me this means communicating respect, faith and openness. I am eager to discover, with the person writing, what is there on the page. Fresh perception? Creative expression can help break up habitual patterns of thought, even of noting things "mindfully." Poem-making can awaken us to a feeling of aliveness. You might imagine this by remembering as a nine-year-old what your most wonderful Saturday morning was like.

Yet it is not so easy for adults to step back into that kind of excitement. So, I like to use poems by children with adults to convey this felt sense of fresh perception, and by doing that, build trust between us. It is also a matter of bringing playfulness and pleasure with words into the writing experience. Play and pleasure come through in the poetry of children. Adults can accept children's poetry with a greater sense of appreciation and enjoyment. Usual defenses are disarmed. I believe children's poetry stirs that child voice in an adult.

Alice Miller (1990) poignantly describes this: "Only when I make room for the child's voice within me do I feel genuine and creative" (p.2). This truth is expressed and caught on a different slant by D.W. Winnicott (1990): "Creativity is inherent in playing and perhaps not to be found elsewhere" (p.64).

In addition to offering poems by children, I use a poem entitled "As They Are" by Barbara McEnerney (1998). This poem encourages deep acceptance by calling on the protective and loving instincts of adults. This poem is useful for initiating reflections about playfulness, holding back and developing self-trust:

As They Are

And what if my words,
my fledgling poems,
were children, were toddlers
trying first steps,
tumbling, skinning knees,
squealing with glee,
splashing mud,

making a mess,
discovering themselves?

Would I hold them
at arm's distance,
disown them, hide them,
say what I imagine
others will think —
that, after all, they
really aren't very good?

And could that be
a way of protecting them —
shielding, holding back?
I know the mockery
odd children can face.

Instead, could I let
them ramble along weedy
paths only they know?
Lean close to hear
them whisper secrets,
learn what they
need from me?
Could I love them
as they are,
give them room
to grow, a chance
to shine?

"As They Are" equates images of writing poems to allowing children freedom to play. This is the metaphor I want adults to integrate as they approach writing even about painful things. It is about why we may not be comfortable expressing ourselves—or feel afraid and embarrassed about our creations. The messiness and even the joy of exuberance can cause adults to pull back.

Why? Barbara McEnerney's poem bravely acknowledges an adult desire to play but also she knows that a need for self-protection is serving a purpose and is worthy of respect and exploration. When an adult is able to soften their defenses, "soften the belly" (Levine 1982), they are better able to listen to secrets their poems are whispering. By "secret" I don't only mean something that can't be spoken, that is unspeakable and hidden, but also simply has gone unnoticed.

We become more present to a poem, allow it to have an impact, and that is a very powerful act of mindfulness.

To create a relationship with this poem (and with any poem) I ask people to mirror back lines or name stanzas that speak to them. For well over 15 years I have found that every part of Barbara's poem speaks to people and their experience. "As

They Are" has the capacity to free up a person's willingness to trust their process. Barbara's metaphor does its job!

Another metaphoric poem I find profoundly useful to encourage self-permission and to gain someone's trust is "These Days" by Charles Olson (1997):

These Days

Whatever you have to say, leave
the roots on, let them
dangle

And the dirt

Just to make clear
where they come from

Here, Olson compares self-expression—what is spoken—with roots and dirt. It is an astonishing metaphor that offers surprisingly diverse and generative possibilities. People in my workshops voice all kinds of things about what the image of this poem evokes. They say:

- let go of being "nice"

- speak in a raw way

- remember heritage

- allow for the unknown embedded in dark earth

- remain close to what feeds me.

Over the years I have heard hundreds of different responses to what this poem is about!

The Therapeutic and Transformative Path

I begin by separating *therapeutic* and *transformative* into different dimensions of life because I want to honor these distinct approaches to how poetry therapy can help someone grow. I want to honor how poetry as healer might be appropriately applied in a given circumstance.

However, I absolutely do not believe the therapeutic and transformative are actually, at depth, separate. As I've said, I see them occurring on a continuum. Rather, I would like to explore how mindfulness, introduced into the practice of expressive arts/poetry therapy, may help the therapeutic and the transformative grow closer within a revived psychology that is not held separate from spirituality, beauty and interdependence.

I would like to show that we can better understand, through poetry and poem-making, that the therapeutic and transformative can inform one another and thus help us view our lives in a whole way.

Bridging the Human and the Timeless with Creative Expression

Something both human *and* timeless is involved in creative expression. What do I mean by the word "timeless"? While theology claims the "timeless" as its domain, psychology generally ignores the timeless altogether. We might better approach the word "timeless" simply with curiosity and wonder felt in the present moment, in essence, mindfully.

How can we loosen the strict separation between the human and the timeless? Between the psychological and the spiritual? How can windows between these two be opened up? I want to name what human beings already use to lift those windows. This *something* is essential to creative expression—and to the making of a poem. We do it through the use of metaphor, the great WD40 of consciousness!

Metaphor makes opening the windows between mind and heart, soul and somatic reality, easier. Our attempts to broaden consciousness and link disparate realities is not something we must go to school for. Artistic expression is an impulse that goes far beyond what we learn in school. It is, unfortunately, often times, in pre-school and elementary education where our uniquely artistic expression is wounded. Many lose access not only to this birthright, but to what is an attribute of soul.

Laura Golden Bellotti, editor of my books, told me the sweetest story about creative expression. Laura said her nephew, Ian, was two and a half and driving along in a car with his mom, Laura's sister. Suddenly Ian points out the window and exclaims, "Look! The clouds are like mashed potatoes!"

I believe we can assume Ian had not studied simile! He was, I suspect, not aware that you make a simile by using the words "like" and "as." However, when he saw those piled up fluffy clouds, and being familiar with mashed potatoes on his dinner plate, he arrived instantly in perception at the heart of simile/metaphor. Ian expresses, as T. Alan Broughton (cited by Behn and Twichell 1992) describes: "Only metaphor can be both precisely concrete and richly suggestive, both utterly mundane and mysterious at the same time" (p.49). Ian was discovering a way of perceiving reality that makes life creative, surprising, connected, expressive, expansive, relational and fun. These positive benefits alone make the use of metaphor tremendously useful to healing and therapeutic processes.

Two Expressions of Mindfulness: Bare Attention and Compassionate Presence

Bare attention and compassionate presence are in themselves another way of saying that the human and the timeless live and breathe close together. I am drawing parallels between definitions provided by Marlatt and Kristeller earlier in this chapter—bare attention as moment-to-moment attention—and Kabat-Zinn's definition of developing intimacy with the core of being with compassionate presence.

What is it to be truly held and seen? Do compassion and attention play a part? How can we, in a therapeutic way, in a healing way, attend to a human person so that, like the grain of sand and that wildflower, we see something more whole and even mysterious in the human person? I am told there is a Cuban proverb: "Listening looks easy, but it's not that simple. Every head is a world." This is not unlike seeing the whole world in a grain of sand.

If we do not slow down it is difficult to cultivate and practice bare attention and compassionate presence. People slow down in different ways. Some people find that having a meditation practice helps to nurture the sensitivity to notice what slowing down offers. For others, a prayer or affirmation repeated silently and slowly, offers that. Taking time to slow down could also come from an activity like gardening or walking.

Clinical Application

Thirty Minutes of Mindfulness in a Hospital Activity Room

In March 2010, I was invited to present at the University of Medicine and Dentistry of New Jersey, and University Hospital in Newark. My host was the far-sighted psychiatrist, Dr. Diana Kaufman. Dr. Kaufman is the guiding light and healing force behind the expressive and creative arts program in the hospital and medical school. The hospital has given Dr. Kaufman an office and that office is not a hole-in-the-wall!

During my visit I presented to students in the medical school, child psychiatrists, administrators in patient services, people in waiting rooms and patients on the floor of the hospital. Patients in the hospital ranged in ages from 20 to 70. Our multi-generational group included family members, nurses and a physician.

A few moments after sitting down and greeting people, I centered myself and made a decision to begin the session by reading a poem based on the Psalms of David from the Holy Bible. This psalm-like poem was written by Roberta de Kay (1997) a woman living with and fighting a very aggressive cancer. I felt Roberta's poem would connect with my listeners, and that this theme of asking for help when one is close to despair, would feel real to the situation of these patients.

PSALM 13

Oh Lord, I am sinking in despair
　　fearing you have forgotten me.
How long will my mind be confused
　　and my heart in grief?
Turn toward me, mothering Healer, bring
　　light to move me from despair before my heart closes.
Gently comes your healing hand
　　across my mind bringing what was needed
　　before I knew myself.
Trust in your mercy opens my heart

and I realize again your grace.
I am richly renewed.
Your mercy is deeper than my despair. (deKay 1997, p.177)

After reading this poem, I let there be quiet. Then, I asked people to speak into the circle a line or word in Roberta's poem that touched them. While it was slow, it was not tedious. People responded thoughtfully.

How long will my mind be confused
and my heart in grief?

Nurses present were drawn in, feeling, I believe, their own "mothering healing" instinct.

Turn toward me, mothering Healer, bring light

We didn't rush. We took time. I can't overstate the importance of slowing down. In this work with poetry as healer, one recognizes and feels interiority within each person, a depth felt within the moment itself. Much of what we bear witness to is that interiority within an individual. It is like a silent and unseen bowing to something sacred. A person feels *seen*.

I believe there is something in poetry and poem-making akin to prayer or like the healing songs of indigenous people. Poetry can restore to medicine aspects related to our spiritual self and the languages of soul, which are often ignored and forgotten in that technologically dense environment.

Let us return to the circle at University Hospital. Gradually people mirror back lines and words. We listen to one another, not in a style of distracted chit-chat or chart-taking questions, but with care and attention.

Trust in your mercy opens my heart
Your mercy is deeper than my despair.

Silences weave into this intimate quiet, and imbue our listening with presence. Not silences of boredom, the dead tedium of languishing in or visiting a hospital. It is a silence of precious attention. A silence of graceful space that rests between green leaves of thought, or a rippling quiet sensed after a wave of thought draws back from the shore of the mind. A conscious respect expressed for another person simply by listening. I won some of their trust, and together we began to create a healing environment.

After our speaking and silence, I read a poem about listening deeply, about being deeply listened to:

When Someone Deeply Listens to You

When someone deeply listens to you
it is like holding out a dented cup
you've had since childhood
and watching it fill up with
cold, fresh water.

When it balances on top of the brim,
you are understood.
When it overflows and touches your skin,
you are loved.

When someone deeply listens to you,
the room where you stay
starts a new life
and the place where you wrote
your first poem
begins to glow in your mind's eye.
It is as if gold has been discovered!

When someone deeply listens to you,
your bare feet are on the earth
and a beloved land that seemed distant
is now at home within you.

I asked people: "What is it like for you as a patient, as a person, to be listened to? What did this poem evoke in you? If you could speak a word or two that reflects what you feel about being listened to, what would your word or those words be?"

Seated to my left was an elder man with a neatly trimmed grey beard, a black man, who had up to that point, looked abstracted, sad and distant. He spoke up quietly. I say this gentleman "spoke up quietly" and that sounds like an oxymoron. Indeed his quiet and simple word lifted something up before all of us. His word carried deep intention, rich with a sense of meaning even though he wasn't proclaiming it loudly—he said one word: "enlightenment."

And then this man paused and said "…and that *enlightenment* could be conveyed to you by a person, place or thing and in a variety of ways."

It sounded as if this gentleman's lung capacity was compromised because he was wheezing. Yet I also heard an unmistakable clarity, dignity and directness in his voice and words. He spoke in a way that caused us all of us to lean toward him. We became more aware of his presence.

Next to speak was a young Latina woman, probably in her mid-twenties, who was sitting politely, quietly. She was a visitor (perhaps a sister or girlfriend) of a young man whose bald head indicated he was in the throes of chemotherapy. In a strong voice, she said, "not being listened to could cause me to feel invisible, as if I don't exist," then she said the listening poem evoked in her a sense of "belonging."

She spoke with confidence and composure, as if she had rung a bell with her voice. Our session with poetry as healer gave this young woman the opportunity to be heard and speak out. Her voice mattered.

Then a middle-aged man with an IV (intravenous) in his arm, tucked into a corner of the room, yet within our circle, said the poem evoked in him "a sense of caring, a sense of ease." Darryl (this is not his actual name) had been quiet. He appeared shy. Even with my perception of shyness, I asked Darryl, because his voice sounded like liquid amber, a beautiful quality I felt could go unrecognized in this hospital. I asked him to read the listening poem out loud. He blushed, took a deep breath and read. It was clear people enjoyed his way of speaking the poem. I felt he took in our appreciation.

It's important to say how much the nurses joined in. They leaned forward, elbows on their knees to hear their patients. They appeared at ease, to use Darryl's word ease. Willing to listen from their hearts, this is the blessing of nurses and nursing, attending to the matter at hand and to the person who is present.

Soon this session concluded. Two hours later, via one of the nurses in the circle, I received a poem written by that so-called "shy" fellow, Darryl. I was told by that nurse he wrote the poem immediately after our session.

Our Human Heart

Why don't people talk?
Sharing their feelings, their thoughts
Why don't people listen?
Hearing the heart's human treasures
To feel, love, hurt, and heal
Why don't we listen to our own self?
This is what we need.
It is life!
Just one person
To tell why we feel
What is beating from within
Asking
to be heard.

Darryl knows how a whole world, which is, after all, rooted in a whole person, can be changed by "one person" who hears you, hears why you feel "the way you do."

Darryl is posing existential questions and declaring what his inner voice says. In living a life with meaning, mindfully, we can *live into* our own deep questions (Rilke 1986), and act upon the prompting of that inner voice.

Conclusion

What facilitates, nurtures, encourages this practice of mindfulness and the use of poetry for therapeutic purpose and healing?

- *My own practice of centering*
  There is a plumb-line within myself that I can feel when paying attention to my breath. This practice centers me. Feeling it in my body brings me into balance and deeper focus. That plumb-line quiets my mind and opens my heart.

- *A loving and skillful use of silence and quiet*

    Bringing that quietness of mind into the room and around the poem, expressed by a simple and thoughtful pause before any speaking, allows for deep honoring to be felt. This builds safety and trust. All of that in turn makes more room for feeling. This kind of listening/quiet is generative. It is a direct way to slow down and create an interior space in the therapeutic relationship.

- *The embodied and intentional reading out loud of poems*

    Like a body, poems have dimension—depth and breadth. Like living organisms, they breathe, move, feel, think and express consciousness. Reading them in a way that draws all of this out enhances their capacity to heal and act as catalysts for creativity.

- *A respect, openness and attention for the person or persons*

    This triad makes for real listening. Respect for the unique nature, creativity and integrity of each person. Sensitive openness to whatever is expressed. Giving bare attention to the exact particulars and entire spectrum of that expression. This creates a sacred container and bows to the interior life.

- *Unconditional acceptance and nonjudgment*

    By remembering the plumb-line practice of centering I stay freer of objectification and dualism. To recall the poem by Charles Olson, roots and dirt are left on. To recall the poem by Barbara McEnerney, poem and person, are accepted *as they are*. They can "whisper secrets" and a client can "learn what they need from me."

- *Curiosity, creative collaboration, commitment, love and caring*

    The foundation of this unconditional acceptance is expressed in the "I and Thou" of Martin Buber: "Every person born into the world represents something new, something that never existed before, something original and unique… If there had been someone like her in the world, there would have been no need for her to be born" (Buber in Diamond 2003, p.78).

    When we, with mindfulness, listen to or read poetry, when we, with mindfulness, respond to or write it, there is a slowing down. We reflect on what's written on the page in order to integrate what is present and living in the heart.

    We pour into the healing environment of the blank page, this sacred container: letters, words, pauses, rhythms and sounds of "just this much" of our lives. That is, we give voice to what's true for us right now—an experience we disclose, an insight we discover, a wound we disinfect, a hurt we name and so begin to disentangle ourselves from.

    Poetic language, rich with metaphor, image and symbol, makes it possible for us to express the diverse, paradoxical, vibrant organisms we are—human beings that grow and struggle, sometimes get ill and heal, live and die, sorrow and sing.

References

Behn, R. and Twichell, C. (1992) *The Practice of Poetry: Writing Exercises from Poets Who Teach.* New York: Harper Perennial.

Carter, D. (2001) *Spontaneous Mind: Selected Interviews 1958–1996.* New York: Harper Collins.

de Kay, R. (1997) "Psalm 13." In J. Fox *Poetic Medicine: The Healing Art of Poem-Making.* New York: Jeremy P. Tarcher Inc.

Diamond, J. (2003) *Narrative Means to Sober Ends: Treating Addiction and Its Aftermath.* New York: Guilford Press.

Didonna, F. (ed.) (2009) *Clinical Handbook of Mindfulness.* New York: Springer Science and Business Media.

Fox, J. (1995) *Finding What You Did Not Lose: Expressing Your Truth and Creativity Through Poem-Making.* New York: Jeremy P. Tarcher, Inc.

Fox, J. (1997) *Poetic Medicine: The Healing Art of Poem-Making.* New York: Jeremy P. Tarcher Inc.

Kabat-Zinn, J. (2005) *Coming to Our Senses.* Talk at UC San Diego Medical Center.

Levine, S. (1982) *Who Dies? An Investigation of Conscious Living and Conscious Dying.* New York: Anchor Books.

Marlatt, G.A. and Kristeller, J.L. (1999) "Mindfulness and meditation." In W. R. Miller (ed.) *Integrating Spirituality into Treatment: Resources for Practitioners.* Washington, DC: American Psychological Association.

Mazza, N. (1999) *Poetry Therapy: Interface of the Arts and Psychotherapy.* New York: CRC Press, Taylor and Francis Group.

McEnerney, B. (1998) "As They Are." Personal communication.

Miller, A. (1990) *For Your Own Good: Hidden Cruelty in Child-Rearing and the Roots of Violence.* (Translated by Hildegarde and Hunter Hannum.) New York: Farrar, Straus, and Grioux. Original publication in German: *Am Anfang war Erziehung* © Sukrkamp Verlag Frankfurt an Main (1980).

Morrison, M.R. (1978) "The use of poetry in the treatment of emotional dysfunction" *Arts and Psychotherapy 5*, 2, 93–98.

Moyers, B. (1995) *The Language of Life: A Festival of Poets.* New York: Doubleday.

Olson, C. (1997) "These Days." In Butterick *The Collected Poems of Charles Olson.* Berkeley, CA: University of California Press.

Rilke, R.M. (1986) *Letters to a Young Poet.* (Translated by Stephen Mitchell.) New York: Random House.

Shieman, J. (1985) Personal communication.

Winnicot, D.W. (1990) *Home Is Where We Start From: Essays by a Psychoanalyst.* New York: W.W. Norton and Company.

Chapter 10

The Silent Creative Retreat for People with Cancer

The Assisi Model for Professionals

Paola Luzzatto, David Payne, Bonnie Gabriel, Anna Lagomaggiore,
Lucia Minerbi, Gabriella Ventrella, Gemma Oldrini, Ellen Mullin

A day of Silence
Can be a pilgrimage in itself

(Hafiz, 1315-1390)

The Silent Creative Retreat is a supportive intervention in the field of Psycho-Oncology, based on the integration of mindfulness meditation practice and creative therapies workshops, within an atmosphere of deep silence. The silence functions as a container of all activities; it facilitates an introspective approach and it allows the experience of meditation and creativity to reach a deeper level. The aim is to help patients to get in touch with their inner strength, and to be able to use it as a resource in the future.

After a brief overview of the traumatic effects of cancer, this chapter provides a description of the Silent Creative Retreat that evolved through the years from 2001 to 2010—thanks to the experience the team acquired and to the many discussions that went on with the team before, during and after each retreat. The aim of this chapter is to offer a step-by-step description of this model, in a way that can be easily followed.

Theoretical Framework

Cancer and Trauma

Cancer patients need to heal from the traumatic effects of the experience (Helgeson 2005; Holland and Lewis 2001; Kangas, Henry, and Bryant 2007). Reactions to the trauma of a cancer diagnosis and treatment differ among cancer patients, influenced by personality structure, and social and cultural environment. Patients may be affected on a biological, psychological, social or spiritual level, often showing an impairment in a sense of trust, safety, hope, self-identity and self-confidence (Van der Kolk, McFarlane, and Weisaeth 1996). The diversity of patients' needs is reflected in the varied support groups that are offered to cancer patients (Cooper and Watson 1991; Spira 1997). Some groups focus on the body; others explore educational issues; reactivate social ties; develop artistic skills; search for inner serenity; etc. Some patients need to recall, others need to understand, while others need to explore new states of mind and new approaches to life.

History and Development of the Silent Creative Retreat

In 1998, three of the authors who were working in the Psycho-Oncology Service at Memorial Sloan Kettering Cancer Center in New York met to discuss their patients' needs. They were offering separate interventions where silence was an essential therapeutic tool. David Payne, a psychologist, was facilitating a Meditation Group; Paola Luzzatto and Bonnie Gabriel, art therapists, were leading a Drop-In Art Therapy Open Studio (traditionally based on free-image making without verbal interaction among the patients), and Art Therapy Groups where verbal interaction was intentionally kept to a minimum. The patients appreciated these art therapy interventions, where they could reveal themselves symbolically, while maintaining their privacy (Luzzatto and Gabriel 2000). As several patients expressed a need for more silence, David Payne, Paola Luzzatto and Bonnie Gabriel decided to collaborate and offer an innovative intervention. They created a monthly "silent day retreat"—a day of full silence incorporating meditation, art-making and creative writing, with a short verbal sharing at the end of the day. This daylong experience was well received, and stimulated the idea for a longer, residential Silent Creative Retreat for cancer patients. The silence factor would allow the participation of cancer patients coming from different countries and speaking different languages; therefore the project soon became international and was endorsed by the International Society for Psycho-Oncology at their 2000 Melbourne Conference.

DEVELOPMENT OF THE INTERNATIONAL TEAM

We looked for another art therapist, a dance-movement therapist and a person with expertise in creative writing. We also needed a person who could do the administrative work and keep in touch with the patients before, during and after the retreat. The cohesion within the team was most important. We all had some experience in silent retreats or a special interest in a meditative and mindful approach. A monastery seemed to be an appropriate setting because monasteries usually have a silent environment, a nice natural surrounding, and many small single rooms. We selected one in Assisi, Italy, an international center for spirituality.

In September 2001, the team organized the first five-day International Silent Creative Retreat. The patients came from different countries, spoke different languages, were different ages and at different stages in their illness. Within ten years, we offered this retreat eight times. There were between 16 and 20 participants at each retreat, a total of 154 participants (136 cancer patients, 6 relatives and 12 professionals all coming from various parts of the world). Many participants repeated the retreat experience two or three times, and a few of them attended all the eight retreats. In the feedback expressed after the retreat, several participants pointed out that the silence helped them to feel very connected, and several mentioned that they would have liked a longer retreat.

Overview of the Silent Retreat

The basic concepts of the Silent Creative Retreat are: (1) the therapeutic use of silence; and (2) the multi-disciplinary approach integrating meditation practice, arts therapies and creative writing.

THE THERAPEUTIC USE OF SILENCE

The aim of the silent retreat is to help patients to get in touch with their own psychic space as a source of strength and resilience inside themselves. The hope is that they will be able to use their internal resources and practices at any time in the future for their own self-care and well-being. The belief in the relevance of a personal psychic space is therefore a prerequisite of anybody who intends to organize a silent retreat for cancer patients.

Our team was committed to working very closely, with the goal of creating a space and time for the retreat to be therapeutic. Since the Silent Creative Retreat combines mindfulness meditation practice and creative arts therapies, it has an affinity with support groups that address existential and spiritual needs (Breitbart 2000; Smith 1995), and with support groups that encourage creative expression (Klagsbrun et al. 2005).

A specific feature of this intervention is the emphasis on silence. All participants respect the silence throughout the retreat, including during meals and in their free time. Silence functions as a container and a connecting, protective and even nourishing element but demands from the participants an intense commitment, as it stimulates an intense inner process. Through silence, the intentions of mindfulness are emphasized—the receptive attention to self-awareness in the here and now, and the open and non-judgmental attitude toward self and others.

In silence, the participants move, write, draw, meditate, express themselves, sit in circles, perform rituals, eat their meals, rest in the garden, disappear into their bedroom at night and emerge from their bedroom in the morning. The transformation of silence from negative (e.g. upsetting memories or disturbing affects) into positive, where the healthy and resourceful aspects of the self may be accessed, is both an aim and a challenge. Patients experience many different types of silence. For example, individual silence during free time is different from silence during mindfulness practice; silence during creative activities is different from silence during meals; and again, all are different from the silence while sitting in candlelight during the evening meetings. Through the experience of different perspectives of silence, the retreat participants become familiar with the use of silence as a therapeutic tool. Essentially, silence will be understood by them not as an escape, or the absence or lack of something, but as a way of strengthening, enriching, or even "making" the personal, psychic self (Maitland 2008; Storr 1994).

THE MULTI-DISCIPLINARY APPROACH: MEDITATION PRACTICE, ARTS THERAPIES AND CREATIVE WRITING

The retreat day schedule is highly structured and includes morning movement, sitting and walking meditation, art therapy, dance/movement therapy and creative writing. Each day is organized around a specific theme that connects all of the activities.

We often select three themes—Identity, Imagination and Integration—which reflect three basic features of psychotherapeutic work with traumatized individuals (Hurlbut 2004). We address the themes for three central days of the retreat. On the first day, we encourage a free and genuine expression of self-*identity*; the second day focuses on the use of *imagination* and the awareness of a core positive self; the third day emphasizes *integration* of positive and negative, as well as physical, emotional and mental experiences. Throughout the retreat, participants are helped to focus their attention on the coherence and the continuity of the self, thereby healing the experience of fragmentation, which often results from the illness (Malchiodi 1999).

In the arts therapies, the main tools for healing are the creative process on one end of a continuum, and a stepping back for self-reflection on the other (Appleton 2001; Chapman *et al.* 2001; Lahad *et al.* 2010; McNiff 1998). Both aspects become especially powerful when conducted in silence, with the support of a group. The possibility of moving from one creative modality to another (e.g. from art to creative writing to movement and to art again) functions as an ongoing translation of affects and moods, increasing awareness of the same affects and moods.

The meditation practice follows Kabat-Zinn's (1990) Mindfulness-Based Stress Reduction (MBSR) approach, which, although originally based on Buddhist teachings, is not explicitly connected to any religious tradition. Through specific breathing and mental techniques, the MBSR approach to cancer care may help patients to move beyond the stressed, anxious and depressed moods toward a more resilient, stable, calm, deep sense of self. The role of silence helps patients to pay attention, to hear, to see, to feel and to think (Bloom 2006; Luzzatto 2005; Monti *et al.* 2006).

The Silent Creative Retreat

Preparation Before the Participants' Arrival

The team meets at the retreat site one day in advance. The preparatory work is labor-intensive and unrelenting with the following goals: to build a cohesive team; to prepare the setting; to share and discuss the form and content of all workshops; and to take care of many organizational details.

Two members of the team are in communication with the participants—from the initial contact of responding to inquiries about what the retreat can offer (which is different and deeper than just "making art" or "socializing"), to giving special attention to their medical and psychological needs. They also welcome each participant on arrival day, liaise with the director of the monastery, and are available if any of the participants feel uneasy or unwell during the retreat. For some patients, the booking process is straightforward; for others, their enthusiasm is paralleled by their anxieties, consequently needing time, reassurance and support before committing to the retreat.

Preparing the Space and Materials

The team cooperates in preparing the spaces to be used during the retreat:

- *Bedrooms:* In order to facilitate silence, participants stay in single rooms. We place name signs on the doors (first name only); inside the room, we place a welcome letter.

- *Activity rooms:* The participants have individual panels made of hard cardboard (1 × 1.5 meters) on which to place their images and words during their workshops (Figure 10.1).

    They are also given individual folders (size A3), to keep images that are removed from the panel. For dance/movement therapy, it is useful to have colorful scarves (one for each person), and a large piece of white paper placed on the wall, where participants may write some words to share feelings and thoughts before leaving the room.

Figure 10.1: Workshop room with individual panels

- *Meditation practice and evening meetings:* A room may be used both for meditation practice and the evening meetings. We sit in a candlelit circle; in the center is one candle, surrounded by small candles, one for each participant (Figure 10.2).

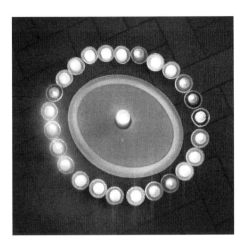

Figure 10.2: Candles for each member

- *Dining room and the "Silence Basket":* Silence during meals may be difficult for some participants. It is helpful to provide quotes about silence (from poets, writers, philosophers and theologians). They may be written on pieces of paper, folded and placed into a basket at the entrance of the dining room. Each person may pick one, and read it silently during the meal.

- *The outside space:* An outside space (a garden or a field), even if small, is essential for movement and walking meditation in the morning, and for individual silent free time.

- *Questions and Comments (Q and C) Box:* A small box, containing pens and paper, is placed near the activity room. Participants are encouraged to write their personal questions and comments at any time during the day. The team collects them before dinner and discusses how to reply. During the evening meeting, one team member reads the comments to the group and replies to the questions.

Arrival Day

As this is an international retreat and many participants travel from abroad, the first general meeting on the arrival day is at 5pm. At the beginning, we introduce our team and each facilitator's role. Participants introduce themselves saying only their first name and the city they come from. Paper and pastels are given to participants to make their own nametag. We suggest they select colors and shapes to express something about themselves.

We talk about the two basic concepts of the retreat—Silence and Creativity. We encourage the participants to share something about what silence and creativity mean to them. We tell them we are committed to help them reach a positive experience of silence and a personal form of creativity, within a mindfulness approach. We read together the daily schedule and answer their questions about it.

Supper on the arrival day is approached as "an experiment in silence." We ask participants to observe their state of mind during the silent meal. At the evening meeting we discuss the experiment of the silent dinner and we have time for more questions. The meeting ends with a ritual to help participants experience the retreat community as a safe container, and to develop confidence about moving toward their silent self (Hammerschlag and Silverman 1997; Pugh 2004):

> We stand up in a circle and each person takes a small candle from the basket. Each participant lights the candle from the person on the left, and says aloud one word, which is personally meaningful in that moment. We then place our small candles on the floor, all around the candle in the center. After a short meditation, we leave the room. Silence starts in that very moment.

Schedule and Description of Retreat Day

In our retreat we follow a similar daily schedule for three days; however, each day is based on a different theme. The following daily schedule explores the theme: Identity.

6:30AM: THE TIBETAN BELL/WAKE-UP

The day starts with the sound of the Tibetan bell. One team member walks along the corridors, ringing the bell gently in front of every door. This bell sends a vibration—which is especially evocative, and helps the participants to get into the right mood for a day of concentration, awareness and discovery. One facilitator will ring the same bell throughout the day, five minutes before each activity.

7:30–7:45AM: MORNING MOVEMENT IN NATURE

The movements are symbolic of the human relationship with natural elements—Earth, Water, Fire, Sky, Stars, the Sun and the Moon. The movement is performed outdoors, with participants forming a circle, followed by repeating the leader's movements. One movement flows into the next, supported by breathing, and becomes a dance enriched by the expressive input of each participant. The sequence is easy to repeat and it is conducted in *crescendo*. Over the days, this dance becomes a morning ritual that facilitates individual body–mind awareness, awareness of the group and a connection with nature.

7:45–8:00AM: WALKING MEDITATION

Immediately after the dance-movement ritual, the meditation leader teaches the group about mindful walking. The approach to meditation used in the retreat is based upon the concept of mindfulness. The leader helps participants to use their body in motion as a focus of their attention, suffusing an ordinary activity like walking with the aspects of intentional and non-judgmental awareness in the moment.

8:00am: Breakfast

9:00–10:00am: Art Therapy Workshop: Something About Me

The participants are shown the basic principles of collage (Landgarten 1993). Images from a magazine take on a personal and symbolic meaning when they are selected for a collage. Participants are asked to select 12 illustrations that attract their attention because they seem to say something about them. They cut out the images, explore different arrangements on a sheet of paper, and then combine them into a collage, which becomes a form of symbolic self-presentation. They give a title to the final product and attach the collage to their personal panel. The last 15 minutes are used to walk around in silence, observing the collages made by the other participants, with full attention and respect for every image made in the group.

10:15–10.45am: Mindfulness Meditation: Breathing as an Anchor to the Present

The basic elements of mindfulness meditation are explained and practiced—contact with the body and the senses; attention to breathing; and attention to the wandering mind, in order to bring the mind back to the breath. The leader focuses on meditation as a way of opening to the reality of one's experience, encouraging the participants to use their breath as an anchor to the present, throughout the course of the day.

11:00am–12:00pm: Creative Writing: Memory as a Source

The leader talks to the group about memory as one of the richest sources of writing (Bradbury 1992). Old and recent memories shape each person's identity and may be accessed through specific techniques. At the top of a sheet of paper, participants are invited to write the words as a prompt—"I remember"—and to continue spontaneously, writing memories, as they flow. Participants may also go outdoors and write while in contact with nature. After everyone is back in the room, they re-read what they have written, underline a sentence that is especially meaningful for them, write it on a strip of paper and place it on their personal panel. The last 15 minutes are spent moving around the room in silence, looking at the sentences selected by the other participants, with full awareness and without judgment.

12:30pm: Lunch

1:00–3:00pm: Personal Silent Free Time

During free time, participants may rest in their bedroom, enjoy the garden or attend the drop-in Open Studio.

Drop-In Open Studio: Freedom of Expression
The Open Studio facilitates an atmosphere of relaxed and free creativity. Participants are advised that they may use any art material and stay as long as they like. They may work without a specific aim, or they may intentionally visualize a feeling, a dream or memory. They may go out and paint from nature. Afterwards, they may come back to

the art room and complete or transform the image. Participants may also use the Open Studio just to "be" in the art room, as a safe and containing space.

3:00–4:00PM: DANCE/MOVEMENT THERAPY: A PLACE FOR ME

The leader writes on a board the following words: "A place—My place—A place from where something new may emerge." The workshop is structured into three phases:

1. Participants use the first 15 minutes for warming up, moving around the room, becoming aware of themselves, others and the room itself.

2. They are encouraged to move from the space of the room toward their personal space with mindful awareness and acceptance, without judgment toward themselves.

3. When they reach their personal space, they are encouraged to stop, listen to their body and to their heart, and allow a gesture to be born from the awareness of their center of life. Then, they move into a circle, and in turn, they offer their personally meaningful movement to the group. The others mirror the movement, and each person feels seen and recognized (Adler 2002).

4:15–4:45PM: MEDITATION PRACTICE: MOUNTAIN MEDITATION

The classic meditation of focusing on the image of a mountain (Kabat-Zinn 1990, pp.126–127) helps participants to become aware of a core, stable Self. This is particularly important for cancer patients. It helps them to see that their emotional storms and crises are much like the weather on the mountain. The weather of our lives is not to be ignored or denied; it is to be encountered, honored, felt and known for what it is. In holding an image of the mountain, we can come to know a deeper silence and stillness and wisdom, right within the storms. The meditation leader helps the participants to identify and strengthen the enduring aspects of their personalities that may remain strong and permanent despite external circumstances.

5:00–6:00PM: CREATIVITY WORKSHOP—MY TREE

The leader shows the group several photographs and paintings of trees, explaining how artists establish a relationship with inspiring landscapes and trees, including their roots, trunk, bark, branches, leaves, fruits, colors, smell and sounds. The leader invites participants to imagine their "personal" tree—to describe the tree and what is happening around it. In this slow process of image making, the tree becomes a symbolic representation of the participants' thoughts, memories, emotions and hopes. After titling their drawing, they are encouraged to write about how it feels to be that particular tree. By deepening their relationship with nature, participants are offered an opportunity to achieve greater insight and to feel stronger (Figure 10.3).

8:00PM: DINNER

9:30PM: EVENING MEETING/CLOSING MEDITATION

We sit on chairs in a circle, in candlelight. The team has opened the Q and C Box. We read the comments and reply to the questions. Comments and questions vary a great deal in content and style, ranging from: personal sharing about most basic issues (i.e. food; sleep); suggested improvements to the day's schedule or to an activity; requests for advice about the best use of silence and creativity; and philosophical themes (i.e. meditation and mysticism).

The meeting closes with a guided meditation, in which participants are helped to focus on their breath and contact their source of peace and strength. Then, we ring the Tibetan bell and say good night. The participants are told that if any of them would like to stay longer in silence around the candles, one member of staff will be present until all have left the room. People leave the room slowly, at different times.

Figure 10.3: Personal tree

Last Day of the Retreat

The last retreat day (before the departure on the next morning) follows a different schedule in order to facilitate each participant's closure of the retreat experience.

9:00AM–12:00PM

In the morning, each participant has space and time to reflect on the entirety of their retreat experiences—and to integrate them into one visual composition, along with a final title (Figure 10.4). These are three hours of relaxed but intense physical, mental and psychological involvement. The following examples from participants' titles of their visual images reflect the rich meaning of the retreat: *Hope through tears; I stretch my arms; Trusting the unknown; The key is inside me; As long as I breathe I live; To find myself; This is Me; I am my candle; Take off your mask; Embrace; Very Colourful Butterflies; Stop, Go inside; Trust; Use your many colors and... GO!*

2:00–5:00PM

In the afternoon, participants have three additional hours of mindfulness attention—this time focused on the work of other participants. We ask each participant to move around, look at the final compositions and give written feedback. The meaning and technique of giving feedback is explained as a personal response: "how I feel—or what comes to my mind—while I am looking at this work." Each person writes one sentence on a white lined page that has been placed near each person's work. This special time of witnessing and interacting with each person's work provides an opportunity to be seen, respected and responded to, before leaving the retreat.

Figure 10.4: Final integrative art and title

5:00PM: BREAKING THE SILENCE

We all sit around in a circle. Each person reads the personal feedback—which is always an enriching experience—selects one sentence that feels useful, and reads that sentence aloud to the group. Afterwards, some time is devoted to filling out the anonymous questionnaire to evaluate the retreat experience. At supper time participants enjoy talking to each other, and are always surprised they feel they already know each other so well!

CLOSING EVENING MEETING

At the beginning of the meeting, there is time for sharing more personal reflections. Then we stand in a circle and repeat the candle ritual of the first evening, with each person expressing with one word the "here and now" awareness. The meeting ends with a guided meditation and the silent time around the light of the candles, to help participants to take the experience of the silence away with them.

Conclusion

A qualitative analysis of the completed questionnaires showed that the participants used the retreat experience to get in touch with their inner resources and to reach a new awareness of existing in the present, along with a new sense of hope for the future. Participants felt helped to deal with the negative side of their cancer experience:

- I unlocked my feeling of paralysis.

- Every day we looked at ourselves and our pain from a different perspective.

- I contacted the negative side of me, I looked at it and saw the boundaries.

- I tend to feel a victim, here I was able to move away from that vicious circle.

- We have avoided the self-narrative, symbolic imagery is stronger.

Participants felt helped to strengthen their positive side:

- I feel better, which means I feel alive and in transformation.

- Silence has now moved inside myself, as a deep source of strength.

- In the silence we are all the same!

- During the first retreat I felt free, but this time I was able to go deeper inside.

- I have experienced joy, trust and energy.

The experience of leading these retreats confirmed to us that the need for silence, often mentioned by cancer patients at the end of their treatment, may be a significant seed for a form of healing. We hope that other professionals who wish to respond to this need for a positive silence will be inspired by our model.

Acknowledgments

We thank Jimmie Holland, MD, former Chairman of the Department of Psychiatry, Memorial Sloan Kettering Cancer Center, New York, for her inspiring leadership and for supporting this intervention from the very beginning; Marcia Plevin (dance-movement therapist) and Birgitta Englung (art therapist) for generously giving their time and professional contribution; the nuns of the monasteries in Assisi and in Florence for their respectful cooperation. We feel particularly grateful to all the participants on our retreats, for their commitment and for their thoughtful feedback.

References

Adler, J. (2002) *Offering from the Conscious Body: The Discipline of Authentic movement*. Rochester, VT: Inner Traditions.

Appleton, V. (2001) "Avenues of hope: Art therapy and the resolution of trauma." *Art Therapy 18*, 1, 6–13.

Bloom, K. (2006) *The Embodied Self: Movement and Psychoanalysis*. New York: Karnac Books.

Bradbury, R. (1992) *Zen in the Art of Writing*. New York: Bantam.

Breitbart, W. (2000) "Spirituality and meaning in supportive care: Spirituality and meaning-centered group psychotherapy intervention in advanced cancer." *Support Care Cancer 10*, 4, 272–278.

Chapman, L., Morabito, D., Ladakakos, C., Schreier H., and Knudson, M. (2001) "The effectiveness of art therapy interventions in reducing post traumatic stress disorder (PTSD) symptoms in pediatric trauma patients." *Art Therapy 18*, 2, 100–104.

Cooper, C. and Watson, M. (eds) (1991) *Cancer and Stress: Psychological, Biological and Coping Studies*. New York: Wiley and Sons.

Hammerschlag, C.A. and Silverman, H.D. (1997) *Healing Ceremonies: Creating Personal Rituals for Spiritual, Emotional, Physical and Mental Health*. New York: The Berkley Publishing Group.

Helgeson, V. (2005) "Recent advances in psychosocial oncology." *Journal of Consulting and Clinical Psychology 73*, 2, 268–271.

Holland, J. and Lewis, S. (2001) *The Human Side of Cancer: Living with Hope, Coping with Uncertainty*. New York: Harper.

Hurlbut, G. (2004) "Healing and Art: Personal Expression, Resolution of Emotional Traumas, and Growth." In H. Thomashoff and N. Sartorious (eds) *Art against Stigma: A Historical Perspective*. New York: Schattauer.

Kabat-Zinn, J. (1990) *Full Catastrophe Living, Using the Wisdom of Your Body and Mind to Face Stress, Pain and Illness: The Program of the Stress Reduction Clinic at the University of Massachusetts Medical Center*. New York: Delta.

Kangas, M., Henry, J.L. and Bryant, R.A. (2007) "Correlates of acute stress disorder in cancer patients." *Journal of Traumatic Stress 20*, 3, 325–334.

Klagsbrun, J., Rappaport, L., Marcow-Speiser,V., Post, P., Stepakoff, S., and Karman, S. (2005) "Focusing and expressive arts therapy as a complementary treatment for women with breast cancer." *Journal of Creativity and Mental Health 1*, 1, 107–137.

Lahad, M., Farhi, M., Leykin, D., and Kaplansky, N. (2010) "Preliminary study of a new integrative approach in treating post-traumatic stress disorder." *The Arts in Psychotherapy 37*, 5, 391–399.

Landgarten, H. (1993) *Magazine Photo Collage: A Multicultural Assessment and Treatment Technique*. New York: Brunner/Mazel.

Luzzatto, P. (2005) "Musing with Death." In D. Waller and C. Sibbett (eds) *Art Therapy and Cancer Care*. New York and London: McGraw Hill.

Luzzatto, P. and Gabriel, B. (2000) "The Creative Journey: A model for short-term group art therapy with post treatment cancer patients." *Art Therapy 17*, 4, 265–269.

Maitland, S. (2008) *A Book of Silence: A Journey in Search of the Pleasures and Powers of Silence*. London: Granta.

Malchiodi, C.A. (ed.) (1999) *Medical Art Therapy with Adults*. London: Jessica Kingsley Publishers.

McNiff, S. (1998) *Trust the Process: An Artist's Guide to Letting Go*. Boston, MA: Shambala.

Miccinesi, G. (2011) "La riabilitazione psico-oncologica in un'ottica multi-disciplinare. Il Ce.Ri.On. di Firenze." *Il Giornale Italiano di Psico-Oncologia 13*, 1, 41–47.

Monti, D., Peterson, C., Shakin Kunkel, E., and Hauck, W.W., *et al.* (2006) "A randomized, controlled trial of mindfulness-based art therapy (MBAT) for women with cancer." *Psycho-Oncology 15*, 5, 363–373.

Pugh, M. (2004) "Transpersonal Approach to Trauma." Paper presented at the AATA Conference, San Diego, CA.

Smith, C.M. (1995) *Psychotherapy and the Sacred: Religious Experience and Religious Resources in Psychotherapy*. Chicago, IL: Center for the Scientific Study of Religion.

Spira, J. (ed.) (1997) *Group Therapy for Medically Ill Patients*. New York: Guilford Press.

Storr, A. (1994) *The School for Genius*. London: Harper Collins.

Van der Kolk, B.A., McFarlane, A.C., and Weisaeth, L. (eds) (1996) *Traumatic Stress: The Effects of Overwhelming Experience on Mind, Body and Society*. New York: Guilford Press.

Chapter 11

Mindfulness-Based Stress Reduction and the Expressive Arts Therapies in a Hospital-Based Community Outreach Program

Patricia D. Isis

Mindfulness-Based Stress Reduction (MBSR) is an eight-week course that integrates formal meditation practices, such as sitting meditation, body scan and yoga, with informal practices designed to heighten awareness (Kabat-Zinn 1994, 2005). Since 2000, I have facilitated MBSR with Expressive Arts Therapies at a community outreach program for a large urban hospital system. The expressive arts are used as additional tools to enhance self-discovery, acceptance, and empathy.

To be an MBSR teacher, one needs to first go through the MBSR courses as a participant and be committed to mindfulness as a practice. To teach mindfulness, we, as clinicians, need to understand and embrace our own suffering with compassion. This chapter includes a brief sharing of a personal crisis that eventually led me to the healing aspects of meditation and learning MBSR, and eventually to integrating the expressive arts with MBSR. I then discuss key theoretical aspects of MBSR and expressive artsin a community setting followed by the eight-week curriculum that I use with groups in an outpatient community hospital.

Personal Significance

I was in crisis when I first encountered meditation. In 1979, my mother was diagnosed with colon cancer. Within four months, it had spread to her liver. Although she lived in Miami, and I was in Boston working on my graduate degree in the expressive therapies, we remained very close. I flew back and forth frequently to care for her. In researching alternative treatments for cancer, I became familiar with the research of oncologist, Dr. Carl Simonton (1974), using meditation and imagery as adjuncts in cancer treatment. In studying 152 patients over a two-year period, Simonton found that response to the treatment was directly related to having a positive attitude and practicing a visualization regularly. The technique is reported to have led to striking remissions of far-advanced cancer. It appears that the manner in which a person sees their illness, and the amount of control that these processes have on their bodily functions, is indicative of their perceptual ability to fight it.

After discovering these concepts, I began to chant daily in meditation and prayer while creating internal images focused on healing myself and my mother. I also created images with paint, pastels, and found objects to serve as healing tools in my own process. At one point, I blended salt water and watercolors along with seaweed to depict my mother's visualization of fighting her cancer with the ocean washing it away against the rocks from the coast of Maine where she grew up (Figure 11.1).

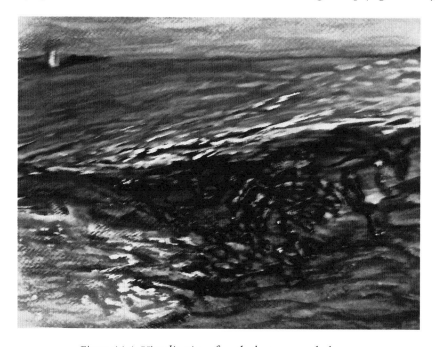

Figure 11.1: Visualization of mother's cancer washed away

During this period, I also attended a weekly meditation group where each of us brought our psychic awareness and spiritual faith together to heal those with emotional and/ or physical ailments who we cared about, both close by and far away. Periodically, I also took part in an open psychodrama group. One of my first experiences as a protagonist became a turning point in my grief process. In this drama, I enacted my mother's funeral. It was here that I received a glimpse of her death and my acceptance of that event. I gave myself the opportunity to rehearse my response to her death with my family and receive support for it, upon hearing similar experiences by those present in the sharing process. It was a profound piece of work that helped me to cope with the reality of life without my mother.

Before she died on Memorial Day, in a lucid moment, my mother told me that she had done all that she wanted to do in her life. She was only 53 years old! Shocked and angry initially, I also realized that this message was a gift to me. All of us have a choice to savor each moment of our lives, for none of us actually know how many moments we have left. To this day, my art and meditation practice remind me to approach and accept many of the experiences of my life, both pleasant and unpleasant.

In 2000, I had the privilege of studying MBSR for healthcare professionals with Jon Kabat-Zinn and Saki Santorelli (1999), the current executive director of the program at University of Massachusetts Medical Center. Ever since this training, I have been fortunate to teach MBSR at a hospital outreach program. In fact, the hospital where I work is the same one that I took my mother to for her chemotherapy treatments! It was that past experience that informed my intention to assist in bringing alternative treatment options to this healthcare setting integrating meditation and the expressive arts therapies.

Theoretical Framework

MBSR and Expressive Arts in a Hospital-Based Outreach Program

Teaching the MBSR course as part of a hospital-based community outreach effort attracts people with an array of mental and emotional challenges. Some participants suffer from chronic pain, fertility issues, panic attacks, complicated grief, and adrenal fatigue. Others simply have a new years resolution to be a "better _____ " (fill in the blank—it could be person, partner, employee, mother, etc.). There are a number of reasons that one would be drawn to mindfulness as a stress reduction practice. It seems that the greatest crises bring the most adherence to the commitment and discipline critical to a mindfulness practice. Certainly, my crisis with my mother's illness served to reinforce my commitment and discipline to the work of mindfulness.

There is extensive evidence-based research using MBSR with a variety of populations and settings (Davis and Kurzban 2012; Denton and Sears 2009; Kabat-Zinn 1990; Mars and Abbey 2010). In particular, there are numerous studies demonstrating decreases in stress, depression, and anxiety, as well as improved mood applied to community-based hospital settings (Carmody *et al.* 2009). According to Chaskalson (2011), "MBSR training…enhances interpersonal relationships…develops emotional intelligence, increases resilience, enhances innovation and creativity, and extends one's attention span" (p.5).

EXPRESSIVE ARTS

With the evidenced-based support validating the efficacy of this model, the integration of expressive arts therapy interventions further offers participants a creative experience designed to deepen self-awareness, emotional regulation, compassion, empathy, self and social esteem. Kabat-Zinn (1990) describes a connection between this mindful awareness and its expression through poetry:

> Mindfulness is a lifetime's journey along a path that ultimately leads nowhere, only to who you are. The way of awareness is always here, always accessible to you, in each moment. After all is said and done, perhaps its essence can only be captured in poetry, and in the silence of your own mind and body at peace. (p.443)

All of the expressive arts offer a vehicle for expression as their sensory nature invites us to see, hear, smell, feel, touch, and taste the true nature of our being from moment to moment. Langer (2005) maintains that "…leading a more mindful and rewarding life is readily available to anyone who can put evaluation aside and just engage in new, creative endeavors" (p.xxi).

I developed the addition of expressive therapies with conventional MBSR practices to inspire, validate, and integrate styles of thought, feeling, and habitual behaviors, both pleasant and unpleasant. Blending expressive arts therapy interventions into the MBSR course offers participants many opportunities for increased self and social awareness. As a result of the creative and playful experiences inherent in the expressive arts, many participants have indicated increased engagement and motivation within the structure of the course, which in turn serves to reinforce both regular attendance and home-based practice.

The expressive arts inspire inner awareness through the creation of outer forms (Levine and Levine 1999). Art is the quality that allows us to witness our own inner forces from moment to moment (Allen 1995, 2005; Langer 2005; Rubin 1984). Consequently, the arts are natural agents for drawing awareness and validating experience internally and externally.

Clinical Application

MBSR and Expressive Arts Curriculum

OVERVIEW

Each week, the MBSR class typically begins with a sitting meditation, on the edge of a straight back chair or cushion. Participants are invited to pay kind, curious attention to each breath: "Take a deep breath into your body…notice as it comes in your body and moves out of your body…just noticing, being curious about it, without judgment." Following this formal practice, participants are invited to use simple art materials (e.g. markers, oil pastels) and to create an artistic representation of their breathing in response to the sitting experience.

As Maggie held up her breath drawing (Figure 11.2) for the rest of the class to see, she was amazed at the various multi-colored lines and movement of the composition.

Maggie said, "I cannot believe how unique each breath is!" As a result of the art-making experience, the actual experience of making and then observing the illustration served to reinforce the original and extraordinary nature of each breath, which we tend to take for granted. This fosters an awareness and acceptance of how thoughts can impact our experience of our breath and body. We often do not notice as we are conditioned to react habitually to stressful scenarios.

After completing their drawings, participants share their art work and experience— first in dyads and then as a whole group. The group members have an opportunity to practice witnessing the other members' breath experiences as they view each other's drawings, without judgment. In later sessions, to deepen awareness, participants may be invited to think of a current challenging situation in their lives followed by drawing their breath. Laura visualized a current stressor in her life while focusing on her breath (Figure 11.3). The boat and the waves symbolize the breath simultaneously as a guide and life-force.

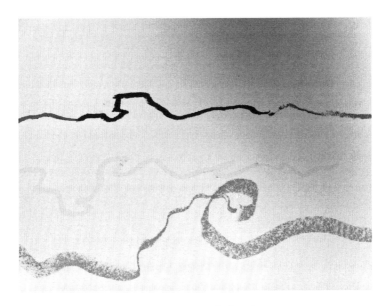

Figure 11.2: Breath drawing

Figure 11.3: Breath drawing with challenging event

Eight-Week MBSR and Expressive Arts Sessions

In addition to learning formal sitting practice and doing breath drawings at the beginning of each group, the expressive arts are integrated throughout an eight-week curriculum in order to bring greater awareness, compassion, and skill enhancement through a creative means. In the next section, I outline the eight-week curriculum that is an abbreviated version of Kabat-Zinn's theme for each session; the intention and expressive arts therapy intervention for each week is included.

GUIDELINES FOR INSTRUCTORS

It is extremely important to realize that a significant amount of what participants learn within an MBSR course comes from their experience of mindfulness as embodied and delivered by the instructor. Consequently, to most effectively and safely apply this material, I strongly recommend that the instructor maintain an ongoing mindfulness practice, be trained in MBSR, and have extensive clinical and Expressive Arts Therapy training. Participants from the community are often seriously challenged with delicate physical, mental, and emotional stressors.

The MBSR instructor needs to have a kind, open, and receptive attitude with an authentic presence. Facilitating mindfulness requires an ability to allow what *is* rather than the usual knee-jerk reaction to "fix" or "smooth over" issues. For example, one woman in a recent class spoke about her anxiety following a sitting practice. In helping her to change her relationship to the experience, I asked her to further describe how and where she felt it in her body. Did it have a color, sound, smell, taste, or texture? The intention is to bring elements of curiosity and hospitality to the difficulty and offer a change in the relationship or perspective to the problem. In the process of helping individuals alleviate distress, this approach takes great skill and flexibility since no one size fits all. It is also imperative that the MBSR instructors first experience each Expressive Arts Therapy intervention prior to offering it to the participants. In this way, one can then have a keen personal awareness of the value and potency of these modalities prior to sharing them with the class.

A variety of modalities are purposely offered here in order to cater to a spectrum of personal preferences. Please note that each class composition creates a particular climate dependent upon the themes that tend to arise out of physical, emotional, and psychological needs. The intentions and directives of the interventions provided here are group-sensitive and flexible in order to accommodate the group as a whole, while promoting safety and authenticity. Based on the original MBSR program, these interventions have been integrated within the evidenced-based curriculum.

Curriculum
Week 1: There is More Right with You Than Wrong with You

- *Intention:* To invite participants to regularly "check in" with themselves and allow all that is present in their internal and external awareness.

- *Expressive arts:* Spectogram/sociodrama.

- *Modality:* Action-method from psychodrama.

The facilitator guides group members to envision an imaginary line, and to then place themselves along it according to how they feel in relation to specific questions or topics. In this example, participants explore their response to stress:

Silently choose a place to stand in a line extended across the room with one end symbolizing maximum stress and the opposite end symbolizing minimal stress. Where you choose to stand reflects your appraisal of the current stress level in your body and in your life. Once standing in the line, take a moment to check inside… If your stress level is primarily a result of an internal source, raise your right hand; or, if it's primarily from an external source raise your left hand or both, raise both hands.

Week 2: How You Do or Don't See Things (Present Moment Awareness)

- *Intention:* To notice how bringing compassionate awareness to our breath allows for an experience based on our senses, opening us to fully experience our life-force from moment to moment.

- *Expressive arts:* Breath drawings.

- *Modalities:* Art, movement, sound.

Following a brief sitting practice, participants are invited to create breath drawings (as in Figure 11.2), and/or use movement and sound to follow one to three breath cycles—full inhalation and full exhalation.

- *Sharing:* The work is then shared in dyads and then within the whole group.

The universality of breath work, concretized through an image (art), movement, or sound, serves both to document the experience and link the community of practitioners on a deeper level.

Week 3: Cultivating Equanimity: Pleasant, Unpleasant, and Neutral

- *Intention:* For participants to notice pleasant, unpleasant, and neutral events inside and outside their bodies. The way we react to undesirable events and respond to desirable events in our lives determines our stress levels.

- *Expressive arts:* Positive experience breath drawing and negative experience breath drawing.

- *Modalities:* Visualization and art.

The facilitator says:

You are invited to visualize a situation in your life right now that is pleasant. Utilize your senses and allow a clear picture to arise in your mind's eye. Notice your breathing. When you feel ready, render your experience of the breath with line, shape, and color (oil pastels, markers, colored pencils). On the other side of the paper, first, visualize a situation in your life now that is unpleasant. Feel it completely in your body. When you are ready, give form to it through the experience of your breath.

- *Sharing:* Participants are asked to share their art and experience in dyads and then in the large group, to notice responses of pleasant, unpleasant, and neutral, to practice nonjudgmental acceptance toward themselves and others.

Week 4: Stress Reactivity and Stress Hardiness

- *Intention:* For participants to bring awareness to pleasant and unpleasant events in their bodies, knowing the experience as it is, the thoughts and feelings around it, and their response or reaction to it.

- *Expressive arts:* Body scan awareness drawing and response.

- *Modalities:* Visualization and Art.

Following the body scan meditation (see Body Scan in Formal Practice in Appendix 1) participants are given paper with pre-drawn figures (see Figure 11.4) and a box of markers or oil pastels.

The facilitator invites the group:

As you reflect on the body scan experience, express what you experienced in the body scan exercise onto the paper, using line, shape, color, and size (see Figure 11.5a).

After the first drawing, the facilitator hands out a blank piece of paper. Members are invited to re-draw the same forms in the identical placement areas without the body outline (Figure 11.5b). The facilitator adds:

Now, reflect on this composition. Without judgment or an agenda, trust your inner self and respond with line, shape, color, and form to nurture the images. What does the image need from you right now to be cared for?

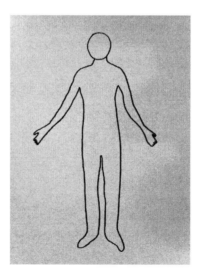

Figure 11.4: Body outline

Stephanie shared the sensations and emotions she experienced during the body scan (Figure 11.5a) and then transformed the original visual forms into a butterfly image (Figure 11.5b). She shared with the group that this symbol represented her strength and resilience to free herself from the negative judgment of the initial experience and provided her a greater opportunity toward self-acceptance and independence.

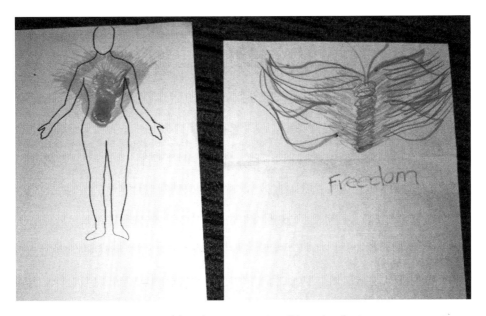

Figure 11.5: (a) Body scan sensation; (b) Caring for image

- *Sharing:* Participants are asked to share in a dyad and large group and to focus on bringing awareness and acceptance to what is inside and outside their bodies. Participants will be asked to become aware of real-life situations that parallel the art work process in order to clarify habits and belief systems regarding stress management and self-care.

Week 5: Everyday Stress and Life-Changing Events and Their Relationship to Our Health

- *Intention:* Awareness of coping styles and patterns of dealing with stressors.

- *Expressive arts:* Don Jones Assessment.

- *Modality:* Art.

This exercise is Jungian in nature and based on an assessment tool developed by art therapy pioneer, Don Jones (Jones, Vinton, and Wernick 1999). Four different adventures are presented to the group. Each adventure represents challenges that we encounter from moment to moment in our daily lives. After each adventure is heard, group members respond to it with a drawing. The response indicates each member's coping style to the challenge.

- *Materials:* drawing paper; choice of pencils or markers. The paper is folded in half and participants number it as 1 on the front page, 2 on the left inside page, 3 on the right inside page, and 4 on the back page.

- *Story* (allot specific time for each of the four parts):

Drawing 1: You are going on a journey, down a path that leads into a forest. You come to a rushing river. You must get across the river to resume your journey. On page 1, draw how you get across the river.

Drawing 2: Now, imagine yourself returning to the trail and leaving the forest. You begin to climb up a mountain. The trail switches back and forth due to the steepness of the slope. You stop for a moment to catch your breath…and notice a wild animal coming toward you. On page 2, show how you get past the animal.

Drawing 3: Imagine you are back on the mountain trail and encounter a massive hail storm. You need to find shelter…and you see a cave close by. There is a monster on both sides of the entrance. On page 3, draw how you manage to get into the cave.

Drawing 4: Once in the cave, you are tired and need to rest. Before you close your eyes to rest, you hear something and realize that you are no longer alone in the cave. Page 4 reflects your experience in the cave and however you choose to end the story.

- *Sharing:* Participants are asked to share in dyads and in the large group.

This exercise helps members to become aware of coping styles. The first adventure can be handled either independently or with support. This parallels how one handles obstacles in one's life. The second situation offers a confrontation (by the wild animal). There are four common ways people tend to cope with this scenario, particularly since one is not in control or prepared for this situation. We either avoid, become aggressive, passive, or passive aggressive. The same is true for the third adventure. However, in this case, we are empowered to access resources to manage the threats. The fourth scene provides a metaphor to reflect on our relationship with ourselves and others.

Week 6: To Recognize Stressful Communication

- *Intention:* Acknowledge origins and styles of coping with conflict.

- *Expressive arts:* Strategies for Conflict Management.

- *Modality:* Sociometry.

Members are invited to stand in a circle. Each person takes a turn by stepping into the center of the circle and sharing one way that they handle conflict. For example, one person steps into the center and says, "I avoid it." Others who also believe they avoid conflict will step in and join the first person. Each person in the center of the circle briefly shares how they avoid conflict. For example, "Do you actually leave the situation, ignore the conflict, or change the subject?" Members are asked to consider who they learned this behavior from. Other group members are encouraged to identify habits of dealing with conflict with support and empathy.

- *Sharing:* Members share their work and insights in a large group. There is no advice giving. Rather, group members support each other through common experiences in order to enhance awareness of ingrained patterns of behavior around difficult communications. Discussion is deepened with self-selected group members offering constructive conflict resolution skill sets.

Week 7: Awareness of Significant Relationships and Social Support

- *Intention:* To take responsibility for our relationship choices and patterns.

- *Expressive arts:* Social atom.

- *Modalities:* Art and sociometry.

A social atom, developed by the founder of psychodrama, Jacob Moreno (1972), is a way to map out and explore significant relationships in one's life.

- *Materials:* Drawing paper; oil pastels, graphite pencils, markers.

The facilitator says:

> Reflect on your life right now and the significant relationships in it. You are going to create an artistic map of your most significant relationships, including you. Use circles to represent females and triangles to represent males. Place the circle or triangle that symbolizes you on the paper to indicate where you see yourself in your life now (i.e. in the center, off center, below center, above center etc). Consider how big or small you feel in your life at this time. Use colors that resonate with your perspective of your relationship to yourself currently. Write "Me" under the symbol. Continue to use the circles, triangles, and selected colors to demonstrate how close or far, big or small, wide or narrow each prominent relationship is for you right now (Figure 11.6). Pets can be part of this picture as can deceased individuals. Use a slanted line through the circle or triangle to show that the person is deceased.

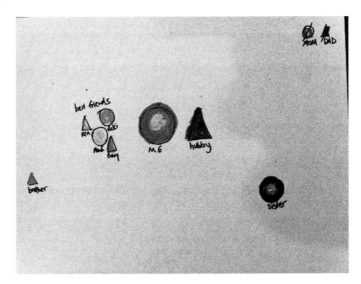

Figure 11.6: Social atom

- *Sharing:* Participants are asked to share in dyads and later in a large group. They are asked to notice the picture of their most significant relationships without judgment. They are asked, "Do you feel crowded, or lonely? If you could have it exactly the way you wanted it, what would it look like?" This exercise helps to clarify one's current support system and offer a way to look at it dispassionately. Further discussion is encouraged regarding what is needed for optimal social support.

Week 8: Claiming the Practice as Your Own

- *Intention:* To carry the skills and tools from the course into daily life.

- *Expressive arts:* There to here.

- *Modalities:* Movement, drama, sounds and gesture.

The facilitator invites the group to:

Imagine a continuum with one end of the room representing "there" and the other end "here." "There" represents the first MBSR class and "here" represents the final class (or first class of the rest of your life). Each of you will take a turn and move through the space to express your journey of learning through the MBSR and Expressive Arts course. Feel free to use movement, sounds, and gestures to reflect your experience.

The group members witness, without judgment, the experience of each member.

- *Sharing:* In dyads and within the large group, members give voice to the impact of the individual movement experiences, along with the effects of witnessing that experience for the group as a whole. Members share how they will carry the experience from the group into their daily lives.

Conclusion

The eight-week MBSR and Expressive Arts course can be adjusted in many ways. As I have found, after 12 years of teaching, each class member brings a unique presence and contribution to the community. Some groups are very quiet and respond well to more structure, others are in need of greater amounts of processing time. The MBSR curriculum must be respected and followed within the parameters developed by Kabat-Zinn. However, using expressive art therapy modalities can be modified according to the current needs of the participants. These exercises can be quite evocative and inspirational. It is important for the MBSR instructor to seek supervision or consultation whenever necessary. Breath work, art work, movement, and sociodrama can elicit underlying emotional challenges and promote insight and transformation.

Setting aside time daily for meditation is critical to the efficacy of this work on the body and the mind. Similarly, one can consider utilizing the expressive arts regularly as vehicles for further self-exploration and validation. Offering MBSR and the expressive arts therapies to the community with support from a well-regarded hospital, underscores the value of mindfulness and the arts, for wellness and prevention.

References

Allen, P.B. (1995) *Art is a Way of Knowing*. Boston, MA: Shambhala.

Allen, P.B. (2005) *Art as a Spiritual Path*. Boston, MA: Shambhala.

Carmody, J., Baer, R.A., Lykins, E.L., and Olendzki, N. (2009) "An empirical study of the mechanisms of mindfulness in a Mindfulness-Based Stress Reduction program." *Journal of Clinical Psychology 65*, 6, 613–626.

Chaskalson, M. (2011) *The Mindful Workplace*. West Sussex, UK: Wiley-Blackwell.

Davis, L. and Kurzban, S. (2012) "Mindfulness-based treatment for people with severe mental illness: A literature review." *American Journal of Psychiatric Rehabilitation 15*, 2, 202–232.

Denton, R. and Sears, R. (2009) "The Clinical Uses of Mindfulness." In J. Allen, E. Wolf, and L. VandeCreek (eds) *Innovations in Clinical Practice*. Sarasota, FL: Professional Resource Press.

Jones, D., Vinton, M., and Wernick, W. (1999) Panel presentation, American Art Therapy Association Conference, November 21. Orlando, FL.

Kabat-Zinn, J. (1990) *Full Catastrophe Living*. New York: Dell Publishing.

Kabat-Zinn, J. (1994) *Wherever You Go, There You Are*. New York: Hyperion.

Kabat-Zinn, J. (2005) *Coming to Our Senses*. New York: Hyperion.

Langer, E. (2005) *On Becoming an Artist*. New York: Ballantine Books.

Levine, S.K. and Levine, E.G. (eds) (1999) *Foundations of Expressive Arts Therapy*. London: Jessica Kingsley Publishers.

Mars, T.S. and Abbey, H. (2010) "Mindfulness meditation practice as a healthcare intervention: A systematic review." *International Journal of Osteopathic Medicine 13*, 2, 56–66.

Moreno, J.L. (1972) *Psychodrama*. McLean, VA: American Society of Group Psychotherapy and Psychodrama.

Rubin, J.A. (1984) *Child Art Therapy*. New York: Van Nostrand Reinhold.

Santorelli, S. (1999) *Heal Thy Self*. New York, NY: Bell Tower.

Simonton, C.O. (1974) "Management of the emotional aspects of malignancy." Lecture delivered at the University of Florida, Gainesville, FL. Reprint.

Chapter 12

Mindfulness-Based Expressive Therapy for People with Severe and Persistent Mental Illness

Daniel Herring

Mindfulness-Based Expressive Therapy (MBET) is an approach to teaching mindfulness by using multiple expressive and artistic modalities. It was developed within a psychosocial rehabilitation day treatment program for adults with severe and persistent mental illness (SPMI). This chapter includes a brief overview of mindfulness-based approaches with SPMI, an overview of the MBET protocol and its efficacy, highlights of MBET exercises, and clinical vignettes emphasizing the importance of adapting the curriculum to individual needs.

Theoretical Framework

Mood disorders, psychotic disorders, personality disorders, severe anxiety disorders, and addictions comprise the majority of the diagnoses in day treatment programs (Herring 2005). A number of mindfulness-based treatment protocols have been developed and studied specifically for the aforementioned diagnoses and problems, however, at this time there are no known studies in day treatment. Dialectical Behavior Therapy (DBT) (Linehan 1995) was developed and validated for persons diagnosed with borderline personality disorder and later adapted for substance use disorders (Davis and Payne 2003; Dimeff and Linehan 2011). Marlatt *et al.* (2004) developed effective mindfulness-based protocols for treating substance use disorders. Mindfulness-Based Cognitive Therapy for Depression (Segal 2002; Ma and Teasdale 2004; Segal, Williams and Teasdale 2002) has been shown to halve the recurrence of depression in those persons who have experienced three or more episodes of major depression. Acceptance and Commitment Therapy (ACT) (Bach and Hayes 2002) has demonstrated efficacy in reducing hospitalizations in persons with psychotic disorders. Mindfulness-informed Cognitive Behavior Therapy or MiCBT (Cayoun 2011) has also demonstrated efficacy in treating those with psychotic disorders. In addition, Mind–body medicine (Benson 1976) and Mindfulness-Based Stress Reduction (MBSR) (Kabat-Zinn 1990) have demonstrated efficacy in treating anxiety and co-occurring medical problems.

Because all of these approaches suggested the potential efficacy of mindfulness-based treatment with SPMI, I developed a 16-week protocol for teaching mindfulness within a day treatment program and introduced mindful activities, such as meditation and mindful movement, as part of the daily curriculum in the program. The protocol was based on my training in Vipassana (Insight Meditation) and the meditation instructions included in *The Middle Length Discourses of the Buddha* (Bodhi and Nanamoli 1995)—on much of which MBSR (Kabat-Zinn 1990) is based.

Efficacy of Mindfulness Training within Day Treatment Programs

The 16-week mindfulness protocol was tested at two different day treatment centers using the "Treatment Outcome Package" or "TOP" developed by Behavioral Health Laboratories. It reduced symptoms by 32 percent over treatment as usual (TAU) at the original center (which included some degree of mindfulness for all participants) and 72 percent at the second center—which had no mindfulness program prior to the introduction of the 16-week protocol. In a questionnaire designed to measure quality of life indicators given at the original program, the mindfulness group reported marked increases in quality of life (Herring 2005). Since these studies, Luanne Davis and colleagues have been studying the use of mindfulness with persons diagnosed with schizophrenia at the Richard L. Roudebush Veterans Administration Medical Center and have concluded that:

> mindfulness-based intervention was acceptable, and it was perceived as having the intended effects of providing symptom relief, initiating cognitive changes, and providing stress management through relaxation. Reactions were generally positive, and there were no reports of psychiatric symptoms worsening during meditation or as a result of the mindfulness training. (Brown *et al.* 2010, p.241)

The Development of MBET

The ideas for MBET began as discussions with two graduate interns from Lesley University (Ben Fox and Stephanie (Sordillo) Ryan) and was further inspired by Caroline Peterson's development of Mindfulness-Based Art Therapy (MBAT) for women with cancer (Monti *et al.* 2005).

We had been discussing ways to use multiple artistic modalities to introduce mindfulness to clients who had difficulty with the 16-week mindfulness protocol and to enhance the understanding and application of mindfulness for those who were beginning to develop mastery in the protocol. After some initial sessions which were applied with some success by Fox and Sordillo and with the help of interns and staff clinicians over the next few years, I developed a 16-week MBET protocol which could be used either as a supplement or as an alternative to the original 16-week mindfulness protocol, for both experienced and new meditators. The addition of expressive arts with mindfulness seems to provide an easier way for clients to witness and learn about the contents of their mind, emotions, and senses without over-identification or reactivity.

Since mindfulness is essentially the act of directing and redirecting attention, it increases basic executive functioning and provides relief from painful feedback loops (Segal *et al.* 2002). Persons with SPMI are frequently caught in such loops.

Mindfulness helps participants to change their relationship to sensory and mental experience from one of fear, attachment, and reactivity to one that is more aware, tolerant, and accepting (Hayes, Strosahl, and Wilson 1999). MBET can be a valuable tool in promoting all of the above.

Clinical Application

MBET Protocol

Sixteen one-hour sessions occur weekly. There are eight to ten participants with a mixture of diagnoses related to SPMI. There is always at least one co-leader.

At the outset of treatment, participants are told that the goal is not on the final artistic product and that there is no expectation or necessity for "talent" in any art form. We encourage participants to think of each session as a guided meditation, keeping communication (especially verbal communication) to a minimum and maintaining a meditative mind-set. This reduces the amount of internal chatter and distraction. We talk about approaching the expressive portions of the exercises with friendly curiosity and openness.

To further promote present-moment focus with minimal distraction, we give each participant their own set of art supplies. If art supplies and paper are being used in the exercise, they are handed out before the meditation and participants are asked to wait for instructions before opening their personal container.

MBET Group Exercises

Due to the limitations of the chapter, I describe a few exercises from the MBET protocol that provide a sense of the kinds of experiences that are emphasized.[1]

The mindfulness exercises follow a progression beginning with the least anxiety provoking and moving toward those that produce more anxiety. The exercises begin with attending to objects that are clearly "outside" oneself (such as visual or auditory objects), then move toward internal objects (sensations, mind-states such as sleepiness or restlessness), then to mind objects (such as thoughts and internal images), and lastly to mindfulness of our interactions with each other.

Each group begins with mindfulness of breathing instructions:

> Notice the sensations of the breath. Make a mental note of each in-breath and each out-breath. We can let the breath occur naturally and don't need to change or control it. It is normal for our attention to wander. When we find that this has happened, we simply return to noticing the breath. It's OK if we're aware of background thoughts, noises, sensations or anything else. We simply keep returning to a gentle and friendly awareness of the sensations of our breathing and let our experience be just as it is, with awareness and acceptance.

MBET EXERCISE 1
Introduction/Exploring Media

Goals
Observation; non-judgment; becoming familiar with the different media; spontaneity; introduction to process orientation versus product.

Materials
Personal container with art supplies; all-purpose paper.

Meditation
Mindfulness of breathing.

Expressive Arts
After meditation, the participants are invited to try each medium, in order, noticing the differences, what is evoked from each (attraction or aversion), what kinds of shapes, textures, or colors they are inclined toward creating with each media. The facilitator decides on the order of materials, keeps time and leads a two to three-minute meditation between media.

Sharing
Initially the group is asked to hold up the paper(s), to simply view and "take in" each other's work. Alternatively, each person can put up their work on the wall and members of the group can view them silently, or the art can be left on the table and the group can slowly walk around the table. After, the leader invites verbal sharing—encouraging awareness and non-judgment:

> Take time to carefully notice each other's work. Note similarities and differences in the shapes, colors, textures, and patterns that emerge. Note any feeling responses you have. Practice using a non-judgmental perspective by describing what you experience without rating it or each other's work as "good" or "bad." Instead, describe your experience of their work. This may take some practice so I hope you don't mind if I keep reminding you.

MBET EXERCISE 2
Observing and Describing a Visual Object

Goals
Direct experience of sensory objects; differentiating the experience of visual objects from thoughts about them; observation; non-reactiveness.

Materials
Art supplies; all-purpose paper.

Discussion
Prior to meditating, have a conversation with the group about sensory awareness. Note that there is a difference between noticing something and thinking about it (Herring 2005). Elicit from the participants a list of "what can be seen" (i.e. shape, color, texture, light, shadow, line, space, etc.). Try to emphasize the difference between what one sees,

and what one thinks about what one sees. Usually we miss the experience of seeing and only notice our thoughts about what we've seen, such as "that's a bowl" or "I like/hate that color."

Meditation
Five-minute mindfulness of breathing meditation.

Expressive Arts
Put out an object (e.g. singing bowl, cushion, and striker) on the table. Invite participants to observe the objects, just taking in the colors, shapes, textures, light, shadow, and patterns, etc. (three to five minutes).

Invite participants to reproduce the colors, shapes, textures, light, shadow, and patterns they observe while looking at the object. Emphasize that this is not a still life and the goal is not to produce an accurate rendition of the object. The intention is for them to explore the different visual qualities that they notice and are experiencing: "You are essentially taking the bowl apart—breaking it down into its various visual components— red triangle, golden circle, smooth curve, shiny black square, etc."

Sharing
Share in the manner described in Exercise 1.

MBET EXERCISE 3
Observing and Describing an Auditory Object
Goals
Direct sensory experience; fully experiencing what one hears; use of visual imagery to clarify what is heard; seeing the similarities between what is heard and visually represented.

Materials
Gongs, singing bowls, rain sticks, hand-held percussion instruments, and other sound-producing instruments; art supplies; all-purpose paper.

Meditation
Begin with the mindfulness of breathing and gradually introduce noticing sounds and letting sounds become the objects of the meditation.

Discussion
Review the visual sensory observation exercise from the week before, reminding participants of the value of experiencing our senses without the over-lay of thoughts or judgments. Review the difference between noticing something and thinking about it. Give some examples from the previous week. Possibly create a list of what can be heard— volume, pitch, timbre, rhythm, etc. Pass out art supplies. Have several gongs, singing bowls, rain sticks, and other sound objects available. Pass out as many pieces of paper as there are instruments. Ask participants to number each piece of paper. Keep track of the order in which you made each sound so that when viewing the visual forms, you will know which sounds they correspond to.

Meditation

Lead a two-minute mindfulness meditation moving into five minutes of mindfulness of sound. Inform participants that you are going to make a sound and invite them to experience sound directly and mindfully, as possible. Use one of the instruments to make a series of sounds.

Expressive Arts

Ask participants to make a line, shape, or pattern, in whatever color seems to fit, in the medium of their choice, to represent the sound they have just heard. Invite them to return to the mindfulness of breathing when they have finished. Then repeat as above until all of the instruments have been used, and visual representations of each sound has been made.

As people finish their drawings, invite them to stay in the mindfulness of breathing for a minute or two. Sometimes it is necessary to cue people to finish with statements such as: "Take all the time you need in the next 60 seconds, to finish your drawing and return to the mindfulness of breathing when you hear the gong."

After a few moments of the mindfulness of breathing, introduce the next sound. Repeat as above. Continue as above until all of the sounds have been heard and visually represented by each participant.

Sharing

Invite each participant to hold up their drawings in order, repeatedly making the sound while the drawings of each sound are being held up. Verbal sharing is optional and is best left at a minimum for this exercise as the experience of hearing while seeing the visual representations is very powerful and too much verbiage may dilute it.

After the sharing, a wonderful way to end the class is by passing out the instruments and inviting each participant to experiment a bit with making sound and then making sound together. I like having one person begin and the others join in one at a time. Then invite the person who began to fade out and the other participants fade out in the order in which they came in. This requires a high level of attentiveness and ends the group in a playful and grounding way.

MBET EXERCISE 4
Mindfulness of the Body

Goals

Awareness of body sensation; development of the sense of being an "embodied" being; increased interest and decreased reactivity to body sensations, leading to increased sense of wellbeing; enjoyment of the body as an organ of expression and communication.

Materials

Chairs placed in a circle with enough room between them so that participants can stand and have enough space to move freely.

Meditation

Mindfulness of breathing followed by an active body scan.

Expressive Arts

After a few minutes of mindful breathing, participants are invited to move, pat, shake, or rub certain parts of the body, beginning with the feet and working their way up to the top of the head. They are invited to stop after each movement/body-part and to feel the sensations they are experiencing in that part of the body. I usually alternate between sitting and standing so the more sedentary or exercise-resistant participants don't get too tired or overwhelmed. The intention is to go systematically through the body experiencing the sensations or lack thereof in each part of the body. As much as possible, I introduce each movement in a light and humorous manner so as to engender a sense of playfulness and fun.

Sharing

Instead of processing in the usual way, participants are introduced to a bit of mindful interaction by making and passing movement around the circle and responding either in tandem or in unison. One person makes a movement followed by the group repeating the movement; sound can be added to the movements and participants can be allowed to be playful, silly, embarrassed—whatever emotions or impulses arise for them. This encourages mindful awareness, non-judgment, authenticity, and spontaneity.

MBET EXERCISE 5
Mindful Eating
Goal

Increased awareness and comfort with reactions and responses to food; increased ability to slow down the eating process and experience each stage in the process; shifting one's relationship from one of intense craving or ambivalence to one of curiosity and enjoyment.

Materials

Paper and pencils or pens. A platter of food (fruits, vegetables, and other foods that are small and easily handled and eaten).

Meditation

Mindfulness of breathing shifting to mindfulness of eating.

After a five-minute meditation put out the tray and ask and guide the participants:

Observe the contents of this tray. Notice your reactions. Perhaps you are experiencing anticipation, anxiety, judgment, craving, confusion, or aversion. Just sit with these feelings for a minute and hold them in a space of openness and friendliness if you can. If not, notice space in which these reactions are occurring.

Expressive Arts

Continue guiding the participants:

Now feel free to share your reactions if you'd like…after a few moments… Pick one of the food items from the platter and put it on a paper plate or napkin in front of you, but do not do anything with it yet. Look at the food item in front of you…after about 15 seconds, take a moment to write down words you may have that describe the item's visual appearance. Now touch the food item and write down words you may discover that describe how it feels… Bring it to your nose and smell it… If you have words to describe the smell, write those down… When you're ready, put the food in your mouth—but don't chew yet. Write down words you may find to describe both the sensations of the food and what happens in your body (especially the mouth) when the food is introduced. Now begin chewing but see if you can resist the urge to swallow. If you can, write down words to describe the chewing process before you swallow. Notice your experience after swallowing and write down any words that may come to describe that.

Think about the experience of eating that you've just had…and look at the words before you. If you'd like, using these or any other words, write a description of the eating process you've just completed. Some people find it easier to get started by using one word from each list (or stage in the eating process). Your writing can be either poetry or prose. You might want to try to capture the immediacy of the experience and see if you can get someone else to feel it. If you're familiar with Haiku, you might try that form or you may wish to find your own form (see Table 12.1 for examples).

Sharing
Have participants share their writing if they're willing. Allow plenty of time for verbal processing.

Table 12.1 Examples of writing

Wrinkly brown Sticky Sweet smell Tickles my mouth Juicy sweetness Can't wait Swallow	I want it! I don't want it! Give me! Get it away! Can't do it anymore Gulp, gulp, gulp

MBET EXERCISE 6
Observing Emotions and Mind-States
Goals
To understand how mind-states can color our perceptions; recognize when we are under the influence of a mind-state; notice the impermanent nature of mind-states. To recognize that we don't need to act according to how we feel in the moment.

Materials
Art supplies; large multi-purpose paper.

Meditation
Mindfulness of breathing with observation of mind-states added.

Discussion
A mind-state is a pervasive condition of the mind that becomes the environment in which our thoughts and perceptions occur. An emotion can become a mind-state when we become saturated by it. For instance, we may be feeling very happy when something

happens to make us angry. The anger may pass quickly and allow us to return to our happiness. If we dwell on the anger and allow memories and images of anger to flourish, the anger may become pervasive and begin to affect all of our perceptions. It may seem as if we can feel nothing but anger, have always felt it, and always will feel it. This is anger as a mind-state.

Another way of thinking about mind-states is that they are like the weather of our minds. The world looks very different when it's cloudy than when it's sunny. A raindrop is a small thing but a rainstorm is a force we have to reckon with.

Mind-states can also be conditions, such as sleepiness, restlessness, sense craving, doubt, or agitation. There may not be a specific emotion behind it and the cause may even be physical—such as a lack of sleep or the side effects of a medication.

We can also think of a mind-state as a mood. It's hard to look outside of it because it's everywhere you see. If you look carefully, however, you can begin to see that your depression (for example) is not operating all of the time. There are moments of humor, comfort, satisfaction, pleasure, and many other kinds of experiences happening even in some of the deepest depressions. We have to learn to see them.

To see that mind-states are less substantial than they appear, we first need to get to know them and watch how they operate in the environment of our minds.

Meditation
Guide the participants:

> As we engage in the mindfulness of breathing, I'd like to invite you to notice the environment in which you perceive the breath. What is the weather like in your mind? Is it bright and cheerful, or dull and dreary? Is it clear or cloudy? Are there persistent themes that keep emerging in your thoughts? What does your body feel like? Is there a relationship between what you're thinking and what you're feeling in the body? Is the mind very busy and active, or is it quiet or calm? Think for a moment of all the different ways we can experience our minds and notice if any of those experiences are present in your mind today.

Expressive Arts
At the end of the meditation, invite each participant to depict the mind-state or states they experienced during the meditation either in the form of a landscape, a weather map, or an abstract. Share and process similarly to Exercise 1. Encourage participants to describe the mind-states they have depicted and discuss how they influenced their experience of the meditation. Particularly notice if there were changes during the meditation or inconsistencies in the depictions of the mind-states, which would illustrate the aforementioned idea that mind-states are not as solid and persistent as they might seem.

MBET EXERCISE 7
Mirroring Visual Movements
Goals
Increased attentiveness and attunement to another person; increased comfort with movement; concentration. Allowing events to occur and participating in them with greater acceptance and spontaneity.

Materials
A spacious room with chairs for each person.

Meditation
Mindfulness of breathing.

Expressive Arts
Ask group members to form dyads and sit facing each other. They should be approximately five feet from each other and five feet from the dyad on either side. Facilitate a five-minute mindfulness meditation. At the conclusion of the meditation, invite participants to make eye contact with their partners. Ask one of the partners to begin by moving slowly. This person will be known as the "leader." In this exercise the term "leader" will always refer to the participant whose movements are being mirrored by another. The other partner will try to mirror the movement. The one who mirrors will be known as the "follower." The follower observes the leader and then imitates the movements of the leader. It is the leaders' responsibility to move in such a way that the followers can simultaneously replicate the movements. After a while, the group facilitator can suggest different movements to mirror, such as facial expressions. Partners can also stand, which may feel more vulnerable so it's important for the facilitator to be attuned to safety needs.

After a few more moments, ask the pairs to switch being leaders and followers. Repeat the exercise as previously described. Invite them to begin switching leaders and followers as you direct them; alternate for varied lengths of time. Then, ask participants to see if they can mirror each other without a leader.

Group Mirroring
Ask participants to stand in a circle. Take turns being leaders, with the rest of the group following. Experiment with mirroring each other without a designated leader. I consider the group leaderless mirror to be the ultimate mindfulness exercise. It requires that one stay alert, open, and receptive, while waiting to see what will emerge. This is the true attitude of mindfulness. Afterwards, sit down and check in verbally.

Clinical Considerations
For all people practicing mindfulness, numerous challenges arise while becoming aware of various mental and emotional states. In a day treatment setting with people with SPMI, it is essential to tailor the MBET protocol to the individual needs of group members. The following vignettes provide a glimpse into some of the ways that MBET can be adapted to support greater emotional regulation.

Provide Individual Members with Greater Structure and Increased Time
Mary, a 35-year-old woman, is diagnosed with schizoaffective disorder. She also experienced significant pre-verbal sexual abuse. She is a wonderful artist, has a playful sense of humor and has a beautiful, radiant presence. Mary is easily overwhelmed by complex tasks and needs to take her time. When she becomes overwhelmed, she can quickly freeze or disintegrate into weeping or unresponsiveness. Quick transitions

can be difficult for her. Some of the tasks (such as numbering the pages in Exercise 3) caused her confusion and distress. In such cases, this can be ameliorated by having a co-leader assist her or by preparing all the pages and papers before the exercise. We also allowed Mary to continue working for as long as she needed—even drawing when the class had moved on.

Provide a Safe Space to Listen to Client Difficulties

Tom is 55 years old and suffers from depression and has a long history of alcohol dependence, in remission. His neuropsychological testing indicated signs of dementia.

Both Tom and Mary felt compelled to draw the bowl as a still life in Exercise 2, which caused them frustration—Tom because he lacked the mastery necessary to accurately portray the object and Mary because she didn't have time to finish. Once they were able to verbalize their frustration and receive support from the group, they were able to describe what they saw and clearly differentiate the process of seeing from the process of thinking, which was the object of the exercise.

Provide Options for Exercises; Validate Client's Experience

Susan is 37 years old with a history of sexual trauma, an eating disorder, and a diagnosis of bipolar disorder and borderline personality disorder. She is a very intelligent and energetic woman who could also be quite volatile emotionally. The eating exercise was quite difficult for her. She felt exposed and reluctant. Giving her choices about how she wanted to proceed, validating her emotional responses and explaining the purpose of the exercise (to slow down eating process and become more aware and less reactive to food and consumption) enabled her to remain in the room and participate enough to get some benefit out of the exercise—enough that she was able to contemplate the possibility of doing it when she was alone.

Susan also found some of the body-oriented exercises to be quite evocative and again, by allowing her to have control over when and in what way she participated, she was able to stay in the room, tolerate her distress, and participate enough to benefit from the exercise.

Conclusion

As mindfulness training becomes increasingly part of the range of tools available to therapists, MBET can play a significant role in bringing mindfulness not only into the realm of activity but also into the realm of interaction. Participants in MBET witness each other struggle, learn, and triumph. They mindfully engage each other through activities that are less susceptible to the misunderstandings and judgments that verbal communication so often engenders. In the space of openness and awareness, there is a much greater tendency to respond to each other with spontaneous kindness and compassion. Mindfulness training has been noteworthy for its ability to change our relationship not only to our experience, but to ourselves as well—to one of less criticism and judgment and more kindness and compassion. MBET facilitates this change in ourselves, and also helps us transfer that learning into our interactions and relationships. If mindfulness is, as Steven Hayes put it, "the third wave of CBT" (Hayes, Follette, and Linehan, *et al.* 2004, pp.5–6) then MBET, MBAT, and the arts-based mindfulness approaches are perhaps the next wave of mindfulness-based treatment.

Note

1   The entire protocol is outlined in Herring (2005) and is available at www.mindfullyunfolding.com (accessed May 1, 2013).

Acknowledgements

Many different expressive therapists and expressive therapy interns participated in this project and have my deepest appreciation and thanks for their influences, particularly: Ben Fox, Stephanie (Sordillo) Ryan, Marika Shimkus, Fiona Logusch, Bev Thurkelsen, Un Chu Lee Hoyle, and Naomi Altman. I would also like to thank Caroline Peterson whose workshop at the Annual Symposium of the Center for Mindfulness, at the University of Massachusetts Medical School, in 2005 helped inspire the inception of MBET and had a large influence on Exercise 1.

References

Bach, P. and Hayes, S. (2002) "The use of acceptance and commitment therapy to prevent re-hospitalization of psychotic patients: A randomized clinical trial." *Journal of Counselling and Clinical Psychology 70*, 5, 1129–1139.

Benson, H. (1976) *The Relaxation Response.* New York: Hearst Books.

Bodhi, B. and Nanamoli, B. (1995) *The Majjhima Nikaya: The Middle Length Discourses of the Buddha.* Boston, MA: Wisdom Publications.

Brown, L.F., Davis, L.W., LaRocco, V.A., and Strasburger, A. (2010) "Participant perspectives on mindfulness meditation training for anxiety in schizophrenia." *American Journal of Psychiatric Rehabilitation 13*, 224–242.

Cayoun, B. (2011) *Mindfulness Integrated CBT.* Chichester: Wiley-Blackwell.

Davis, G. and Payne, A. (2003) *Dialectical Behavior Therapy for Substance Abusers.* Workshop Presentation. Seattle, WA: Behavioral Tech LLC.

Dimeff, L.A. and Linehan, M.M. (2011) *Dialectical Behavior Therapy for Substance Abusers.* (Kindle edition).

Hayes, S.C., Follette, V.M., and Linehan, M.M. (eds) (2004) *Mindfulness and Acceptance: Expanding the Cognitive-Behavioral Tradition.* New York: Guilford Press.

Hayes, S.C., Strosahl, K.D., and Wilson, K.G. (1999) *Acceptance and Commitment Therapy: An Experiential Approach to Behavior Change.* New York: Guilford Press.

Herring, D. (2005) *The Mindfulness Workbook for the Treatment of Severe and Persistent Mental Illness.* Unpublished manuscript. Available via www.mindfullyunfolding.com, accessed May 1, 2013.

Kabat-Zinn, J. (1990) *Full Catastrophe Living: Using the Wisdom of Your Body and Mind to Face Stress, Pain, and Illness.* New York: Dell Publishing.

Linehan, M.M. (1995) *Treating Borderline personality disorder: The Dialectic Approach.* New York: Guilford Press.

Ma, S.H. and Teasdale, J.D. (2004) "Mindfulness-based cognitive therapy for depression: Replication and exploration of differential relapse prevention effects." *Journal of Consulting and Clinical Psychology 72*, 1, 31–40.

Marlatt, G.A., Witkewitz, K., Dillworth, T.M., Bowen, S.W., *et al.* (2004) "Vipassana meditation as a treatment protocol for alcohol and drug use disorders." In S.C. Hayes, V.M. Follette, and M.M.

Linehan (eds) *Mindfulness and Acceptance: Expanding the Cognitive-Behavioral Tradition.* New York: Guilford Press.

Monti, D., Peterson, C., Shakin Kunkel, E., Hauck, W.W., *et al.* (2006) "A randomized, controlled trial of mindfulness-based art therapy (MBAT) for women with cancer." *Psycho-Oncology 15*, 5, 363–373.

Segal, Z.V., Williams, J.M.G., and Teasdale, J.D. (2002) *Mindfulness-Based Cognitive Behavioral Therapy for Depression: A New Approach to Preventing Relapse.* New York: Guilford Press.

Teasdale, J.D., Segal, Z.V., Ridgeway, V.A., Soulsby, J.M., *et al.* (2000) "Prevention of relapse/occurrence in major depression by Mindfulness-Based Cognitive Therapy." *Journal of Consulting Clinical Psychology 68*, 4, 615–623.

PART IV

Mindfulness-Based Arts Therapies Approaches

Chapter 13

Authentic Movement and Mindfulness

Embodied Awareness and the Healing Nature of the Expressive Arts

Zoë Avstreih

Authentic Movement is a self-directed movement practice in which one or more move in the presence of a witness. With eyes closed, the mover focuses inward—bringing attention to sensation, impulse, image, and feeling, as it emerges into awareness in the present moment. The witness sits at the side, with eyes open, creating a safe container for the mover to listen deeply to the wisdom of the body.

Mindfulness, the practice of maintaining one's attention on the immediate experience with curiosity, openness, and acceptance, is the very essence of Authentic Movement. As a practice, it is rooted in trust that the direct experience of one's body is a source of wisdom, a portal to the voice of the "inner teacher." Allowing each embodied moment to unfold, noticing all that arises with a quality of spacious openness, willingness, and non-judgmental acceptance, the practice nurtures the capacity for compassion for self and others.

This chapter discusses Authentic Movement and the cultivation of the inner witness in relationship to therapeutic process and the sense of well-being that stems from increased capacity to enter fully and intimately into each moment of our lived experience.

Theoretical Framework

Authentic Movement

Authentic Movement is a practice rooted in the work of Mary Starks Whitehouse, one of the early pioneers in the field of Dance/Movement therapy (Chodorow 2007; Levy 2005; Lowell 2007). Her work evolved from the intersection of her roots in dance and her own experience in Jungian Analysis; it combined a "thorough understanding of dance with the principles of depth psychology" (Chodorow 2007, p.33). It was a form of active imagination in movement, a process in which one focuses attention inwardly engaging with "the impulses and images of the unconscious" while simultaneously maintaining a self-reflective stance (Chodorow 1997), providing a way for unconscious aspects of our being to be embodied and integrated in our life. Since active imagination involves direct contact with the powerful energies of the unconscious, Jung thought that the work was best suited for psychologically mature individuals with both ego strength and capacity for self-reflection (Chodorow 1997).

Whitehouse used the word "authentic" to describe the particular movements that she felt were genuine, true for the mover in the moment. She stated:

> When movement was simple and inevitable, not to be changed no matter how limited or partial, it became what I called "authentic"—it could be recognized as genuine, belonging to that person. Authentic was the only term I could think of that meant truth—truth of a kind unlearned. (Whitehouse 1979, pp.81–82)

These "authentic" movements serve the process of individuation—what Whitehouse referred to as the "slow unfolding of a wholeness already there" (Whitehouse 1979, p.78).

It was Janet Adler, one of Mary's students, who began to use the words "Authentic Movement" to describe a formalized practice in which a mover moves in the presence of a witness (Lowell 2007, p.54). Authentic Movement is a profoundly simple form. Its outer structure is defined by two roles—a mover and a witness and the relationship that exists between them. For both the mover and the witness, the work of Authentic Movement "is centered on the development of an inner witness, which is one way of understanding the development of consciousness" (Adler 2002, p.xvi). It is this cultivation of the inner witness that both defines Authentic Movement as a practice and links it to the ancient lineage of mindfulness awareness practices.

AUTHENTIC MOVEMENT: THE FORM

The work usually begins in dyads, with one mover and a trained witness; it may develop to include work in triads and groups. In the beginning, the movement time may be ten minutes or so. As the inner witness develops within the mover, supporting an increased capacity to stay present and conscious of the unfolding movement experience, the movement time will gradually increase. In a group of experienced movers and witnesses, the movement time may last for 40 minutes or longer. Following movement, a time to write, draw, and speak supports the integration of direct experience into consciousness.

The Mover

The instructions to the mover are quite simple and are offered as an invitation, a way to support the mover to enter the school of the body and meet the inner teacher. The instructions may vary depending on the individual or group and their comfort or capacity to make direct contact with their embodied experience in the present moment. As a teacher/witness, I might say: "As you enter the space, allow yourself to walk around the room with eyes open, becoming familiar and comfortable in the space. Now slowly allow your focus to turn inward; it often helps to close one's eyes. Begin to notice what is happening in your body right now, the sensations, impulses, energy flows that are here right now, listening for what wants to move, trusting that the body has wisdom that is ready to speak to you and guide you. Remember, there is no right or wrong way to move, no standard of performance, allow yourself to open to the teacher within as it begins to speak through sensation, impulse, gesture, image and affect that are arising in this moment."

Some people find their way in more easily than others. For some, a bit of structure is helpful. I might suggest that they begin by exploring a movement polarity in their body. For example, lying on the floor and exploring "open" and "closed": "Feel these words in this moment, what form does 'open' take in your body right now. When you are as open as feels true for you in this moment, allow your body to find its way to feel and express 'closed.' The expression may involve your whole body, it may happen in a finger, it may be visible to the external witness or not. Remember there is no right way to do this; you are listening for what is impeccably true for you in the moment."

Often during this exploration, the mover will begin to have a sense of listening to and allowing sensation and impulse to guide the movement; they are now on their way to developing a deeper capacity to listen to and be guided by the kinesthetic sense, the technical term for experiencing one's body moving. In the words of Mary Whitehouse:

> The kinesthetic sense can be awakened and developed using any and all kinds of movement, but I believe it becomes conscious only when the inner, that is, the subjective connection is found… It is the concrete, specific awareness of one's own act of moving which is so satisfying. (Whitehouse 1958, p.46)

The mover, echoing the three interwoven moment-to-moment aspects of mindfulness—intention, attention, and attitude (Shapiro and Carlson 2009)—enters the movement time with the intention to remain present and attentive to the specifics of the movement experience, remaining open to image, words, feeling, and memories that might arise.

The Witness

The core of the work of Authentic Movement is rooted in relationship: the relationship between the mover and the external witness; the relationship between the moving self and the internal witness; between the individual and the collective; and between the individual and the greater mysteries of life itself (Adler 1992, 1995, 2002; Avstreih 2005, 2007, 2008).

EXTERNAL WITNESS

The external witness sits at the side of the movement space with eyes open, initially holding the larger responsibility for consciousness. The quiet, non-intrusive presence of the witness creates a safe space for the mover to enter the process, to listen deeply inward and yield to sensation, impulse, image, and feeling as it emerges into consciousness and sequences into movement, visible or invisible to the external witness. Through years of practice, the external witness has cultivated a strong inner witness, capable of tracking both the mover and tracking their own embodied experience, including sensations, impulses, images, feelings, memories, and thoughts.

> The witness brings to the practice a willingness to be present, to be receptive, and to observe without judgment, free from the need to know or define. Most importantly, the witness embodies a willingness to learn from whatever arises, to relinquish answers and to be totally attentive to the present moment. Witnessing is an act of mindfulness and a gift of nonjudgmental presence to another. There is

profound intimacy in witnessing and being witnessed. To see and be seen is the intimacy of true presence, which invites healing. (Avstreih 2007, p.272)

INNER WITNESS

In the practice of Authentic Movement, the words "inner witness" are used to describe the innate capacity of awareness, that which notices. Mindfulness, the practice of intentionally and gently focusing attention on the direct experience of the moment with open receptivity to all that arises, is the practice of cultivating and strengthening one's relationship to the inner witness. It is this focus on the cultivation of the inner witness for both the mover and the witness that defines Authentic Movement as an embodied mindfulness awareness practice.

THE RELATIONSHIP BETWEEN MOVER AND WITNESS

At the core of the practice is the experience of seeing and being seen—which reflects the paradox that we are birthed into the fullness of our being through the attuned presence of another. The early caregiver acts like a mirror for the infant, "giving back the baby the baby's own self" (Winnicott 1964 cited in Philips 1988, p.128). The open, receptive attentiveness and non-judgmental presence of the witness provides an environment of "holding" (Winnicott 1965), a metaphor for an affectively attuned relational field that provides a felt sense of safety and trust. This supports the mover to yield to the deepest levels of her kinesthetic reality, to know one's truth in the presence of another and to have it received by another free from projection.

The movement time is usually followed by a time for the mover and witness to speak. Here, the training and experience of the external witness is critical in order to protect the mover from unconscious witnessing. As Adler (1994) states, "The witness practices the art of seeing" (p.194), which entails not simply "looking at" the mover, but rather allowing oneself to receive and attune to the mover while also attending to one's own experiences in response to the mover. As a practice, Authentic Movement cultivates the ability to witness oneself (intrapersonal attunement) while witnessing another (interpersonal attunement). "Practicing internal attunement makes us more likely to be empathically attuned to others" (Siegel 2012, p.23).

Adler introduced "Percept Language" (Weir 1975), the use of the pronoun "I" into the sharing process to encourage witnessing which is free from judgment, interpretation, and projection (Adler 2002). For example, the witness may see a mover making gentle circular movements on the floor with her hands and it brings to mind an image of playing in the sand as a child. The witness notices a feeling of sadness arising within and remembers a particular experience at the beach and sadness associated with that memory. The witness may share, "As I see you sitting on the floor making gentle circular movements on the floor, I feel a sadness well up in me related to a memory of an early time in my life." The witness owns the experience of sadness, making no assumptions that the mover is also experiencing sadness. This careful attention to speaking as witness is an essential aspect of the practice enhancing its commitment to nurture and protect the integrity and authenticity of expression and being.

It is this emphasis on clarity of seeing and speaking in Authentic movement that makes it an ideal training modality for psychotherapists, promoting what Silverberg (1988) refers to as "therapeutic resonance," a way of "being with" another person rooted in receptivity, openness and quiet attention (Silverberg 1988, p.25).

Authentic Movement as an Embodied Mindfulness Practice

Fundamental to the discipline of Authentic Movement is the understanding that transformation must be rooted in the body. The body is simultaneously the doorway to the unknown and an anchor in the present moment. "Although the impulse to move may spring from a source in the unconscious, the body, which allows the impulse to manifest itself, remains firmly rooted in the fact of its own existence" (Chodorow 1978, p.246).

Mindfulness, the direct, pre-symbolic experience of the lived moment, "is fundamentally a way of being—a way of inhabiting one's body, one's mind, one's moment-to-moment experience" (Shapiro and Carlson 2009, p.5). This non-conceptual awareness or "bare attention" (Gunaratana 2011) is like a mirror, open, alert, non-judgmental, receiving the moment as it births into existence. This is the invitation that the discipline of Authentic Movement has offered since its inception. When Mary Whitehouse introduced her work to a class of dance students at UCLA who were interested not in performance but in dance as rehabilitation and therapy, she began by asking how they might practice without her instruction.

> My impression was of a great deal of activity and movement but of nothing individual, reflective, discovered or spontaneous. It has all been learned. I asked them to sit with their legs crossed and to close their eyes. I described the open waiting, which is also a kind of listening to the body, an emptiness in which something can happen. You wait until you feel a change—the body sinks or begins to tip, the head slowly lowers forward or rolls to one side. As you feel it begin, you follow where it leads, like following a pathway that opens up before you as you step. … The ego learns slowly an attitude toward *what* wants moving. (Whitehouse 1987, pp.52–53)

Whitehouse, guided by a deep intuitive knowing, her keen powers of observation and her open curiosity, was articulating the ancient wisdom of mindfulness in an embodied form she called *Authentic* movement. The heart of the practice is deep listening, right here, right now, paying attention and opening to the wisdom of the inner teacher as it bubbles up into consciousness as sensation and impulse emerging into movement visible or invisible to the external witness.

Jon Kabat-Zinn (2005) refers to this ancient innate wisdom as follows:

> It turns out that we all have, lying deep within us, in our hearts and in our bones, a capacity for a dynamic, vital, sustaining inner peacefulness and well-being, and for a huge, innate, multifaceted intelligence that goes way beyond the merely conceptual… We gain access to them starting from wherever we are, which is always here, and in the only moment that we ever have, which is now. (pp.7–8)

This is the essence of Authentic Movement; we begin with the direct experience of the body in this present moment.

Clinical and Training Application

The School of the Body: The Wisdom of the Inner Teacher

I have engaged in the practice of Authentic Movement for 40 years as both a therapist and a teacher, utilizing the form in in-depth individual and group therapy and in the graduate and post-graduate training of therapists with various theoretical orientations. For both clients and students training to become therapists, Authentic Movement has provided an education rooted in the wisdom of the inner teacher as it speaks through the body as illustrated in the following "lessons."

LESSON 1: GROUNDING IN THE PRESENT MOMENT AND WELCOMING WHAT IS

Authentic Movement, like meditation, requires both surrender and discipline. It requires impeccable attention to impulse, sensation, image, and feeling, and allowing what arises to sequence from awareness into movement. Joyce, a woman in her mid-fifties, who elected to enroll in my Authentic Movement class to fulfill the body-awareness requirement in her graduate psychology program, describes her initial experiences with the practice and the changes and healing that occurred in the following way:

> During my first experiences as a mover, and I listen for what is here, in my body right now. I am aware of a deep-seated pain in my upper right back. I notice I am moving with a force as if to cut through the knotted tangle, rather than to allow the experience to be there. My left side feels numb and unmoving as my right side, particularly my right upper back and arm twist and struggle. At times, I feel like someone is pulling on my right arm. This pattern continues to emerge for a few weeks.
>
> Around my third session, I begin to relax somewhat and allow my awareness to drop into the discomfort in my right side rather than struggle with it. Following the movement time, I take time to write. Here is what my right arm had to say:
>
> > Oh, I'm busy, busy. I feel the cool smooth wood floor. But I am so busy, restless. Now I start to sew. I sew up old wounds with yellow thread. I sew, sew, sew, so busy. Sewing here and there, chest, arm, neck, head. Oh these eyes are sore. They need circular movements and out the forehead and top of the head. Oh yes, yes, I'm a busy old crone. No one believes me that I can sew up this and that old wound. But I do see the internal fabric of the soul and I can sew it up. That is a skill I have, very skillful and very busy.
>
> The following session, I lay on my back, but this time my whole body is awake and active, and feels whole, as if the old crone had indeed sewn up the two sides. I sense my body from inside and outside at the same time. One half of me is meeting and touching the other half. One foot touches the other foot; one

arm twines around the other, as though one entity or being meets another. I experience this meeting both from inside and from outside—both experiences— feeling and being felt. Feeling my face—the bony prominence of the nose, the soft squishiness of the eyelids, the coarse softness of the hair. How the hair feels from the outside through my fingers and hands, and how it feels from inside my head to have my hair gently pulled by my hands.

The mover reported that this session marked the awakening of a true kinesthetic sense of self, a direct, subjective connection to her own moving body, which she found provided a new sense of security and ease. As she grounded in the present-moment experience of the body, "the sewing up of old wounds" revealed a path for healing, integration, and a felt sense of security and trust.

LESSON 2: TURNING TOWARD

Sensation becomes the guide or doorway to the wisdom of the inner teacher. As we develop the capacity to stay present with open, receptive attention, the body speaks, revealing the fixed patterns that restrict our lived experience. "Acknowledging present-moment reality as it actually is, whether pleasant or unpleasant, is the first step toward transforming that reality and your relationship to it" (Kabat-Zinn 1993 cited in Christopher *et al.* 2006, p.497). Authentic Movement provides a safe container for these constricting patterns to emerge into consciousness and release naturally and organically, as the words of this mover, a man in his forties in the midst of career change, so poignantly demonstrate:

> I enter the space and wait with open, receptive attention to what is arising in my body, letting twitches, impulses, feelings just come. I feel nervous, and notice my right shoulder is pulled back, head turned to the front, right hand lightly holding left wrist. This is an old comfortable stance that I fall into many times a day. The movements alternately fade and exaggerate, as if they have their own intention. Then my right hand grasps the left wrist tighter and tighter, desperately, as if hanging on, while the right shoulder twists back. Suddenly my right arm pulls free, swings behind as if defending me from behind. I realize it has not been comforting my left hand, but hanging on to keep from swinging back, hanging on for dear life.
>
> I remember a recurrent childhood nightmare of being chased by a wild animal and then remember for the first time in many decades being chased around the house by my drunken father leather belt in hand ready to attack me. I am sweating; the continuous movements of my right arm behind me and the powerful rhythmic twisting of my torso support me in the moment. Instantly, surprising myself, I whirl around to face what is behind. All the twists in my shoulder, arms and neck relax. I feel my feet on the floor. I explore the strength of my feet, legs and hips and the freedom in my arms. I hear the words inside, "What a choice, humiliation or injury." I am not sure what they mean.

Since this movement time, the habitual stance has dropped away almost entirely. When it does emerge again, I am aware of it and invariably can find something in the immediate context that feels threatening. Awareness brings choice andopportunities to respond in new ways. I am no longer confined to the old belief that there are only two possibilities in life—humiliation or injury.

As this mover demonstrates, the capacity to remain in direct connection with the body, in this case exploring a familiar posture with openness and receptivity supports the mover to open to life in new ways creating possibility based on choice rather than unconscious reaction.

LESSON 3: DEVELOPING COMPASSION FOR ONESELF

The essence of Authentic Movement is rooted in the cultivation of a compassionate and spacious inner witness, which enables us to meet the present with openness; "we come to trust our capacity to open to life without armoring" (Kornfield 2009, p.31). Illness, when met with mindfulness, can be fertile soil for the cultivation of compassion for oneself as demonstrated by the words of this mover, a young man in his thirties training to become a psychotherapist:

Since being diagnosed with Lyme disease, I have dealt with and thought about my body constantly. Paradoxically, all this attention paid to my body has not brought a real experience of my body. Instead, I have ignored my body out of fear of knowing the full toll of the disease. Through the practice of Authentic Movement, I have been learning to relate to my body in a deeper way. In this movement session, I am lying on the floor, rocking my legs and hips in a soothing motion. I begin to sink in and listen to the pain in my body, the pain I often try to ignore. After I finish the movement time, I write these words:

My movements are meant to soothe, soothe the pain that lies in my hips, my knees, my back, my shoulders, wrists, and ankles—deep in my heart. Seven years of disease coursing through me in outwardly silent pain. My movements are meant to soothe, so I can contain the hurt, the burden—soothe the heart and soul and mind—soothe my innards. Soothe my family; soothe my eyes, my face, my shoulders, my chest. Soothe my legs. So I am tall, erect, open. So I can face the world.

It is the first time in a very long time that I am truly present with my body. The effect is that I can feel myself on a deeper level, below the pain. (Avstreih 2008, p.217)

Here practice leads to the direct experience of the inner witness, which remains present to, with, and in spite of the pain, offering the possibility "to access a deep, and perhaps inviolable, sense of who we are at the center of ourselves" (Wallin 2007, p.165).

LESSON 4: BEARING WITNESS: EXTENDING COMPASSION TO OTHERS

As stability of the inner witness develops, there comes a time when one is both ready and longing to sit as witness for others. Having been seen, there is the desire and the capacity to see others.

> The relationship between mover and witness is subtle and complex. Although the witness does not engage in her own experience, her inner mover remains alive and resonant, nurturing the ability to be empathically attuned with another and with the potential to experience another directly…When the illusionary boundaries between self and other dissolve, there is only compassionate seeing. (Avstreih 2008, pp.218–219)

Following are the words of an experienced student of the form as she sits as witness to a group of movers:

> I sit along the edge and yet feel intimately connected to the movers. I see one mover lying on her stomach, her hand on the top of her head, her fingers gently touching, caressing her hair. I am filled with a sense of tenderness, and caring. On the other side of the room, I see another mover also with hands on head. This mover is curled in a tight ball, both hands tightly wrapped around the top of his head. I feel fear, sadness, and a profound sense of aloneness. My heart opens to both. I am deeply connected to both movers, and recognize the universality of our shared human existence. I feel rooted in myself and at the same time connected to something larger.

Authentic Movement cultivates the ability to witness oneself while witnessing another. *Self-knowing awareness* enhances the capacity to resonate with another and yet maintain one's own differentiated sense of self, supporting the capacity to make empathic contact and maintain the equilibrium necessary to stay present for others in distress, an essential therapeutic skill (Siegel 2012, pp.22–23).

Conclusion: Coming Full Circle

Authentic Movement invites us into the school of the body. Here, we have an opportunity to cultivate "intimacy with how things actually are" (Kabat-Zinn 2005, p.545) and to embrace this "utter gift of a human life" (Kabat-Zinn 2005, p.608). This is the first step in healing and a call to live life fully with consciousness, compassion, and mindful awareness, to individuate and actualize our innate wholeness. As Jung said, "Individuation does not shut one out from the world, but gathers the world to one's self" (Jung cited in Preece 2006, p.74). Individuality blossoms into interconnectedness. We "dance" into the fullness of our being for ourselves and for the world.

References

Adler, J. (1992) "Body and Soul." In P. Pallaro (ed.) (1999) *Authentic movement: Essays by Mary Starks Whitehouse, Janet Adler and Joan Chodorow.* London and Philadelphia, PA: Jessica Kingsley Publishers.

Adler, J. (1994) "The Collective Body." In P. Pallaro (ed.) (1999) *Authentic movement: Essays by Mary Starks Whitehouse, Janet Adler and Joan Chodorow.* London and Philadelphia, PA: Jessica Kingsley Publishers.

Adler, J. (1995) *Arching Backward.* Rochester, VT: Inner Traditions.

Adler, J. (2002) *Offering from the Conscious Body: The Discipline of Authentic movement.* Rochester, VT: Inner Traditions.

Avstreih, Z. (2005) "Authentic movement and Buddhism." *A Moving Journal 13,* 3, 8–10.

Avstreih, Z. (2007) "Achieving Body Permanence: Authentic movement and the Paradox of Healing." In P. Pallaro (ed.) (2007) *Authentic movement: Moving the Body, Moving the Self, Being Moved.* London and Philadelphia, PA: Jessica Kingsley Publishers.

Avstreih, Z. (2008) "The Body in Psychotherapy: Dancing with the Paradox." In F. Kaklasuskas, S. Nimanheminda, L. Hoffman, and M. Jack (eds) *Brilliant Sanity: Buddhist Approaches to Psychotherapy.* Colorado Springs, CO: University of the Rockies Press.

Chodorow, J. (1978) "Dance Therapy and the Transcendent Function." In P. Pallaro (ed.) (1999) *Authentic movement: Essays by Mary Starks Whitehouse, Janet Adler and Joan Chodorow.* London and Philadelphia, PA: Jessica Kingsley Publishers.

Chodorow, J. (1997) (ed.) *Jung on Active Imagination.* Princeton, NJ: Princeton University Press.

Chodorow, J. (2007) "Inner-Directed Movement in Analysis: Early Beginning". In P. Pallaro (ed.) (2007) *Authentic movement: Moving the Body, Moving the Self, Being Moved.* London and Philadelphia: Jessica Kingsley Publishers.

Christopher, J.C., Christopher, S.E., Dunnagan, T., and Schure, M. (2006) "Teaching self care through mindfulness practices: The application of yoga, meditation, and qiqong to counselor training." *Journal of Humanistic Psychology 46,* 494–509.

Gunaratana, B. (2011) (First published 1991) *Mindfulness in Plain English.* Boston, MA: Wisdom Publications.

Jung, C.G. (1969) "The Structure and Dynamics of the Psyche." In *The Collected Works of C.G. Jung.* Vol. 8. London: Routledge and Kegan Paul.

Kabat-Zinn, J. (1993) "Mindfulness Meditation: Health Benefits of an Ancient Buddhist Practice." In D. Goleman and J. Gurin (eds) *Mind/body Medicine.* New York: Consumer Reports Books.

Kabat-Zinn, J. (2005) *Coming to Our Senses: Healing Ourselves and the World Through Mindfulness.* New York: Hyperion.

Kornfield, J. (2009) *The Wise Heart: A Guide to the Universal Teachings of Buddhist Psychology.* New York: Bantam Books.

Levy, F. (2005) *Dance/movement therapy: A Healing Art.* Reston, VA: American Alliance for Health, Physical Education, Recreation and Dance.

Lowell, D. (2007) "Authentic movement." In P. Pallaro (ed.) (2007) *Authentic movement: Moving the Body, Moving the Self, Being Moved.* London and Philadelphia, PA: Jessica Kingsley Publishers.

Philips, A. (1988) *Winnicott.* Cambridge, MA: Harvard University Press.

Preece, R. (2006) *The Wisdom of Imperfection: The Challenge of Individuation in Buddhist Life.* Ithaca, NY: Snow Lion Publications.

Shapiro, S.L. and Carlson, L.E. (2009) *The Art and Science of Mindfulness: Integrating Mindfulness into Psychology and the Helping Professions.* Washington, DC: American Psychological Association.

Siegel, D. (2012) *Pocket Guide to Interpersonal Neurobiology: An Integrative Handbook of the Mind.* New York and London: W.W. Norton and Company.

Silverberg, F. (1988) "Therapeutic resonance." *Journal of Contemplative Psychotherapy 5,* 25–42.

Wallin, D. (2007) *Attachment in Psychotherapy.* New York and London: The Guilford Press.

Weir, J. (1975) "The Personal Growth Laboratory." In K.D. Benne, L.P. Bradford, J. R. Gibb, and R.O. Lippitt (eds) *The Laboratory Method of Changing and Learning: Theory and Application.* Palo Alto, CA: Science Behavior Books.

Whitehouse, M.S. (1958) "The Tao of the Body." In P. Pallaro (ed.) (1999) *Authentic movement: Essays by Mary Starks Whitehouse, Janet Adler and Joan Chodorow.* London and Philadelphia: Jessica Kingsley Publishers.

Whitehouse, M.S. (1979) "C.J. Jung and Dance Therapy: Two Major Principles." In P. Pallaro (ed.) (1999) *Authentic movement: Essays by Mary Starks Whitehouse, Janet Adler and Joan Chodorow.* London and Philadelphia, PA: Jessica Kingsley Publishers.

Whitehouse, M.S. (1987) "Physical Movement and Personality" In P. Pallaro (ed.) (1999) *Authentic movement: Essays by Mary Starks Whitehouse, Janet Adler and Joan Chodorow.* London and Philadelphia, PA: Jessica Kingsley Publishers.

Winnicott, D.W. (1964) "Mirror-Role." In *The Family and Individual Development.* London: Tavistock.

Winnicott, D.W. (1965) "The Theory of the Parent–Infant Relationship." In *The Maturational Processes and the Facilitating Environment.* London: Hogarth Press.

Figure 3.1: Anger (tempera paint on paper 21"x 26")

(p.58)

Figure 4.8: Eternal Nourishment

(p.77)

Figure 5.4: (a) Enlargement of the surrounding space

(p.89)

Figure 10.3: Personal tree

(p.151)

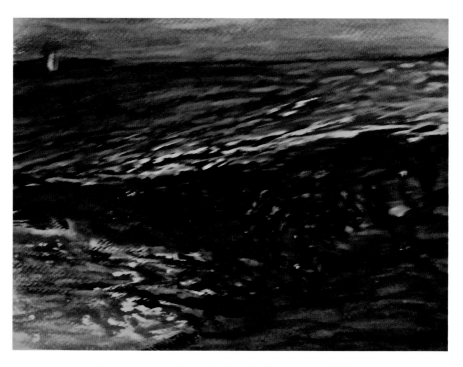

Figure 11.1: Visualization of mother's cancer washed away

(p.156)

Figure 14.6: What does it need?

(p.206)

Figure 15.2: Nick's surrounded orb

(p.216)

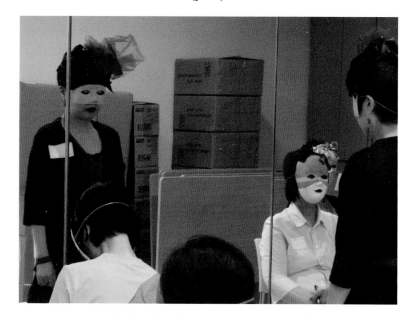

Figure 16.9: The voice from my half-mask

(p.231)

Figure 18.5: Prayer flags: "What I Want to Carry With Me"

(p.257)

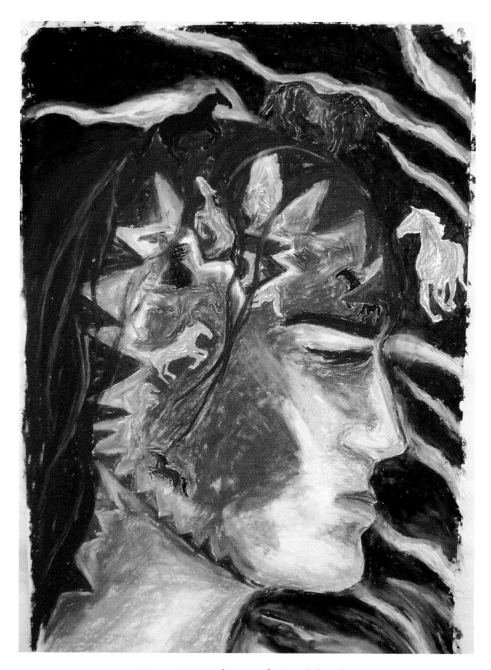

Figure 19.1: Student art of agitated thoughts

(p.273)

Chapter 14

Focusing-Oriented Arts Therapy
Cultivating Mindfulness and Compassion, and Accessing Inner Wisdom

Laury Rappaport

Focusing-Oriented Arts Therapy (FOAT) is a mindfulness-based approach that integrates Eugene Gendlin's Focusing with the arts therapies (Rappaport 2014, 2013, 2012, 2010, 2009, 2008). Focusing adds a mindfulness aspect to the expressive arts therapies, grounds the experience in the body, accesses the client's inner knowing, cultivates greater compassion, and enhances the skills to stay attuned to the moment-to-moment unfolding of the client's experiential process. Rome and Martin (2010) describe Focusing as "a contemplative practice drawing from Western philosophy and psychology that cultivates three vital inner skills: self-knowing, caring presence, and intuitive insight" (p.60). Other Focusing professionals describe parallels between Focusing, Buddhism, and other spiritual traditions (Chutroo 2003; Focusing Institute 2013).

My training in mindfulness meditation derives from the teachings of Thich Nhat Hanh, Vietnamese Buddhist mindfulness teacher. Although FOAT is not a traditional mindfulness practice, there are interconnections between Thich Nhat Hanh's teachings and FOAT theory and practices. In this chapter, I present a theoretical overview of FOAT as a mindfulness-based approach, interconnections between Thich Nhat Hanh's practices of mindfulness and FOAT, followed by training and clinical examples.

Theoretical Framework
FOAT as a Mindfulness-Based Approach
DEVELOPMENT AND OVERVIEW OF FOAT

I developed Focusing-Oriented Arts Therapy (FOAT) after 30 years of applying Focusing to the expressive arts therapies with a wide variety of clinical populations in different settings with individuals, couples, families, groups, and organizations. FOAT is based on the original six-step method that Eugene Gendlin (1981, 1996) developed to teach people Focusing, and on the practices of Focusing-Oriented Therapy (FOT). FOAT consists of a set of foundational principles and four main approaches: FOAT Check-In; Clearing a Space with the Arts (CAS-Arts); Theme-Directed FOAT; and Focusing-Oriented Arts Psychotherapy.

The interconnections between FOAT and mindfulness are summarized in Table 14.1 (see p.194).

Table 14.1 Interconnections between FOAT and mindfulness

FOAT	Mindfulness
Foundational principles: presence, grounding; felt sense; Focusing Attitude; clinical sensitivity; listening/reflection	Establishes mindfulness; deep listening
FOAT Check-In	Cultivates mindful awareness; compassion; and insight (wisdom)
Clearing a Space with the Arts	Names feelings and experiences without identifying with them; accesses qualities of mindfulness
Theme-Directed FOAT	Cultivates mindfulness, compassion, and insight (wisdom)
Focusing-Oriented Arts Psychotherapy	Cultivates mindfulness, compassion, and insight (wisdom)
Transforming feelings: see Clinical and Training Application of four FOAT approaches, (pp.197–206)	See Thich Nhat Hanh's five steps for transforming feelings (p.197)

FOAT FOUNDATIONAL PRINCIPLES: ESTABLISHING MINDFULNESS

The foundational principles of FOAT—presence, grounding, Focusing Attitude, listening and reflection, and clinical sensitivity—serve to establish mindfulness and are designed to ensure the respect and safety of clients throughout all phases of treatment.

Presence

Mindful awareness begins with the therapist's sense of presence: Are you here and ready to receive the client? Are you present in your own body, heart, mind, and spirit? Are you ready to listen compassionately? Are you aware of your own issues—and can you set them aside to be present? Presence in FOAT is similar to mindfulness practices of being aware with compassionate acceptance in the present moment.

The Focusing Attitude

The Focusing Attitude is characterized by qualities of "being friendly," accepting, nonjudgmental, and welcoming toward one's inner felt sense—and it cultivates self-compassion. Rome (2004) describes the Focusing Attitude as "akin to the Buddhist virtue called maître—lovingkindness or friendliness directed toward oneself. It is a potent and at times quite magical way of making friends with oneself" (p.63).

Grounding

During Focusing, unexpected feelings and issues may surface. It is helpful for therapists to teach clients grounding or centering practices—such as, mindful breathing, body awareness of feet on the ground— before Focusing. Thich Nhat Hanh (1991, 2001,

2012) describes the importance of mindful breathing to calm the body and mind prior to working with strong feelings.

Listening and Reflection

In FOAT, the therapist demonstrates compassionate understanding through experiential listening, artistic reflection, and nonverbal communication (e.g. gesture, energy, movement). Deep listening is a fundamental mindfulness practice. Hanh (2001) states, "Listening with compassion can help the other person to suffer less… Compassionate listening is a very deep practice" (p.4).

Clinical Sensitivity

It is important to be mindful of each client's needs, vulnerabilities, and strengths, and to adapt FOAT accordingly. For example, Focusing and mindfulness are often done with eyes closed. However, clients in early stages of trauma, or people in an acute phase of severe mental illness, may not feel comfortable closing their eyes (Rappaport 2009, 2010). Both FOAT and mindfulness can be done with eyes open—for example, inviting clients to keep their gaze toward the group and keep a soft focus.

FOAT Approaches and Mindfulness Interconnections

The four FOAT approaches cultivate mindfulness in unique ways.

FOAT Check-In: Focusing Attitude and Felt Sense

A FOAT Check-In provides an opportunity for clients to pause—bringing mindful awareness and the Focusing Attitude of being "friendly" to their felt sense of their experience. A felt sense is one's inner bodily sense of an experience, feeling, or issue. Taking time, the Focuser is invited to see if there is a "symbol/handle" (Gendlin 1981, p.44)—a word, phrase, image, gesture, or sound—that matches the felt sense. The Focuser checks it or "resonates" it for a sense of rightness. After, the Focuser is invited to express the felt sense handle/symbol through expressive arts.

From a felt sense, a word or phrase naturally unfolds into writing or poetry; an image into art; a gesture into movement or dance; and a sound into music, voice, or sound exploration. Alternatively, the Focuser can simply do a Focusing Check-In without the artistic expression. A FOAT Check-In is similar in intention to Thich Nhat Hanh's (1991) description of meditation: "Meditation has two aspects: stopping and calming is the first, and looking deeply is the second" (p.89).

Clearing a Space with the Arts

In Clearing a Space with the Arts (CAS-Arts), the Focuser is guided to take a mindful inventory of what's in the way of feeling "All Fine" (or present) right now (not every issue or stressor in one's entire life but rather, about three to six things that are affecting one's well-being in the present moment). As each stressor arises, it is kinesthetically sensed—and the Focuser either uses the arts to symbolically place it outside of one's body and at a distance that feels right, or imagines doing so. The expressive arts concretize placing the stressor outside of the body.

Setting the stressor outside of the body, either through the imagination or use of the arts, helps the Focuser to dis-identify with it. The Focuser senses a *me* that is separate from those stressors. Once the issues are set aside, the Focuser is guided to sense the place inside that is "All Fine" or clear—and to find a handle/symbol that matches the "All Fine Place." This helps the Focuser to access and ground an aspect of self that is intrinsically whole (Castailia 2010; Lee 2011; Rappaport 2009; Weiland 2011; Weiner 2012).

As Thich Nhat Hanh (1991) says, "Calling a feeling by its name, such as 'anger,' 'sorrow,' 'joy,' or 'happiness,' helps us identify it clearly and recognize it more deeply" (p.51). CAS-Arts helps to name each issue and to access an inherent place of well-being, that is often described as peaceful, calm, and vast. There are four variations of CAS-Arts so that a range of client needs can be met: nondirective, directive, concrete and hybrid (a combination of concrete with nondirective or directive). The nondirective and directive approaches are often done with the eyes closed, whereas the concrete CAS is conducted with eyes open (see Rappaport 2009 for detailed descriptions).

Theme-Directed FOAT
Mindfulness themes of compassion, gratitude, forgiveness, generosity, and so forth can be offered to the group to Focus on. For example, the Focuser can become aware of something in their life that has been a teacher of compassion—perhaps a person, pet, spiritual source, or something from nature. The Focuser is guided to bring mindful awareness into the body along with an attitude of friendly curiosity, and to get a felt sense of the teacher of compassion. Next, the Focuser is guided to see if there is a symbol that matches the felt sense—a word, phrase, image, gesture, or sound—followed by artistic expression.

In Theme-Directed FOAT, I often teach mindfulness exercises—mindful breathing, mindful walking, and Pebble Meditation (based on the teachings of Thich Nhat Hanh) followed by Focusing and expressive arts (see Appendix 1 and Rappaport 2009).

Focusing-Oriented Arts Psychotherapy
In Focusing-Oriented Arts Psychotherapy, Focusing, listening, and the expressive arts are interwoven throughout the unfolding psychotherapy process. The Focusing Attitude helps clients to simultaneously be in touch with a witness aspect of self while also experiencing their felt sense of an issue, situation, or experience. This is especially beneficial when working with strong or overwhelming feelings. The Focusing Attitude helps to achieve what Thich Nhat Hanh (1991) describes as mindful observation and the ability not to be overwhelmed by feelings:

> Mindful observation is based on the principle of "non-duality": our feeling is not separate from us or caused merely by something outside us; our feeling *is* us, and for the moment we *are* that feeling. We are neither drowned in nor terrorized by that feeling, nor do we reject it. (p.52)

The expressive arts also provide tools for strengthening the ability to access a calm center while also being engaged in the felt sense experience.

TRANSFORMING FEELINGS: MINDFULNESS AND FOAT

Thich Nhat Hanh describes five mindfulness steps for transforming feelings: (1) recognize feelings; (2) be one with the feeling; (3) calm the feeling; (4) release the feeling; and (5) look deeply. To clarify Step 2, Thich Nhat Hanh describes "being one" with the feeling, that is similar to the Focusing Attitude and felt sense:

> It is best not to say, "Go away, Fear. I don't like you. You are not me." It is much more effective to say, "Hello Fear. How are you today?" Then you can invite the two aspects of yourself, mindfulness and fear, to shake hands as friends and become one. (pp.53–54)

He elaborates on "looking deeply": "Calming and releasing are just medicines for symptoms… By looking you will see what will help you to begin to transform the feeling" (p.55). The arts therapies provide methods for looking deeply.

Thich Nhat Hanh's five steps for transforming feelings are reflected in the following clinical and training examples of the four FOAT approaches.

Clinical and Training Application

Like mindfulness, Focusing is a practice that deepens over time. It is more than a technique to apply to psychotherapy—but rather a life skill for living with greater compassion and wisdom. To become a Focusing or FOAT practitioner, the training incorporates learning from the inside out. The exercises and examples presented here are used for training therapists and also working with clients.

FOAT Check-In: Focusing Attitude and Felt Sense

A FOAT Check-In can be done at the beginning of a session so that a client can become mindful of how they are right now; during the session when on the edge of a feeling in order to get a bodily felt sense of it; before or after an expressive arts intervention; and at the end of a session.

Example: Heather

Heather was in her late twenties when she was diagnosed with a rare illness that caused chronic pain, weakness, and a myriad of other symptoms. To manage the illness, she needed to take many medications and undergo chemotherapy infusions. During a training group, I led the group in a FOAT Check-In:

Box 14.1 FOAT Check-In exercise

Take a few deep breaths down inside your body. Notice the breath as it comes into your body and moves out of your body, feeling the support of whatever you're sitting on…the support of the earth…and sky. When you're ready, gently bring your awareness to the inside of your body, just noticing how you are right now—sensations, energies, feelings, etc. Just notice…being friendly to whatever you find right now (*pause*). See if there's a word, phrase, image, gesture, or sound that matches the inner felt sense. Check it for a sense of rightness. When you have it, express the felt sense through an artistic modality.

Heather drew an image of a red outline of a body with a smaller black figure clawing it (Figure 14.1).

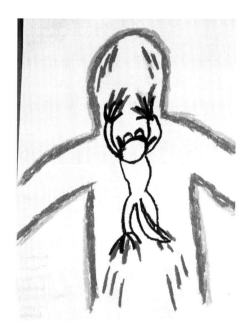

Figure 14.1: FOAT Check-In

She shared:

> Before I began using Focusing with art, I thought of my pain and anger with hatred. The illness is symbolized as a creature with black claws inside of the human figure in red.

> The creature was clawing and scratching inside the body, leaving bloody, red scratch marks.

Later, Heather continued to work with the Focusing Attitude. She imagined and sensed into her body, "What would it be like and feel like to be more accepting of the illness?" This time Heather's felt sense symbol came as a blue figure surrounded with bright, yellow light holding a small figure (Figure 14.2).

She shared:

As I brought an attitude of "being friendly" to it, I began to understand, that the creature was clawing and scratching inside the body because it was trapped and scared and confused. It wasn't evil and it meant no harm. It was innocent and trying to get free.

Now the figure is blue surrounded by yellow light…and is cradling that same creature, now buried and sleeping softly in its arms. Seeing my pain as innocent and frightened led me to have more compassion for myself. In cradling the creature, I was actually cradling the vulnerable part of myself that was frightened and hurting. The claw marks are still visible inside the figure…but now they are black rather than red… symbolizing healing scars rather than fresh wounds. (Rappaport 2013, pp.229–230)

Figure 14.2: Focusing Attitude toward illness

In this example, we see all of Thich Nhat Hanh's steps for transforming feelings. By bringing mindful awareness into her body through Focusing, Heather was first able to *recognize* her feelings. Next she was able to *become one* with the feeling by taking her time to get a felt sense. The Focusing Attitude of "being friendly" helped her to *calm* the feeling. Heather was able to release the feeling through the expressive arts. Both Focusing and art helped her to *look deeply*—first, to notice that the creature was scared and meant no harm. Bringing greater acceptance to the illness opened an inner sense of self-compassion toward this vulnerable part of self. In FOAT the transformation or felt shift (Gendlin 1981) can be both seen in the art and experienced in the body.

Clearing a Space with the Arts

CAS-Arts is a beneficial practice for stress reduction, emotion regulation, and strengthening one's connection to the calm peaceful center within each of us. It can be used as a practice on a daily basis and is useful for therapists' and clients' self-care.

Example: Indra

Indra was a student in a training group. I led the group in CAS-Arts (nondirective).

Box 14.2 CAS-Arts exercise

Take a few deep breaths inside to your body…being friendly and accepting to whatever is happening within right now. Imagine yourself in a peaceful place. When you're ready, ask, "What's between me and feeling 'All Fine' right now?" As each concern comes up, just notice it, without going into it. Imagine a way to set the issues at a distance from you outside of your body—such as, wrapping each concern up and setting it at a distance from you; placing it on a park bench nearby, or any imagery that comes to you. As you put each issue aside, sense how it feels inside. Check again… Except for all of that, am I "All Fine"? and see if anything else comes up.

   Once you set aside the concerns or stressors, notice how you are inside.

   See if there is an image that matches your inner felt sense of the "All Fine Place." When you're ready, express your experience through the arts. Some people prefer to only create the "All Fine Place" while others like to include the stressors they are setting aside and the "All Fine Place." Trust what is right for you.

After the guided Focusing, Indra shared her experience (Figure 14.3):

> As I became aware of each issue, I imagined wrapping each one in a package. First, I imagined placing the anger at my boss in an orange wrapper. As I placed it, I noticed myself taking a deeper breath with a slight sigh of relief. Next, I took the "me" that has been eating all this junk food, and wrapped that up in a brown paper bag. I imagined tossing it across a river. I noticed a huge sense of lightness come into my body. I also wrapped up the anxiety of worrying what others think of me; and not exercising enough. When you asked us to inwardly ask, "Except for all of that, I'm all fine?" a sadness came up about how hard it is to find work that is meaningful to me. I wrapped that up in a purple wrapper and imagined placing it at a distance but not too far from me.

Figure 14.3: Clearing a Space with the Arts

After, keeping all of that separate, I sensed a place of warmth in my body…with a sense of being supported. The image that came and matched the felt sense was of myself being held in a circle, like the sun or moon. I felt a feeling of surrender as I rested in a field with fresh flowers around me. Clearing a Space with the Arts helped me to feel in touch with something that was peaceful and calmer—and that I could then go and pick an issue when I felt ready to deal with it.

Indra's example demonstrates *transforming feelings* through CAS-Arts. Bringing awareness to what was in the way of feeling "All Fine" helped Indra to *recognize* the feeling. She became *one* with each feeling by sensing into each issue and *calmed* the feeling by bringing acceptance toward it. Indra *released* the feeling by setting it at a distance (externalizing it through the arts). In *looking deeply* Indra was able to find a peaceful, calm center from where she could view each issue to work on when she felt ready.

Theme-Directed FOAT

In Theme-Directed FOAT, a topic attuned to a client or group's needs is presented, followed by Focusing and expressive arts. In this example, mindful breathing is taught as a theme.

Example: Rita

Rita, a client in her fifties was a survivor of childhood abuse. After working through a good amount of the trauma, Rita was still pulled into repetitive patterns of anger and mistrust. She was interested in mindfulness and so I taught her mindful breathing as a tool to deepen her connection to a peaceful center.

Mindful Breathing

We began each session with listening to the bell. I guided Rita: "As you hear the sound of the bell, enjoy your breathing. Breathing in, I know I am breathing in. Breathing out, I know I am breathing out. Coordinating the phrase awareness of the breath moving in and out of the body—noticing thoughts, feelings, and sensations pass by like the clouds in the sky."

Additional words or phrases can be substituted, such as, "Breathing in calm, breathing out peace." Thich Nhat Hanh (2001) also teaches ways to work with difficult emotions: "Breathing in, I am aware anger is in me; breathing out, anger is leaving me." I tailor these *gathas* (short phrases) to match the client's needs.

FOAT

After 5 to 20 minutes, I guided Rita to access a felt sense from the mindful breathing, and to see if there is a word, phrase, image, gesture, or sound that matched the felt sense (see Box 14.3). Rita expressed the felt sense of mindful breathing in a collage (Figure 14.4). She continued this practice of mindfulness, Focusing, and expressive arts as a daily practice.

Box 14.3 Accessing a felt sense

Now, as you're noticing your breath moving in and out of the body, bring your awareness to your body sense…noticing how you are on the inside right now… just being friendly or welcoming to however it is right now. See if there's a word, phrase, image, gesture, or sound that matches the inner felt sense (*pause*). Check against your body for a sense of rightness. When you have it, create an artistic representation (any modality) to express your felt sense symbol.

Rita found that the expressive arts and writing helped her to hold on to the meditation experience. Over time, Rita was more able to notice when her past trauma was triggered, to notice the arising feelings of anger and fear, and to use mindful breathing and the expressive arts to stay rooted in an inner place of calm.

Figure 14.4: Felt sense mindful breathing collage

Focusing-Oriented Arts Psychotherapy

In Focusing-Oriented Arts Psychotherapy, clients typically bring their attention to an issue that needs attention (often beginning with a FOAT Check-In). The session continues to unfold moment-to-moment—interspersing the Focusing Attitude, listening reflections, and expressive arts attuned to the client's experiential process.

Example: Kristie

Kristie was a client in her thirties who had been in a car accident with her boyfriend. She suffered minor injuries but her boyfriend died as a result of the crash. She felt both guilt that she survived and overwhelming grief from the loss.

After establishing safety through presence, empathic listening, and grounding, I guided Kristie in a FOAT Check-In (see instructions on p.198):

Kristie (K): There's a big gooey tar-like substance…sitting right here…in my chest… penetrating into my heart (*felt sense and handle/symbol*).

Therapist (T): A big gooey tar-like substance in your chest and penetrating your heart (*listening reflection*).

K: It's too scary though… It's so dense and dark and heavy.

T: Can you see if you just be curious about it…oh that's interesting…and perhaps take a tiny step of being friendly toward it (*Focusing Attitude*).

K: (*sensing*)…It feels a little easier…like there's a part of me with it and a little part next to it.

T: Oh. Can you and I just sit here and keep it company?

Here I am reinforcing the Focusing Attitude to help Kristie maintain the delicate balance of staying present with the feeling without being overwhelmed by it. With very vulnerable places it can be helpful to join the client in keeping company with the strong feeling.

K: (*Kristie is quiet for a while. Her face seems more relaxed and I sense that she is feeling calmer with the tar-like substance.*)

T: Sometimes it's helpful to express the felt sense image through the arts. Would you like to?

Kristie takes a sponge, and dips it into black Sumi ink. She places it on a large sheet of paper and begins to add more black ink and paint. She pushes the paint all around the paper, getting it thicker and gooey-er (Figure 14.5). When she reaches a stopping place, we both look at the art. I ask, "Is there anything you would like to share?" Kristie says, "This is how it feels inside of me. It's heavy and stuck, sticky, and dense. It's all I see and feel."

Figure 14.5: Kristie's felt sense

T: Inside it feels heavy, stuck, sticky, and dense everywhere (*reflection*).

K: Yeah.

T: Would it be OK to go back inside for a moment, to ask it something? (*K nods yes.*)

"Asking" is a Focusing term in which the Focuser is sitting with the felt sense and can ask it something. The Focuser is engaging an inner dialogue with the felt sense. "Receiving" is a Focusing term for accepting what the felt sense offers.

T: Imagine sitting down next to it and ask it, "What makes it so heavy, stuck, sticky, and dense?" Just listen…and hear what it has to say.

K: (cries deeply) It says, "That was so scary. I thought I was going to die. Then I was OK but Ian died. Everything went dark. The death is inside me."

T: Yes…that was terrifying. And you were afraid that you were going to die. Then you saw that you didn't but Ian died. In that moment it's like the world went dark and now it feels the death is trapped inside of you (listening reflection).

K: Yeah. Exactly. I don't know how to live with this.

T: You don't know how to go forward in life with this profound traumatic loss (reflection).

K: Yes.

T: Can we take a moment and go back inside and ask it one more thing? (asking)

(Kristie nods yes.) Take a few deep breaths down into your body. As you breathe, sitting down next to this place inside that doesn't know how you will be able to live with this; when you're ready, ask it, "What do you need?" Just wait, allowing an answer to come from the body sense. It might come in words, images a gesture, or sound. See if you can be friendly and receive what comes (receiving).

K: I got an image.

Kristie reaches for the pastels. First, she draws a yellow circle around the black painting and sponge. She then adds another sheet of paper and adds a figure embracing the black shape. Next Kristie adds a heart that touches the black shape (Figure 14.6).

Kristie shares: "When I asked what it needed, I felt a warmth in my center surround the darkness. As I sat with it, I then sensed myself holding the blackness. I heard the words, 'It's horrible but I am here. Ian doesn't want you to die too. He is here with you. He's in your heart with you. It's important for you to live.'"

Focusing-Oriented Arts Psychotherapy requires that the therapist stay carefully attuned to the moment-to-moment unfolding of a delicate experiential process. There is often an alternation between Focusing, listening reflection, and expressive arts. Thich Nhat Hanh's five steps for transforming feelings are seen repeatedly throughout the example with Kristie—recognizing the gooey tar-like substance, being one with it through Focusing and the art-making, calming it through the Focusing Attitude; releasing it through the art, and looking deeply using Focusing and expressive arts. Kristie was able to access her inner knowing that carried forward a warm healing light, access a figure for holding the grief, and to hear her heart's message conveying her boyfriend's wishes.

Figure 14.6: What does it need?

Conclusion

As can be seen, there are a number of parallels between FOAT and mindfulness, although there are also differences. The Focusing Attitude is crucial for adding a mindfulness component and deepening self-compassion, and for helping to stay in the calm eye of the storm. The skillful use of listening fosters compassion for others. Clearing a Space with the Arts teaches how to dis-identify with issues and access a spacious peaceful, awareness that is within each of us. Integrating mindfulness qualities through Theme-Directed FOAT waters the positive seeds that are there as a resource during challenging moments, and expands a sense of well-being. In Focusing-Oriented Arts Psychotherapy, therapists are challenged to stay present, compassionate, and creative in the moment-to-moment attunement with the client. Both FOAT and mindfulness help clients to access their inner wisdom. As Thich Nhat Hanh (2012) affirms: "When you have enough energy of mindfulness you can look deeply into any emotion and discover the true nature of that emotion. If you can do that, you will be able to transform that emotion" (p.89).

References

Castalia, A. (2010) "The effect of Clearing a Space with Art on stress reduction in sign language interpreters." (Unpublished Master's thesis.) Notre Dame De Namur University: Art Therapy.

Chutroo, B. (2003) "On Focusing and Buddhism." Available at www.focusing.org/spirituality/chutroo_buddhism.html, accessed May 1, 2013.

Focusing Institute (2013) "Focusing into spirituality." Available at www.focusing.org/spirituality.html, accessed on May 1, 2013.

Gendlin, E.T. (1981) *Focusing*. New York: Bantam Books.

Gendlin, E.T. (1996) *Focusing-Oriented Psychotherapy: A Manual for the Experiential Method*. New York: Guilford Press.

Hanh, T.N. (1991) *Peace is Every Step: The Path of Mindfulness in Everyday Life*. New York: Bantam Books.

Hanh, T.N. (2001) *Anger: Wisdom for Cooling the Flames*. New York: The Berkley Publishing Group.

Hanh, T.N. (2012) *Fear: Essential Wisdom on Getting through the Storm*. New York: Harper One.

Lee, H. (2011) "Focusing-Oriented Art Therapy and bookmaking to promote protective resiliency of children living in a homeless shelter." (Unpublished Master's thesis.) Notre Dame De Namur University: Art Therapy Department, Belmont, CA.

Rappaport, L. (2014) "Focusing-Oriented Arts Therapy: Working on the Avenues." In Madison, G. (ed.) *Theory and Practice of Psychotherapy: Beyond the Talking Cure*. London: Jessica Kingsley Publishers.

Rappaport, L. (2008) "Focusing-Oriented Art Therapy." *The Folio 21*, 1, 139–155.

Rappaport, L. (2009) *Focusing-Oriented Art Therapy: Accessing the Body's Wisdom and Creative Intelligence*. London: Jessica Kingsley Publishers.

Rappaport, L. (2013) "Focusing-oriented art therapy with people who have chronic illnesses." In C.A. Malchiodi (ed.) *Art Therapy and Health Care*. New York: Guilford Press.

Rappaport, L. (2010) "Focusing-oriented art therapy with trauma." *Journal of Person-Centered and Experiential Psychotherapy 9*, 2, 128–142.

Rappaport, L., Ikemi, A., and Miyake, M. (2012) "Focusing-oriented art therapy and experiential collage work: History and Development in Japan." In D.Kalmanowitz, J.S. Potash, and S.M. Chan (ed.). *Art Therapy in Asia: To the Bone or Wrapped in Silk*, London: Jessica Kingsley Publishers.

Rome, D. (2004) "*Searching for the truth that is far below the search*." *Shambhala Sun*, 60–63 and 91–93.

Rome, D. and Martin, H. (2010) "Are you listening?" *Shambhala Sun*, July, 56–61.

Chapter 15

Hakomi and Art Therapy

Merryl E. Rothaus

"Hakomi," a word from the Hopi Native American language, means "How do you stand in relation to these many realms?" or simply "Who are you?" (Kurtz 1990, p.i). Hakomi Experiential Psychotherapy is a mindfulness-based, body-centered psychotherapy that emphasizes somatic awareness and experiential techniques (Mischke Reeds and Perrin 2011), designed to allow unconscious core material to gently and safely surface for the purpose of healing. The inspiration for Hakomi derives in part from Buddhism and Taoism, emphasizing mindfulness, non-violence, compassion, spiritual presence and mutuality (Mischke Reeds and Perrin 2011). According to its founder Ron Kurtz (1990), Hakomi also integrates aspects from Reich, Bioenergetics, Focusing, Neurolinguistic Programming, Gestalt, Ericksonian Hypnosis and Feldenkrais. Hakomi's emphasis on mindfulness, the body and creative experimentation distinguishes it as a unique therapeutic approach that, in many ways, marries creativity with mindful wisdom of the body.

Personal Significance and Influences

During my first year in Graduate School as an art therapy student, I struggled as I questioned whether or not I had chosen the "right" profession. My love for art therapy rivaled my love for dance and movement therapy. I wanted to study both, yet due to the nature of a specialized graduate program, the interface of these two disciplines was not possible. This led me into my own inquiry of how I might create a bridge between these two passions. I recall slowly smoothing a white oil stick over a large piece of thick, black tar paper and noting how my body followed this rhythm, as I began to dance line, shape, color and texture into image. Simultaneously, I felt the creaminess of that oil stick internally, as if it was smoothing edges of my insides. In that moment, I was deeply tuned into my body, the art and my internal still process. I located this moment as embodied mindfulness.

Around this same time, I was introduced to the work of one of the founders of art therapy, Florence Cane (1951). A woman ahead of her time, Cane was an artist and art educator who noted "the release of the creative faculty through the free rhythmic use of the body" as necessary to "true art expression" (p.37). Cane also underscored the need for the creative process to have both "active and receptive states" (p.21) where the artist oscillates between turning inward for rest, reflection and closed-eyed attention to imagery, with the outward art expression of this imagery. This is also referred to as surrender and initiative (McNiff 1998) or doing and reflecting (Rubin 2011).

Cane and others were addressing elements of my interest in the body, art therapy and mindfulness. And, I needed more. Inspired to fill in the missing pieces theoretically and practically I trained in Gestalt therapy—which was a step closer. Years later, as a practicing therapist, I felt the puzzle inside of me complete itself when I trained in the Hakomi Method of Experiential Psychotherapy.

This chapter includes a brief introduction and overview of Hakomi, along with its foundational principles and the principal role of mindfulness. In addition, the chapter describes the flow of a traditional Hakomi session, along with the benefits of synthesizing Hakomi and art therapy. A case study of a young man in private practice illustrates the application of Hakomi as a mindfulness-based practice with art therapy. The chapter concludes with the parallels between Hakomi and art therapy, and the significance of mindfulness.

Theoretical Framework

The Hakomi Method of Experiential Psychotherapy: Overview

The Hakomi Method of Experiential Psychotherapy was developed in the United States by the late Ron Kurtz (1990) and colleagues in the mid-1970s as a body-oriented psychotherapy. Hakomi recognized the body "as a resource that reflects and stores formative memories and the core beliefs they have generated, and also provides a 'doorway' to core material" (Barstow and Johanson 2007, p.79). Additionally, Hakomi may employ consensual, therapeutic touch from therapist to client or may simply involve helping the client to access what is happening in their body moment to moment. Mindfulness is central to Hakomi in its entirety and both informs and supports all aspects of the work as will be discussed further in this chapter.

Hakomi principles are "basic, foundational assumptions" adapted from contemporary scientific philosophy and religious traditions (Barstow and Johanson 2007, p.78) that guide every aspect of the therapeutic work in Hakomi. These principles are: organicity, mindfulness, non-violence, mind–body–spirit holism and unity (Kurtz 1990).

The Hakomi Principles

ORGANICITY: LIVING SYSTEMS

The principle of *organicity as a living system* honors a client's inherent wisdom and ability to heal, including an inner knowing of what is needed in order to grow. The client's authentic process is honored and tracked by the therapist. Kurtz (1990) describes living systems as: "a lusty affirmation of personal freedom and the natural intelligence of all life" where the creativity that is life will "self-organize, self-create, self-maintain, and…direct their own evolution" (p.26).

MINDFULNESS

In Hakomi, mindfulness refers to being a spacious, experimentally and experientially based therapy, as well as "a distinct state of consciousness, characterized by relaxed volition, a surrender to and acceptance of the happenings of the moment, a gentle, sustained focus of attention inward, a heightened sensitivity and the ability to observe and name the contents of consciousness" (Kurtz 1990, p.3). It is present-moment awareness where there is a turning of one's attention and focus inward, toward the body with mindful self-study.

Kurtz (1990) also referred to mindfulness in Hakomi as "assisted meditation" (p.27) where, with the help of the therapist, clients are assisted in slowly studying themselves in a non-judgmental and phenomenological way (Keller 2005). By slowing down and quieting one's system through mindfulness, the unconscious core material (Mischke Reeds and Perrin 2011) that lies under the surface may slowly and gently be brought into conscious awareness.

NON-VIOLENCE: REVERENCE FOR LIFE

Closely related to organicity, *non-violence* refers to allowing the client's therapeutic process to unfold as it is, without interfering with its natural rhythm. Kurtz (1990) describes non-violence: "Non-violence is born of an attitude of acceptance and an active attention to the way events naturally unfold. It works hand in hand with mindfulness, which helps us to understand without interfering. It takes a long time to learn" (p.29).

The therapist holds a view or a light touch to the direction that the therapy takes, as opposed to being wed to definitive directives or an absolute agenda. The therapist is present, mindful and respectful of the client's moment-to-moment unfolding.

MIND–BODY–SPIRIT HOLISM

In conjunction with the unity principle, the principle of *mind–body–spirit holism* purports that these three qualities constantly inform and influence one another, as well as being reflected in one's beliefs about self, others and the world.

UNITY: A PARTICIPATORY UNIVERSE

The *unity* principle adheres to the belief that all things are connected. It is expressed "through the therapist's wordless understanding of the client's experience… It is shared pain and sympathetic joy. It shows up as the ability to create cooperation and intimacy" (Kurtz cited by Myullerup-Brookhuis 2008, p.74) to parts of oneself and others that are unintegrated or in conflict (Kurtz 1990, p.33).

The Flow of a Hakomi Session

Aligned with the Hakomi principles, there is a typical sequence of stages or flow to a Hakomi session: *contact, accessing, processing and integration* (Mischke Reeds and Perrin 2011). A brief overview of these stages and concepts follows and will be further illustrated in the clinical case study described later in the chapter.

CONTACT

Contact consists of the therapist establishing and maintaining an environment of loving presence that ideally fosters safety and trust between therapist and client, and within the therapeutic field. Contact is fundamental to the establishment of mindfulness as without the safety and rapport, the vulnerable, open state that often occurs in mindfulness may likely not occur. The therapist offers *contact* statements— non-interpretive, direct statements about the client's current experience (Kurtz 1990). Examples of contact statements might be: "I notice your brow furrowing"; or "Lots of sadness, huh?"

ACCESSING

Once contact is established, *accessing* refers to using mindfulness in order to study present experience and deepen toward core material so that the unconscious material may move into conscious awareness. For example, the therapist may say, "Close your eyes and turn your attention toward your inward experience. Just notice what is happening." As the clients' system quiets and slows down in mindfulness, they are supported to notice and focus on present experience; to pay attention to what is happening within and to study it phenomenologically, without judgment. Within a safe space, clients are encouraged to be mindfully aware of what is present—which may include vulnerable and sensitive places, as defenses fall (Kurtz 1995). The therapist stays in loving presence and contact—tracking, or mindfully watching and following clients, as they share their unfolding present-moment awareness: "As much as you can, stay with and notice whatever is happening…and let me know what is happening so I can follow you."

To further explore ideas or beliefs about the client's current life situation (Kurtz 2007) the Hakomi therapist may "evoke experience" (Kurtz 1990, p.72) through creating "experiments" using mindful exploration, with the consent of the client. For example, the therapist may offer a "probe," a potentially nourishing statement that usually results in responses that show something about how the client is organized around that specific belief or concept (Kurtz 1990). For example, "Just notice what happens when you hear a voice that says, 'It's OK to relax.'" Often, memories, body sensations, emotions or images arise through experiments and then these things are studied. Another type of experiment may be to invite the client to engage in making art (Mischke Reeds and Perrin 2011).

PROCESSING

During the *processing* stage, the client and therapist study the responses to the various experiments. Barriers to nourishment and satisfaction are explored. For example, in response to the aforementioned probe, "It's OK to relax," clients may notice that they cannot believe this statement. In processing, this struggle may be explored. The therapist's loving presence and tracking of the client's beliefs and responses that get in the way of satisfaction (e.g. relaxing) may assist in the personal transformation that can happen by helping to provide missing experiences and nourishment for the client. The therapist may offer an experience in the session that results in the client having an experience of relaxation in the session—which may then be applied outside of the therapy session through concrete steps. Thus, processing leads to transformation and change.

INTEGRATION

Lastly, during the final stage of *integration*, often done with the eyes open, the therapist helps the client to make sense of what occurred in the session by weaving together the various themes that occurred in the session.

Benefits of Integrating Hakomi and Art Therapy

Integrating art therapy into Hakomi, and Hakomi with art therapy, has numerous benefits. Hakomi brings mindful awareness and a finely tuned somatic approach to art therapy while art therapy provides a creative means to externalize, contain and observe a concrete expression of the client's internal experience.

Hakomi's emphasis on mindfulness is an important contribution to art therapy. There is a deep richness in mindful self-study that characterizes a Hakomi session. Learning to intentionally turn attention toward what is happening, even that which is unpleasant, is a part of Hakomi's mindfulness prototcol. It is an inner act of lovingkindness to pay close attention, listen to, follow and remain with oneself in this way. Bringing these compassionate qualities to art therapy offers a sacredness and respect toward oneself and to one's personal imagery as a client learns to slowly stay with an arising image, mindfully studying its messages, meanings and impact. As Franklin (2012) notes, just as in sitting meditation, when unpleasant thoughts arise, the goal is to stay present, observe and move toward the content, in art, the goal is the same—to stay present and "move toward the imagery with fresh, open-minded perspective" (p.90).

The addition of art therapy to Hakomi helps to hold and expand imagery that comes during mindfulness of what is happening within the body and/or mind—which, in turn, may lead to an increased depth of healing. As stated by Morgan (2006), "The hypnotic quality, present in mindfulness induction, has been shown to heighten mental imagery" (p.17). Hakomi provides a gentle slowness that supports mindful self-study. From this quiet inner space, images often arise and reveal themselves to the client. Art therapy offers Hakomi a toolbag to "actualize these representations" (Riley 2004, p.184) through the use of art media. Doing so can help to consolidate insights (Lo 2011) gathered during the mindful state. The integration of Hakomi and art therapy has a cycle of flow—from self to the image to the artmaking and then cyling back from the artmaking to self, the image and back to artmaking again. Art therapist Bruce Moon (2009) writes: "Artistic expression leads to mindfulness, mindfulness leads to creative anxiety, which leads to change/action, which fosters expression that deepens mindfulness" (p.11). As Kurtz (2010) stated, images can be contained without being repressed and expressed without going to extremes.

Clinical Application
Case Study: Nick

Nick, 21, pierced and tattooed, sits cross-legged in a comfortable posture across from me. Given that we've worked together for two years and have established rapport and *contact*, he is ready to begin our session as we usually do, with an invitation to enter into mindfulness: "Nick, take a moment to just settle into yourself." This helps him arrive into the therapy space and more deeply into his body and present-moment, authentic experience. Nick closes his eyes, which is customary for entering into mindful self-study. Doing so allows him to reduce distraction, slow down his mind and mindfully study his inner experience and what is happening in his body.

Accessing with a gentle voice and slow pacing, I encourage him to study his somatic experience and what happens in his system as he settles into himself: "Nick, let's see what happens as you turn your attention inward and toward your body. Take your time. Just notice what's happening on its own." There is space and silence between our connection, while Nick studies his experience and I witness him, closely, tracking his body movements. I notice his breath slow down. Shoulders relax. As Nick remains in mindfulness, I offer him a "drop-down menu" (DelPrince 2006) from which he might choose what he is aware of: "Nick, notice what you are aware of—any sensations, feelings, impulses, memories, images." As an art therapist, I am most interested in the personal imagery that forms here. Scrunching his brow, Nick describes a black and brown orb that he feels and sees spinning there.

I *contact* this "indicator," or involuntary somatic cue (Kurtz 2010): "Your brow furrows." "Yeah," he responds, "Sharp pain." Embracing the experimental attitude and spirit of curiosity of Hakomi, I ask if he has an interest in studying any of this further. He nods his head, "Yes."

Applying the principle of *organicity*, I encourage Nick to notice this spinning orb just as it is and to see whether it has an effect in any other area of his body. His brow furrows further. "Uck. Makes me nauseous." I ask him whether it is OK to stay with that. I want to make sure he knows that at any time, if the experience becomes too uncomfortable, he can choose to stop. Honoring the Hakomi principle of *non-violence*, Nick is in charge. He nods his head, "Yes." Expanding Hakomi's reliance on loving contact with the body, I suggest that Nick make contact with the "Uck" by putting his hand on his brow. I am working to deepen Nick's experience by creating experiments that may help us to see what beliefs he is holding about self and the world (Kurtz 1995).

As Nick places his right hand on his brow, he releases a large sigh. Tears come. I support what I see by compassionately *contacting* them: "Big sigh. Tears. Yes. Let those happen." In mindfulness, Nick's defenses soften. Facilitated by my offering encouragement for what is occurring, a spaciousness for expression emerges. Nick begins to cry deeply. I let him know I am there with him. I give Nick space and time to be with his experience, and ask him, "Nick, when you're ready, let me know what is happening for you so I can be there with you." Through a veil of tears, Nick shares a memory of being seven years old. His parents screaming at one another resulted in Nick wanting to just shut down and go away. This core material that has previously existed under Nick's surface awareness is now safely moving toward consciousness. His body folds over. Going with what is in the moment, I invite Nick to mindfully study his folded body. Memories of hiding under a coffee table while his parents fight emerge. A choice-point arrives. I can either go with the memory and contact the little boy within him now, or I can contact the body. Both would suffice. I choose to go toward the body. I ask Nick, "What are you aware of as you hold your body?" "It's like I gotta protect." I encourage him to keep studying this. I am tracking his barriers or "beliefs that block the normal organic process of attaining sensitivity and satisfaction" (Barstow and Johanson 2007, p.77). Nick studies how it feels to remain folded and reports feeling "scared." Wanting to deepen his experience, as another experiment, I offer a probe:"I'm going to offer you a statement. You don't need to believe it or disbelieve it. Just notice what happens all by itself when you hear a voice that says, 'Nick, you are safe here.'" I allow space for Nick to have his response. He sighs deeply. His body raises up just slightly, which I point out to him or *contact*: "Your shoulders and face lift a bit." Not surprisingly, given the impact of this memory on his life, he shares that part of him believes the statement, and part does not. We are now in the *processing* stage. I suggest we explore both, beginning with the part that does not believe this nourishment is true. We briefly explore this part but there is not much there and Nick expresses that he's "not interested in it." It's as if that part is habitual; a cobweb that is ready to be wiped away. I ask him, "What is happening in your body?" as I also point out, "I notice that you went from being folded over to now sitting up and your brow is no longer furrowed." His breath is slow and steady. I offer the probe again from this place: "Nick, you are safe here." He nods his head indicating "Yes." I ask, "How do you experience safety right now? What does safety feel like in your body?" He reports feeling a warmth in his belly and that the orb is now there but in different form that "feels good…surrounded by purple…here." He places his left hand on his abdomen. I slow down the process to give the imagery and his body-sense time to catch up with the rest of his experience.

In this session, there were many points where moving into the art therapy would have been fruitful and, as there are many choice-points within the experimental attitude of a Hakomi session, I trust there is no "wrong" or "right" way. I trust the process implicitly. Now feels like a perfect time to depart from the Hakomi structure in order to allow exploration through art therapy. In front of him are a variety of art media—chalk and oil pastels, oil sticks, watercolor paints and colored pencils. Nick is invited to choose media that will best articulate the orb, as well as its felt sense in his body. He chooses black and brown chalk pastels and begins creating the orb on textured watercolor paper.

As he draws, I bring mindfulness to his moment-by-moment experience by offering prompts such as, "Notice how you are feeling the movement of the pastels on the paper, in your own body." Or, I *contact* what I am seeing: "Your breath deepens as you smooth the chalks with your hands." I also offer that Nick periodically close his eyes, check back in with his body and the imagery living there, and then come back out to express his internal experience though the art image: "See what happens, Nick, when you check back in with that orb in your body. How does it inform the art image on paper?" Here, I am assisting Nick in moving between active and receptive states (Cane 1951) during the creative process. I then inquire about the purple part he mentioned in response to the part that felt safe after the experiment with the "probe." He picks up a purple pastel and gently begins applying it to create a circle form around the orb. His breath deepens. After working quietly, Nick completes his image (Figure 15.1). I *integrate* the bullet points of a powerful session. We are done for today.

It is our next session. After our mindfulness exercise, I hang the image on the wall. I am unsure of its relevance today. If it is not present, I will not push it. Nick studies it with curiosity and smiles. As he does, I welcome mindfulness of his body: "What are you aware of in your body—sensations and otherwise—right now as you look at your image?" He reports feeling "deeply peaceful inside." I invite Nick to close his eyes and internalize the deep peacefulness, to ingest what he created through the art: "Let yourself have the peacefulness of that image. Sense how it lives and feels inside of your body; its qualities, its texture…" His hand moves to his abdomen and he breathes deeply. Moment by moment, he mindfully tracks his internal experience with eyes closed, alternating with looking at his image. Within the scope of the open-minded, experimental attitude that characterizes mindful Hakomi study, I help Nick to shuttle back and forth from internal exploration of the imagery in his body to external exploration. We continue this back and forth "zig-zag" (Rappaport 2012) of taking the created image back into his body, mindfully studying what happens there and returning to looking at it. His hand remains on his abdomen and he begins to rub his tummy in what appears to be an act of nurturance. I offer a contact statement: "Feels good to rub the tummy, huh?" I invite Nick to add this felt sense experience to his image. He picks turquoise blue chalk. I encourage him to use the chalk in the same rhythmic motion that he used to rub his tummy. I have him practice doing so with eyes opened and closed—again going from internal to external. He breathes deeply and his body gently sways from side to side with the chalk on paper and his fingers smoothing the lines. He completes the image (see Figure 15.2).

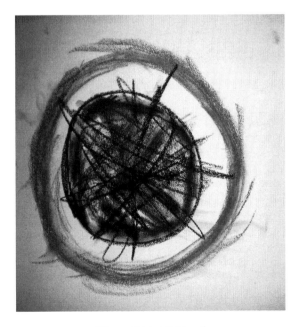

Figure 15.1: Nick's orb

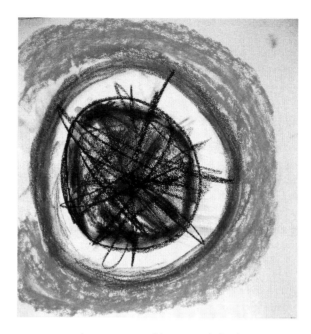

Figure 15.2: Nick's surrounded orb

To help Nick to anchor this healing more, I offer him various art therapy techniques—dialoging with the image (McNiff 1992) and witness-writing (Allen 1995), that help him to explore his image further and access its meaning. I integrate the experience by recapping where we began, what happened and where we are now. I check in with Nick about the childhood memories and how he is doing now. Nick reports feeling "really good." I encourage him to live with the orb image at home by hanging it on his wall. I also encourage him to practice this back-and-forth exchange between viewing the image and taking it into his body mindfully and perhaps continuing to write or dialogue with it.

This case study illustrates the efficacy of the application of Hakomi principles and processes integrated with art therapy. From working with Nick, it was clear that Hakomi with art therapy myelinated the growth that he was ready and able to achieve. The combination of Hakomi and art therapy anchored the work in his body on the felt sense level, as he reported feeling "strong and peaceful" somatically. Additionally, it anchored the work externally through the creation of an embodied image that came out of that strong and peaceful somatic experience. The image serves as a talisman now (Schaverien 1992), transferring its healing properties back to Nick's inner bodily felt experience, simply from viewing it. In essence, this work resulted in healing and growth for Nick emotionally, mentally, physically and spiritually.

Conclusion

As seen in the case study, Hakomi and art therapy, both integrative therapies, are poised as "mutually supportive frames of reference" (Rubin 2011, p.288) that can and do "energize and shape one another" (McNiff 1997, p.37) through their complementarity and shared aspects of mindfulness. Mindfulness allowed Nick's nervous system to relax so that he could become aware of his core material and pay attention to his "integrated, embodied knowing" (Rappaport 2009, p.23) or felt sense (Gendlin 1981). This allowed him to calmly move toward and stay present with the strong feelings there. Doing so ushered in significant meaning and insight for him (Gendlin cited by Myullerup-Brookhuis 2008) accessed in response to an emerging image. Through the Hakomi structure, Nick's imagery was courted and explored both verbally and somatically in order to deepen his process. Both modalities acknowledged the healing benefits of this imagery, and utilized the wisdom and healing potential inherent in the imaginal realm (Bachelard 1971; Hillman 1979; Jung 1961; Kurtz 1990; McConeghey 2003; McNiff 1992).

Through mindfulness, Nick was able to "trust the process," as his "creative intelligence" organically unfolded (McNiff 1998, pp.2–3). Staying present with his experience, authentic imagery emerged in Nick's psyche. Art, followed by witness-writing (Allen 1995) and dialoguing with the image (McNiff 1998), provided a means for Nick to express and contain this powerful, embodied experience. In its entirety, Hakomi and art therapy as collaborative disciplines are indeed "the basis of the creative process" (McNiff 1997, p.37).

References

Allen, P. (1995) *Art is a Way of Knowing*. Boston, MA: Shambhala.

Bachelard, G. (1971) *On Poetic Imagination and Reverie*. New York: G.P. Putnam's Sons.

Barstow, C. and Johanson, G. (2007) "Glossary of Hakomi therapy terms." *Hakomi Forum 18*, 77–79.

Cane, F. (1951) *The Artist in Each of Us*. London: Thames and Hudson.

DelPrince, P. (2006) Personal communication.

Franklin, M. (2012) "Know thyself: Awakening self-referential awareness through art-based research." *Journal of Applied Arts and Health 3*, 1, 87–96.

Gendlin, E.T. (1981) "Movement therapy, objectification, and focusing." *The Focusing Folio 1*, 2, 35–37.

Hillman, J. (1979) "Image-sense." *Spring*, 130–143.

Jung, G. (1961) *Memories, Dreams, Reflections*. New York: Pantheon.

Keller, R. (2005) "Hakomi simplified: A new view of Ron Kurtz's mindfulness-based psychotherapy." *Hakomi Forum 14–15*, 5–18.

Kurtz, R. (1990) *Body-Centered Psychotherapy: The Hakomi Method*. Mendocino, CA: LifeRhythm.

Kurtz, R. (1995) "The origins of the Hakomi method." *Hakomi Forum 11*, 23–28.

Kurtz, R. (2007) "Three recent essays." *Hakomi Forum 18*, 5–10.

Kurtz, R. (2010) Personal communication (April).

Lo, Pui Yin (2011) "A heuristic and art-based inquiry: The experience of combining mindfulness practice and art-making." *Australian and New Zealand Journal of Art Therapy 6*, 1, 51–67.

McConeghey, H. (2003) *Art and Soul*. Dallas, TX: Spring Publications.

McNiff, S. (1992) *Art as Medicine: Creating a Therapy of the Imagination*. Boston, MA: Shambhala.

McNiff, S. (1997) "Art therapy: A spectrum of partnerships." *The Arts in Psychotherapy 24*, 1, 37–44.

McNiff, S. (1998) *Trust the Process: An Artist's Guide to Letting Go*. Boston, MA: Shambhala.

Mischke Reeds, M. and Perrin, J. (2011) *Training Manual for the Comprehensive Training in the Hakomi Method*. Sydney: Lorella Ricci Marriott.

Moon, B. (2009) (First published 1997) *Existential Art Therapy: The Canvas Mirror*. Springfield, IL: Charles C. Thomas.

Morgan, M. (2006) "Neuroscience and psychotherapy." *Hakomi Forum 15–17*, 9–22.

Myullerup-Brookhuis, I. (2008) "The principles of Hakomi." *Hakomi Forum 19–21*, 69–83.

Rappaport, L. (2009) *Focusing-Oriented Art Therapy: Accessing the Body's Wisdom and Creative Intelligence.* London and Philadelphia, PA: Jessica Kingsley Publishers.

Rappaport, L. (2012) Personal communication (July).

Riley, S. (2004) "The creative mind." *The American Journal of Art Therapy 21*, 4, 184–190.

Rubin, J. (2011) (First published 1984) *The Art of Art Therapy.* London: Routledge.

Schaverien, J. (1992) *The Revealing Image; Analytical Art Psychotherapy in Theory and Practice.* London and Philadelphia, PA: Jessica Kingsley Publishers.

Chapter 16

Mindfulness and Person-Centered Expressive Arts Therapy

Fiona Chang

Person-Centered Expressive Arts Therapy (PCEAT), developed by Natalie Rogers (1993, 2011), integrates the humanistic principles of Person-Centered Therapy (Rogers, C. 1951, 1980) with the expressive arts. The core conditions of person-centered approaches—unconditional positive regard, congruence and empathy—are closely aligned with principles of mindfulness. In PCEAT, a safe, supportive and non-judgmental environment is created in order to cultivate an atmosphere where people can engage with their body, emotion, thoughts and spirits fully through the Creative Connection®. PCEAT incorporates presence, listening, congruence and the arts to help people cultivate authenticity and compassion with self and others in the present moment. PCEAT is applied to psychotherapy, personal growth and social transformation.

This chapter presents an overview of the interconnections between PCEAT and mindfulness. It also includes clinical examples of integrating PCEAT with mindfulness in a hospital outpatient group with people living with cancer.

Theoretical Framework

PCEAT and Mindfulness: Interconnections

Although different practices and approaches, PCEAT and mindfulness cultivate similar qualities, including being present, deep listening and non-judgmental awareness. Table 16.1 further delineates these properties including: full attention, listening, openness, compassion and congruence. In the next section, I discuss the principles of PCEAT and how they are interconnected with mindfulness.

FULL ATTENTION TO THE PRESENT MOMENT

In PCEAT, we often begin with meditation to calm the mind, center ourselves, listen to our inner messages and receive guidance from our higher self (Rogers, N. 1993). We often begin with open awareness meditation (Hanson 2009):

> Take a few deep breaths into your body…becoming aware of how you are in this moment…allow your shoulders to relax…noticing and opening to what is there… thoughts, sensations, sounds, images, feelings. Just allowing…accepting what is there, free from judgment.

The meditation is a mindfulness exercise and helps to inspire possibilities for creative expression. For those who find it difficult to engage in a prolonged meditation state, we incorporate peaceful music and aim to access the contemplative arena in the space of imagination and creativity.

Table 16.1: Shared practice wisdom of mindfulness and PCEAT

Practice Wisdom	Mindfulness Practice	PCEAT Practice
Full attention	Full attention to the present moment	Full presence to each individual and the expressive arts process
Listening	Deep listening to ourselves, others and the environment	Empathic understanding of the person(s), the expressive arts process and artistic creation
Openness	Beginner's mind—embrace whatever is emerging at each moment	Openness to experience with unconditional positive regard
Compassion	Lovingkindness Concern for the suffering of beings	Understanding empathically with a caring heart
Congruence	Being true to yourself	Being genuine

DEEP LISTENING

In PCEAT, active listening is a core practice. We listen with our heart and compassionately say back the essence of what the person shares with us. The Chinese word "聽"—"Listen" captures the essence of deep listening. It includes six Chinese characters: ears (耳); king (王); ten eyes and one heart (十目一心)—reminding us to listen to people with an undivided heart, respecting them like a king (Figure 16.1).

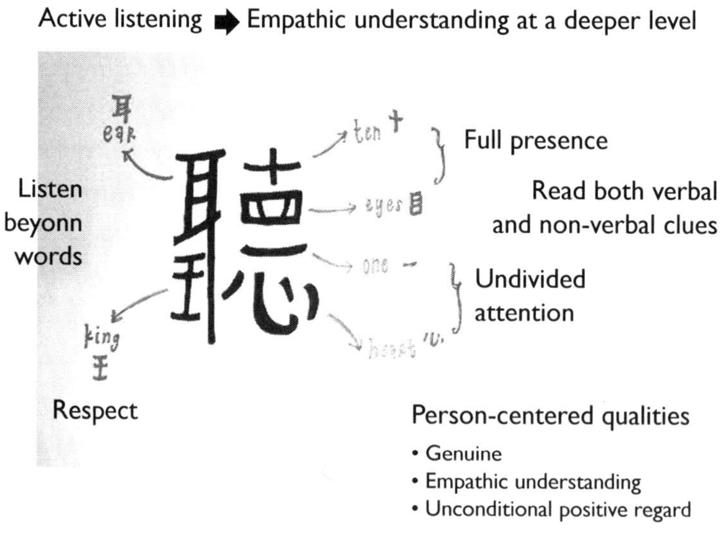

Active listening ➡ Empathic understanding at a deeper level

Listen beyonn words

Full presence

Read both verbal and non-verbal clues

Undivided attention

Respect

Person-centered qualities
• Genuine
• Empathic understanding
• Unconditional positive regard

Figure 16.1: Chinese word, "Listen"

We listen beyond words. Our eyes see both verbal and non-verbal cues. With a genuine heart, full concentration and unconditional respect, we deeply listen to others, ourselves and the unknown. Thich Nhat Hanh (2009), Buddhist monk and mindfulness teacher, includes deep listening as a practice. He says, "Compassionate listening brings about healing. Sometimes only ten minutes of listening deeply can transform us and bring a smile back to our lips" (p.149).

OPENNESS

The humanistic principles of PCEAT emphasize looking at life and experiences through a non-judgmental lens. When we are free of the desire to impose our perceived truths, we respect the capacity of people to discover the true nature of their own issues and find ways toward their goals (Rogers, N. 2011). When we experience a positive and accepting attitude to whatever emerges at that moment, a therapeutic change is more likely to occur (Rogers, C. 1980).

Mindfulness practice helps teach us to stay open to the unknown—moment to moment, with an accepting heart. With an infant's eye and a beginner's mind, we look at things with curiosity, openness to possibilities, receptiveness and readiness to learn (Goodman 2005; Suzuki 1987). This allows us to see things in a refreshing light, where we can gain clarity from new perspectives.

COMPASSION

In PCEAT, we provide a loving presence that helps to cultivate understanding, sensitivity, acceptance and forgiveness within ourselves and others. As we are empathically heard, we can understand more accurately the flow of our moment-to-moment inner experience, becoming congruent and enjoying the freedom to become a whole person (Rogers, C. 1980). We express compassion through therapeutic witnessing and aesthetic responses. We try to sense precisely the feelings and personal meanings that people have in the creative process and express this understanding through creative means (Rogers, C. 1980; Rogers, N. 1993). The arts also serve as our compassionate listener. Our being is contained and reflected in the presence of a creative act that touches our soul, engages our thought and emotion (Knill, Barba, and Fuchs 1995). At the same time we listen to the arts, hearing their messages (McNiff, 2009; Rogers 1993).

In mindfulness, the practice of non-judgmental awareness in the present moment helps to cultivate qualities of compassion, allowing a space for all that is within us to be welcomed.

CONGRUENCE

Congruence is being aligned with our genuine, authentic self and speaking from that place (McCown, Reibel, and Micozzi 2010). Bolton (1979) points out that genuineness has three ingredients—self-expression, self-awareness and self-acceptance. When we meet our aesthetic, playful and novel selves in the arts for self-expression, we become more aware of our true selves and convey acceptance to ourselves. The therapeutic qualities of the arts stimulate our physical, emotional, intellectual and spiritual aspects of self, and facilitate the integration of our inner and outer reality. This creative transformation process helps us to be more congruent. Mindfulness also helps us to become more aware and more congruent with our authentic self.

Clinical Application

The following examples are from a group of adults in an outpatient cancer support group at a hospital. The group integrated mindfulness practices with PCEAT.

Therapeutic Objectives of Mindfulness-Based PCEAT

1. To utilize one's inner self-healing strengths and hidden creativity to improve body–mind–spirit well-being.

2. To safely release worries and suppressed feelings.

3. To explore, understand, embrace and become more accepting of one's whole self.

ATTITUDINAL FOUNDATIONS

We begin the group with the following foundations as guidelines for the group (Box 16.1). They are based on core attitudes and principles of PCEAT (Rogers, N. 1993) and mindfulness practice (Kabat-Zinn 1990).

Box 16.1 PCEAT and mindfulness practice reminder

1. Be aware of your own body, and take care of yourselves.
2. All instructions are invitations/suggestions. You have the option not to follow. Be your own master, here.
3. Expressive arts experiences may stir up inner feelings—sadness, happiness, known and unknown feelings may arise. Allow yourself to experience with openness and express happenings mindfully in the safe containment of the arts!
4. Be aware of your feelings as an energy source of creativity. Emerging visuals and words, loud sounds, dramatic acts and tears are a natural manifestation of your creative expression at the present moment.
5. Listen with compassion. Notice your own body–mind–spirit experience from within and the feelings of others.
6. Maintain beginner's mind to embrace and create the infinite possibilities.
7. Drop your critical lens; accept yourself and others truly with an open attitude.
8. If you choose to observe, notice your present feelings. Respect the group dynamics, surrounding environment and others' experiences.
9. Keep personal events confidential. Feel free to share the activities outside of the group without mentioning names and disclosing personal information.
   Thank you for keeping our trust and respect!

PREPARATION

We encourage participants to bring musical instruments, found materials, tactile supplies, images, songs and words that reflect their felt sense.

Mindfulness-Based PCEAT Activities

TEA MEDITATION

We use tea meditation (Plum Village 2010, p.12) as an opening ritual. Practicing tea meditation is being truly present with our tea and friends to dwell happily in the present moment, despite sorrows and worries. The expressive arts help to enrich the meditation experience. In return, the tea meditation refreshes awareness and grounds the soul to mindfully experience the creative process.

Participants are invited to draw their names and create an intention for the day on a white paper cup. We then pour the tea, holding the cup to feel the temperature. We enjoy the tea—sip by sip, bringing awareness to the taste with all of our senses. We savor the aroma. We feel the flow of the warm-hearted tea filling our bodies. The art, tea and meditation become a fine amalgam to appreciate ourselves.

Alternatively, you can start the tea meditation with a blank paper cup. We stay observant with an open attitude. We welcome and create whatever emerges in the process. We can articulate our felt sense tangibly in the arts through drawing, writing, humming and moving our body. Sometimes we play soothing music to slow down our body–mind, dissolve our ego and become more relaxed. On occasion, we follow our senses and improvise with music. We feel connected with our spirit. Our soul is enlightened. Tea meditation can also be a closing ritual to calm and clear our mind. The arts are used to contain our learning at the end.

Case Studies: Ah Wah and Mei Fung

Ah Wah (a woman, age 50) described her joy in the tea meditation as an image of relaxing on a grassland with a smiling face (Figure 16.2).

Figure 16.2: Image drawn on a cup for tea meditation

Mei Fung (a woman, age 45) shared her intention of taking care of herself. Participants in our cancer group expressed their hope of being free from sickness, through images of nature. Our participants enjoyed this creative tea meditation. We could be both absorbed and aware in the process. Sometimes people without prior arts experience are resistant. We found this activity helped them to attune to their body, feel connected with others in sharing tea together and clear the resistance in a relaxed way. It helped the creative process to be more liberating.

AWARENESS EXPLORATION—SELF, OTHER AND CONTEXT (CONGRUENCE)

Virginia Satir presented congruence as a circle in which self, others and context (Figure 16.3) are all honored (Satir *et al.* 1991).

Figure 16.3: Congruence: self, others and context (Satir et al., 1991)

When we are truly aware, we sense what is happening both within ourselves and outside in our environment (Kyle 1998, p.173).

In mindfulness, we observe our self, others and context. Inspired by the work of Michael Franklin (2012), we invite participants to do a creative mindfulness observation of self, other and environment. We begin with a partner mindfulness observation exercise. Two people pair up and sit facing each other. Each of them takes a few moments to be attentive in silence to their own self, to the other and to the environment. Afterwards, they use arts to express the experience.

Case Study: Mei Ling

Mei Ling, a 48-year-old woman, became aware that she spent most of her awareness in being alert to the environment (shown in her observation in Figure 16.4 as the purple, three-quarters part of the circle); then toward others (peach, quarter of the circle) with very little attention paid to herself (yellow, line in circle). Mei Ling learned that her emotions were easily triggered by others and the social environment. In the paired meditation, she became aware and inspired to put more attention on herself and to let go of the expectations from the surroundings on her.

Figure 16.4: Mei Ling's "self, others and context" observation

Case Study: Siu Man

Siu Man, a woman, age 56, had a more balanced observation in these three aspects (see Figure 16.5). She felt the calmness within (smiling face) while paying attention to herself and others. She was aware of the anxiety in her partner (upper left shape in circle, in red) who was looking around, perhaps to distract herself from the tension (black dots). She perceived the environment as hopeful, in yellow (bottom left shaded area in circle), and added the grey cloud because it was a rainy day.

Figure 16.5: Siu Man's balanced observation

The participants found this exercise helpful in giving them both an experiential and visual understanding of their awareness including self, other and environment. It is a mindful practice of full presence, compassion and congruence. We listen attentively from the heart with our whole being—allowing what is said to "sound" from within (McCown *et al.* 2010) connecting with one's true self, while also listening compassionately to others and staying respectful of the earth (Plum Village 2010).

BODY SCAN PORTRAIT PAINTING

In view of the benefit of mindfulness to physical health (Langer 1989) and the initial research on the effect of Mindfulness-Based Art Therapy (MBAT) in improving quality of life in women with cancer (Monti *et al.* 2006), we combine a mindfulness body scan with portrait painting to explore the triangle of awareness—body sensation, thought and emotion (Figure 16.6) (McCown *et al.* 2010).

Figure 16.6: Triangle of awareness through body scan and portrait painting

Participants are guided in a body scan to bring awareness to the moment-to-moment unfolding of sensations, emotions and thoughts in the body:

> Take a few deep breaths into your body. Gently notice what is there, gradually from the top of your head, slowly down to the toes… Just notice, letting go of any judgment. Notice sensations…thoughts in your mind…and feelings that are present.

After the body scan, the participants express their experience in a visual form of body portrait painting. They are welcome to express the experience as it was or allow continued unfolding through the creative exploration. At times we vary the body scan, to include a more structured invitation, such as, (1) noticing body parts that are unpleasant, or pleasant; (2) becoming aware of different emotions inhibited in these body parts; (3) listening to any thoughts that are positive or negative; and (4) noticing our spiritual source inside us. They then create those through the arts after each exploration.

Case Study: Sin Yuet

Sin Yuet, a woman, age 46, felt solid in facing the seasonal changes and enjoyed going with the flow in life. Throughout the body scan, she received a message of encouragement from her body to bring a flavor of acceptance and warmth alongside a sense of exploration, curiosity, aliveness and adventure (Kabat-Zinn 1990). She found both her tears and smile, distress and peace. Sin Yuet felt that the organic, creative process of arts expression, deep breathing and mindfulness enabled her to stay with the complex feelings. She preferred doing the arts in silence, without music, thereby allowing the energy of mindfulness to penetrate her body and mind (Plum Village 2010). Sin Yuet accepted both pleasurable and painful experiences as they arose.

EMOTION LANDSCAPE PAINTING

In Suzuki Roshi's book, Zen Mind, Beginner's Mind, he intentionally left several pages blank to remind us of emptying our mind. To express the empty space, we use a large roll of blank Xuan paper (Chinese painting paper) in an "emotion landscape" painting. Before painting, each participant is encouraged to mount the Xuan paper on the wall in front of them.

We begin with a brief mindfulness exercise. Meditation helps in keeping our minds pure and learning fresh. After a time of noble silence with the paper, the participants are encouraged to cultivate an open-minded state by allowing positive and negative emotions to dance on the paper. We express the variation of emotions through colors, lines, shapes and images. Xuan paper is a wonderful container for emotions because it has the perfect absorbency for ink, paints and motion from the strokes. The length of the paper offers a great amount of space for expression.

Case Study: K.S.

Free from control and judgment, K.S., a man, age 61, let go of his inner critic, relaxed and enjoyed arts spontaneously. He painted with full attention as if he was discovering what he was painting for the first time (Figure 16.7).

Figure 16.7: My emotion landscape

This is the way of practicing moment by moment (Suzuki 1987). Usually K.S. has difficulty concentrating but this time he was fully attentive. He could not stop painting. He was glad to witness his sadness, guilt, fear, anger, happiness, gratitude and hope as they were expressed in visual form in his art. K.S. enjoyed the process of being open and receptive to his feelings. Our feelings and emotions are an energy source for creativity and transformation (Rogers, N. 1993). K.S. discovered that he could embody his full self through the art and channel his emotions into healing energy.

BUDDHA BOARD

A Tibetan meditation master Yongyey Mingyur Rinpoche (2007, cited by Gilbert and Tirch 2009, p.102) described mindfulness as "the key, the how of Buddhist practice [that] lies in learning to simply rest in a bare awareness of thoughts, feelings and perceptions as they occur." A "Buddha Board" (see www.buddhaboard.com) is a product where you simply paint water on the surface of the board; the images come to life in a darker color and then gradually fade away. It is a wonderful vessel for us to stay still with our moment-to-moment awareness. We can paint, enjoy and observe the moment. It is based on the Zen concepts of living in the present moment and impermanence. It is a healing process of being present in the moment, appreciating each precious moment, letting go, and clearing our mind. It is a wonderful teacher that things change and are not permanent.

Case Study: Star

Using the Buddha Board, Star, a woman, age 53, drew her mother with her favorite food (Figure 16.8a). Star's mother had passed away a week earlier. On the Buddha Board, Star used the water and painted an image of her mother and herself. Star meditated on the fading image, saying goodbye to her mother (Figure 16.8b).

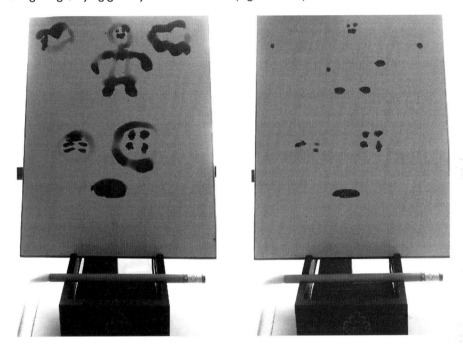

Figure 16.8: (a) Buddha Board; (b) Letting go and forgiving ourselves

Star realized how quickly her mother was gone. During this process, Star became aware of her own patience in taking care of her mother for years, as well as her own resilience.

MINDFUL SELF-EXPLORATION THROUGH MIRROR, MASK-MAKING AND AUTHENTIC MOVEMENT

A mask serves the function of helping to symbolizing our persona—who we present on the outside, as well as our shadow—the parts that are more hidden. This helps us to bring acceptance to the whole of who we are—our true self. Mindfulness practice helps us to contemplate, keep still and concentrate on this inner journey. We begin with a guided mindful exploration of our face in a mirror (see Box 16.2) for looking into ourselves phenomenologically and finding the compassionate space to transform, before mask-making.

Box 16.2 Guided instructions: mindful masks

Assume a comfortable posture, keep your spine straight, slow down your breathing…

Let go of your burden, psychologically and physically…

Try to relax your body…let your shoulders drop.

Enjoy this precious moment to get in touch with your inner self…

Put the mirror in front of you…

Be curious of the reflected face image, observe and explore it without any judgment,

Just being with this familiar image,

Breathing in…I know I am breathing in…

Breathing out…I know I am breathing out…

Just look at it deeply with your breathing…

If you find your mind has been wandering away,

Just gently bring your attention back to this image.

Be aware of your feelings, you may feel unusual, unfamiliar and quite strange.

But these are the feelings you own at the present moment.

Just accept it gently and be with it…

You are willing to accept these feelings as they are…

As best you can, keep your mind concentrated on this image and

Try to make friends with it. No matter whether you like it or dislike it,

Become aware of your sensations and feelings on this image…

Slowly give full attention to the hair, eyes, nose, ears and mouth on this familiar face.

Breathing in… Breathing out…

You may want to get close to this face, get in touch with it through

Seeing, listening, smelling and tasting…

If you want, you may know more about it gradually and

Follow your pace without a hurry…

Breathing in… Breathing out…

You may use your sensations to experience the feelings of

The person in the mirror. Feel what it felt…

Be aware of your own feelings at this present moment…

The feelings can be happy, sad, worry, hope, guilt, pleasant…

Try to explore what these feelings are…and be with it without reacting on it…

Just look at it with your breathing…

Breathing in, I know I am breathing in… Breathing out, I know I am breathing out…

The face in the mirror may want to talk to you. You may relax your mind and

Just listen to it with your heart… How does it feel? Any thoughts?

Try to listen and understand this face at this present moment…

Feeling is just a feeling only, it comes and it goes, no right or wrong.

You are the master of these feelings. You own your feelings.

If you wish, you may use your hands to touch and explore this face…

Feel your eyes, ears, nose, mouth, lip and neck…

Gently, use your hands and whole body to feel…

Breathing in… Breathing out…

Any feelings you found, any discoveries?

You may have suggested to have two minutes for free exploration…

Through this exploratory process,

You may get closer to yourself and have some discoveries.

If you want to stay a little bit longer for exploration, we certainly respect your need.

If you are ready, you can follow your heart to further explore this experience by making a mask or you can do writing about this process.

After mindful exploration of the face, most participants preferred creating a mask to express their felt experience. From their dialogue with the mask they decorated the mask with words, colors, symbols, images and ideas. To observe their mask from a new perspective, they put it on the table and freely described it.

Then, they put the mask on, listening to its feelings and thoughts. When having a dialogue with it, they looked into their own feelings and thoughts as well. We used music to support staying open to the voices of self from within. Some allowed their body to move as they felt and sensed what was happening inside (authentic movement). As a therapist, we maintain a safe, supportive and open space for spontaneous and authentic expression. We remind the participants to listen to themselves mindfully with compassion, staying open to this evolving process. They slow down to experience each moment. After, the group members write to integrate the experience. We close the session with a short statement to the mask. We begin with, "Thank you, mask. I have learned_____ from you."

Case Study: Fong

Fong, a woman, age 38, reflected that it was a fruitful experience to mindfully observe herself using all her senses. She struggled hard as to whether to show her vulnerable side. She felt sad losing her true voice beneath her social mask (Figure 16.9).

Figure 16.9: The voice from my half-mask

Fong followed her inner voice to cut the mask into a half-mask to show her mouth. Through this creative exploration, Fong experienced the freedom to speak up. It was a profound breakthrough when she accepted her courage to sing "The Phantom of the Opera" loudly. As Fong became more aware of her senses, she got closer to her inner self and accepted herself intimately. She thanked me at the end because of my full presence.

Reflections and Conclusion

In the mindfulness-based expressive arts process, we need to be able to be fully present with openness, acceptance and compassion to the four elements of PCEAT: people (participants and therapist); process; context; and creation. These elements are interactively related (see Figure 16.10).

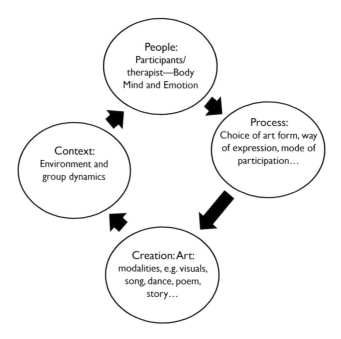

Figure 16.10: Four elements of PCEAT

People

The PCEAT with mindfulness practice is developed and reviewed collaboratively with the people involved in the process. This respectful, empowered quality is also practiced in Thich Nhat Hanh's mindfulness community (Hanh 2002). Additionally, genuineness, compassion, unconditional positive regard and congruence cannot be taught as a cognitive skill. It is truly an "I–Thou" relationship (Ryback 2006) and a way of being. As we go through our life challenges, practicing mindfulness, arts and person-centered being, we practice from the heart with clarity and compassion.

Process

Some may ask about ready-made recipes and step-by-step protocols. As practitioners, we always stay open to the present moment, listen deeply to the participants in our groups, and adapt expressive arts to best meet their needs.

Context

Practicing mindfulness and PCEAT is not just for our work, it is our own life practice. Our work is not to demonstrate our professional expertise. Our intention is to actualize awareness, creativity and healing potential for personal growth and social transformation. As shared by Suzuki Roshi, the Japanese Zen Master, "In the beginner's mind, there are many possibilities, but in the expert's there are few" (cited by Kabat-Zinn 2012, p.9). We hope our experience sharing here can open up the possibilities in your practice.

Creation

Both mindfulness and PCEAT are not only methods of psychotherapy but are also ways of being in relationship with others and the world. It is a beneficial life practice to be congruent, listen with compassion, uncover inhibitions, calm our mind and connect to our spirit–soul–body–mind. Mindfulness strengthens our awareness and presence in the Creative Connection® process. At the same time, the healing potential of expressive arts also guides us to go inside and realize what arises from the unconsciousness.

The interactive effects of mindfulness and PCEAT foster self-awareness and healing, not just for serving the participants, but also for the therapists. Zen mind is wisdom seeking wisdom (Suzuki 1987, p.xxi). In this chapter, we (my colleague Josephine Cheng and myself) shared our evolving understanding of integrating mindfulness and Person-centered Expressive Arts Therapy. We learn every day from beginner's mind and gain from my moment-to-moment practice. We are humbled to keep up the journey of seeking for wisdom through our practices of mindfulness, expressive arts and openness.

Acknowledgements

Through this chapter I offer my deepest gratitude to my dear colleague, Josephine Cheng. We have been facilitating expressive arts since 1994. She and my cohort Gregg Kerlin guided me to the avenue of relating mindfulness and Zen Buddhism to my practice. I would like to express my speechless appreciation to my teacher Natalie Rogers for her passionate teaching of Person-Centered Expressive Arts Therapy; my supervisor Jack Weller and Anin Utigaard; and my mentors Kate Donohue, Benedikte Scheiby, Christine Evans and Laury Rappaport. Jack always holds my hand at his heart mindfully in my expressive arts pathway. I also appreciate the unconditional positive regard of my mom, William, Celina, Helena and my dogs, Chips and Fries. With the consent of the participating individuals, we are grateful for having their support in telling their unfolding stories in an authentic way using creative names.

References

Bolton, R. (1979) *People Skill: How to Assert Yourself, Listen to Others, and Resolve Conflicts.* New York: Simon and Schuster, Inc.

Franklin, M. (2012) Personal communication.

Gilbert, P. and Tirch, D. (2009) "Emotional Memory, Mindfulness and Compassion." In F. Didonna (ed.) (2009) *Clinical Handbook of Mindfulness.* New York: Springer.

Goodman, T.A. (2005) "Working with Children: Beginner's Mind." In C.K Germer, R.D. Siegel, and P.R. Fulton (eds) (2005) *Mindfulness and Psychotherapy.* New York: The Guilford Press.

Hanh, T.N. (2002) *Friends on the Path: Living in Spiritual Communities.* Berkeley, CA: Parallax Press.

Hanh, T. N. (2009) *Happiness: Essential Mindfulness Practices.* Berkeley, CA: Parallax Press.

Hanson, R. (2009) *Buddha's Brain: The Practical Neuroscience of Happiness, Love, and Wisdom.* Oakland, CA: New Harbinger Publications, Inc.

Kabat-Zinn, J. (1990) *Full Catastrophe Living: Using the Wisdom of Your Body and Mind to Face Stress, Pain, and Illness.* New York: Bantam Dell (a division of Random House, Inc.).

Kabat-Zinn, J. (2012) *Mindfulness for Beginners: Reclaiming the Present Moment—and Your Life.* Boulder, CO: Sounds True, Inc.

Knill, P.J., Barba, H.N., and Fuchs, M.N. (1995) *Minstrels of Soul: Intermodal Expressive Therapy.* Toronto: Palmerston Press.

Kyle, D.T. (1998) *The Four Powers of Leadership: Presence, Attention, Wisdom and Compassion.* Deerfield Beach, FL: Health Communications, Inc.

Langer, E.J. (1989) "Minding Matters: The Consequences of Mindlessness—Mindfulness." In L. Berkowitz (ed.) (1989) *Advances in Experimental Social Psychology, Vol. 22.* Cambridge, MA: Academic Press Inc.

McCown, D., Reibel, D., and Micozzi, M.S. (2010) *Teaching Mindfulness: A Practical Guide for Clinicians and Educators.* New York: Springer Press.

McNiff, S. (2009) *Integrating the Arts in Therapy: History, Theory and Practice.* Springfield; IL: Charles Thomas Publisher Ltd.

Monti, D., Peterson, C., Shakin Kunkel, E., Hauck, W.W., *et al.* (2006) "A randomized, controlled trial of mindfulness-based art therapy (MBAT) for women with cancer." *Psycholo-Oncology 15,* 5, 363–373.

Plum Village, The (2010) *Practice from the Heart: Zen Master Thich Nhat Hanh in Hong Kong 2010.* Awaken to Joy at Mindfulness Retreat, Hong Kong.

Rogers, C.R. (1951) *Client-Centered Therapy: Its Current Practice, Implications and Theory.* Boston, MA: Houghton Mifflin.

Rogers, C.R. (1980) *A Way of Being.* New York: Houghton Mifflin Company.

Rogers, N. (1993) *The Creative Connection: Expressive Arts as Healing.* Palo Alto, CA: Science and Behavior Books.

Rogers, N. (2011) *The Creative Connection for Groups: Person-Centered Expressive Arts for Healing and Social Change.* Palo Alto, CA: Science and Behavior Books.

Ryback, D. (2006) "Self-determination and the neurology of mindfulness." *Journal of Humanistic Psychology 46,* 4, 474–493.

Satir, V., Banmen, J., Gerder, J. and Gomori, M. (1991) *The Satir Model Family Therapy and Beyond.* Palo Alto, CA: Science and Behaviour Books.

Suzuki, S. (1987) *Zen Mind, Beginner's Mind: 40th Anniversary Edition.* Boston, MA: Shambhala Publications, Inc.

Chapter 17

Creative Mindfulness

Dialectical Behavioral Therapy and Expressive Arts Therapy

Karin von Daler and Lori Schwanbeck

Creative Mindfulness combines Expressive Arts Therapy with Dialectical Behavior Therapy (DBT). This model was developed by the authors in 2004 as a means to integrate the effectiveness of DBT with the creative and sensory modes of self-expression and learning of Expressive Arts Therapy. We created it as a way to work creatively *and* effectively with highly reactive clients presenting with emotional vulnerability and self-harm impulses. We have been encouraged to see that bringing our passion for Expressive Arts Therapy to the more structured DBT therapy has led to positive outcomes for clients and inspired non-expressive arts-oriented therapists to use creativity in their clinical work.

As some clinicians have experienced, there are limits to traditional creative modalities when working with highly emotionally dysregulated clients who need immediate behavioral and cognitive change for their very survival and fundamental well-being. For example, following the client's lead into their imagination or free movement can result in emotional flooding and re-experiencing of trauma. At these times, client and therapist can both feel overwhelmed and at a loss. Even when unstructured creative expression evokes emotional catharsis, there may be no learning of new behaviors or skills, which could be used in the client's life when emotional triggers threaten to destabilize any therapeutic growth. Huckvale and Learmonth (2009) point out how "Working with chaos, deep distress, acute disturbance and imminent life-threatening danger to the person demands containing structures... Approaches that have emphasized the art-based root have tended to also emphasize the organic, non-directive and spontaneous elements of art-making" (p.62).

On the other end of the continuum, the more structured and evidence-based therapies such as DBT that are often required in mental health settings, favor the cognitive to the exclusion of the sensory, creative and imaginal where resources, connection and embodied learning can be experienced. In integrating expressive arts with DBT, Creative Mindfulness suggests a way of working therapeutically that is as containing and structured as DBT and as creative, embodied and multi-sensory as expressive arts.

Theoretical Framework

Dialectical Behavior Therapy

DBT was developed by Marcia Linehan (1993a) to treat suicidality and Borderline personality disorder (Linehan 1993a). It has also demonstrated efficacy in treating addictions, eating disorders and mood disorders, and emotional vulnerability (Telch, Agras, and Linehan 2001). Emotional vulnerability shows up in clients who struggle with the aforementioned disorders and those who present with inappropriate anger, relationship problems and Post Traumatic Stress Disorder. DBT is a behavioral mindfulness-based psychotherapy that teaches clients life-skills (Safer, Telch, and Chen 2009).

DBT views impulsive behaviors, including self-harm and addictions, as a result of faulty emotion regulation systems and maladaptive attempts to manage disturbed emotions. Emotion regulation systems can be negatively shaped by early environments, specifically those that are invalidating (Linehan 1993a). These environments can create confusion about emotions and what is appropriate or safe to feel and express and can lead one to become more reactive to stimulation, and unable to soothe oneself effectively once aroused.

DBT theory posits that self-harm behaviors, such as cutting or other self-destructive behaviors, are learned coping strategies for unbearable emotions. DBT assists people with severe emotional dysregulation by reducing emotional sensitivity and encouraging more effective ways to handle emotions when they do arise.

DBT Skills

There are four skill modules in DBT: Core Mindfulness, Emotion Regulation, Distress Tolerance and Interpersonal Effectiveness. DBT assumes that these important life-skills must be learned and consciously practiced in order to find emotional balance. Some people learn these skills naturally in their development and others do not. DBT focuses on actively building skills in a psycho-educational group setting and in individual therapy.

CORE MINDFULNESS SKILLS

Mindfulness is paying attention with intention—not the intention to judge, but to notice with openness and curiosity. Mindfulness skills are at the core of DBT skills because increased awareness in the moment leads to increased flexibility in responding. Mindfulness is cultivating an awareness of the current moment with acceptance and creates an observing perspective that allows one to become aware of thoughts, emotions and triggers, as *events*, not as facts, thus creating distance from them. This allows a moment of space and time to assess and respond, rather than react to the moment.

EMOTION REGULATION SKILLS

These skills help clients to develop adaptive skills that will enable them to more effectively manage negative emotional states, and cultivate a greater capacity for positive emotional experiences (Linehan 1993b). Emotions can be viewed as problematic, mysterious and dangerous by those who have experienced intense emotional invalidation. Teaching that emotions are natural responses to stimuli, affect our body, mind and behaviors, and are functional in getting us to respond to situations, is essential. The goal of emotion regulation is not to eliminate negative and unpleasant emotions, but to reduce suffering that arises from either denying emotions, being too reactive or unable to regulate emotions once they arise (Linehan 1993b).

DISTRESS TOLERANCE SKILLS

We all experience pain in life. Some responses to pain, while alleviating it in the short term, may cause further distress. Self-harm behaviors and addictions may numb or soothe but are not adaptive coping skills. Distress tolerance skills provide clients with a variety of strategies to use in the present moment when experiencing pain, difficulty or distress that cannot be changed right away (Linehan 1993b). At the heart of distress tolerance skills is learning to develop patience, tolerance and equanimity in response to difficult situations (Linehan 1993b).

INTERPERSONAL EFFECTIVENESS

One of the most significant sources of both emotional well-being, and distress, is our interactions with other people (Siegel 2007). It is therefore essential to learn how to be effective in relationships. Interpersonal effectiveness skills help with assertiveness, boundary setting, building connection, assessing the health of a relationship and with letting go of relationships that are harmful (Linehan 1993b).

Creative Mindfulness: Integrating Expressive Arts with DBT

Teaching DBT skills, prior to developing Creative Mindfulness, we found that the skills were highly effective in supporting positive change in people's lives, yet we longed to include the creativity and sensory engagement that we knew from Expressive Arts Therapy. As efficacious as DBT is in helping clients change behaviors, regulate emotions and create a life worth living, we wanted to integrate the wealth of possibility that comes from the sensory engagement, imagination and creativity of expressive arts—that might augment growth and deepen engagement and transformation.

Conceptually, we were also curious to investigate the family resemblance (Wittgenstein 1998) between the pure and detailed sensory focus of mindfulness and the expressive arts approach of "staying on the surface" (Knill, Barba, and Fuchs 1995). In addition, recent neurobiological findings have pointed to the benefit of multi-sensory learning (Ackerman 2004).

Integrating DBT with expressive arts became a creative experiment in our skills training sessions. One was a group of people struggling with emotion dysregulation and self-harm impulses with borderline personality disorder, bipolar disorder and other diagnoses. The other group focused on healing from eating disorders. The first unsystematic attempts at integration quickly hinted at its effectiveness. Clients engaged positively with the learning in sessions and in *in vivo* application outside of sessions. We had expanded beyond a conceptual didactic discussion of the skills into an enriched, creative and embodied immersion that enhanced the learning. For example, when teaching about the Wise Mind (Linehan 1993b), we found that many clients understood the concept but did not have access to the state. We hypothesized that the experiential and imaginal realms needed to be involved in order for clients to access such resources.

We also found that using creativity to learn is enlivening and engaging. The novelty and engagement of sensory stimulation creates more interest, a sense of playfulness, and openness to exploring new concepts. Playing can bypass the defenses and resistance (Nachmanovitch 1990) in clients who might respond with willfulness and hopelessness.

A group member had been struggling to adopt self-soothing skills because, as she put it, "they wouldn't work for me." No persuading on our part had convinced her even to try. After experiencing being able to soothe herself while shaping some clay *in* session, she was able to begin the necessary learning process of using her senses to soothe herself *outside* of sessions, as we kept referring back to the lump of clay as an anchor for her growing ability. In this way, the new skill could be *played out* and thereby learned *in vivo*, instead of just theoretically, and was reinforced in the interpersonal setting of the therapy room.

It became apparent that learning was enhanced, and that skills integrated more easily in clients' lives. During our weekly skills check-in, clients reported having used more skills than usual. Since developing Creative Mindfulness we have gained substantial experience and support for our initial findings through systematic and consistent use of the method in clinical work.

Principles of Behavioral and Neurological Change

Exploring advances in brain research validated the changes we were witnessing. The concept of neuroplasticity (Hebb 1949) illustrates how experience shapes our reality. The wiring of the brain changes with each experience and neural links are formed between every sequence of activity in the brain (Siegel 2007). Every action, thought, sensation, memory and emotion becomes linked with other simultaneous neural events, creating a network of stimulus and response patterning. The more we follow a certain stimulus with a certain response, the stronger the neural link between the two become. If every time a person has the emotion of loneliness, they turn to food for soothing, the link between loneliness and eating is reinforced, making this response more and more automatic. While this makes a good explanation for the difficulty in changing long-standing emotional response patterns, it also suggests that by intentionally creating adaptive responses to stressful thoughts and emotions and reinforcing these over time, we have the ability to rewire the brain.

Other research has shown that when the new response is multi-sensory (Kabat-Zinn 2005), we are using more parts of the brain while responding, thus creating a variety of links or associations in the neural network that strengthen the new response. This creates more sensory doorways or reminders of a new response. For example, when feeling flooded with loneliness, a client is instructed to choose something self-soothing, such as working with clay rather than binge eating. In doing so, the client is likely to be engaging the somato-sensory cortex and creating somatic associations between the feeling of loneliness and an adaptive response of tactile engagement with the clay. The full spectrum of sensory experiences of the clay—the color, the smell, the visual and the feel—can act as somatic markers to help access the skillful behavior.

Research also suggests that new responses must be reinforced in order to become as accessible as older but less adaptive ones (Hanson 2009). The change does not happen overnight, and new responses must be reinforced through validation and repetition to weaken the default mode of responding and strengthen the new one.

Clinical Application

Clinical Model of Creative Mindfulness

Following the logic of these neurobiological findings, we structured the treatment into three phases:

1. DISTRACTION

The initial focus in building new responses to adverse stimuli is to direct attention away from the client's habitual patterns of negative behavior and thought.

2. CREATING A NEW EXPERIENCE

A more regulating and adaptive experience is focused on, with an emphasis on sensory immersion in the new experience.

3. APPLICATION OF THE NEW SKILL IN THE CLIENT'S LIFE

After the steps of refocusing attention, and regulating emotions, reinforcement is needed to anchor this adaptive response and make it as compelling and easy to choose as the older, less adaptive ones.

Correlation between DBT and Expressive Arts (EXA) and Core Concepts

In practice we found that these phases can also be understood in terms inherent to both DBT and EXA (Knill *et al.* 1995) (see Table 17.1).

Table 17.1: DBT and Expressive Arts Therapy (EXA)

DBT	EXA
Distraction	Decentering
Creating a new experience	Range of play
Application	Rehearsal and performance

1. Distraction—Decentering

In DBT distraction is the intentional shifting of attention away from a distressing experience. Refocusing attention helps break the cycle of rumination and obsession. In EXA terms, we are helping the client to "de-center." According to Knill, Levine, and Levine (2005) "decentering activities can open the door to unexpected surprises and often emerge with spontaneity or intuition. They point in the direction of an alternative world experience through a distancing effect" (p.64). Instead of focusing on the problem represented in the client's art piece, attention is directed to another area.

2. Creating a New Experience—Range of Play

In DBT, building a new positive or regulating experience is an attempt to deliberately increase positive emotions or reduce the intensity of negative ones. This parallels the EXA strategy of expanding the "range of play" by offering a broader aesthetic repertoire and nourishing the imagination, thereby increasing access to resources such as flexibility, creativity and new perspectives and ways of responding.

3. Application—Rehearsal and Performance

The third stage is the application of the new skill in the client's life; in DBT this is observed through weekly skills check-ins. In EXA terms, the art created in session is a tangible, sensory manifestation of the learning that took place. Performing, touching, hearing or viewing the art piece outside of session reactivates the felt sense and beliefs associated with creating it.

At a meta-theoretical level the approaches of DBT and EXA are similar when we juxtapose dialectics and creative conflict. A dialectical perspective takes the stance that reality is not static or balanced but comprised of internal opposing forces (Linehan 1993b). Similarly, creative imagination expressed in concrete art forms enables clients to better hold the tension and conflict inherent in life even when the issues cannot be resolved (Levine 1995).

The overall goal of DBT skills training is "creating a life worth living" (Linehan 1993b). This parallels EXA's focus on resources and creativity in contrast to therapeutic models that operate from a pathology/cure paradigm. Creative Mindfulness says that the ultimate act of creation is creating a life worth living. Our goal is to support clients by increasing their life-skill palette.

Case Study: Accessing and Embodying the Wise Mind

Cindy, a 25-year-old woman, suffers from frequent binge eating and occasional cutting following painful interpersonal interactions. She judges herself for having these behaviors, leading to crippling guilt and shame. Her negative self-judgment has reinforced hopelessness and doubt that she will ever be able to change her behavior and feel better. She has labeled herself "treatment resistant." After years of trying to change, Cindy is skeptical of therapy and describes her challenges as "insurmountable boulders that block the path of my life."

We introduced the skill of Wise Mind, initially through discussion. Cindy understood the concept but was adamant that she did not have access to this internal voice of wise guidance saying, "If I did, why would I still be here working on all this?" Working with her image of the boulders, we asked Cindy to create a visual representation of the boulders. Using an adapted form of sculpture making, to stay within the language of her boulder image, we suggested that she place pillows and chairs around the room to represent the boulders. We invited Cindy to imagine how Wise Mind would interact with the boulders. With some hesitation Cindy imagined Wise Mind to be like a stream of water, flowing around the boulders. To help her practice and embody this new way of approaching the boulders, we asked her what this might look like in simple movements.

Cindy began to move around the room, meeting the "boulder" pillows and then moving around them. After she had practiced this new movement pattern for a few minutes, we led her more deeply into awareness of her present experience: "Cindy, I invite you to notice what it is like for you to move around the room and the boulders in this way. What thoughts, feelings or sensations are you noticing in yourself in this moment?" Cindy reported feeling a bit more confident and open in relation to the boulders. To reinforce this felt state we invited Cindy to become more mindful: "Let yourself notice what is happening in your body as you feel more confident and open." Cindy said she felt more strength in her arms and legs and that this felt sense made her aware that she might actually have access to an inner Wise Mind. To further anchor this new experience, we engaged her visual sense and asked her to choose an object in the room to represent this new experience. She picked a peacock blue scarf, which she held on to for the rest of the session.

Next week, Cindy reported having gone to a family gathering. Her experience was that as soon as she got near her family, she would binge eat to try to ease her pain and fear, resulting in shame and guilt. The combination of Cindy's anxiety, anticipating difficult interactions and the ensuing "boulder" of pain, led her to automatically look to the buffet in the dining room for comfort.

Across the room, however, she noticed a woman wearing a peacock blue scarf. Cindy immediately recalled the experience of the Wise Mind water flowing around the obstacles. This memory, triggered by the color, brought back the feeling of strength, openness and flow. Feeling connected to these Wise Mind qualities helped her to choose not to binge, but instead to go outside for some fresh air. When she re-entered the family gathering, she was able to stay more open and curious to the in-the-moment connection with her family and for the moment not to binge eat. The blue color became a resource Cindy continued to use to access strength and inner guidance.

Creative Mindfulness in Practice

Following are some of the Creative Mindfulness exercises we use in our skills groups. Most can be used for individual clients with slight adaptations. They are categorized according to the DBT skills modules: Core Mindfulness, Emotion Regulation, Distress Tolerance and Interpersonal Effectiveness. After a definition of each skill, we suggest ways of integrating EXA to teach the specific skill.

Core Mindfulness Skills

WISE MIND

Wise Mind is the meeting place between the rational and emotional mind. It is the place of intuition or knowing what is right action.

- *Sculpture/drama:* Imagine what your "Wise Mind" might look like if it were here in the room. What posture does your Wise Mind have? How does it move? How does it sound?

- *Collage:* Create a collage of images that represent wisdom and balance.

OBSERVE

Awareness of one's moment-by-moment internal and external experience.

- *Movement:* Bring awareness to the sensation of movement in the body as client slowly moves about the room.

- *Visual art:* Observe the colors of an image that a client or fellow group member has created one color and shape at a time.

DESCRIBE

To put words to one's experience as objectively and factually as possible using sensory language.

- *Painting/sculpture:* Invite clients to describe with art something they observed in the previous exercises. This could be a sound from the street, a warm sensation in one's belly, a shape in a painted image.

- *Movement/sculpture:* Have clients close their eyes and open their hands to feel an object you hand them. Ask them to put words to the experience their hands are having in touching the object (hard/soft, round/sharp, warm/cold, etc.).

NON-JUDGMENTAL STANCE

Open receptivity. Not judging or evaluating a phenomenon, or experiencing a moment as good or bad.

- *Visual art:* Ask clients to pair up and non-judgmentally describe their partner's art, noticing the objective qualities, for example, "I see a blue shape, surrounded by little dots of brown."

- *Visual art:* Have clients close their eyes and paint with their fingers. With eyes open, ask them to notice judgment and then practice speaking non-judgmentally about their piece.

ONE-MINDFULLY—IN THE MOMENT

Doing one thing at a time with full awareness.

- *Sculpture:* Ask clients to explore a lump of clay with all their senses, inviting them to become fully absorbed in the experience.

- *Music:* Play various pieces of music. Invite clients to stay fully present with the sounds and return to the music when their minds wander.

EFFECTIVELY

Focus on doing what works in each moment, keeping in mind long-term goals, rather than what you think is "right" or "fair."

- *Sculpture:* Divide materials (paper, glue, clay, popsicle sticks, etc.) unevenly among group members (i.e. more paper for one than another). Ask each to construct a tower (or other shape) given the materials they have.

- *Visual art:* Paint a group painting one by one. Begin with one person and pass the painting around, instructing each to add to the painting as they are inspired.

Emotion Regulation Skills

POSITIVE EXPERIENCES

Intentionally pursuing enjoyable activities in order to increase the likelihood of inducing *positive* emotions.

- *Multiple art forms:* Create a weekly structure of engaging in creative processes the client most enjoys. Using *observe* and *describe* skills, have clients journal about the impact on their mood.

OPPOSITE-TO-EMOTION ACTION

Acting in a way that is opposite to an emotional urge, to decrease the presence or intensity of an emotion.

- *Movement:* Instruct clients to find and hold a body position that represents sadness, and then shift into a position that represents joy. Use *observe* and *describe* to notice the difference in mood and energy with each body position.

- *Drama:* Have clients dramatize a situation from their lives in which they acted on their mood with negative consequences. Describe the effects this action had on both them and the other person(s). Create an alternative "script" in which they choose an alternative behavior; for example instead of yelling, stop, take a time out, or practice a communication skill. Rehearse the new script several times.

Distress Tolerance Skills

DISTRACT

Shifting attention away from distressing thoughts or emotions in order to prevent emotional overwhelm.

- *Music:* Listen to or create music that shifts emotional state. Use skill of *one-mindfully* to anchor attention with the music.

- *Movement:* Move energetically to music that invites dancing, shifting attention away from negative thoughts, into the body.

SELF-SOOTHE

Intentionally engaging in acts of comfort, nurturance and kindness toward oneself.

- *Music:* Listen to calming music. Ask clients to put together a tape of music they love, encouraging them to use it whenever they need soothing.

- *Movement:* Move gently and rhythmically, perhaps with rocking, gentle patting or by giving their own body a gentle hug.

IMPROVE THE MOMENT

Getting through a difficult moment by deliberately making it better:

Improve stands for **I**magery: Imagine relaxing scenes or things going well.

Meaning: Find some purpose or meaning in the experience.

Prayer: Pray to whomever one worships or chant a personal mantra.

Relaxation: Relax muscles, breathe deeply.

One thing in the moment: Focus entire attention on what one is doing in the moment.

Vacation: Take a break from it all for a short time.

Encouragement: Cheerleading oneself: "You can make it through this."

- *Visual art:* Ask clients to practice working with what is in the moment. Complete a quick imperfect drawing, and then ask what else it "needs" in terms of colors or shapes in order to make it just a little better.

- *Guided imagery with all senses:* Guide clients to experience colors, images, shapes, body sensations, sounds that are pleasing.

PROS AND CONS

Assessing the potential positive and negative consequences of an action, curbing impulsivity and reactivity.

- *Movement/sculpture:* Invite reflection on consequences of various choices by experiencing each choice through the body. Make "islands" around the room with colored scarves to represent different choices. Ask clients to step onto the first "island" and observe and describe how it is to have made the choice this represents, then step onto another and notice the difference between them. After they have visited all the choices, have clients step aside and reflect on what they noticed.

RADICAL ACCEPTANCE
Accepting circumstances as they are, regardless of whether one likes them or agrees with them.

- *Visual art:* Have clients draw or paint the experience exactly how it is for them, not how they wish it were, how bad it is, but allowing themselves to get immersed in how it *is*; experience and express that in colors and shapes.

- *Movement:* Invite clients to practice being a blanket receiving falling leaves or dance/move this feeling or situation just as it is.

Interpersonal Effectiveness Skills
DEARMAN
Steps to effectively communicate and address a problem with another person.

D: Describe the facts of a situation.

E: Express how you feel.

A: Ask for what you want.

R: Reinforce the benefits to the other person.

M: Stay mindful and on topic.

A: Appear confident.

N: Negotiate. Come up with a solution that you both can agree on.

- *Drama:* Have clients role-play in dyads to practice communicating ineffectively and then effectively, using the steps of DEARMAN. Emphasize and experiment with finding the appropriate tone of voice, body posture and facial expressions as they go through the steps and track how each feels in their body. Have some of the group members help by directing the scene and giving feedback.

- *Movement:* Go through the same steps as described for the drama exercise, but this time do it just with movement—no words, to anchor the new experience non-verbally in the body.

RELATIONSHIP EFFECTIVENESS (GIVE)

Communication tool used when keeping the relationship is a priority.

G: Be gentle. Be courteous.

I: Be interested in their point of view.

V: Validate. Let the other person know that you understand how he or she is feeling.

E: Easy manner. Don't be too intense; introduce humor if appropriate.

- *Drama:* Clients role-play making a request, playing with finding the right voice and body stance for them, practicing how to express themselves as they appear gentle, interested, validating and easy in their manner. Ask clients to be mindful of how their inner state changes as they practice.

RELATIONSHIP EFFECTIVENESS (FAST)

Communication tool that enhances self-respect.

F: Be fair to yourself and the other person. Don't be judgmental.

A: No apologies if you tend to over-apologize.

S: Stick to your values. Don't change your feelings just to make the other person happy.

T: Be truthful. Don't lie to yourself or the other person.

- *Drama:* Clients role-play in dyads holding a position when challenged. For example, Person A wants to borrow money from Person B. Person B's job is to insist on saying "no" to the request regardless of what Person A says. Guide clients to hold somatic awareness of their center, observing boundaries as they go through the four letters.

- *Movement:* Experiment with body postures that reflect the qualities of the FAST acronym.

Conclusion

Creative Mindfulness was developed through a playful yet systematic experimentation with DBT skills and EXA. We have gained substantial experience through the development and practice of the method in clinical work and the training of other clinicians. We are encouraged to see that using the method has led to significant positive changes for clients who present with emotional vulnerability and self-harm impulses. They report decreased maladaptive behavior, an expanded skill-set for handling distress and increased positive moods. Developing and using Creative Mindfulness has also enlivened the therapy process with challenging clients. Research in neurobiology, mindfulness and core EXA tenets support our work. However, additional practice by other clinicians as well as empirical qualitative research is needed to more solidly establish its efficacy and usefulness.

References

Ackerman, D. (2004) *An Alchemy of Mind.* New York: Scribner.

Hanson, R. (2009) *Buddha's Brain.* Oakland, Ca: New Harbinger Publications.

Hebb, D.O. (1949) *The Organization of Behavior.* New York: Wiley and Sons.

Huckvale, K. and Learmonth, M. (2009) "A case example of art therapy in relation to dialectical behavior therapy." *International Journal of Art Therapy 14,* 2, 52–63.

Kabat-Zinn, J. (2005) *Coming to our Senses.* New York: Hyperion.

Knill, P., Barba, H., and Fuchs, M. (1995) *Minstrels of Soul.* Ontario: Palmerston Press.

Knill, P., Levine, E., and Levine, S. (2005) *Principles and Practice of Expressive Arts Therapy.* London: Jessica Kingsley Publishers.

Levine, E. (1995) *Tending the Fire: Studies in Art, Therapy and Creativity.* Ontario: Palmerston Press.

Linehan, M. (1993a) *Cognitive Behavioral Treatment of Borderline personality disorder.* New York: Guilford Press.

Linehan, M. (1993b) *Skills Training Manual for Treating Borderline personality disorder.* New York: Guilford Press.

Nachmanovitch, S. (1990) *Free Play.* New York: Tarcher Penguin.

Safer, D., Telch, C., and Chen, E. (2009) *Dialectical Behavior Therapy for Binge Eating and Bulimia.* New York: Guilford Press.

Siegel, D. (2007) *The Mindful Brain.* New York: W.W. Norton and Company.

Telch, C.F., Agras, W.S., and Linehan, M.M. (2001) "Dialectical behavior therapy for binge eating disorder." *Journal of Consulting and Clinical Psychology 69,* 6, 1061–1065.

Wittgenstein, L. (1998) *Culture and Value. Revised Edition.* (Edited by Henrik von Wright.) London: Wiley-Blackwell.

Chapter 18

Mindfulness and Focusing-Oriented Arts Therapy with Children and Adolescents

Emily Tara Weiner and Laury Rappaport

Today, mindfulness practices are being taught to children in school-based programs, summer camps, meditation programs, and family life. The arts can be used as inspiring means to teach mindfulness to children and adolescents (Coholic 2010, 2011; Saltzman and Goldin 2008). While many children are able to learn formal mindfulness practices, such as sitting and walking meditation, the arts often provide an enjoyable, tangible route to access and express mindfulness practices. For example, a child can choose a color and draw a line coordinated with their in-breath followed by creating another line on their out-breath. Children can notice how it feels in their body after mindful breathing, and then draw the feeling onto a body outline or cut-out figure.

Focusing-Oriented Arts Therapy (FOAT) (Rappaport 2009)—a mindfulness-based approach that incorporates the expressive arts with Gendlin's Focusing (1981, 1996)—helps to deepen the experience of mindfulness. The core elements that contribute to FOAT's mindfulness foundation are: the Focusing Attitude—being welcoming and "friendly" toward inner experience, and Clearing a Space with Art—setting stressors aside and accessing a place that is "All Fine," or separate from these stressors. From a mindfulness-based perspective, being able to create a healthy distance from thoughts and emotions with a witnessing presence is key, and the addition of art to the Focusing process facilitates this externalization and crystallization of emotions. Integrating mindfulness practices with Focusing-Oriented Arts Therapy (FOAT) (Rappaport 2009) provides an arts-based method for children and adolescents to learn the fundamentals of mindfulness skills—becoming more accepting of their inner experience, developing a healthy relationship with their emotions, accessing a place of wholeness, and cultivating both self-compassion and compassion toward others.

Before teaching mindfulness to children, it is important to cultivate one's own mindfulness practice. Thich Nhat Hanh (2011) describes the importance of teaching mindfulness to children:

> I have learned that the most important thing to transmit to the children is our way of being… So our presence, calmness, gentleness, and peace are the most important things we can offer them. Therefore, we need to really practice in order to have these things to transmit to them. (p.37)

This chapter provides an overview of research on mindfulness with children and adolescents, a brief summary of approaches that integrate art with mindfulness for youth, and a description of a week-long Mindful Art Program that integrated mindfulness and FOAT at the Omega Institute's Teen Camp in New York (Weiner 2012).

Theoretical Framework

Mindfulness and Art with Children and Adolescents

There is increasing evidence of the benefits of mindfulness for children and adolescents. Research has demonstrated that mindfulness training with children and adolescents leads to increased cognitive attention and learning (Biegel and Brown 2011; Flook *et al.* 2010; Siegel and Bryson 2011), social and emotional learning (Lantieri 2008), emotional self-regulation (Coholic 2011; Flook *et al.* 2010; Saltzman and Goldin 2008), resiliency and coping skills (Coholic 2011), overall psychological well-being (Huppert and Johnson 2010), and decreased stress and anxiety (Biegel *et al.* 2009; Burke 2010; Ryan 2012; Semple *et al.* 2010; Sibinga *et al.* 2011; Thompson and Gauntlett-Gilbert 2008).

The integration of art with mindfulness has also demonstrated positive outcomes. Saltzman and Goldin (2008) integrated art into the standard Mindfulness-Based Stress Reduction (MBSR) curriculum for children (MBSR-C). They found that the use of metaphors and art helped the mindfulness exercises to be more fun and engaging for children. Coholic (2010, 2011) developed an arts-based mindfulness group with children that has been found to increase self-awareness, acceptance of feelings, emotional regulation, problem-solving, coping and social skills, and resiliency at school and at home. Coholic (2011) also found that mindfulness practices taught through arts-based methods were more fun, engaging, and effective than the mindfulness practices alone.

Focusing-Oriented Arts Therapy (FOAT)
with Children and Adolescents

Focusing-Oriented Arts Therapy (FOAT), developed by Rappaport (2009), has recently been adapted for children and adolescents. Lee (2011) conducted research using FOAT and positive psychology with children in a homeless shelter, and Weiner (2012) designed a research grant using mindfulness and FOAT with fourth and fifth graders. Other Focusing trainers have also incorporated Focusing with art with children and/or adolescents (Marder 1997; Merkur 1997; Murayama and Yuba 1988; Neagu 1988; Novek 2009; Santen 1990, 1999, 2007; Stapert 1997a, 1997b; Stapert and Verliefde 2008).

Clinical Application

Mindful Art Program with Teens

With the collaboration and guidance of Dr. Laury Rappaport, I (Emily) created a Mindful Art Program for children and adolescents that integrates mindfulness practices with FOAT. The program is based on both FOAT and the curriculum of Mindful Schools, a non-profit organization in the San Francisco Bay Area, which offers professional training, in-class instruction, and other resources to support mindfulness in education. The Mindful Art Program is framed within a wellness and prevention model to teach tools for stress reduction, relaxation, and compassion for oneself and others. The Mindful Art Program is also very much aligned with the Center for Mindful Self-Compassion, which combines skills of mindfulness and self-compassion (Neff and Gerner 2013). The program was piloted at the Omega Teen Camp in Rhinebeck, New York, Summer 2012. Seven adolescents (ages 14–17) participated, and the class met for one hour and a half on five consecutive days.

OVERALL STRUCTURE OF MINDFUL ART PROGRAM

Each day included a mindfulness and FOAT exercise. We began with an opening ritual of sitting in meditation for five minutes. Because the teens had previous meditation experience, they were able to practice for this length of time. Groups new to meditation and/or mindfulness may need to begin with one to two minutes of mindfulness exercises, building up to longer periods with practice. At the end of each day, we concluded with a closing ritual of art sharing for 10–15 minutes; teens were invited to share anything from their art and/or art process that they wished to share with the group—but always with the option to "pass" and not share.

MINDFUL ART PROGRAM WEEKLY SCHEDULE

Day 1: Mindfulness Fundamentals

- FOAT Exercise: Clearing a Space with Art

- "All Fine Place" journal covers

Day 2: Mindfulness Fundamentals (continued)

- FOAT Exercise: Clearing a Space with Art

- Complete journal covers

Day 3: The Focusing Attitude with Oneself

- Self-compassion meditation and mandalas

Day 4: The Focusing Attitude with Others

- Self-compassion mandala group poems

Day 5: FOAT Exercise: Carrying It Forward

- Prayer flags

Description of Themes and Exercises
Days 1–2: Mindfulness Fundamentals and FOAT

- *Goals:* Create safety, introductions; mindfulness—to learn mindfulness tools for grounding, centering, and witnessing their experience; FOAT—to teach Clearing a Space with Art as method for stress reduction, healthy dis-identification with feelings, and access to an inner place of well-being.

- *Materials:* Tibetan bell, blank journals, pre-cut peaceful magazine images, inspiring words/quotes, pens, scrapbooking paper, glue sticks, glue guns, glitter glue gun sticks, scissors, etc.

Mindfulness Practice: Anchors

After introducing ourselves and sharing our intentions for the program, I guided the teens through various mindfulness exercises (Mindful Schools 2010). The concept of having an "anchor" to the present moment was introduced. An "anchor" is an object of attention that helps to keep the mind from moving away from the present moment (like a boat's anchor that keeps it from moving away from its docking place). I taught the teens three anchors—sound, breath, and body sensations—that we practiced on the first two days:

- Sound (mindful listening): "What does a boat's anchor do? An anchor helps keep the boat right where it is, right? If the boat starts to drift away, the anchor pulls it back in. Sound can be your mind's anchor to the present moment. When your mind starts to drift off in thought, the sound of the bell or the sounds in the environment can help bring your mind's attention back to this moment, here and now. Let's try mindful listening to the sound of the bell. See if you can pay attention to the sound of the bell from the very first moment you hear it until the sound is completely gone for you. Raise your hand when you do not hear the bell at all anymore" (*ring Tibetan singing bowl or bell*). Practice ringing the bell with mindful listening several times; share experiences of the exercise.

- Breath: "Your breath can be another anchor for your mind, helping your mind stay in the present moment. See if you can notice your breath near your nostrils. What sensations are there? Is it cool? Warm? Or what? Next, see if you can notice your breath in your chest. What sensations are there? Is it tight? Relaxed? Now, see if you can notice your breath in your belly. What sensations are there? Try to just notice and accept however it is right now. See if you can keep your attention and focus on your breath, for one full cycle (inhale/exhale). When your mind wanders, see if you can gently bring your attention back to your breath. The mind likes to think and have thoughts. There is nothing wrong with this. This is actually the mind's job! However, sometimes it is nice to give the mind a rest or break from working! Remember—the goal is not to try to stop thinking; the goal is just to simply notice when your mind is thinking and gently bring your attention back to your breath."

- Body sensations or the body scan (flashlight of attention): "Imagine you have a flashlight. Shine your flashlight down into your body. First, stand back…open the lens of your flashlight wide, and let the flashlight shine light on your entire body. See if you can sense your entire body as a whole. Then, come in closer…

narrow the lens, and begin to shine the flashlight on different parts of your body. Shine the light on your feet. What sensations do you feel in your feet? Are they hot? Cold? Now shine the light on your ankles." Repeat with each body part, scanning up the entire body (i.e. calves, knees, thighs, hips, bottom, back, belly, chest, shoulders, arms, fingers, neck, head, etc.).

Sharing

After practicing, the teens were invited to share how the experience was for them. I reminded them that the goal of this practice is not to have a certain type of experience, but rather to just notice and accept whatever experience is present. These mindfulness fundamentals then helped provide a foundation for going deeper into the mindfulness-based FOAT practices.

FOAT Exercise: Clearing a Space with Art

Clearing a Space with Art teaches how to set stressors outside of the body (metaphorically) and to sense the place inside that is already and always whole, or "All Fine" (Rappaport 2009). I led the teens in a guided Clearing a Space (see Chapter 14, p.200). The teens were reminded that they were not "banishing" or "getting rid" of their issues, but rather, gently and lovingly setting them aside, just for now, in order to gain some healthy distance from them. I asked the teens to focus on four to five minor issues, rather than larger life issues, since this was a camp program and not a therapy setting. At the end of the guided Focusing, the teens were invited to create "All Fine Place" journal covers. The teens were reminded that it was OK if they did not feel "All Fine" or peaceful at the end of the exercise—and they could represent however they were feeling through the art.

Sharing

One teen, Mollie, excitedly shared her experience during Clearing a Space: "I imagined sitting in a peaceful place, near a lake I like to go. As I was setting things aside, I felt a breeze go by, and then I got chills…and I felt my body relax." I explained that this is what is known as the "felt shift" in Focusing, and I encouraged her to express this felt shift into relaxation by drawing and/or writing in her journal.

Ria drew her "All Fine Place" as a beautiful landscape with a blue sky, a waterfall, and a periwinkle hummingbird hovering over it (Figure 18.1).

Ria shared that after she drew her "All Fine Place" in her journal, it felt "more real." This is the power of the arts with Focusing—the art concretizes the bodily felt sense and helps it to "come alive" and become more vivid. The art journal serves as a tangible reference point and reflection of Ria's internal experience, that she can carry with her and return to as a reminder.

Figure 18.1: "All Fine Place" journal cover

Liza drew her "All Fine Place" as a picture of herself touching a lightning bolt, with a blue, iridescent light behind her (Figure 18.2).

Figure 18.2: "All Fine Place": The Protector

She shared the following: "The first night here, our cabin was struck by lightning and everyone was saying we have a guardian angel—and it kind of freaked me out. But, it helped to put it down on paper, in a drawing. It made it less scary. I could see that we did have a protector…and I felt more relaxed after I drew it." The act of art-making helped Liza to concretize the experience of having a protector, which helped the experience to feel more manageable and helped her relax. Clearing a Space with Art helped Liza gain some healthy distance from the experience and from the fear.

Mikhail drew his "All Fine Place" with a collage of peaceful nature scenes. Above his collage, he wrote the words: "Home, but in a different world." Mikhail described how the word "home" was his "handle"—the word that matched the felt sense of his "All Fine Place"—but that it was different from his actual home. Finding the "All Fine Place" can allow teens to come home to their bodies and find a spiritual home within themselves. They can experience a place of "inherent wholeness" (Rappaport 2009) or "fundamental okayness" (Ferraro 2012) within themselves that they may not have known was there.

Day 3: "The Focusing Attitude" with Oneself

- *Goals:* To cultivate greater self-acceptance and self-compassion.

- *Materials:* Tibetan bell, journals, construction paper for mandalas, markers, oil pastels, etc.

Mindfulness Practice

I guided the teens in mindfulness practice for the opening five minutes of the meeting. The teens were encouraged to choose one anchor that they resonated with the most and to practice with it for the remainder of our meetings.

FOAT Exercises: Self-Gratitude or Self-Kindness Journals (Writing); Self-Compassion Meditation and Focusing; Self-Compassion Mandalas (Art)

The teens were invited to start a daily practice of writing three things they are grateful for about themselves and/or three ways they can show kindness to themselves. Mollie wrote: "I am grateful for my creativity, open heart and perspective." Liza wrote: "1. Eat right. 2. Accept yourself for who you truly are. 3. Know that you will be loved for who you are." After journaling, I guided the teens in a self-compassion meditation with Focusing.

Self-Compassion Meditation and Focusing

Imagine someone living,[1] who you see regularly in your life right now; someone who it is easy for you to have loving thoughts and feelings about, and someone who helps you feel loved. Feel in your body how it feels when you think about and/or imagine this person standing in front of you. Imagine this person telling you loving things and giving you a hug/smiling at you. (*Pause for about 30 seconds*). Now imagine loving yourself the way this person loves you. See if you can tell yourself these same kind and loving things. See if you can give yourself a loving hug and smile. Many people often find it harder to feel and give love to themselves, as compared to others. It can take time to cultivate this sense of love toward yourself. Be patient, gentle. Even when you are not able to be loving toward yourself, see if you can find a way to be loving toward this part that is finding it difficult and learning how to love! Even if you don't feel compassionate toward yourself right now, that is OK. Whatever you feel is OK...just notice and be accepting. Sense inside what it feels like in your body right now, and see if there is an image, word, or phrase that matches your felt sense.

Afterwards, the teens were invited to symbolize their felt sense from the self-compassion meditation in art by creating a self-compassion mandala (mandalas were also used in Day 4).

Sharing
The teens shared their experiences during the self-compassion meditation and/or their mandala.

Day 4:"The Focusing Attitude" With Others: Self-Compassion Poems

- *Goal:* To cultivate kindness and compassion for others.

- *Materials:* Tibetan bell, mandalas from previous session, strips of paper, pens, markers.

Mindfulness Practice
As before, this was practiced for the opening five minutes of the meeting.

FOAT Exercise: Self-Compassion Mandala Group Poems
Each group member was given small strips of paper, one for each member of the group and one for themselves. The mandalas were arranged around the room so that members could walk around and stand in front of each one. I guided the teens:"As you view each mandala, see if you can get a sense of something about it—a quality that you can affirm. Notice the felt sense in your body. Write down a word or phrase on the strip of paper that matches your felt sense when looking at the mandala—and leave the strip of paper as a gift for the mandala's creator, including your own. Remember to write only positive messages as gifts."

Afterwards, the teens returned to their own mandala to receive their gifts. I guided them:"Notice the felt sense in your body as you receive these gifts from others and yourself. Create a poem using the words/phrases on the strips of papers.You can use the actual words/phrases written on the strips, some of them, part of a phrase, none of them, and/or add your own words and phrases."

Sharing
Many of the self-compassion mandalas and accompanying poems centered around the themes of peace, love, interconnectedness, and acceptance of all emotions and facets of life (see Figures 18.3, 18.4 and poems).

Self-Compassion Poem: Waves of Love and Light
May your mind flow like water
from the core waves of love and light
calming peaceful
relaxed
rich with energy and life—rushing power
Freedom.

Figure 18.3: Self-compassion mandala: Waves of Love and Light

Self-Compassion Poem: Heartful Web of Life

Joyously, she navigates the many facets of being, through the colorful web of life.
Her calming illusion, the sensation of being around her brings you on a journey of
energy, power and inner peace. Together your elegance is nothing but interminable and
heartful.

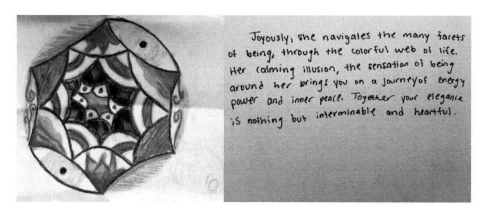

Figure 18.4: Self-compassion mandala: Heartful Web of Life

Day 5: Closing Ritual: "What I Want to Carry With Me" Prayer Flags

- *Goals:* To integrate the experiences from the week and identify tools to bring
into daily life.

- *Materials:* Tibetan bell, small square pieces of cloth, string, glue guns, glitter glue gun sticks, jewels, markers, scissors, etc.

Mindfulness Practice
Again, this took up the opening five minutes of the meeting.

FOAT Exercise: Carrying It Forward
I guided the teens:

> Think and feel back over our entire week together. Remember first arriving here…all of the mindfulness and art activities we have done throughout the week. Ask inside: "What do I want to carry with me from the Mindful Art Program into my life?" Listen to the felt sense inside your body, and see what comes. See if there is a word, phrase, and/or image that matches this felt sense and/or represents something you want to take with you.

After the Focusing, the teens were asked to express the word, phrase, or image on prayer flags that we strung and hung together as one (Figure 18.5).

Figure 18.5: Prayer flags: "What I Want to Carry With Me"

Sharing
Many teens wrote variations of the word "peace"—"Inner Peace" and "Circle of Peace." Another teen, Madilynn, drew a wishing flower (also drawn in her self-compassion mandala) and shared that her wish was for "everyone to find peace."

Findings From the Mindful Art Program
In their program evaluations, almost all of the teens reported that the Mindful Art Program helped to decrease stress, and increase relaxation, self-compassion, and compassion for others. Five of the six teens completed program evaluations (one left early) and all reported that the Mindful Art Program helped them to decrease their stress levels. They also reported that the program increased their self-compassion

and/or compassion for others. One teen reported, "During the course of the week my stress level has gone down so much and also meditation got much easier. This class really helped me see myself in a different light and increased my compassion for myself and others." Two of the teens described feeling "calmer" and "clearer" after the class: "I liked that we meditated for five minutes at the beginning of each class because it was calming. I also liked making and writing in the journals... If I'm feeling under pressure, meditating or clearing my mind for a few minutes can make me feel better and more relaxed." Another teen reported, "My stress level was very low in the beginning, but now my mind is cleared." In addition, three of the teens reported that they felt less judgment and more acceptance of themselves, their own art and/or the artwork of their peers. One teen reported, "I learned not to be so hard on myself." Another reported, "I learned that no one's art is perfect, but accept what it is." And another, "I didn't ridicule myself and my art."

Additional Suggestions for Pre-teens and Adolescents (ages 11–17)

Daniel Rechtschaffen (2012), who helped form the curriculum for Mindful Schools and their new year-long Mindfulness in Education Certification, suggests:

- "Counsel Practice": The teens can break into small groups and each share in response to a specific topic, quote, poem, phrase, or question. During counsel practice, borrowed from Native American traditions, each teen shares for a set amount of time, uninterrupted by others. The teens do not respond to each other's shares but rather practice a deep, mindful listening and witnessing presence.

- Tai Chi and Yoga: These mindful movement practices provide balance to the sitting during mindfulness and art activities. Expressive arts modalities— art, dance, music, sound, and gestures—can be integrated as a way to add movement and offer another non-verbal, fun, and active way to be witnessed.

Adaptations for Younger Children (ages 5–10)

- Shorter time frames for mindfulness and art activities.

- Concrete and directive art activities, for example, Clearing a Space Concrete (Rappaport 2009) in which the children symbolize their stressors using objects and put them inside a container.

- Movement activities and games using mindfulness metaphors. Examples include catching thoughts like butterflies in a net; thoughts swirling like glitter in a jar; thoughts going by like floats in a parade or sticks in a stream. These can all be turned into movement games and/or art activities.

- Parent/guardian participation and at-home practice.[2]

Conclusion

The earlier children and teens learn these mindfulness and FOAT skills, and the earlier they become reinforced neural pathways in the brain, the more easily they will be able to access and remember to use them later in life (Siegel and Bryson 2011). As Thich Nhat Hanh (2011) teaches, "We each have a seed of mindfulness, but we usually forget to water it" (p.16). Programs like these are planting and watering the seeds of mindfulness, social-emotional learning, compassion, and peace in children and adolescents. "The seed is already there. A good teacher touches the seed, allowing it to wake up, to sprout, and to grow" (p.15). Practicing mindfulness can help the innate seeds of unconditional presence take root and grow, first in ourselves, and then in the children and adolescents whose lives we touch. This unconditional presence is a way of being with—simply being with—whatever is here, now, with kindness. Children and adolescents who have these seeds tended to early in their lives, who receive this quality of presence from adults in their lives and learn how to treat themselves with this kind presence, will be more likely to bloom into joyous, compassionate adults.

Notes

1   Since the program was only one week and there would not be regular follow-up, I decided to have the teens focus on a living person in case there were unresolved emotions about someone who was deceased.
2   For school-based programs, it may also be necessary to keep the language and content completely secular (i.e. "mindfulness exercise" rather than "meditation," Vibra-Tone bell rather than Tibetan bell, etc.).

References

Biegel, G.M., Brown, K.W., Shapiro, S.L., and Schubert, C.M. (2009) "Mindfulness-Based Stress Reduction for the treatment of adolescent psychiatric outpatients: A randomized clinical trial." *Journal of Consulting and Clinical Psychology 77*, 5, 855–866.

Biegel, G.M. and Brown, K.W. (2011) *Assessing the Efficacy of an Adapted In-Class Mindfulness-Based Training Program for School-Age Children: A Pilot Study.* Available at www.mindfulschools.org/aboutmindfulness/research, accessed May 9, 2013.

Burke, C.A. (2010) "Mindfulness-based approaches with children and adolescents: A preliminary review of current research in an emergent field." *Journal of Child and Family Studies 19*, 2, 133–144.

Coholic, D. (2010) *Arts Activities for Children and Young People in Need: Helping Children to Develop Mindfulness, Spiritual Awareness and Self-Esteem.* Philadelphia, PA: Jessica Kingsley Publishers.

Coholic, D. (2011) "Exploring the feasibility and benefits of arts-based mindfulness-based practices with young people in need: Aiming to improve aspects of self-awareness and resilience." *Child Youth Care Forum 40*, 4, 303–317.

Ferraro, V. (2012) Personal communication, Mindful Schools.

Flook, L. Smalley, S.L., Kitil, M., Galla, J., *et al.* (2010) "Effects of Mindful Awareness Practices on executive functions in elementary school children." *Journal of Applied School Psychology 26*, 1, 70–95.

Gendlin, E.T. (1981) *Focusing.* New York: Bantam.

Gendlin, E.T. (1996) *Focusing-Oriented Psychotherapy: The Experimental Method.* NY: Guilford Press.

Hanh, T.N. (2011) *Planting Seeds: Practicing Mindfulness with Children.* Berkeley, CA: Parallax Press.

Huppert, F.A and Johnson, D.M. (2010) "A controlled trial of mindfulness training in schools: The importance of practice for an impact on well-being." *The Journal of Positive Psychology 5*, 4, 264–274.

Lantieri, L. (2008) *Building Emotional Intelligence: Techniques to Cultivate Inner Strength in Children.* Boulder, CO: Sounds True.

Lee, H. (2011) "Focusing-Oriented Art Therapy and bookmaking to promote protective resiliency of children living in a homeless shelter." (Unpublished Master's thesis.) Notre Dame De Namur University: Art Therapy Department, Belmont, CA. Available at www.focusingarts.com.

Marder, D. (1997) "Sarah: Focusing and play therapy with a six-year-old child." *The Focusing Folio 16*, 1–2, 51–54. Available at www.focusing.org/chfc/article_index.html, accessed May 9, 2013.

Merkur, B. (1997) "Focusing using art with adolescents." *The Folio 16*, 1–2, 51–55. Availanle at www.focusing.org/chfc/article_index.html, accessed May 9, 2013.

Mindful Schools (2010) *Level II Curriculum Training: August 21–22.* Oakland, CA. Available at www.mindfulschools.org, accessed May 9, 2013.

Murayama, S. and Yuba, N. (1988) "Clearing a Space with drawing in play therapy." *The Folio 7*, 1. Available at www.focusing.org/chfc/article_index.html, accessed May 9, 2013.

Neagu, G. (1988) "The Focusing Technique with children and adolescents." *The Focusing Folio 7*, 4. Available at www.focusing.org/chfc/article_index.html, accessed May 9, 2013.

Neff, K. D., Germer, C. K. (2013) "A Pilot Study and randomizes controlled trial of the mindful self-compassion program." *Journal of Clinical Psychology 69*, 28−44. Available at www.centerformsc.org.

Novek, M. (2009) "An after school program: the inside space explorers club." April 21 to June 9, 2009, at the 14th Street Y of the Educational Alliance, New York City. Available at www.focusing.org/chfc/article_index.html, accessed May 9, 2013.

Rappaport, L. (2009) *Focusing-Oriented Art Therapy: Accessing the Body's Wisdom and Creative Intelligence.* Philidelphia, PA: Jessica Kingsley Publishers.

Rechtschaffen, D. (2012) Personal Communication. Contact at www.mindfulchildren.com.

Ryan, T. (2012) *A Mindful Nation: How a Simple Practice Can Help Us Reduce Stress, Improve Performance, and Recapture the American Spirit.* New York: Hay House.

Saltzman, A. and Goldin, P. (2008) "Mindfulness-Based Stress Reduction for School-Age Children." In L. Greco and S. Hayes (eds) *Acceptance and Mindfulness Treatments for Children and Adolescents.* Oakland, CA: New Harbinger Publications.

Santen, B. (1990) "Beyond good and evil: Focusing with early traumatized children and adolescents." Leuven University Press. Available at www.focusing.org/chfc/article_index.html, accessed on May 9, 2013.

Santen, B. (1999) "Focusing as a therapeutic technique with children and adolescents." In Charles E. Schaefer (ed.) *Innovative Psychotherapy Techniques in Child and Adolescent Therapy.* New York: Wiley and Sons, Inc. Available at www.focusing.org/chfc/article_index.html, accessed on May 9, 2013.

Santen, B. (2007) "Into the fear factory: Treating children of trauma with body maps." *The Folio 20*, 1, 60–78.

Semple, R.J, Lee, J., Rosa, D., and Miller, L.F. (2010) "A randomized trial of Mindfulness-Based Cognitive Therapy for children: Promoting mindful attention to enhance social-emotional resiliency in children." *Journal of Child and Family Studies 19*, 2, 218–229.

Sibinga, E.M, Kerrigan, D., Stewart, M., Johnson, K., Magyari, T., and Ellen, J.M. (2011) "Mindfulness-Based Stress Reduction for urban youth." *Journal of Alternative and Complementary Medicine 17*, 3, 213–218.

Siegel, D. and Bryson, T. (2011) *The Whole-Brain Child: 12 Revolutionary Strategies to Nurture Your Child's Developing Brain.* New York: Delacorte Press.

Stapert, M. (1997a) "Focusing in school: Reader from Children's Focusing Corner." *The Folio 16*, 1–2.

Stapert, M. (1997b) "Children Focusing: Guiding and teaching children to Focus." Reader from Children's Focusing Corner. Available at www.focusing.org/chfc/article_index.html, accessed May 9, 2013.

Stapert, M. and Verliefde, E. (2008) *Focusing with Children: The Art of Communicating with Children at School and at Home.* Ross-on-Wye: PCCS Books.

Thompson, M. and Gauntlett-Gilbert, J. (2008) "Mindfulness with children and adolescents: Effective clinical application." *Clinical Child Psychology and Psychiatry 13*, 3, 395–407.

Weiner, E.T. (2012) "A Mindful Art Program: Using mindfulness and Focusing-Oriented Art Therapy with children and adolescents to decrease stress and increase self-compassion." (Unpublished master's thesis.) Notre Dame De Namur University: Art Therapy Department, Belmont, CA. Available at www.mindfulartprogram.com and www.focusingarts.com.

PART V

Mindfulness and the Arts Therapies in Education and Training

Chapter 19

Mindful Considerations for Training Art Therapists

Inner Friendship—Outer Professionalism

Michael A. Franklin

Since its inception in August 1992, the graduate art therapy program at Naropa University has incorporated mindfulness meditation training into its core curriculum. To my knowledge, no other graduate program in our field has integrated meditation so thoroughly into its program of study. This core educational and institutional value began with Chögyam Trungpa, the founder of Naropa University. Trungpa Rinpoche was a prolific scholar and modern master of Tibetan Buddhism who taught about the basic goodness and the "brilliant sanity" of intrinsic health that exists in all people (Fabrice 2004). Trungpa coined the term "brilliant sanity," which infers the following three innate, unconditional qualities of mind: spaciousness (emptiness), clarity (wisdom), and compassion (clarity + warmth and empathy) (Wegela 2010). Meditation for him was a way to cultivate awakened, brilliantly sane qualities of mind that could be integrated into daily life, including art (Trungpa 1996).

Looking even further back in time, the namesake of our school, the great eleventh century sage, Naropa, was an accomplished practitioner and teacher of tantric Buddhism at the legendary Nalanda University in India. I mention this brief historical perspective at the outset of this chapter since it offers a glimpse into the contemplative education lineage that inspired Naropa University, as well as our art therapy program.

The intention of this chapter is to discuss clear reasons for integrating mindfulness meditation within a blended counseling and art therapy curriculum. Simply, in advance of sitting with another as a therapist, we need to discover how to sit with ourselves, particularly when our mind becomes stressed and restless. Before offering unconditional positive regard to our clients, it is important to be unconditionally present with ourselves.

By combining meditation with clinical training, our students and faculty learn to cultivate inner poise when predictable as well as unexpected events emerge in therapy. Mindfulness meditation, when combined with professional clinical training, prepares students to apply specific awareness skills to their work. Whether practicing in a traditional counseling setting or community-based art studio, meditation training is a sensible subject to include in any counseling/art therapy curriculum.

Throughout this chapter, contemplative approaches to counseling are generally viewed as the mindful application of cultivating, engaging, and sustaining present-centered awareness (Baer *et al.* 2006; Germer, Siegel, and Fulton 2005; Kabat-Zinn 1990; Siegel 2007) in art and art therapy (Farrelly-Hansen 2001; Franklin

1999a,1999b, 2010b; Franklin *et al.* 2000; Rappaport 2009). Essentially, mindfulness can be defined as relaxed, flexible attentiveness to the "reflective self," including non-judgmental "moment-to-moment awareness" of emerging thoughts and sensations (Davis and Hayes 2011, p.198).

Given this summary of mindfulness and meditation, several questions emerge concerning counseling education for art therapists. Why is learning mindfulness meditation and other contemplative practices essential for clinical training? How does mindfulness meditation help art therapy students to become reliably present with themselves and their clients? How does mindfulness meditation practice help us to manage ambiguous clinical, cultural, and intellectual course material? These questions begin to define the focus of this chapter, especially since meditation and art describe a set of practices that can refine various forms of awareness. For example, perceptual wakefulness, focused absorption in the moment, creating an awakened studio space, and increased awareness of inner narratives, are all outcomes of both art and mindfulness practices.

This chapter outlines theoretical connections between meditation and art therapy and discusses the integration of meditation within a combined art therapy/counseling clinical training program. It also includes responses from advanced Naropa University meditation teachers who address the efficacy of combining mindfulness meditation with counseling training. The chapter ends with a student example that illustrates the mindful use of art during a studio class. The final conclusion summarizes the main points highlighted throughout the chapter.

Theoretical Framework

Framework, Freedom, and Meditation

With elegant simplicity, Rubin (2009) sums up the practice of art therapy as offering a framework for freedom. This koan-like aphorism starts to define the practice of mindfulness in art therapy. Whether we are working in video or in clay, each medium simultaneously offers both emotional containment and freedom for expression. Similarly, in contemplative practices like meditation, we learn how discipline and structure (posture and focused attention) supports openness to the freedom of each rising moment. Said another way, meditation incorporates various frameworks in order to freely meet emerging moment-to-moment experiences.

Chögyam Trungpa (1976) spoke of mindfulness and awareness in meditation and the importance of creating space around agitated thoughts, stating, "Meditation is giving a huge, luscious meadow to a restless cow" (p.49). Restlessness becomes mollified when surrounded by space. The agitated cow in the vast pasture is another way to think about Rubin's notion of framework for freedom. In art, as in meditation, we learn to use the elements of figure and ground together. Figure is like a thought and ground is the space that can gently hold it. The problem is, when difficult thoughts emerge, we often forget to surround the agitation with space. In these situations, figure/thought becomes prominent while ground/space is ignored. By intentionally placing room around restless thoughts we provide an opening for the disturbance to breathe. The result is that the thought, while still present, is less cramped, less claustrophobic. In art and meditation, there is a dynamic relationship between figure/thought and space/ground. We always mix the two together.

Defining Mindful and Concentrative Meditation Practices

In general, meditation consists of practices that "self-regulate the body and mind" in such a way that it affects "mental events" through attentional focus (Cahn and Polich 2006, p.180). Among the many approaches to meditation are mantra recitation (Feuerstein 2003), yantra gazing (Khanna 1979), mindfulness practice (Baer *et al.* 2006; Germer *et al.* 2005; Kabat-Zinn 1990; Siegel 2007), and practices from yoga and tantric traditions (Feuerstein 2001, 2003; Yogananda 2003).

It is interesting to note that there are meditation practices that reference the expressive therapies. For example, related to music therapy, sound is used in mantra and chanting. Paintings of deities are used in yantra and mandala gazing. Movement is incorporated into walking meditation and hatha yoga. Writing supports contemplative self-inquiry exercises. In general, there are many connections to make between the expressive therapies and meditation traditions (Franklin 2010b).

Walsh and Shapiro (2006) offer a concise definition of meditation. They describe it as "a family of self-regulation practices that focus on training attention and awareness in order to bring mental processes under greater voluntary control and thereby foster general mental wellbeing and development and/or specific capacities such as calm, clarity, and concentration" (p.229). Meditation practices fall into two basic categories: mindfulness and concentrative (Cahn and Polich 2006). According to these authors, mindfulness involves allowing whatever is emerging at the conceptual or sensory level to surface. The practitioner maintains non-judgmental attention to these events while sustaining open, unattached awareness of the unfolding phenomenal field.

Concentrative approaches work with conceptual or sensory material by coordinating focused awareness, sometimes in combination with a sound mantra, a visual yantra, and/or the breath. Another aspect of concentrative approaches is the cultivation of witness awareness. Similar to the observing capacity of the ego (Sterba 1934), the conscious, neutral, self-observation process of meditation cultivates the inner witness function. Mantra recitation, for instance, fills the field of the mind with a repeated sound or phrase. With focused attention, the practitioner returns to the recited phrase with the aid of witness awareness (Franklin 1999a). This organizing framework minimizes cognitive distractions while maximizing moment-to-moment attentiveness and freedom of choice. Again, Rubin's aphorism comes to mind.

All meditation approaches from various traditions basically strive toward the same results—the cultivation of attention as awareness, observation as awareness, concentration as awareness, insight as awareness, non-judgment as awareness. In essence, remembering to remember to return to wakeful attention. Our art therapy program incorporates both mindful and concentrative approaches throughout the curriculum.

Evenly Suspended Attention and Informed Intuition

It is important to state that all art therapy programs train their students to be self-observant. For example, our field of expressive therapies is uniquely poised to reflectively study clinical material stemming from transference and countertransference material (Lewis 1992). Response art (Fish 2012; Franklin 2012; Moon 1999) and empathy art (Franklin 1990, 2010a) practices are established methods to become good students of ourselves (Franklin 1999a). As artists, we know that art trains awareness. For example, in a figure drawing class we learn to evenly distribute our attention between the model and the corresponding marks we are making on our paper. We even use language like "I captured the exact expression on the model's face," implying attuned absorption in our focused observational process. In art, as in counseling, we utilize the panoramic awareness practices (Speeth 1982) of simultaneously being the experiencer and the observer while hovering our attention between the model, ourselves, and our drawing; or, the client, ourselves, and their artwork.

Speeth distinguishes between panoramic and focused attention. Mantra recitation is a focused attention practice. Panoramic awareness, as demonstrated in the figure drawing example, strives to be equally attentive to the field of occurring events. This impartial distribution of awareness is similar to Freud's notion of evenly suspended or hovering attention and Reik's elaboration of freely floating attention (Epstein 1984). When attention is unencumbered and evenly distributed, unconscious awareness can access informed intuitive resources.

Throughout training, students cultivate many clinical reflexes that can inform their work, especially when they relax their fear of mistakes, the need to know, or panic around performance in general. Informed intuition is often behind many spontaneous therapeutic interventions and is accessed by evenly suspending and hovering attention. Additionally, when ambiguity is welcomed, counselors can relax their conceptual agendas as random events come alive in any given session. The skill of evenly hovering attention, which is an outcome of meditation and art, is essential to cultivate in clinical training.

Training Application

Cultivating Mindful Awareness in Clinical Training

All throughout our program, concentrative and mindful approaches to meditation are incorporated into each course. In our first year all students take two courses on the psychology of meditation. The catalogue description of the first course follows:

> Mindfulness, the ability to be fully present, is essential for the skillful counselor. This course introduces the practice of mindful breathing (shamatha-vipashyana) sitting meditation drawn from the Buddhist tradition as a means of developing moment-to-moment awareness. Methods for cultivating wakefulness within daily life situations are explored. (Naropa University 2012–2013)

Four meditation instructors from these courses were asked to respond to the following two questions. Below are selected excerpts from their responses.

1. *Why is it important to include meditation training in the education of counselors/art therapists?*

2. *What outcomes or results have you noticed for our students as a result of this training?*

Acharya Dale Asrael, MA

Why is it important to include meditation training in the education of counselors/art therapists?

Mindfulness meditation is a body–mind practice that teaches us to return to the direct experience of physical sensations. Furthermore, it trains the capacity to recognize what is occurring in the present moment of sensations, thoughts, emotion, or mood and that the human mind has a self-reflective quality of awareness; that is, the mind can be aware of what it is aware of by asking the question—"What am I aware of?" There is tremendous potential in this question. In addition, mindfulness meditation cultivates an attitude of interest and acceptance in whatever is arising in the present moment, including one's own mind, body, and external events. The repeated discovery of mindfulness meditation is that what is occurring in the body–mind, even when uncomfortable, is always relevant and full of information.

The first day of the Psychology of Meditation class, Acharya Asrael asks her students: "What are we doing when we sit with another person in counseling? What do you need to know in order to be a good, helpful counselor?" From the answers, discussions unfold about presence, clear seeing, acceptance, attention, and the needed ability to relax within the uncertainty of ambiguity. People need to know what the mind is and how it works. Toward this end, the Psychology of Meditation class unravels questions about what *mind* is through direct practice.

During these early discussions, students quickly learn that they are not there to fix clients—that they are more of a mid-wife than a mechanic. The core value of inherent sanity and basic goodness is addressed as a cornerstone concept intrinsic in all people. Even within the most extreme and disturbed states of mind, there is inherent sanity, which needs to be acknowledged.

Students also learn that mindfulness meditation surfaces an awareness of behaviors that impede happiness and living a satisfied life. Discussions then turn to what students need to know in order to accomplish the work of a counselor. Over the semester and through personal practice, the class explores the relationships between ingrained patterns of thought, emotion, and behavior and how habitual patterns can be released. As the course evolves and a sitting practice is established, students realize that new patterns of behavior can be developed through mindfulness meditation.

In terms of states of mind, the capacity or attitude of friendliness toward oneself is part of any healing process. Certain types of intelligence are not accessed in a linear way—there is a need to hold an open question and tolerate confusion and ambiguity in the process of discovery. Students therefore learn about their own conditioning— what belongs to them and to another person in the counseling relationship. Another important realization concerns how to mindfully resource themselves at the same time they are offering themselves to another person without becoming confused with judgments and opinions.

What outcomes or results have you noticed for our students as a result of this training?

As a result of a sitting practice, there is an increased reorganization in terms of personal regard. This is essential since one needs to be able to pay attention to one's own mind, thoughts, speech, and behavior with inquisitiveness and kindness. Additionally, there is change in how students embrace themselves. They learn to have an appropriate sense of humor with their mistakes. Overall, students display a great softening around personal struggle and a presence that is more available to the client.

CATHY HUBIAK ZIMMERMAN, MA

Why is it important to include meditation training in the education of counselors/art therapists?

Unconditional presence is the most helpful gift a therapist can offer a client. I consider mindfulness meditation practice to be the quintessential training in unconditional presence... When we slow down and create the conditions for mindfulness, we begin to discern when we are present and when we are not... One of the most important contributions that this kind of practice offers is warmth and acceptance of our own self-judgment. We call this *maître*, which is friendliness to one's own complex subject matter. When we meditate we begin to see and develop a relationship to our self-judging mind. Over time, it is this relationship to seeing what *is* and letting it *be*, that sets the stage for acceptance of our own unwanted material... When we are new to our therapy practice, it can be challenging to sit with another's pain. We may find ourselves strategizing, problem-solving, lost in our own associations. Our mindfulness practice brings us back to the present moment in our therapeutic relationship.

What outcomes or results have you noticed for our students as a result of this training?

I have witnessed relief and relaxation from my students. Coming face to face with our own mind is not for the weak of heart. It takes courage to do this. When students truthfully meet who they are, joy emerges. Students also feel more grounded. They can relax and know that they can be present for what comes up; that they don't have to be armored with theories or techniques. This is an extraordinary form of authentic confidence.

JOHN W. STEELE, PH.D.

Why is it important to include meditation training in the education of counselors/art therapists?

Cultivating Evenly Hovering Attention and Affect Tolerance

Freud wrote that therapists should have "evenly hovering attention" during the therapy hour... It is hard to stay engaged with an emotionally disengaged client. Likewise it is difficult to follow clients whose thought process is confused or whose emotions are difficult to bear. If we can't tolerate our own feelings, we may end up distancing ourselves from clients who display troubling emotions. Mindfulness practice trains us to sustain evenly hovering attention, sometimes called equanimity...and cultivate our capacity to face and accept both our own and our clients' difficult emotions.

Cultivating Attention, Empathy and Unconditional Positive Regard

Carl Rogers' counseling approach focused on the curative factors of whole-hearted attention, genuine interest, empathy, and unconditional positive regard... By practicing focused curiosity, non-judgmental, present-centered awareness, and compassion, mindfulness meditation cultivates this capacity for unconditional positive regard and genuine interest.

Cultivating Clear Seeing

Mindfulness practice cultivates our ability to be less identified with our thoughts, concepts and theories... We notice the gaps in our logic and free ourselves from conventional ways of construing the world... We open to not knowing and become free from self-limiting beliefs so that we can aid clients in the process to free themselves from their self-imposed limitations.

Self-Care

Scientific evidence is demonstrating that mindfulness meditation reduces stress-related symptoms, strengthens parts of the prefrontal cortex related to concentration, develops empathy and positive emotion while shrinking the amygdala, which is related to fight/flight reactivity. From these findings it seems clear that meditation can play an important role in counselor/therapist self-care.

What outcomes or results have you noticed for our students as a result of this training?

Feedback and personal observation from graduate students that I have mentored convinces me that the combination of mindfulness training and psychological work enables students to gain insight into their personal and cultural conditioning while cultivating spacious awareness, radical acceptance, and genuine compassion toward self and others.

LISA SCHAEWE, LPC, ATR-BC

Why is it important to include meditation training in the education of counselors/art therapists?

A definition for mindfulness used in our classes is, "awareness of the present moment with acceptance." Another definition for mindfulness is, "attending to the complex process of being." A variety of techniques such as mindful breathing, sitting meditation, walking meditation, body scans, and awareness of daily activities are introduced in the Psychology of Meditation class. These mindfulness practices cultivate qualities of being non-conceptual, present centered, non-judgmental, intentional, participatory, and exploratory... Students are asked to maintain a regular meditation practice... which as an integral part of training, cultivates self-inquiry, wakefulness, and the ability to be present with clients. In addition, mindfulness practice provides self-care tools to combat burn-out and compassion fatigue.

Overall, mindfulness meditation develops awareness of habitual cognitive patterns. This in turn allows students to recognize countertransference and discriminate between internal responses and objective observations of a client's expressive communication.

What outcomes or results have you noticed for our students as a result of this training?

I once supervised a student in an art therapy group at a treatment facility for adults coping with severe mental illness. One client was overtaken by an aggravated psychotic state and needed to be hospitalized, so an ambulance was called. City protocol required that the police and fire department also be dispatched. Once they arrived, confusion ensued and our group was further disrupted. While engaging with the client in crisis and the emergency response workers, the practicum student skillfully attended to the group that was in progress. His equanimity in the midst of this chaos helped the remaining clients feel safe and supported. I am convinced his training in meditation helped him maintain clear presence during this chaotic situation.

These accomplished teachers and practitioners have noticed similar results. To summarize their observational conclusions, mindfulness promotes unconditional presence and positive regard for oneself, especially during ambiguous situations. Another way to summarize this outcome is that there was an increase in self-compassion or *maître*—friendliness toward oneself. Another outcome is the use of mindfulness meditation for self-care. Part of self-care is cultivating self-reflective awareness. According to these instructors, mindfulness meditation teaches our students to observe and monitor their thoughts without judgment. Students and faculty notice that practicing mindfulness untangles cognitive habits and patterns. Additionally, witnessing inner sensations, thoughts, and moods softens self-judgment and increases tolerance for ambiguity. Overall, mindfulness practice cultivates a greater availability within the therapist to be present for clients by learning to evenly distribute attention.

Like meditation, art helps the practitioner to cultivate equanimity and not to reject or defend against provocative stimuli (Walsh and Shapiro 2006). Baer *et al.* (2006) observed similar results of meditation practice, such as the softening of inner reactivity while staying aware of the ebb and flow of sensations, thoughts, and feelings. The authors also address how the meditation practitioner learns to describe and observe thoughts and sensations and refrain from judging inner experiences.

Similarly, Kabat-Zinn (1990) outlines seven fundamental qualities of mindfulness meditation practice. They are non-judging, patience, beginner's mind, trust, non-striving, acceptance, and letting go (pp. 33–40). These seven factors are consistently recycled throughout the art process.

States and Traits of Art and Meditation

Specific somatic and cognitive states result from meditation practices. States refer to the emergence of sensory, cognitive, and self-referential awareness that is altered while meditating. Traits refer to enduring changes that result from meditation. Similar state and trait outcomes exist for art and meditation (Cahn and Polich 2006). Walsh and Shapiro (2006) observe that mindfulness meditation enhances perceptual sensitivity along with creativity and the reduction of stress. Practitioners of meditation become adept at observing rather than reacting to thoughts, a skill known as *disidentification* (Walsh and Shapiro 2006). Just as the meditator becomes the skillful witness of the mind, the artist too does the same through careful observation of externalized thoughts and feelings directly reflected in their work. Art is externalized thought or experience fixed in the aesthetic language of symbol and form. Rather than observe thoughts on the inner screen of the mind only, the artist observes these cognitions as they materialize in an outer form, through paint, clay, or other art media. Seeing and actually holding thoughts fixed in tangible forms offer additional access to inner contemplative awareness, especially when thoughts and feelings are ambiguous and confusing.

Csikszentmihalyi's (1997) notion of flow and the autotelic personality offer additional connections between state and trait outcomes of art and meditation. He defines *flow* as effortless engagement whereby full attention is directed toward an activity for its own sake, which is the essence of the autotelic personality. Art is often described this way; that is, creating work, in the here and now for its own sake and intrinsic reward. Joy emerges out of full absorption in these activities. Simply, happiness is to be found in absorbed immersion; in this case with art materials, processes, and products. Unlike the "exotelic" (p.117) personality, which is reinforced by an outside seeking of public acknowledgement, the autotelic personality is self-fulfilled as a result of absorbed engagement.

Case Study: Student Example of Mindfulness and Art

The following example illustrates how these combined factors of meditation, outlined in the studies mentioned above, can directly surface in the art process.

A student in our program came to the studio in an agitated state due to relationship problems with her partner. Distraught, rather than become hijacked by her discomfort, she decided to literally face and lean into these emerging emotions by directly rendering them. Rather than reject her discomfort, she moved toward the provocative stimuli.

She began by first drawing a large head that filled up a 22 x 30 inch piece of paper (Figure 19.1).

Next she drew her ruminating thoughts swirling about both inside of her mind and also outside of her skull. By initiating this process and sustaining her engagement with these uncomfortable thoughts, she was practicing softened non-reactivity to her inner experience. What was so impressive was that she was literally creating and therefore seeing before her eyes the exact disturbing narrative she was feeling inside. As the artwork confronted her back with its truthful turbulence, she remained in a state of poise and equanimity. This form of restraining judgment and maintaining "beginner's mind" kept the process fresh and ripe for further investigation.

As the process unfolded, she remained in the observer role, witnessing and accepting her charged emotions made visible through the art process. She also mindfully externalized and contained in her drawing the multiple themes that were initially upsetting her. While noticing the in-and-out breath and the figure/ground elements in her artwork, she oscillated between being the experiencer and observer of these stimulating emotions by letting them go into the actual artwork. She was poised and aware of her sensations and reactions throughout the progression of her imagery. With an eye toward her judging mind, by making images of her irritations, she was visually labeling them.

Figure 19.1: Student art of agitated thoughts

After her process, she reflected on her work and began to listen deeply to the narrative set in motion by her imagery. This part of the sequence offers yet another encounter with the outcomes of meditation listed above. When observing her product and unexpectedly triggered by her imagery, she again practiced a form of non-judgmental presence where she observed her thoughts, proceeding onward with greater awareness to receive the layers of her experience presented through the art.

Within this single artwork, this student practiced non-judging, patience, beginner's mind, inner friendship, non-striving, acceptance, and letting go. She softened her reflexes of inner reactivity while staying aware of the ebb and flow of sensations, thoughts, and feelings. This example underscores how the counselor and art therapist use the art process to sit with and manage powerful emotions in preparation for working with future clients. Not only was she the observer of her physical sensations, she was also observing her various thoughts as they emerged in her work. Trungpa Rinpoche's comment that meditation is a practice of providing a spacious meadow for an agitated animal is readily apparent in this example. The 22 x 30 inch piece of paper was like a vast pasture where the student's restless thoughts and emotions could wander and eventually settle once the troubling experiences were honestly expressed in her artwork. Art is the conscious mind externalized. Consciousness can be defined as the introspective, felt properties of states of awareness. Mind, and its vital characteristics of "monitoring and modifying," according to Siegel (2010), is defined as "an embodied and relational process that regulates the flow of energy and information" (p.25). In this example, art served as a self-regulation process to mindfully subjectify and objectify the informational activity of personal thoughts, insights, and emotions. This brief example illustrates Siegel's notion of mindsight which fosters neural integration through "openness, objectivity, and observation" (p.xxi)—all of which were part of this student's art process.

Conclusion: Taking One's Seat as an Art Therapist and Counselor

While probably controversial to some, it is my belief that in order to fully absorb the benefits of mindfulness meditation, one has to practice the practice. This includes a disciplined commitment to sitting. Year after year I have noticed the magical moment when our students shift from wanting to jump off of the meditation cushion and bolt out of the room when restless, to taking their seat and remaining poised and present with whatever arises. They become at ease as their flexible mind observes moment-to-moment inner and outer events.

It is true that mindfulness can be practiced while washing dishes, gardening, or painting. And there is great benefit to sitting and observing instead of doing and observing. While I do not value one over the other, I do see both approaches as necessary to cultivating mindful presence. Any way we can develop moment-to-moment awareness is worth pursuing. Overall, by acknowledging the brilliant sanity of basic goodness that exists in all people we promote inner and outer friendship. Ultimately, these are the fundamental moral and ethical conditions behind unconditional positive regard for self and other.

References

Baer, R.A., Smith, G.T., Hopkins, J., Krietemeyer, J., and Toney, L. (2006) "Using self report assessment methods to explore facets of mindfulness." *Assessment 13*, 1, 27–45.

Cahn, B.R. and Polich, J. (2006 March) "Meditation states and traits: EEG, ERP, and neuroimaging studies." *Psychological Bulletin 132*, 2, 180–211.

Csikszentmihalyi, M. (1997) *Finding Flow: The Psychology of Engagement with Everyday Life.* New York: Basic Books.

Davis, D.M. and Hayes, J.A. (2011) "What are the benefits of mindfulness? A practice review of psychotherapy-related research." *Psychotherapy 48*, 2, 198–208.

Epstein, M.D. (1984) "On the neglect of evenly suspended attention." *The Journal of Transpersonal Psychology 16*, 2, 193–205.

Fabrice, M. (2004) *Chogyam Trungpa: His Life and Vision.* Boston, MA: Shambhala.

Farrelly-Hansen, M. (2001) *Spirituality and Art Therapy: Living the Connection.* Philadelphia, PA: Jessica Kingsley Publishers.

Feuerstein, G. (2001) *The Yoga Tradition: Its History, Literature, Philosophy and Practice.* Prescott, AZ: Hohm Press.

Feuerstein, G. (2003) *The Deeper Dimension of Yoga: Theory and Practice.* Boston, MA: Shambhala.

Fish, B.J. (2012) "Response art: The art of the art therapist." *Art Therapy: The Journal of the American Art Therapy Association 29*, 3, 138–143.

Franklin, M. (1990) "Aesthetics and empathy: A point of convergence." *American Journal of Art Therapy 29*, 2, 42–47.

Franklin, M. (1999a) "Becoming a student of oneself: Activating the Witness in meditation, art, and super-vision." *The American Journal of Art Therapy 38*, 1, 2–13.

Franklin, M. (1999b) "Art practice/psychotherapy practice/meditation practice: Sitting on the dove's tail." *Guidance and Counseling 15*, 3, 18–22.

Franklin, M.A. (2010a) "Affect regulation, mirror neurons and the 3rd hand: Formulating mindful empathic art interventions." *Art Therapy: The Journal of the American Art Therapy Association 27*, 4, 160–167.

Franklin, M.A. (2010b) *Aesthetic Mind – Meditative Mind: Reflections on Art as Yoga and Contemplative Practice.* Ph.D. dissertation. Cambridge, MA: Lesley University.

Franklin, M. (2012) "Karuna – Ahimsa – and Relational Aesthetics: Empathic Art Interventions for Contemplative Approaches to Psychotherapy." In P. de Silva (ed.) *Buddhist Psychotherapy*. Ayuthaya, Thailand: Mahachulalongkornrajavidyalaya University. Available at www.undv.org/vesak2012/iabudoc/15FranklinFINAL.pdf, accessed May 9, 2013.

Franklin, M., Farrelly-Hansen, M., Marek, B., Swan-Foster, N., and Wallingford, S. (2000) "Transpersonal art therapy education." *Art Therapy: The Journal of the American Art Therapy Association 17*, 2, 101–110.

Germer, G.K, Siegel, R.D., and Fulton, R.F. (2005) *Mindfulness and Psychotherapy*. New York: Guilford Press.

Kabat-Zinn, J. (1990) *Full Catastrophe Living: Using the Wisdom of Your Body and Mind to Face Stress, Pain, and Illness*. New York: Delacorte.

Khanna, M. (1979) *Yantra: The Tantric Symbol of Cosmic Unity*. New York: Thames.

Lewis, P.P. (1992) "The creative arts in transference/countertransference relationships." *The Arts in Psychotherapy 19*, 3, 317–323.

Moon, B.L. (1999) "The tears make me paint: The role of responsive artmaking in adolescent art therapy." *Art Therapy: The Journal of the American Art Therapy Association 16*, 3, 78–82.

Naropa University (2013–2014) *Course Catalog 2013–2014*. Available at http://coursecatalog.naropa.edu, accessed October 10, 2013

Rappaport, L. (2009) *Focusing-Oriented Art Therapy: Accessing the Body's Wisdom and Creative Intelligence*. London: Jessica Kingsley Publishers.

Rubin, J.A. (2009) *Introduction to Art Therapy: Sources and Resources*. New York: Taylor and Frances.

Siegel, D.J. (2007) *The Mindful Brain*. New York: Norton.

Siegel, D.J. (2010) *The Mindful Therapist: A Clinician's Guide to Mindsight and Neural Integration*. New York: W.W. Norton and Company.

Speeth, K.R. (1982) "On therapeutic attention." *The Journal of Transpersonal Psychology 14*, 2, 141–160.

Sterba, R.F. (1934) "The fate of the ego in analytic therapy." *International Journal of Psychoanalysis 18*, 117–126.

Trungpa, C. (1976) *The Myth of Freedom and the Way of Meditation*. Berkeley, CA and London: Shambhala.

Trungpa, C. (1996) *Dharma Art*. Boston, MA: Shambhala.

Walsh, R. and Shapiro, S.L. (2006) "The meeting of meditative disciplines and Western psychology: A mutually enriching dialogue." *American Psychologist 61*, 3, 227–239.

Wegela, K.K. (2010) *The courage to be Present: Buddhism, Psychotherapy, and the Awakening of Natural Wisdom*. Boston, MA: Shambhala.

Yogananda, P. (2003) *Autobiography of a Yogi*. Los Angeles, CA: Self Realization Fellowship.

Chapter 20

Relational Mindfulness and Relational Movement in Training Dance/Movement Therapists

Nancy Beardall and Janet Surrey

In dance/movement therapy, the relationship between client and therapist is a core component in therapeutic work. "Dance Therapy is the psychotherapeutic use of movement as a process that furthers emotional, physical and cognitive integration of the individual" (Levy 2005, p.11). Marian Chace, a pioneer dance therapist, describes the "therapeutic movement relationship" (Chaiklin and Schmais 1993, p.79). This concept was Chace's contribution to dance/movement therapy (DMT)—where the therapist moves with the client, communicating a sense of acceptance and being seen (Levy 2005, p.22). Chace "literally expressed 'I know how you feel' in movement terms, thus establishing affective, empathic interactions" (Chaiklin and Schmais 1993, p.79). The breath, relational flow of movement, and movement in stillness allow for inner and outer attunement between the client and therapist—whether engaged in micro or macro movements—or the flow between them. Relational movement in dance is also reflected in the contributions of other dance/movement therapy pioneers, Whitehouse (Pallaro 1999), Adler (2002) and Canner (1975).

Relational mindfulness is the practice of mindfulness in the flow of relationship between two or more people (Surrey 2005). There are three dimensions of focus in relational awareness. The first offers an opportunity for moment-to-moment awareness of internal experiences, sensations, emotions and thoughts as they are happening within the movement of relationship. The second dimension of awareness focuses on the empathic attunement to the other as it is experienced. The third point of focus is the experienced movement and flow of connection and disconnections within the relationship.

It was the shared recognition of the centrality of relational movement in healing that initially brought the co-authors of this chapter into collaboration. Rather than focus on internal change within the individual, beginning dance/movement therapists need to appreciate the importance of the relationship and to learn how to use the healing power of relationship in movement. As a DMT educator, Dr. Beardall felt that relational cultural theory (RCT) (Jordan *et al.* 1991) and relational mindfulness practice (Surrey 2005) would be valuable tools in the early stages of training of dance/movement therapists.

The collaboration between Dr. Janet Surrey, founding scholar of the Jean Baker Miller Training Foundation and faculty member at the Institute for Meditation and

Psychotherapy, and Dr. Nancy Beardall, Coordinator of the Lesley University DMT program, took place over three years with the DMT graduate students from Lesley University during their first year of training. Students were introduced to RCT in order to provide language and theoretical concepts for understanding the fundamentals of healing relationships. Meditation practice was integrated into learning in order to provide students with a direct experience and an awareness of relationship dimensions.

This chapter presents significant contributions from interpersonal neurobiology and their connection to relational movement, an overview of RCT and relational mindfulness. We also present a model of relational mindfulness and relational movement applied to training graduate students in DMT. Descriptions of the process, discussion of application and reflective comments from the DMT students are included.

Theoretical Framework

Interpersonal Neurobiology

Social-relational neuroscience supports the importance relationships play in our social and emotional development (Siegel 2007) and can be observed through the practice of mirroring, attunement, empathic reflections in training dance/movement therapists and their role in training new therapists and practitioners. Since the 1990s, neuroscience research has helped to underscore and validate the mind–body connection, the plasticity of the brain, the relational brain and attunement to other (Siegel 2007). Research continues to explore the role of the mirror neuron system in supporting empathic reflection and responsiveness. Witnessing, mirroring, empathic reflection, relational mindfulness and relational movement take place within the mind–body experiential way of knowing.

Siegel has researched the relationship between mindfulness and integration of the brain, and the role of secure relational attunement for providing the groundwork for health and resiliency in life. If attunement produces integration in the brain, the interpersonal attunement and intrapersonal attunement will reinforce each other and produce greater neural integration. These can be the neural dimensions linking the ways in which mindful awareness promotes both relational and internal well-being in the promotion of integration (Siegel 2007, p.201). Siegel refers to this process as interpersonal neurobiology.

Creative movement and improvisation responses—with a sense of being open, present, listening, observant and attuned to the client—are relational competencies required of the dance therapist. This empathic process needs to be experienced and practiced by DMT practitioners as it is crucial in developing a sense of mutual connection and trust between the client and therapist.

Relational Cultural Theory (RCT)

RCT is an emerging model of clinical relational practice and offers clinicians-in-training a valuable language and theory to describe their clinical practice and goals. RCT is the psychological framework for human growth developed over the past

30 years at the Jean Baker Miller Training Institute, The Stone Center, Wellesley College. This theory describes the fundamental power of relationships in shaping psychological development and maps the arc of relational movement in growth and healing. Researchers and clinicians at the Stone Center have described healthy human development as occurring within and toward mutual connection. All relationships are seen as moving (never static) either toward or away from psychological connection. The basic human yearning for connection and the power of connection in promoting mental health and physical health over the whole life cycle is well documented today (Miller and Stiver 1997).

The movement toward growth-fostering relationships is created in the ongoing struggle for mutuality—mutual authenticity, mutual empathy, mutual empowerment and mutual responsibility. These processes strengthen individuals through the process of strengthening relationships. Relationships are seen as having a "life" or existence co-created by individuals and then contributing to their growth and development.

Relational awareness, an awareness of the flow of connection and disconnection, is a necessary aspect of development and is crucial. Jean Baker Miller described five positive characteristics of growth-fostering relationships: (1) increased zest (vitality); (2) increased ability to take action (empowerment); (3) increased clarity (a clearer picture of one's self, the other and the relationship); (4) increased sense of worth; and (5) a desire for relationships beyond that particular one. These five characteristics describe the outcomes of growth-fostering relationships—we grow not toward separation, but toward greater mutuality and empathic possibility. In therapy, the focus of attention is primarily on the client's experience, however, both therapist and client experience these five qualities both in and through the relationship.

In addition to describing the benefits of such relationships, RCT explores the impact of disconnection, recognizing that disconnection is an inevitable part of being in a relationship (caused by empathic failures, relational violations, injuries, etc.). When, in response to a disconnection, the injured (especially the less culturally powerful or privileged) person is able to express their feelings and the other person can respond empathically, experiences of disconnection can lead to a strengthened relationship and an increased sense of relational competence. (i.e. being able to effect change and feeling effective in connections) (Jordan 1995). However, when an injured or less powerful person is unable to represent themselves, or receives a response of indifference, additional injury or denial of their experience, they will begin to keep aspects of self out of relationship in order to keep or maintain the relationship. These adaptive strategies are called "strategies of disconnection."

This is the core of the Central Relational Paradox of therapy. It is necessary to honor these strategies of disconnections, as well as to recognize the underlying yearning for connection. In therapy based on RCT, the therapist is guided by this paradox, attending to the ongoing moment-to-moment movements of connection and disconnection and helping relationships move toward reconnection.

Relationships grow through the deepening of connection, which can occur through movement within disconnection and the therapist's skilled negotiation of *being with* the client's experience as a way to move the relationship toward a fuller, more expansive level of connection. This arc of relational movement is addressed in Figure 20.1.

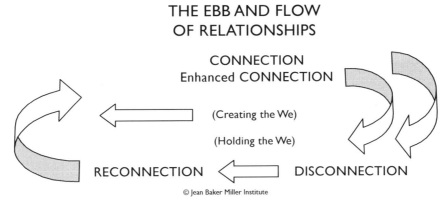

Figure 20.1: Diagram of relational movement

Training Application

In relational mindfulness meditation, awareness is cultivated in the moment of two persons practicing mindfulness of "being together" and "breathing together." Relational movement is at the core of the practice of relational mindfulness. In dyadic relational meditation, two (or more) participants are engaged first in silent meditation and then with mindful speaking and listening.

Relational Mindfulness and Relational Movement Process

The relational mindfulness/relational movement process) (Figure 20.2) includes seven phases: (1) silent co-meditation based on mindfulness of breath; (2) reflection with meditation partner; (3) transitions to moving with partner and witnessing together; (4) group participation in the dance of connection, disconnection and reconnection and (5) observing and reflecting in small and large groups, that leads to (6) greater individual and relational awareness; (7) integration and healing; and then flows back to (1) relational mindfulness meditation, or stillness in movement.

The process increases the clinician's relational awareness of self, partner and the relational movement between them; moment-to-moment awareness within self and partner; and the ability to maintain a caring presence.

MEDITATION WITH PARTNER, MINDFULNESS
OF BREATHING (FIGURE 20.2, #1)

The first practice the students experience is mindfulness of breathing, focused internally with eyes closed, and then with eyes open.

1. Sit facing a partner at a comfortable distance on chair or cushions. Closing your eyes, bring attention to the movement of your breathing in and out (*two to three minutes*). When your mind wanders come back to the breath.

2. Open your eyes, maintain awareness of your breathing. Observe the movement of breathing of your partner. Rest in the awareness of both internal and external experience, noticing what arises, perhaps discomfort or judgment, and simply return to your awareness of the movement of the breath (*three to five minutes*).

3. Allow your eyes to meet the gaze of the other without fixed focus. Be open to eye contact; notice what arises, self-consciousness, discomfort, resistance. Coming back to this moment, explore the shared gaze. Notice the flow of connection and disconnection internally and also in the relationship. What do you notice (*three to five minutes*)?

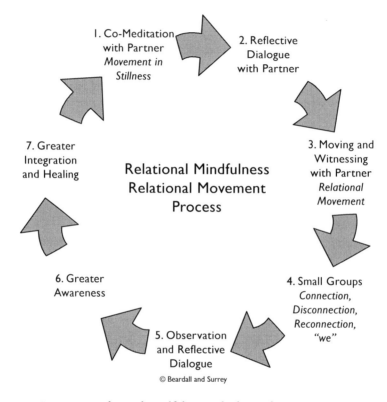

Figure 20.2: Relational mindfulness and relational movement process

At this point in the process a DMT student responded, "We started off with our eyes closed which was a huge relief for me. I find it intimidating to start an exercise staring into another person's eyes. After my partner and I opened our eyes and started looking at one another, I found it strangely comforting. I was not as uncomfortable as I thought I would be. Immediately, I noticed that our breath started to link up. Our breath complemented each other and reminded me to keep breathing."

The intimacy of this practice can bring up both confusion and discomfort and habitual strategies of disconnection, as well as moments of often surprising depth of connection. "Seeing" the other and "being seen" are simple, human, developmental experiences. Babies seek this mutual gaze quite naturally. However, the invitation to see and be seen can come to be uncomfortable and challenging. In a safe and quiet setting, where this discomfort is normalized and investigated, and everyone is supported in "caring" for self and other, relational mindfulness can be cultivated and awareness of strategies of disconnection revealed and released.

Insight Dialogue, Reflective Dialogue (Figure 20.2, #2)

The second level of relational meditation is based on Insight Dialogue Meditation (Kramer 2007). The six guidelines for this practice are taught: Pause, Relax, Open, Trust Emergence, Listen Deeply and Speak the Truth. Mindfulness of authentic speaking and "deep" listening is cultivated and students practice relational awareness of verbal and non-verbal experience in using words and voice to express and investigate their actual experience.

1. Sit facing your partner; remember to pause before speaking, during speaking and after speaking. Let there be spacious awareness of habitual patterns of speech and conversation. Speak the truth of the moment as it happens (body sensations, thoughts, images). Listen deeply to yourself and other.

2. Designate first speaker and second speaker; contemplate "What are you aware of in this moment?" The first speaker is given five minutes to speak and then the listener reflects back what has been heard for two minutes. Then the second speaker speaks for five minutes and the listener reflects back for two minutes.

3. Take a few minutes of silence and then express your gratitude for sharing these moments together. Offer gratitude and appreciation for your partner and wishes for his or her well-being, and remember to receive as well (three to five minutes).

4. The leader rings a chime and gives partners five minutes to share together on this experience.

5. Bring to the large group and share experiences.

Non-conceptual knowing and deep receptivity are cultivated as gateways to relational/kinesthetic connection. Mindfulness of the interactive, co-constructed micro-movements of "being in" and "moving in" relation can be known and explored. Noticing the moment-to-moment flow or movement becomes an attuned theme as the training moves from meditative sitting and stillness to embodied movement or dance in relationship.

Moving with Partner: Relational Movement (Figure 20.2, #3)

The relational movement exercises experienced in class provide the opportunity for practicing mindfulness and the connection to DMT theory, RCT and relational mindfulness, relational movement and dance.

The first movement exercise is based on the authentic movement process (Adler 2002) and the dance of the witness and the mover.

1. Partner with a student; begin with the first student moving and the other following; then the second student dances and is followed, until both are moving relationally without a leader or follower. During the process, they witness and stay in touch with themselves while they are in the movement and flow of relationship between them (four minutes).

2. Each partner shares for two minutes.

Small Groups: Connection, Disconnection and Reconnection (Figure 20.2, #4)

In this stage the students are given an assignment to form small groups and create a dance of "moving toward or away" in the "movement of connection" and "movement of disconnection" (Beardall, Bergman, and Surrey 2007).

1. Divide the class into groups of three or four. One group is given an assignment to choreograph a dance or movement from superficial connection to a painful disconnection and isolation. Another group is to choreograph a dance or movement sequence from connection to disconnection to reconnection resulting in a deeper connection. Each group improvises, kinesthetically expresses and resonates with the movement of relationship as it evolves (*five minutes*).

2. The groups observe movement qualities and the different ways of moving through the exercises. The students become aware of the micro and macro movements as they flow. The dancers feel their attunement with each other, as well as the dissonance of the movement. The students communicate and embody the dance of relational movement.

3. The sharing that follows leads to dialogues related to how differently these exercises are choreographed, felt and experienced.

Two DMT students commented on this exercise: "We broke into groups and expressed connections, painful disconnection and healthy reconnections through body sculptures and movement scenes. It was very interesting to see the different approaches each group took with the exercises reminding me of the many possibilities of human interaction. Because the body can tell so much, it is essential to notice what's happening when making and breaking human connections."

Another student shared, "The process of creating the small duet went really smoothly, and our transitions felt very representative of how truly connected relationships can be formed. It was also interesting to view the other groups' interpretations of the assignment—it's great to see that there are many different ways to achieve the end goal of deeper connection and understanding!"

Observation and Reflective Dialogue (Figure 20.2, #5)

The class participates in a reflective dialogue shared within the group and then between the groups on what they observed and kinesthetically felt during the dances. They also explore how the relational movement creates metaphors—informing the students about the dance of connection and disconnection. Questions include:

1. What did you observe?

2. How did you feel?

3. What did you learn?

Greater Awareness and Integration (Figure 20.2, #6, #7)

After the dialogue, students reflect and write about their experiences regarding the interface between RCT and DMT. The students note any new awarenesses, and how this awareness impacts both their personal relationships and professional development in therapeutic settings.

This entire cycle can be repeated any number of times; each experience builds on the previous. The DMT students' experience of relational mindful meditation and relational movement contributes to embodied awareness and integration of presence in each unfolding moment. Being on the edge of creative emergence—not knowing but trusting in the movement of connection (and disconnection)—the moment-to-moment sense of increased knowing allows the process and the relationship to unfold.

A video clip of pioneer dance therapist Norma Canner is shared at the end of the first cyclical process. In the video of her life and work entitled "A Time to Dance" (Brownell and Wilcoxen 1998). Norma's work with an adolescent with autism parallels and demonstrates the Insight Dialogue process of "Pause, Relax, Open, Trust Emergence, Listen Deeply and Speak the Truth" (Kramer 2007). Norma is present and meets the child where he is, connects, relationally moves/dances with and holds him during his relational disconnection (relational paradox) eventually allowing him to mutually connect with her. It is a beautiful example of a relationally choreographed dance between the two.

Themes from Student Reflections

Three general themes were extracted from the students' reflective written comments after experiencing the progression of relational meditation and movement exercises—including meditation with self and other, witnessing and moving together and dancing the movement of connection, disconnection and reconnection.

Increased Embodiment

DMT students expressed being more fully present in their bodies. One student shared, "I feel that I was not very present in my body at the beginning of the class but as soon as we were asked to find a partner and breathe with them, I allowed myself to relax, my shoulders began to lower and my breath became fuller. I slowly opened my eyes to see my partner's kind eyes. She allowed me to gaze at her, to be seen, as I also allowed myself to be seen by her. The exercise felt comforting to me because my partner and I were able to connect so easily in the first moments of gazing at each other. I enjoyed this exercise so much. It allowed me to center myself as well as welcome a connection."

Another student shared, "Using dance/movement therapy as a means to promote relational mindfulness and relational movement is beneficial because it allows me to feel and internalize the authenticity of a relationship on a body level."

Increased Awareness of Connection and Disconnection

The second theme that emerged was that of relational paradox, longing for connection yet preventing and using strategies to prevent the connection. Three different students responded:

- "I never really thought about relational paradox before. I can especially see it in my own relationships. I tend to stray away from getting close to people. I may push people away, only to realize that I need them in my life. This has unfortunately happened to me far too many times."

- "In my personal life I have observed how I have been disconnected from my parents and this created isolation. I realized through this work that I need to create a better relationship and this would be possible only if I have a conversation with them and that can help me reconnect with them."

- "The connection or creation of the 'we' is very powerful. I have come from another country and I think I have been adapting to the culture here, at the same time following my own culture. I know that there is a constant balance I try to maintain with my culture and the culture here."

Integration, Self, Relationship and Connection

The third theme includes four inter-related aspects—integration; experiencing and embodying relational mindfulness and relational movement; being present and attuning with self and client; and staying sensitive to the closeness and distance of the interactive dance. The following quotes are from three other DMT students:

- "I felt as if there was a universal connection made for me. My brain understood the truth of DMT and why it worked but my body and heart needed a refresher. I needed to embody why I believed it worked. The relational movement exercise helped me. The spiritual reminder of connection and disconnection and the dance is what helped me embody this."

- "Being mindful of how you are connecting or disconnecting with your clients is paramount for a successful group. I thought the experiential where we were just looking at our partner also really exemplified this point. It was sometimes hard to maintain a long connection. Sometimes we both found ourselves looking away from each other or somewhere across the room, but there were also moments of genuine connection. Our breathing and posture were the same, it was almost as if we were moving as one."

- "The mutually empathic relationship is about being able to describe the other's experience, about being moved by the other, and seeing through another's eyes. Wow, this is connection indeed. Just in this moment of reflection, I realized it's not just about dialogue or hanging out together—truly listening to another means leaving yourself and entering that person's experience. It's about entering… entering and coming back out into yourself. You don't ever lose you, maybe that's what freedom is—entering another and understanding the experience of the other and yet being able to come back to yourself, always, and knowing who you are. We must know who we are so we can know others."

Conclusion

This work is currently in the preliminary phases and suggests a teaching protocol in the training of dance/movement therapists. Additional opportunities to observe and evaluate this process are needed. The relational mindfulness and relational movement process can be applied and adapted to the training of expressive arts psychotherapists and counseling clinicians as well.

The students' comments communicate the power of relational mindfulness and relational movement in their DMT training experience and personal process. The students began to embody and integrate an awareness of self, other and the relationship or "we." This relational mindful and movement-in-relationship (Surrey 2005) process allows the students to experience an internal sense of trusting, and the movement in stillness increases their mindful awareness and intention of being present and knowing what is happening moment to moment. "Pause, Relax, Open, Trust Emergence, Listen Deeply and Speak the Truth" informs the students' internal and external process as clinicians. For example, the relational mindful meditation with a partner allows for their moving together in subtle ways where the movement in stillness and movement of connection flow between them.

Guiding clinicians to embody this process also provides an experience on how this relational mindful, relational movement process supports their practice. The interface between relational mindfulness, relational movement, RCT, Insight Dialogue and the neuroscience of relationships is an effective way to guide DMT students and clinicians to embody a mindful presence in the relational movement process. This contributes to an increased sense of awareness and presence to the subtle dance of self, other and the flow of relationship.

As previously stated, this process is in the early stages of investigation and exploration, and the current chapter is a first attempt to present a promising model of relational mindfulness and relational movement in the training of dance/movement therapists and other clinicians. Future exploration and studies will be conducted to further develop a comprehensive protocol in this significant area of guiding clinicians in their mindful awareness and relational development as we move, relate and dance with each other.

Acknowledgment

The authors would like to thank the DMT students at Lesley University for their thoughtful reflections.

References

Adler, J. (2002) *Offering from the Conscious Body*. Vermont: Inner Traditions.

Beardall, N., Bergman S., and Surrey, J. (2007) *Making Connections: Building Community and Gender Dialogue in Secondary Schools*. Cambridge, MA: Educators for Social Responsibility.

Brownell, I. and Wilcoxen, W. (directors) (1998) *A Time to Dance: The Life and Work of Norma Canner* (Documentary/Biography). Somerville, MA: Bushy Theater.

Canner, N. (1975) *And a Time to Dance*. Boston, MA: Plays, Inc.

Chaiklin, S. and Schmais, C. (1993) "The Chace Approach to Dance Therapy." In S. Sandel, S. Chaiklin, and A. Lohn (eds) *Foundation of Dance/movement therapy: The Life and Work of Marian Chace*. Columbia, MD: American Dance Therapy Association.

Jordan, J., Kaplan, A., Miller, J., Stiver I., and Surrey, J. (1991) *Women's Growth in Connection: Writings from the Stone Center*. New York: Guilford Press.

Jordan, J.V. (1995) "Relational Awareness: Transforming Disconnection." Work in Progress, No. 76, Wellesley, MA: Stone Center Working Paper Series.

Kramer, G. (2007) *Insight Dialogue: The Interpersonal Path to Freedom.* Boston, MA: Shambhala Press.

Levy, F.J. (2005) *Dance/movement therapy: A Healing Art.* Reston, VA: AAHPERD.

Miller, J.B. and Stiver, I. (1997) *The Healing Connection.* Boston, MA: Beacon Press.

Pallaro, P. (ed.) (1999) *Authentic movement: Essays by Mary Starks Whitehouse, Janet Adler and Joan Chodorow.* London and Philadelphia, PA: Jessica Kingsley Publishers.

Siegel, D. (2007) *The Mindful Brain.* New York: Guilford Press.

Surrey, J. (2005) "Relational Therapy, Relational Mindfulnes". In C. Germer, P. Fulton, and R. Siegal (eds) *Mindfulness and Psychotherapy.* New York: Guilford Press.

PART VI

Neuroscience, Mindfulness, and the Arts Therapies

Chapter 21

Perspectives from Clinical Neuroscience

Mindfulness and the Therapeutic Use of the Arts

Jared D. Kass and Sidney M. Trantham

The internal composure that can be facilitated through mindfulness and therapeutic use of the arts is foundational to resilient coping and psychospiritual well-being. In the midst of life's inevitable crises, interpersonal conflicts, developmental challenges, and existential anxiety, internal composure helps individuals respond to people and events resourcefully, without unnecessary triggering of the stress response. As the neuroscience in this chapter will demonstrate, dysregulated triggering of the stress response is a defining feature of maladaptive coping and a gateway to psychopathology, health-risk behaviors, and anti-social behaviors. Internal composure, which can be compared to the calm eye in the center of a hurricane, enables people to navigate these stressors constructively and compassionately, maintaining a positive worldview of confidence in life and self (Kass 1998), and strengthening vital social networks.

Internal composure, as we will also explain, is a quality of being that must be cultivated. It is an *innate, emergent property of evolving human consciousness* that requires intentional and skillful nurturance in order to prevail and be accessed during stressful life circumstances. For this reason, mindfulness and therapeutic use of the arts are becoming critical tools in psychotherapy, trauma psychology, and social transformation.

This chapter presents the neuroscience underlying these important ideas and methods. We begin by defining internal composure functionally, using attachment theory and gestalt therapy. Then we discuss the neuroscience of resilient and destructive coping, exploring *the autonomic nervous system* through Porges' (2011b) innovative "polyvagal" perspective, *the brain* through MacLean's (1990) influential triune model, and *somatic memory* through Reich's (1980) pioneering explication of emotional armoring. Finally, we explore specific methods and mechanisms through which mindfulness and therapeutic use of the arts can be used to cultivate our emergent capacity for internal composure.

Internal Composure: A Foundation for Resilient Coping

Internal composure is a state of mindful attunement with self. It can include strong emotions like anger and sadness, as well as inner calm. However, these emotions do not control the person reactively. Rather, internal composure helps individuals respond to their emotions with intentionality, thereby facilitating constructive engagement with people and situations, or healthy withdrawal from them. From gestalt therapy's interpersonal perspective (Woldt and Toman 2005), engagement and withdrawal are the *yin and yang* of human life—necessary for *growth* (relational contact; withdrawal for rest and reflection) and *defense* (fight; flight). Lack of internal composure (fear/anxiety) produces immobilization, an interruption of growth-promoting and defense-oriented efforts to engage or withdraw (Perls 1973).

Relationship to Attachment Theory

From attachment theory's developmental perspective (Bowlby 1969), internal composure has formative roots in the infant–caregiver relationship (Ainsworth 1985; Ainsworth and Eichberg 1991; Ainsworth *et al.* 1978). In secure attachment, a calm loving caregiver is accurately attuned to a child's emotional states, through right-brain to right-brain (i.e. somatic, pre-verbal) resonance. Infants lack regulatory self-structure. The attuned caregiver helps them modulate hyper- or hypo-aroused responses to stimuli, gradually shaping their capacity for emotional self-regulation (Schore 2000, 2009; Schore and Schore 2008). Over time, they develop a flexible self-structure capable of congruent responses—engagement and withdrawal—to stimuli (Rogers 1961), thereby strengthening internal composure.

Current research distinguishes secure attachment from anxious, avoidant, and dissociative/disorganized relational templates (Schore 2009). These templates reinforce hyper- or hypo-aroused responses to people and situations, yielding dysfunctional engagement and withdrawal. Longitudinal research supports this model. Secure attachment contributes to infant mental health and subsequent affect regulation (Schore 2001). Disorganized attachment impairs right-brain self-regulatory processes in children, particularly when paired with early relational trauma (Schore 2002), and reinforces cyclic predisposition to violence in adolescents and adults (Schore 2003a). Both secure and insecure childhood attachment predict quality of adult functioning (Siegel 2012). Men in secure relationships demonstrate better affect regulation, specifically recovery from anger (Diamond and Hicks 2005).

Fortunately, internal composure can be cultivated in subsequent life stages. Adults can develop "earned" secure attachment (Siegel 2003) through psychospiritual growth. Cognitive-behavioral methods can identify attachment templates that trigger dysregulating responses. Mindfulness, therapeutic use of the arts, and meditation can facilitate the ability to witness and tolerate dysregulating emotions, promoting constructive engagement and withdrawal. Gradually, internal composure can promote secure attachment both in interpersonal relationships and a person's experienced relationship with the cosmos. Such *secure existential attachment* is an emergent characteristic of psychospiritual growth (Kass 2007). Thus, cultivation of internal composure and earned secure attachment are primary therapeutic goals.

The Neuroscience of Resilient and Destructive Coping

Neurobehavioral mechanisms that regulate engagement and withdrawal evolved in animals—mammals, reptiles, pre-vertebrates—when these functions were comparatively simple. In humans, however, these mechanisms have evolved to support complex forms of psychological growth and defense. The human brain can construct cognitive models of self, others, and life; modify these models through relational experience, self-reflection, and meditation; regulate emotional reactions; and transmute primitive instincts for protective hierarchical bonds into relational capacities where cooperative problem-solving, empathic attunement, conflict resolution, and love are possible. However, when these emergent cognitive, social-emotional and contemplative skills are impaired through psychological wounds, our advanced coping capacities devolve into the mammalian and reptilian defense systems from which they evolved (Porges 1995, 1998).

These more primitive systems remain useful during life-threatening situations. In addition, human evolution has adapted them to new uses. However, in general, when people apply fight/flight/freeze responses rigidly to complex social stressors, their behavior may become dysfunctional. In psychopathology, "the stress response is a common denominator or at least a shared, contributing circumstance in virtually every disorder" (Lambert and Kinsley 2005, p.78). "The defining features of psychopathology may include either a person's inability to *inhibit* defense systems in a safe environment or the inability to *activate* defense systems in a risky environment—or both" (Porges 2011b, p.12).

Thus, resilient coping through cultivation of internal composure is an emergent neurobehavioral capacity of human evolution. The mechanisms underlying these maturing abilities will become evident as we examine recent research on the autonomic nervous system, brain, and somatic memory.

The Autonomic Nervous System: A New "Polyvagal Perspective"

The autonomic nervous system (ANS) is a key component of the human nervous system, regulating critical metabolic processes that govern stress coping (Figure 21.1). Models of the ANS traditionally focus on the sympathetic nervous system (SNS), highlighting activation of the stress response. However, a new "polyvagal perspective" has altered this focus (Porges 2011b). It gives primacy to the inhibitory parasympathetic nervous system and its major pathway (the vagus nerve) in coping processes, including regulation of social engagement and defense.

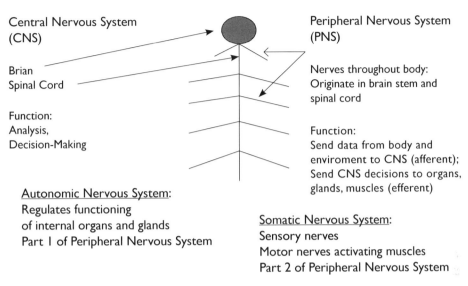

The Autonomic Nervous System
Regulates Critical Metabolic Processes

Central Nervous System
(CNS)

Brian
Spinal Cord

Function:
Analysis,
Decision-Making

Peripheral Nervous System
(PNS)

Nerves throughout body:
Originate in brain stem and
spinal cord

Function:
Send data from body and
enviroment to CNS (afferent);
Send CNS decisions to organs,
glands, muscles (efferent)

Autonomic Nervous System:
Regulates functioning
of internal organs and glands
Part 1 of Peripheral Nervous System

Somatic Nervous System:
Sensory nerves
Motor nerves activating muscles
Part 2 of Peripheral Nervous System

Figure 21.1: Overview of nervous system

PARASYMPATHETIC NERVOUS SYSTEM (PNS) AND RESILIENT COPING

The vagus nerve has two separate branches—the dorsal vagal complex (DVC) and the ventral vagal complex (VVC) (Porges 1995, 1998). The DVC developed in reptiles, cold-blooded animals that need to conserve energy. To lower metabolism and provide camouflage, the inhibitory effect of this vagal branch produces immobilization, in which a reptile's heart rate slows drastically and the animal appears dead. This ancient metabolic strategy works effectively for reptiles. However, messages between the brainstem and heart travel comparatively slowly. Subtle gradations in response to stimuli are not possible. The reptile is either "off" (full vagal inhibition) or "on" (no vagal inhibition).

The VVC developed in mammals, warm-blooded animals that live in social groups (Porges 1995, 1998). To support these evolutionary advances, this circuit is functionally more complex. First, it is faster. Its myelinated sheathing permits rapid communication between brainstem and heart, enabling subtle gradations in mammalian energetic responses to stimuli. Second, the VVC migrated away from the DVC to a different part of the brainstem, the nucleus ambiguous. Here, it became linked to the cranial nerves that regulate striated muscles in the face and head that control facial gestures, vocalization, and hearing. In this way, Porges explains, the VVC became an integrated circuit connecting heart and lungs with expressive musculature in the face and head critical to social engagement and attachment (Porges 1995, 1998).

Through the VVC, subtle gradations in heart rate and breath are linked with subtle gradations in facial expression, voice tone, and hearing (Porges 1998, 2009).

In this way, the attuned mother and child develop a heart resonance; for example, gazing into each other's eyes during nursing and exchanging vocalizations that mutually reinforce secure attachment (Schore 2001). This vagal branch also stimulates hypothalamic-pituitary release of oxytocin—a bonding hormone that elevates pleasure and perceptions of safety—further deepening attachment. In short, this "smart" vagus plays a critical role in the formation of secure attachment by facilitating attuned, loving communication (Porges 1995).

Smart Vagus

The smart vagus plays an equally important role in restorative rest and healthy mobilization of energy (Porges 1998). When internal composure is strong and a person feels safe, the smart vagus keeps the heart rate slow, breathing deep, and digestive processes active. (The stomach and intestines, situated beneath the diaphragm, are regulated by the DVC. During internal composure/perceived safety, the VVC and DVC work together.)

The regulation of the heart by the smart vagus is useful to understand. Heart muscle contracts naturally, governed by a nerve bundle called the sino-atrial node. Its intrinsic rate is 100–120 beats per minute. Such a rate is not healthy over long periods of time (Opthof 2000). During restorative rest and calm functioning, the smart vagus inhibits heart rate to a baseline 60–80 beats per minute, playing the protective role of "vagal brake" (Porges *et al.* 1996). When mobilization is necessary, the smart vagus lets up on the brake, increasing metabolic output. Ultimately, if danger is perceived, the vagus relinquishes control, allowing the SNS to activate fight/flight mechanisms. However, if danger is not perceived, the smart vagus has sufficient latitude to mobilize energy without SNS activation.

This is important for two reasons. First, fight/flight is metabolically expensive. Second, during fight/flight, the social engagement system functions less effectively. The implications for health and resilient coping are significant. When people retain internal composure during life challenges, and do not perceive these challenges as threats, they can mobilize energy and utilize social support to meet challenges constructively and cooperatively—without the physical costs of fight/flight. In addition, if some degree of SNS activation is necessary, a strong vagal brake will inhibit this activity as soon as possible, aiding cardiovascular recovery (Porges 1998).

When the vagal brake is functioning effectively, "vagal tone" is high. This permits a beneficial, wide range of heart rate variability (HRV). Because the smart vagus also regulates respiration, a useful measure of HRV examines the subtle relationship between heart and lungs. During inhalation, the vagal brake relaxes slightly—heart rate increases. During exhalation, the vagal brake increases slightly—heart rate decreases. This variation is called respiratory sinus arrhythmia (RSA). High RSA is an indicator of cardiovascular health (Porges 1998, 2007).

Not surprisingly, high RSA also predicts psychological well-being across the life span. In infants, high HRV predicts more adaptive social behavior at age three (Porges and Furman 2011; Porges *et al.* 1996; Porges *et al.* 1994). In school-age children, vagal tone is associated with prosocial behavior (Eisenberg *et al.* 1995), sympathy (Fabes, Eisenberg, and Eisenbud 1993), and better coping with interparental conflict

(El-Sheikh, Harger, and Whitson 2001). In university students, high resting RSA has been associated with positive mood and optimism across a six–eight-month time span (Oveis *et al.* 2009) and self-regulatory strength (Segerstrom and Solberg-Nes 2007). When university students were confronted with negative stimuli, high resting RSA was associated with internal composure, measured by variations in facial expression (Demaree *et al.* 2006). In adults, low HRV has been associated with elevated levels of anxiety, depression, and hostility (Demaree *et al.* 2004). Over a nine-week period of self-reflection about daily personal experiences, adults who began with high RSA showed greater increases in positive emotions and social connectedness than those with low RSA. Additionally, there was a bidirectional relationship. Increases in positive emotions and social connectedness predicted improvements in vagal tone, independent of initial vagal tone level (Kok and Fredrickson 2010).

These data show that resilient individuals have a high degree of vagal tone—indicating an ability to face life challenges with internal composure, positive emotions, and social support that minimize the costly psychophysiological mechanisms of fight/flight mobilization. Thus, polyvagal theory suggests that resilient coping reflects an emergent stage of human evolution, offering unique human capacities for secure attachment, love, and social engagement (Porges 2011b). It provides a robust foundation for understanding the benefits of mindfulness and therapeutic use of the arts as facilitators of internal composure (Figure 21.2).

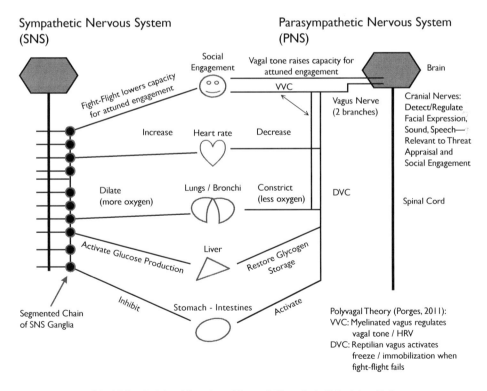

Figure 21.2: Autonomic nervous system pathways—social engagement and defense

SYMPATHETIC NERVOUS SYSTEM (SNS) AND POTENTIALLY DESTRUCTIVE COPING

During life-threatening situations and other challenges that require high-energy output, SNS activation of the stress response is necessary. Still, from the polyvagal perspective, it is a less evolved, second tier of stress coping. It should be activated mindfully, only when necessary. As noted, a defining characteristic of psychopathology is inaccurate appraisal of threat—with dysfunctional triggering of the stress response.

Benefits and Costs of SNS Activation

High-arousal SNS stress coping increases heart rate (often higher than its intrinsic rate). Bronchial passageways dilate to increase oxygen consumption for energy production. Blood pressure increases to speed nutrient transport. Digestion is inhibited because it takes too much time to provide the burst of energy needed for rapid fight/flight. Reproductive capacities are similarly inhibited. To provide glucose for rapid energy production, the liver stops storing nutrients as glycogen (its function during restorative rest), and converts stored glycogen to glucose. Blood flow is directed away from the skin to minimize bleeding. Blood is directed toward large muscle systems that will be used for fight/flight. Mental vigilance and muscle tension increase. Social engagement is minimized, replaced by abbreviated (often tense) communication focused on threat elimination (see Figure 21.2).

This coping strategy presents humans with potentially dangerous metabolic issues. Elevated heart rate, high blood pressure, and inhibition of digestive and reproductive functioning are adaptive during threat, but not when chronic. These health dangers are further heightened because the stress response also activates long-lasting stress hormones.

Hypothalamic-Pituitary-Adrenal Axis (HPA)

The hypothalamus is located in the brain, near the brainstem. It regulates the endocrine system and has direct connections to the adrenal gland through the SNS. Rapid SNS stimulation of the adrenal medulla releases epinephrine (adrenaline) and nor-epinephrine (nor-adrenaline) into the blood stream. These hormones increase heart rate and blood pressure, prolonging the mobilizing effects of the SNS. The hypothalamus is also connected to the pituitary gland (suspended below it). As Figure 21.3 shows, the hypothalamus also transmits CRH (corticotropin-releasing hormone) to the pituitary gland, stimulating release of ACTH (adrenocorticotropic hormone). Traveling through the bloodstream, ACTH triggers the adrenal cortex to release glucocorticoids (a sub-set of corticosteroids).

Cortisol, the stress hormone, is a primary glucocorticoid that floods the body. It has several functions—with both positive and negative effects. First, cortisol stimulates the liver to release glucose, prolonging SNS activation, and amplifying energy for fight/flight. Second, it inhibits the immune system. In fact, short bursts of the stress response increase immune function, protecting the body from bacterial infection during bleeding. However, like digestion and reproduction, fighting pathogens loses priority during life-threatening situations. As cortisol increases glucose production, it directs energy away from protein synthesis, including proteins necessary for immune cell production.

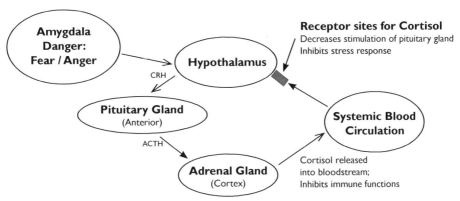

Cortisol Can Regulate the Stress Response

PTSD:
Perceived threat of danger is constant—Stress thermostat does not turn off
Counter-intuitive data: Low cortisol levels in bloodstream (Yehuda, 1997)

Mechanism not fully understood; various theories:
• Genetic predisposition for low cortisol / smaller hippocampus (Stein, et. al., 1997)
• Trauma amplifies negative HPA feedback: sensitivity to lower cortisol levels (Anisman, et. al., 2001)
• Reduced cortisol levels associated with vicious aggression in animals (Haller, et. al., 2003)

© Jared D. Kass, Psychological Maturation and Therapeutic Change; Used with Permission of Author

Figure 21.3: Thermostat for stress response: cortisol levels and post-traumatic stress disorder (PTSD)

If the stress response becomes the individual's default coping strategy, prolonged release of cortisol becomes harmful, depressing immune functions significantly (O'Connor, O'Halloran, and Shanahan 2000; Sapolsky 1998). This problem is common in modern life because social-evaluative threat is a trigger for cortisol release (Dickerson and Kemeny 2004). A further complication: cortisol flooding impairs the hippocampus, leading to atrophy (Sapolsky 1992). As we will discuss, the hippocampus plays a central role in the construction of memory; atrophy has severe negative effects. This problem is exacerbated by a destructive cycle: damage to the hippocampus increases cortisol release (Sapolsky 1996, 2003).

Cortisol has an additional, counter-intuitive, regulatory effect; it suppresses the stress response. As Figure 21.3 indicates, the hypothalamus has receptor sites for cortisol. When a set-point has been reached, cortisol inhibits the release of CRH (O'Connor *et al.* 2000; Sapolsky, Romero, and Munck 2000). Thus, it is an important "stress thermostat," providing negative feedback that returns the body to homeostasis. However, there are many instances when this stress thermostat does not function properly. For example, in nearly 50 percent of depressed patients, the HPA-axis remains hyper-reactive. High levels of urinary cortisol show that the thermostat does not turn off (Southwick, Vythilingam, and Charney 2005).

Paradoxically, in PTSD, urinary cortisol levels are low—despite high levels of epinephrine/nor-epinephrine and persistent symptoms of hyper-arousal (Mason *et al.* 2001; McGirr *et al.* 2010; Yehuda *et al.* 1990a, 1990b). Here, it is likely that the hypothalamus adaptively increases cortisol receptors (Yehuda *et al.* 1991). Despite reduced cortisol, the set-point is not reached; the HPA system becomes acutely reactive to stress (van der Kolk 1994).

Animal studies of cortisol may explain why traumatic violence escalates repetitively. The same pattern of high SNS-adrenaline and low HPA-cortisol is evident in very aggressive animals (Koolhaas *et al.* 1991); particularly those that exhibit the most dangerous types of violence (Haller and Kruk 2003). In animal studies, aggression is considered normal behavior to achieve dominance; but most aggressive behavior is posturing. The dominant warns the subordinate with "angry" behavior (e.g. vocalization, chest-beating) meant to avoid actual fighting. However, animals with low cortisol levels fight differently. They attack without warning. Their attacks are vicious; they strike to kill (Haller and Kruk 2003). Trauma may have similar effects on humans, rendering us more prone to vicious violence and subsequent traumatization of others. This neurobehavioral mechanism would help explain why intergroup violence and conflict become so intractable.

The Dorsal Vagal Complex (DVC) and Immobilization

As trauma psychology has shown, there is a third tier of stress coping—immobilization. When fight/flight is perceived as impossible, and individuals are flooded with overwhelming fear, they freeze—physically and psychologically. Limbs and torso grow numb. Cognitive processes shut down. Fainting or dissociative self-protection may occur. Memories of these events remain implicit, fragmented, somatic, and intrusive, often leading to self-soothing through substance dependence (Herman 1997; Rothschild 2000; Siegel 2003; van der Kolk 1994).

Polyvagal theory explains that during overwhelming threat, SNS-HPA stress coping collapses, devolving into reptilian stress coping—immobilization (see Figure 21.2). The primitive branch of the vagus nerve (DVC) becomes dominant, rapidly diminishing metabolic activity (Porges 2001, 2011b; van der Kolk 1994), producing dissociative, non-communicative states (Schore 2009). While effective for reptiles, and partially protective for humans *during* traumatic events, dissociative responses produce an oscillating pattern of hyper- and hypo-arousal typical in PTSD (van der Kolk 2003). In this psychological pattern, frozen individuals are virtually unavailable for intervention. Not surprisingly, a history of insecure attachment increases vulnerability to PTSD, whereas secure attachment is protective (Schore 2003a; Siegel 2012).

In summary, a polyvagal understanding of the autonomic nervous system provides a three-tiered neurobiological model of coping. It highlights the relationship between inner composure and resilient coping; and underscores the danger of inaccurate threat appraisal.

The Triune Brain: Social Engagement and Threat Appraisal

Cognitive and emotional appraisal takes place in the brain. Figure 21.4 offers a simplified illustration of brain structures, using MacLean's (1990) triune model of reptilian, mammalian, and human/primate components. Although this model does not encompass the full complexity of the brain, it has explanatory power (Cozolino 2006). Like the three tiers of coping in the polyvagal perspective, the brain has evolved from reptilian functionality to our capacities for cognition, self-reflection, emotional regulation, social engagement, and empathic attunement.

BRAIN STEM: THE "REPTILIAN" BRAIN

Reptiles have no social life. They are cold-blooded isolates whose behavior is limited to basic survival functions. While their ability to focus attention on the environment is keen, they have no capacity for reflective cognition or social bonding. In short, their neural systems are primarily autonomic. MacLean (1990) described the human brainstem, which regulates autonomic survival functions and attention on external stimuli as the "reptilian" brain (Figure 21.4).

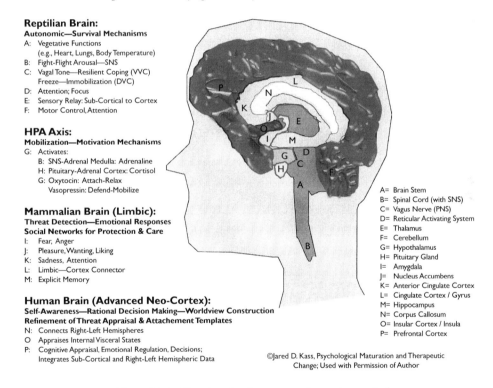

Reptilian Brain:
Autonomic—Survival Mechanisms
A: Vegetative Functions
      (e.g., Heart, Lungs, Body Temperature)
B: Fight-Flight Arousal—SNS
C: Vagal Tone—Resilient Coping (VVC)
      Freeze—Immobilization (DVC)
D: Attention; Focus
E: Sensory Relay: Sub-Cortical to Cortex
F: Motor Control, Attention

HPA Axis:
Mobilization—Motivation Mechanisms
G: Activates:
      B: SNS-Adrenal Medulla: Adrenaline
      H: Pituitary-Adrenal Cortex: Cortisol
      G: Oxytocin: Attach-Relax
         Vasopressin: Defend-Mobilize

Mammalian Brain (Limbic):
Threat Detection—Emotional Responses
Social Networks for Protection & Care
I: Fear, Anger
J: Pleasure, Wanting, Liking
K: Sadness, Attention
L: Limbic—Cortex Connector
M: Explicit Memory

Human Brain (Advanced Neo-Cortex):
Self-Awareness—Rational Decision Making—Worldview Construction
Refinement of Threat Appraisal & Attachement Templates
N: Connects Right-Left Hemispheres
O: Appraises Internal Visceral States
P: Cognitive Appraisal, Emotional Regulation, Decisions;
      Integrates Sub-Cortical and Right-Left Hemispheric Data

A=   Brain Stem
B=   Spinal Cord (with SNS)
C=   Vagus Nerve (PNS)
D=   Reticular Activating System
E=   Thalamus
F=   Cerebellum
G=   Hypothalamus
H=   Pituitary Gland
I=   Amygdala
J=   Nucleus Accumbens
K=   Anterior Cingulate Cortex
L=   Cingulate Cortex / Gyrus
M=   Hippocampus
N=   Corpus Callosum
O=   Insular Cortex / Insula
P=   Prefrontal Cortex

©Jared D. Kass, Psychological Maturation and Therapeutic Change; Used with Permission of Author

Figure 21.4: The triune brain: stress coping and appraisal

The brainstem, which includes the medulla oblongata, is the point of origination for the ANS (smart vagus, SNS, and dorsal vagal complex) and the somatic nervous system. Thus, it controls the inhibition and activation of all metabolic processes. It receives afferent messages (body to brain) about the environment and internal organs.

It sends efferent messages (brain to body) that control responses to the environment (see Figure 21.1). Near the top of the brainstem, the reticular activating system regulates arousal, attention, wakefulness, and sleep. It is connected to the thalamus, a sensory input relay to higher-functioning sections of the brain.

LIMBIC SYSTEM: THE "MAMMALIAN" BRAIN

Mammals have social lives. They are warm-blooded animals who tend their offspring until maturity. They show clear evidence of attachment, bonding, social groups, and hierarchical organization. Their behavior suggests emotional states: anger, fear, happiness, submission, and separation grief. Pups play. They communicate non-verbally and through vocalization—and demonstrate many gradations of approach–avoid behavior. For these reasons, MacLean (1990) designated the limbic system as the "mammalian" brain.

The limbic system sits above the brainstem, around the thalamus. It is a group of structures that generate emotional responses to situations. It appraises threat and attraction with greater complexity than the brainstem, using associative memories. Feelings of fear, disgust, anger, attraction, and pleasure, produce social engagement (approach–withdraw) and defense (fight/flight/freeze) by activating the hypothalamus and brainstem. Each limbic structure is bi-lateral, somewhat comparable to the cortical hemispheres. Research has begun to differentiate left and right activity—but damage to either diminishes functionality in both.

Amygdala

This almond-shaped organ assesses sensory data, generating emotional states of fear (flight/freeze), anger (fight), repulsion (avoid), and attraction (approach). Protective vigilance is its major role. It magnifies the startle response, judges facial expressions for trustworthiness (Adolphs, Tranel, and Damasio 1998), and is more reactive to faces from other races, when compared with responses to "in-group" faces (Hart *et al.* 2000). However, the amygdala also responds to positive stimuli and happy faces. Thus, its primary function is evaluation of emotional stimuli (Luan Phan *et al.* 2004). To aid this appraisal process, it appears to retrieve emotion-laden memories (Rauch *et al.* 1996). Thus, the amygdala imbues human relationships with emotional energy. However, it can produce inaccurate reactivity, when its rapid responses bypass review by the prefrontal cortex.

Nucleus Accumbens (NA)

This hub of dopamine pathways is the pleasure and reward center of the brain. It plays a central role in liking and wanting. Some neuroscientists consider it as separate from the limbic system. However, many consider the NA a limbic structure because it affects motivation and emotional behavior (Lambert and Kinsley 2005). When we feel loved, loving, or engage in addictive behaviors (e.g. alcohol, sex, gambling, video games), the NA creates positive feedback that reinforces these activities. While some of these activities are self-destructive, the NA plays a critical role in approach behavior and social engagement.

Anterior Cingulate Cortex (ACC)

The cingulate cortex (or gyrus) is an ancient portion of the cerebral cortex, peripheral to other limbic structures. The anterior portion has both cortical (cognitive) and limbic (social-emotional) functions, relaying data between these parts of the brain. From the cognitive perspective, the ACC helps maintain focused attention. From the limbic perspective, the ACC is associated with sadness. It is active during recollection of negative autobiographical experiences (Luan Phan *et al.* 2004), and in clinical depression (Liotti *et al.* 2000).

Hippocampus

The hippocampus plays a central role in long-term memory. The neural circuits that "hold" memories are not localized in a specific part of the brain (Lashley 1950). However, severe damage to the hippocampus produces amnesia, including events before and after the damage. Therefore, it seems to play a role in the creation of memory circuits and their retrieval.

There are two kinds of memory—implicit and explicit. An example of implicit, somatically encoded memory is when a child displays anxiety about a past experience but cannot describe it verbally. Conversely, when a person can review an experience verbally and describe its contextual details, the memory is explicit. The hippocampus transmutes daily experience into explicit memory, particularly autobiographical memories. However, stress-induced cortisol destroys hippocampus cells (Sapolsky 1996). During traumatic events that induce dissociative immobilization, the hippocampus does not function. This is why traumatic memories often remain implicit—unavailable for verbal exploration, but psychophysiologically intrusive and stressful (van der Kolk 2003).

In summary, these limbic structures generate emotions and memories that bind and rupture human relationships. *Both in the service of growth and defense, they play a crucial role in engagement and withdrawal.* However, this "mammalian" emotional brain lacks self-reflective capacities. Consequently, it is vulnerable to inaccurate and premature reactivity.

NEO-CORTEX: THE ADVANCED "HUMAN" BRAIN

Reflective capacities that provide accurate appraisal evolved in the cortex. All mammals have a rudimentary cortex. They learn from experiences, and retain learning through associative or consequential conditioning. However, most mammals do not learn by observing others, nor do they recognize themselves in a mirror. These behaviors belong to the primates, and we humans have developed these capabilities most extensively. The human neo-cortex has the self-reflective ability to refine perceptions, and to construct a comprehensive worldview (meaning-system) about self, others, and life. However, cognitive capacities do not guarantee accuracy. Psychological wounds, trauma, socio-cultural oppression, family histories of neglect/abuse, or insecure attachment all shape the worldview-making process. Generalizations from past experience can distort expectations for the future and perceptions in the present.

Therefore, our self-reflective capacities are challenged to examine our worldview, identify distortions, and risk new behavioral responses. Internal composure (high vagal tone) increases our capacity for learning and risk-taking. Conversely, when the neocortex is locked in a worldview that triggers SNS fight/flight or DVC immobilization, the ability to accurately refine perceptions is minimized.

Prefrontal Cortex (PFC)

The prefrontal cortex plays a primary role in these functions. It is located in the anterior section of the frontal lobe (Figure 21.5).

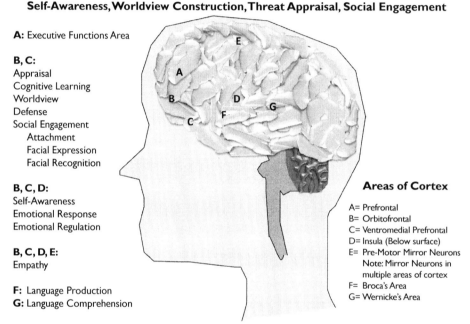

Self-Awareness, Worldview Construction, Threat Appraisal, Social Engagement

A: Executive Functions Area

B, C:
Appraisal
Cognitive Learning
Worldview
Defense
Social Engagement
   Attachment
   Facial Expression
   Facial Recognition

B, C, D:
Self-Awareness
Emotional Response
Emotional Regulation

B, C, D, E:
Empathy

F: Language Production
G: Language Comprehension

Areas of Cortex

A= Prefrontal
B= Orbitofrontal
C= Ventromedial Prefrontal
D= Insula (Below surface)
E= Pre-Motor Mirror Neurons
   Note: Mirror Neurons in
   multiple areas of cortex
F= Broca's Area
G= Wernicke's Area

©Jared D. Kass, Psychological Maturation and Therapeutic Change; Used with Permission of Author

Figure 21.5: Neo-Cortex

The PFC integrates incoming data from all parts of the brain—with direct links to limbic structures and brainstem (Siegel 2007). It provides a final executive appraisal of environmental stimuli, inhibiting or amplifying emotional signals from the limbic system. Drawing on previous life-experience, the PFC employs its cognitive worldview to evaluate specific situations and shape appropriate behavioral responses. For example, if the PFC has developed a nuanced worldview that differentiates various levels of threat, allows previous negative experiences "a voice" but not absolute authority, and identifies positive potential in new challenges, then the PFC is primed to maintain vagal tone and support resilient coping.

As brain scan research has progressed, it has begun to identify specialized areas in the prefrontal cortex and frontal lobe. Current findings are not definitive but offer potentially useful insights about appraisal, self-regulation, and social engagement processes.

Insular Cortex (Insula)

The insula is buried deep within the PFC, near the limbic system, at the junction of the frontal and temporal lobes. It plays a crucial role in self-awareness, through connection to the evolutionarily new Lamina I. This is a neural circuit that runs from the spinal cord, through the brainstem and thalamus, to the insula, transmitting data about the body's physiological states. This process is called interoception (Craig 2002). Examples include awareness of heart beat, limb pain, stomach feeling full, and empathic feelings for a loved one who is experiencing pain.

The anterior insular cortex (AIC) is also activated during self-recognition (viewing image of self), self-awareness of body movement, self-awareness of emotions, time perception, and a feeling of knowing. Therefore, it seems likely that the AIC is central to self-awareness—the knowledge that "I am" and "This is how I feel" (Craig 2009). At the same time, Damasio (1999) suggests that the insula integrates internal somatic feelings with external stimuli—producing "gut" responses that guide emotion-based behavioral decisions. Finally, in patients with PTSD, the AIC is activated when re-experiencing trauma but not activated during dissociative states (Hopper *et al.* 2007). Therefore, the insular cortex plays an essential self-reflective role in appraisal, engagement, and defense.

Orbitofrontal Cortex (OFC)

In the lower forehead, slightly above and behind the eye, the OFC is the pre-eminent decision-making section of the prefrontal cortex. Appraising data from the insula, limbic system, and other relevant areas, the OFC regulates emotional states and responses. As the architect of worldview construction and refinement, it can rapidly learn and unlearn stimulus-associated patterns (Davidson 2004). Integrating new learning with current attachment templates (secure, anxious, avoidant, or dissociative/disorganized), it shapes our responses to people and events (Schore 2000, 2003a, 2009).

Ventro-Medial Prefrontal Cortex (vmPFC)

The terms OFC and vmPFC are sometimes used interchangeably. Technically, the vmPFC is a small area directly below the OFC, sharing responsibility for emotion regulation and threat appraisal. Damage to the vmPFC can cause blunted emotional experience, defective social decision-making, and lack of insight (Hansel and von Kanel 2008). It has also been associated with multiple forms of psychopathology (Schore 2012). Activity in the vmPFC is associated with the elimination of previously learned fearful associations (Phelps *et al.* 2004). Additionally, the vmPFC appears to modulate the vagal brake. It is active when vagal tone is high and individuals are in a restful, mentally alert state (Hansel and von Kanel 2008). Vagal tone is also affected by the insula and limbic structures. However, high vmPFC activity seems to reflect a positive state of perceived safety, attunement to self, and capacity for attunement with others. Therefore, it may be instrumental in secure attachment (Schore 2003a, 2009), as well as a focal point of internal composure.

HEMISPHERIC LATERALIZATION—RIGHT AND LEFT BRAIN FUNCTIONS

Hemispheric control of opposite body sides—contralateral functioning—was first identified in patients with damage to the corpus callosum, the neural circuits that connect the hemispheres. Subsequent EEG research has identified additional distinctions. However, complex activities (e.g. speech) require coordinated effort from both hemispheres. For example, Broca's area in the left hemisphere (LH) controls grammatical speech, while Broca's area in the right hemisphere (RH) controls tone of voice. Wernicke's area in the LH controls language comprehension, while Wernicke's area in the RH recognizes vocal tone. It is easy, therefore, to overstate lateral asymmetry. Nonetheless, these activities reflect different functions. The LH is dominant during verbal expression and conceptual thinking. The RH is dominant during non-verbal expression, somatic experience, and visuo-spatial thinking.

These differences are consistent with the discovery that, during the first three years of life, the RH is dominant (Chiron *et al.* 1997). During this formative period, language is non-existent or rudimentary. Infants learn through somatic experience. Attachment is formed through physical touch and non-verbal attunement. Rapid growth in neural connections between the RH and the limbic system enhance the child's emotional valence and non-verbal alarm system reactivity. Memory encoding is strong—but implicit. At approximately age four, children become capable of LH verbal descriptions of daily experience. However, their descriptions retain a high degree of RH emotionality. When they get frightened, LH verbal and conceptual processes quickly shut down.

This predominance leads Schore (2009) to describe the RH as the functional equivalent of Freud's unconscious—the container for early childhood experience as well as memories repressed by trauma-induced dissociation. EEG research appears to support this model (Allen 2004). In psychopathology, RH activity is associated with fight/flight reactivity and withdrawal behavior; LH activity is associated with improvements in mindfulness, self-reflection, emotional regulation, and approach behavior (Coan and Allen 2004; Davidson 2004). These differences suggest that clinicians must develop right-brain to right-brain attunement with patients, employing left-brain functions to transmute implicit, somatic memory into cogent episodic narratives and self-regulatory learning (Schore 2009).

MIRROR NEURONS

Recent research suggests that mirror neurons may contribute to our capacity for empathic attunement and threat appraisal. They are a broad array of neurons that fire both when an individual is performing an action, and when the individual observes others performing the same action (Gallese *et al.* 1996; Rizzolatti *et al.* 1996). For example, the mirror neurons that fire when we observe someone cry, also fire when we cry. With access to the emotions of the other person, we can feel visceral compassion. Similarly, mirror neurons that fire when we observe someone angry, also fire when we are angry. Recognizing this emotion internally, we realize this person may become a threat. Such "embodied simulation" (Gallese 2001) may provide a neurological foundation for empathy (Gallese 2005).

Empathy, of course, is a complex process. It requires coordinated activity in the prefrontal cortex, insula, and limbic system (Shamay-Tsoory 2009). Still, mirror neurons may play a significant role. They are highly responsive to facial expression, even in early infancy, potentially contributing to attunement between child and caregiver. At the same time, there appear to be individual differences in how effectively the mirror neuron system functions (Gallese 2007). For example, mirror neuron activity is restricted in autism, impairing the ability to give and receive social engagement cues (Gallese 2006). These differences support the potential role of mirror neurons in the empathic process.

In summary, the neo-cortex plays an instrumental role in social engagement and threat appraisal. It shapes the worldview that determines how we respond to the environment, either inhibiting or activating sub-cortical and visceral systems for fight/flee/freeze, or approach. Inaccurate appraisal is figural in psychopathology; accurate appraisal is figural in resilient coping. This explains why cognitive-behavioral methods that help patients identify their worldview and its effects are often effective psychotherapeutically. However, traditional cognitive-behavioral therapy (CBT) is less effective treating complex trauma and severe attachment disorders because disorganized perceptions, implicit memories, and somatically held emotions restrict self-reflective capacities. In this treatment domain, mindfulness and therapeutic use of the arts become particularly useful. To appreciate their value fully, it is necessary to understand the dynamics of somatic memory and emotional armoring in more detail.

Somatic Memory: Emotional Armoring and Neuromuscular Suppression of Memory

While the somatization of emotion-laden memory in trauma survivors is an established phenomenon (Rothschild 2000; van der Kolk 1994), the neuromuscular process of emotion suppression requires further elaboration (Scherer 2000). Current studies emphasize the face and vocalization (Ekman 1993, 2003; Mehu *et al.* 2012) because they are central to infant–caregiver attachment (Schore 2001) and "smart" vagal social engagement (Porges 2011b). However, recent research demonstrates that the entire body is utilized in emotional suppression and expression (Dael, Mortillaro, and Scherer 2011). It suggests that emotion is more than a psychological state. It is an active process in which cortical and limbic structures send efferent messages to psychomotor systems, activating or inhibiting physical movement (Scherer 2000). This body/mind connection is illustrated by patients who describe emotions through somatic metaphors (e.g. shoulders are tight; gut is raging; body is burning). It is also illustrated by patients who benefit from bio-energetic integration of physical movement into psychotherapy (e.g. relaxing shoulder rolls or yoga stretches before talking; hitting a pillow to release pent-up anger) (Conger 1994; Lowen 1975; Wilner 1999).

Current analysis of full body expression is mechanistic, coding for movement in specific parts (e.g. arm, wrist action) (Dael *et al.* 2011) or movement qualities

(Gross, Crane, and Fredrickson 2010; Laban 1988). A more useful approach contrasts neuromuscular systems that regulate suppression and expression. For example, Scherer (2000, p.238) reports that children holding back laughter engage in "*lip press.*" Gross and Levenson (1993) report that adults suppressing disgust *blink* more frequently.

Reich, a pioneer of somatic psychology, explained this phenomenon in a functionally integrative model (Frager and Fadiman 2005; Herskowitz 2008; Reich 1980). When expression is robust, emotional energy is mobilized throughout the body. The laughing child breathes deeply—throat muscles unconstricted, mouth muscles relaxed. Laughter flows out of the child. In uproarious laughter, children may stamp their feet in excitement or "collapse" in hysterics. Reich observed that robust expressive energy moves upward and downward in the body, directionally parallel with the spine. Conversely, when people suppress emotions, psychomotor zones transverse to the spine hold feelings back—the classic *stiff upper lip*. The transverse zones include the eyes, lips, shoulders, throat, diaphragm, abdomen, and pelvis. Reich observed that suppression of emotions and repression of memories invariably includes tension in some or all of these zones. When therapeutically appropriate for patients to explore suppressed material, the release of tension in these zones mobilizes emotional expression and event-specific memory (Conger 1994; Lowen 1975; Reich 1960a; Wilner 1999).

Using an evolutionary perspective (akin to Porges and MacLean, with differences), Reich described this psychophysiological emotion regulation system as *segmented*—a functional adaptation of defense structures developed in pre-vertebrates (segmented exo-skeleton). In humans, structural traces can be found in the segmented chain of SNS ganglia and spine (see Figure 21.2), though this adaptation is primarily functional (Reich 1960b). Segmentation of the spine enables robust movements of expansion and contraction, mobilizing bio-energy for laughter, anger, sadness, social engagement, sexual intimacy, and withdrawal. The transverse, segmental zones provide a neuromuscular mechanism for suppression. SNS-activated muscular tension "holds" emotions in the body (at times, unconsciously) until these implicit memories and stored emotions can be accessed therapeutically (Conger 1994; Ogden, Minton, and Pain 2006). Clinical work with these transverse zones is utilized by many somatically oriented clinicians (Gendlin 1982, 1998; Hazell and Perez 2011; Keleman 1985; Kurtz 1990; Levine 2005; Pesso 1973; Pierrakos 1987; Wilner 1999), illustrating the neuromuscular dynamics of emotional armoring in somatic memory.

Mindfulness and the Therapeutic Use of the Arts: Neuroscience in Action

Internal composure, as we have seen, is a key element in resilient coping. It empowers individuals to respond to stress and existential anxiety resourcefully, maintaining social support and a positive worldview (confidence in life and self; secure existential attachment) associated with high vagal tone. These emergent human capacities must be cultivated. Otherwise, coping devolves into primitive fight/flight/freeze behaviors that, while periodically useful, become destructive when habitual or chronic. The social sciences have reached a critical juncture, learning to facilitate these evolving capacities and transcend primitive defense systems. In psychotherapy, trauma psychology, and social transformation work, the cultivation of inner composure has emerged as a figural goal.

This neuroscientific material also demonstrates that psychological wounds, emotional agitation, and distorted cognitions are rooted in pre-verbal, somatically encoded experience. For this reason, mindfulness and the therapeutic use of the arts provide essential tools for effective clinical work. Individuals who do not feel safe enough to risk self-disclosure, who have lost touch with the visceral sensations and internal messages of their bodies, who have not gained accurate verbal access to their emotions, who live in oscillating states of hyper- and hypo-arousal, or who lack the reflective capacities of an observing self, require experiential, sensorimotor "bottom-up" psychotherapy rather than predominantly verbal, "top-down" forms (Fosha 2003; Schore 2009). Such treatment provides pre-verbal, somatic experiences of safety; increased sensorimotor awareness; somatic emotion-regulation skills that build affect tolerance; titrated unpacking of somatic memories without dissociative regression; internal experience of a calm core; and gradual movement to verbal capacities for self-disclosure and social engagement.

Despite this emerging consensus, these clinical approaches are comparatively new. The integration of verbal and non-verbal therapies requires further exploration. Careful research is needed to substantiate the contributions of non-verbal modalities to therapeutic outcomes (Schore 2003b; Wiener 1999). We offer brief guidelines and a review of current research.

Mindfulness and Meditation

Psychotherapy provides a relational process where insecure attachment, interpersonal emotional dysregulation, and destructive coping can be repaired (Ginot 2012). Meditation, practiced alone, rarely replaces this corrective experience. However, the incorporation of mindfulness and meditation into psychotherapy can contribute to these goals substantively (Germer and Siegel 2012). As we have seen, the capacity to be aware of current experience (somatic, emotional, cognitive) through a non-judgmental stance of observant attention, acceptance, and inner calm constitutes a central feature of psychological congruence (Rogers 1961) and emotional well-being (Davidson 2004; Kabat-Zinn 1990; Siegel 2007).

Kabat-Zinn's (1990) pioneering Mindfulness-Based Stress Reduction (MBSR) program combines active forms of mindfulness (mindful walking, hatha yoga, mindful eating, and body scans) with sitting meditation. The active forms have particular relevance to therapeutic use of the arts because mindfulness-in-action can deepen the quality of awareness and concentration that individuals bring to expressive work and daily tasks. In addition, these activities provide an introduction to the more rigorous process of sitting meditation—the ability to turn inward, learning to observe the conditioned thoughts and emotions that shape worldview and behavior.

As individuals become aware of their current perceptual field, meditation intensifies the therapeutic process through which they can heal distorted cognitive schema, emotional wounds, and insecure attachment. In addition, as meditation calms the dysregulating arousal of emotional wounds and memories, it gradually reveals a peaceful, composed core at the center of self (Kass and Lennox 2005; Kass *et al.* 1991; Siegel 2007). When practiced regularly, meditation strengthens internal composure and resilient coping.

It is intriguing that this "simple" practice can be so useful—and the neuroscience we have explored helps explain this phenomenon. The calm, deep breathing that meditation cultivates increases vagal tone (Gevirtz 2011), inhibits SNS-HPA activity, and activates the VVC social engagement system (Porges 2001). In this case, the mind is turned inward, attuning the VVC to internal experience, producing a state of relaxed, open-ended attentiveness.

The long-term effects of meditation can be further explicated by polyvagal theory. Porges suggests that humans have developed positive adaptations for DVC immobilization. During the shared reverie of nursing, the connected bodies of mother and infant grow still (Porges 1998). This nurturing moment, in which the mother is calmly attentive to the cues of the child, produces a securely attached state of thought-free, loving attunement. It is possible that the reverie of meditation employs this same adaptive mechanism, gradually producing a quiescent state of attentive, thought-free, loving attunement with life itself (see Taylor 2009). Consequently, meditation can become a source of *secure existential attachment* (Kass 2007; Kass 2014).

Research supports these ideas. Meditation increases HRV (Burg, Wolf, and Michalak 2012; Ditto, Eclache, and Goldman 2006; Peng *et al.* 2004; Peng *et al.* 1999) and activates prefrontal and limbic neural structures related to attention and arousal (Lazar *et al.* 2000). It produces left prefrontal activation associated with approach behavior and improved immune function (Davidson *et al.* 2003). In addition, meditation produces increased cortical thickness in the prefrontal cortex and insula (Lazar *et al.* 2005), and increased grey matter in the insula and hippocampus (Holzel *et al.* 2008); reduction in perceived stress among meditators is associated with decreases in the grey matter of the amygdala (Holzel *et al.* 2010). Meditation has been shown to increase theta and alpha EEG activity (Cahn and Polich 2006; Lagopoulos *et al.* 2009) and neural synchrony in high-amplitude gamma oscillations (Lutz *et al.* 2004), potentially explaining its characteristic combination of relaxation, heightened attention, mental clarity, and integration of RH and LH processes (Kass 2014; Siegel 2007). Mindfulness has been found to increase attention skills, empathy, and compassion in mental health clinicians (Davis and Hayes 2011). While further research is needed (Chiesa and Serretti 2010), systematic reviews support these conclusions (Cahn and Polich 2006; Greeson 2008; Holzel *et al.* 2011; Treadway and Lazar 2009).

These impressive effects are associated with key markers of internal composure, psychological well-being, and increased growth in the neural structures that facilitate resilient coping. Meditation, as a self-reflective process *par excellence*, can contribute significantly to therapeutic goals and practice. Intermediary methods, like Focusing (Rappaport 2009) and guided visualizations (Kass 1996a, 1996b) offer further introduction to meditative processes for clients who require more structured guidance.

Therapeutic Use of the Arts

Two themes will emerge in this discussion. First, therapeutic use of the arts is a figural practice in somatically oriented "bottom-up" clinical practice. Second, evidence-based research using neurobehavioral markers to substantiate the efficacy of therapeutic use of the arts is minimal. We propose solutions to this issue as we conclude our review.

MUSIC

Neuroscience has long suspected that language and music developed together. The rhythms of language in ethno-cultural groups often parallel rhythmic structures in their music (Patel 2008). This suggests that culturally syntonic music may facilitate therapeutic bonding and verbal communication. Polyvagal theory provides additional insight. The cranial nerves that regulate auditory and vocal functioning are part of the VVC, intimately linked to vagal regulation of the heart and social engagement system. Gentle, rhythmic music activates pre-verbal neural circuits that increase HRV, perceptions of safety, and affiliative bonding.

   For dissociative trauma patients, music can modulate limbic hyper-arousal (Porges 2011a). This approach has also been tested with autism, which may include functional impairment in social engagement. When autistic children listened to acoustically engineered sound (that enabled their middle ears to distinguish human voices from background noise more effectively), improvements were observed in social behavior and communication skills with peers and parents (Porges 2001). Consequently, polyvagal theory provides conceptual support for Tomatis' research on middle ear dysfunction and the physiological benefits of music (Thompson and Andrews 2000). In a systematic review, Ellis and Thayer (2010) summarize nascent research associating music therapy with improvements in HRV. Mrazova and Celec (2010) highlight the need for additional neurobiological outcome studies.

MOVEMENT AND DANCE

Adler's (1970) classic case study of her work with an autistic child provides eloquent evidence that dance/movement therapy can provide non-verbal clients with the safety and sensorimotor learning necessary for bottom-up therapeutic growth (Ogden 2009; Reich 1960b). Initially, the child's rigid and poignantly awkward self-referential movements reflect segmented, somatic blockage of emotional and physical energy. As Adler mirrors the child's movements with exquisite sensitivity, we can almost "see" the child's mirror neuron system become responsive (Gallese 2007). Gradually, they achieve a degree of behavioral synchrony, indicating empathic attunement (Vacharkulksemsuk and Fredrickson 2012). The child then tentatively explores "approach and withdraw" behaviors, which Adler receives with calm, internal composure, mirroring both types of movement. Over many sessions, the child begins to tolerate the anxiety that her attachment-seeking approach behavior arouses in her. Eventually, the girl settles into Adler's lap tenderly, reflecting her experience of secure attachment. This study illustrates current neuroscientific research impeccably. However, evidence-based research with neurobiological markers is lacking in the dance-movement field.

VISUAL ART

An extensive case study literature in art therapy illustrates numerous applications of a somatically oriented therapeutic approach (Malchiodi 1990, 2008; Rogers 1993, 2011; Steele and Malchiodi 2012). These applications include the cultivation of safety (e.g. draw or visualize a place where you feel nurtured and safe); explorations of sensorimotor experience (e.g. use colors and shapes to show how your shoulder feels); symbolic expression of unconscious emotions (e.g. a tree with broken limbs); representational images of traumatic events (e.g. the scary man); a safe container to express raw emotion (e.g. red slashes across the page); incorporation of verbal expression and self-disclosure (e.g. write a sentence about this drawing); cultivation of a calm core (e.g. now that you feel more calm, draw how this feels); cultivation of an observing self (e.g. let's step back from this powerful drawing and think about how it affects you); and, an internal locus of affect regulation (e.g. let's compare drawings when you feel frightened and when you feel calm).

A growing literature makes conceptual connections between current neuroscience and art therapy (Buk 2009; Gantt 2009; Hass-Cohen and Carr 2008; Klorer 2005; Lusebrink 2004). A small literature reports single-case EEG studies of art-perception and art-making, presenting data that is somewhat contradictory, though consistently suggests bi-lateral hemispheric activity and integration (Belkofer and Konopka 2008; Bhattacharya and Petsche 2002; Ziadel 2005). In summary, a more robust effort to gather outcome data with neurobiological markers is needed within the art therapy field.

DRAMATIC ENACTMENT

Physical enactment of sensorimotor states, emotions, conflicts, and traumatic events is a potent therapeutic tool (Emunah 1999; Haen 2008). Enactment can begin with safety-building activities (e.g. let's pretend we are walking on a tight-rope) that gradually increase in emotional depth to the acting out of imaginary stories and folk tales that have symbolic meaning for participants (e.g. Cinderella) and eventually to group expressive actions that release emotions and build interpersonal bonds (e.g. let's yell at the dragon together). Enactment can also provide integrative therapeutic closure for relationships and events (e.g. although your father is dead, let's imagine talking to him; or, use your body to sculpt how you felt when you were hit, and then let's enact what you would like to do to the person who attacked you). In each example, enactment provides a concrete method to overcome DVC immobilization (Ogden 2009; Porges 2009). It is very likely that these methods have a positive effect on vagal tone. Research in this area is absent and vital.

Neurobehavioral Research in Therapeutic Use of the Arts

There is a concrete reason that research has been lacking. Brain scans and EEG studies require immobility. This is not possible for action-based forms of mindfulness or therapeutic use of the arts. However, the material in this chapter suggests a solution. Resting HRV has become an accepted marker for vagal tone and neurobiological correlates of internal composure (Porges 2011b). Resting HRV could be used in quasi-experimental or randomized designs to generate pre- and post-intervention data that compares experimental and control conditions. This protocol would provide a neurobiological foundation for necessary research.

Conclusion

Internal composure and resilient coping are emergent properties of humanity's evolving neurobehavioral pathways. This chapter highlights the clinical value of mindfulness and therapeutic use of the arts to facilitate internal composure and provides a neuroscientific understanding of these comparatively new clinical practices. As clinicians grow familiar with this neuroscience, they will recognize ways that they already utilize these principles intuitively, while also learning to incorporate them more mindfully.

References

Adler, J. (1970) *Looking for Me.* Berkeley, CA: University of California/Berkeley.

Adolphs, R., Tranel, D., and Damasio, A.R. (1998) "The human amygdala in social judgment." *Nature 393,* 6684, 470–474.

Ainsworth, M.D. (1985) "Attachments across the life span." *Bulletin of the New York Academy of Medicine 61,* 9, 792–812.

Ainsworth, M.D. and Eichberg, C. (1991) "Effects on Infant–Mother Attachment of Mother's Unresolved Loss of an Attachment Figure, or Other Traumatic Experience." In C.M. Parks, J. Stevenson-Hinde, and P. Marris (eds) *Attachment Across the Life Cycle.* New York: Tavistock/Routledge.

Ainsworth, M.D., Blehar, M., Waters, E., and Wall, S. (1978) *Patterns of Attachment.* Hillsdale, NJ: Lawrence Erlbaum.

Allen, J.J.B. (2004) "Frontal EEG asymmetry, emotion, and psychopathology: The first, and the next, 25 years." *Biological Psychology 67,* 1–2, 1–5.

Belkofer, C.M. and Konopka, L.M. (2008) "Conducting art therapy research using quantitative EEG measures." *Art Therapy: Journal of the American Art Therapy Association 25,* 2, 56–63.

Bhattacharya, J. and Petsche, H. (2002) "Shadows of artistry: Cortical synchrony during perception and imagery of visual art." *Cognitive Brain Research 13,* 2, 179–186.

Bowlby, J. (1969) *Attachment and Loss. Volume 1: Attachment.* New York: Basic Books.

Buk, A. (2009) "The mirror neuron system and embodied simulation: Clinical implications for art therapists working with trauma survivors." *The Arts in Psychotherapy 36,* 2, 61–74.

Burg, J.M., Wolf, O.T., and Michalak, J. (2012) "Mindfulness as self-regulated attention: Associations with heart rate variability." *Swiss Journal of Psychology 71,* 3, 135–139.

Cahn, B.R. and Polich, J. (2006) "Meditation states and traits: EEG, ERP, and neuroimaging studies." *Psychological Bulletin 132,* 2, 180–211.

Chiesa, A. and Serretti, A. (2010) "A systematic review of neurobiological and clinical features of mindfulness meditation." *Psychological Medicine 40,* 8, 1239–1252.

Chiron, C., Jambaque, I., Nabbout, R., Lounes, R., Syrota, A., and Dulac, O. (1997) "The right brain hemisphere is dominant in human infants." *Brain 120,* 6, 1057–1065.

Coan, J.A. and Allen, J.J.B. (2004) "Frontal EEG asymmetry as a moderator and mediator of emotion." *Biological Psychology 67,* 1–3, 7–50.

Conger, J.P. (1994) *The Body in Recovery: Somatic Psychotherapy and the Self.* Berkeley, CA: Frog Books.

Cozolino, L. (2006) *The Neuroscience of Human Relationships: Attachment and the Developing Social Brain.* New York: Norton.

Craig, A.D. (2002) "How do you feel? Interoception: The sense of the physiological condition of the body." *Nature Reviews Neuroscience 3*, 8, 655–666.

Craig, A.D. (2009) "How do you feel—now? The anterior insula and human awareness." *Nature Reviews Neuroscience 10*, 1, 59–70.

Dael, N., Mortillaro, M., and Scherer, K.R. (2011) "Emotion expression in body action and posture." *Emotion* (Advanced Online Publication). DOI: 10.1037/a0025737.

Damasio, A.R. (1999) *The Feeling of What Happens: Body and Emotion in the Making of Consciousness.* New York: Harcourt Brace.

Davidson, R.J. (2004) "Well-being and affective style: Neural substrates and biobehavioral correlates." *Philosophical Transactions of the Royal Society London, Biological Sciences 359*, 1449, 1395–1411.

Davidson, R.J., Kabat-Zinn, J., Schumacher, J., Rosenkranz, M., *et al.* (2003) "Alterations in brain and immune function produced by mindfulness meditation." *Psychosomatic Medicine 65*, 4, 564–570.

Davis, D.M. and Hayes, J.A. (2011) "What are the benefits of mindfulness? A practice review of psychotherapy-related research." *Psychotherapy 48*, 2, 198–208.

Demaree, H.A., Pu, J., Robinson, J.L., Schmeichel, B.J., and Everhart, D.E. (2006) "Predicting facial valence to negative stimuli from resting RSA: Not a function of active emotion regulation." *Cognition and Emotion 20*, 2, 161–176.

Demaree, H.A., Robinson, J.L., Everhart, D.E., and Schmeichel, B.J. (2004) "Resting RSA is associated with natural and self-regulated responses to negative emotional stimuli." *Brain and Cognition 56*, 1, 14–23.

Diamond, L.M. and Hicks, A.M. (2005) "Attachment style, current relationship security, and negative emotions: The mediating role of physiological regulation." *Journal of Social and Personal Relationships 22*, 4, 499–518.

Dickerson, S.S. and Kemeny, M.E. (2004) "Acute stressors and cortisol responses: A theoretical integration and synthesis of laboratory research." *Psychological Bulletin 130*, 3, 355–391.

Ditto, B., Eclache, M., and Goldman, N. (2006) "Short-term autonomic and cardiovascular effects of mindfulness body scan meditation." *Annals of Behavioral Medicine 32*, 3, 227–234.

Eisenberg, N., Fabes, R.A., Murphy, B., Maszk, P., Smith, M., and Karbon, M. (1995) "The role of emotionality and regulation in children's social functioning: A longitudinal study." *Child Development 66*, 5, 1360–1384.

Ekman, P. (1993) "Facial expression and emotion." *American Psychologist 48*, 4, 384–392.

Ekman, P. (2003) "Darwin, Deception, and Facial Expression." In P. Ekman, J.J. Campos, R.J. Davidson, and F.B.M. de Waal (eds) *Emotions Inside Out.* New York: New York Academy of Sciences.

El-Sheikh, M., Harger, J.A., and Whitson, S.M. (2001) "Exposure to interparental conflict and children's adjustment and physical health: The moderating role of vagal tone." *Child Development 72*, 6, 1617–1636.

Ellis, R.J. and Thayer, J.F. (2010) "Music and autonomic nervous system (dys)function." *Music Perception 27*, 4, 317–326.

Emunah, R. (1999) "Drama Therapy in Action." In D.J. Wiener (ed.) *Beyond Talk Therapy: Using Movement and Expressive Techniques in Clinical Practice.* Washington, DC: American Psychological Association.

Fabes, R.A., Eisenberg, N., and Eisenbud, L. (1993) "Behavioral and physiological correlates of children's reactions to others' stress." *Developmental Psychology 29*, 4, 655–663.

Fosha, D. (2003) "Dyadic Regulation and Experiential Work with Emotions and Relatedness in Trauma and Disorganized Attachment." In M.F. Solomon and D.J. Siegel (eds) *Healing Trauma: Attachment, Mind, Body, and Brain.* New York: Norton.

Frager, R. and Fadiman, J. (2005) *Personality and Personal Growth.* New York: Pearson Prentice Hall.

Gallese, V. (2001) "The 'shared manifold' hypothesis: From mirror neurons to empathy." *Journal of Consciousness Studies 8*, 5–7, 33–50.

Gallese, V. (2005) "Embodied simulation: From neurons to phenomenal experience." *Phenomenology and the Cognitive Sciences 4*, 23–48.

Gallese, V. (2006) "Intentional attunement: A neurophysiological perspective on social cognition and its disruption in autism." *Brain Research 1079*, 1, 15–24.

Gallese, V. (2007) "Intentional attunement: Mirror neurons and the neural underpinnings of interpersonal relations." *Journal of the American Psychoanalytic Association 55*, 1, 131–176.

Gallese, V., Fadiga, L., Fogassi, L., and Rizzolatti, G. (1996) "Action recognition in the premotor cortex." *Brain 119*, 593–609.

Gantt, L. (2009) "Support for a neurobiological view of trauma with implications for art therapy." *The Arts in Psychotherapy 36*, 3, 148–153.

Gendlin, E.T. (1982) *Focusing.* New York: Bantam Books.

Gendlin, E.T. (1998) *Focusing-Oriented Psychotherapy.* New York: Guilford.

Germer, C.K. and Siegel, R.D. (eds) (2012) *Wisdom and Compassion in Psychotherapy: Deepening Mindfulness in Clinical Practice.* New York: Guilford.

Gevirtz, R. (2011) "Autonomic Nervous System Markers for Psychophyiological, Anxiety, and Physical Disorders." In E. Gordon and S.H. Koslow (eds) *Integrative Neuroscience and Personalized Medicine.* New York: Oxford University Press.

Ginot, E. (2012) "Self-narratives and dysregulated affective states: The neuropsychological links between self-narratives, attachment, affect, and cognition." *Psychoanalytic Psychology 29*, 1, 59–80.

Greeson, J.M. (2008) "Mindfulness research update." *Complementary Health Practice Review 14*, 1, 10–18.

Gross, J.J. and Levenson, R.W. (1993) "Emotional suppression: Physiology, self-report, and expressive behavior." *Journal of Personality and Social Psychology 64*, 6, 970–986.

Gross, M.M., Crane, E.A., and Fredrickson, B.L. (2010) "Methodology for assessing bodily expression of emotion." *Journal of Nonverbal Behavior 34*, 4, 223–248.

Haen, C. (2008) "Vanquishing Monsters: Drama Therapy for Treating Childhood Trauma in the Group Setting." In C. Malchiodi (ed.) *Creative Interventions with Traumatized Children.* New York: Guilford.

Haller, J. and Kruk, M.R. (2003) "Neuroendocrine Stress Responses and Aggression." In M.P. Mattson (ed.) *Neurobiology of Aggression: Understanding and Preventing Violence.* Totowa, NJ: Humana Press.

Hansel, A. and von Kanel, R. (2008) "The ventro-medial prefrontal cortex: A major link between the autonomic nervous system, regulation of emotion, and stress reactivity?" *BioPsychoSocial Medicine 2*, 21. DOI::10.1186/1751-0759-1182-1121.

Hart, A.J., Whalen, P.J., Shin, L.M., McInerny, S.C., Fischer, H., and Rauch, S.L. (2000) "Differential response in the human amygdala to racial outgroup vs ingroup face stimuli." *NeuroReport 11*, 11, 2351–2355.

Hass-Cohen, N. and Carr, R. (eds) (2008) *Art Therapy and Clinical Neuroscience.* London: Jessica Kingsley Publishers.

Hazell, C. and Perez, R. (2011) *What Happens When You Touch the Body? The Psychology of Body-Work.* Bloomington, IN: AuthorHouse.

Herman, J. (1997) *Trauma and Recovery: The Aftermath of Violence.* New York: Basic Books.

Herskowitz, M. (2008) *Emotional Armoring.* Piscataway, NJ: Rutgers University-Transactions Publishers.

Holzel, B., Carmody, J., Evans, K.C., Hoge, E.A., *et al.* (2010) "Stress reduction correlates with structural changes in the amygdala." *Social Cognitive and Affective Neuroscience 5*, 1, 11–17.

Holzel, B., Lazar, S.W., Gard, T., Schuman-Olivier, Z., Vago, D.R., and Ott, U. (2011) "How does mindfulness meditation work? Proposing mechanisms of action from a conceptual and neural perspective." *Perspectives on Psychological Science 6*, 6, 537–559.

Holzel, B.K., Ott, U., Gard, T., Hempel, H. *et al.* (2008) "Investigation of mindfulness meditation practitioners with voxel-based morphometry." *Social Cognitive and Affective Neuroscience 3*, 55–61.

Hopper, J.W., Frewen, P.A., Van der Kolk, B.A., and Lanius, R.A. (2007) "Neural correlates of re-experiencing, avoidance, and dissociation in PTSD: Symptom dimensions and emotion dysregulation in responses to script-driven trauma imagery." *Journal of Traumatic Studies 20*, 5, 713–725.

Kabat-Zinn, J. (1990) *Full Catastrophe Living.* New York: Dell Publishing.

Kass, J. (1996a) "Coping with life-threatening illnesses using a logotherapeutic approach, stage I: Health care team interventions." *International Forum for Logotherapy 19*, Spring, 15–19.

Kass, J. (1996b) "Coping with life-threatening illnesses using a logotherapeutic approach, stage II: Clinical mental health counseling." *International Forum for Logotherapy 20*, Fall, 10–14.

Kass, J. (1998) "The Inventory of Positive Psychological Attitudes: Measuring Attitudes which Buffer Stress and Facilitate Primary Prevention." In C. Zalaquette and R. Wood (eds) *Evaluating Stress: A Book of Resources.* Lanham, MD: University Press of America.

Kass, J. (2007) Spiritual maturation: A developmental resource for resilience, well-being, and peace." *Journal of Pedagogy, Pluralism, and Practice 12*, Summer, 56–64.

Kass, J. and Lennox, S. (2005) "Emerging Models of Spiritual Development: A Foundation for Mature, Moral, and Health-Promoting Behavior." In W.R. Miller and H. Delaney (eds) *Judeo–Christian Perspectives on Psychology: Human Nature, Motivation, and Change.* Washington, DC: American Psychological Association.

Kass, J. (2014) "Person-centered spiritual maturation: A multidimensional model." *Journal of Humanistic Psychology.* Accepted for publication.

Kass, J., Friedman, R., Leserman, J., Zuttermeister, P., and Benson, H. (1991) "Health outcomes and a new measure of spiritual experience." *Journal for the Scientific Study of Religion 30,* 2, 203–211.

Keleman, S. (1985) *Emotional Anatomy.* Berkeley, CA: Center Press.

Klorer, P.G. (2005) "Expressive therapy with severely maltreated children: Neuroscience contributions." *Art Therapy: Journal of the American Art Therapy Association 22,* 4, 213–220.

Kok, B.E. and Fredrickson, B.L. (2010) "Upward spirals of the heart: Autonomic flexibility, as indexed by vagal tone, reciprocally and propsectively predicts positive emotions and social connectedness." *Biological Psychology 85,* 3, 432–436.

Koolhaas, J.M., Korte, S.M., De Boer, S.F., Van Der Vegt, B.J., Van Reenen, V., and Hopster, H. (1991) "Coping styles in animals: Current status in behavior and stress physiology." *Neuroscience and Behavioral Reviews 23,* 7, 925–935.

Kurtz, R. (1990) *Body-Centered Psychotherapy: The Hakomi Method: The Integrated Use of Mindfulness, Nonviolence, and the Body.* Mendocino, CA: LifeRhythm.

Laban, R. (1988) *The Mastery of Movement* (Fourth edition). Plymouth: Northcote House.

Lagopoulos, J., Xu, J., Rasmussen, I., Vik, A., *et al.* (2009) "Increased theta and alpha EEG activity during nondirective meditation." *Journal of Alternative and Complementary Medicine 15,* 11, 1187–1192.

Lambert, K. and Kinsley, C.H. (2005) *Clinical Neuroscience.* New York: Worth Publishers.

Lashley, K.S. (1950) "In search of the engram." In *Physiological Mechanisms in Animal Behavior: Symposia of the Society for Experimental Biology 4,* 454–482.

Lazar, S.W., Bush, G., Gollub, R.L., Fricchione, G.L., Khalsa, G., and Benson, H. (2000) "Functional brain mapping of the relaxation response and meditation." *NeuroReport 11,* 7, 1581–1585.

Lazar, S.W., Kerr, C.E., Wasserman, R.H., Gray, J.R., *et al.* (2005) "Meditation is associated with increased cortical thickness." *NeuroReport 16,* 17, 1893–1897.

Levine, P.A. (2005) *Healing Trauma: A Pioneering Program for Restoring the Wisdom of Your Body.* Boulder, CO: Sounds True.

Liotti, M., Mayberg, H.S., Brannan, S.K., McGinnis, J., Jerabek, P. and Fox, P.T. (2000) "Differential cortico-limbic correlates of sadness and anxiety in healthy subjects: Implications for affective disorders." *Biological Psychiatry 48,* 1, 30–42.

Lowen, A. (1975) *Bioenergetics.* New York: Penguin Books.

Luan Phan, K., Wagner, T.D., Taylor, S.F., and Liberzon, I. (2004) "Functional neuroimaging studies of human emotions. *CNS Spectrums 9,* 4, 258–266.

Lusebrink, V.B. (2004) "Art therapy and the brain: An attempt to understand the underlying processes of art expression in therapy." *Art Therapy: Journal of the American Art Therapy Association 21,* 3, 125–135.

Lutz, A., Greischar, L.L., Rawlings, N.B., Ricard, M., and Davidson, J.M. (2004) "Long-term meditators self-induce high amplitude gamma synchrony during mental practice." *Neuroscience 101,* 46, 16369–16373.

MacLean, P.D. (1990) *The Triune Brain in Evolution.* New York: Plenum Press.

Malchiodi, C. (1990) *Breaking the Silence: Art Therapy with Children from Violent Homes.* New York: Brunner-Mazel.

Malchiodi, C. (ed.) (2008) *Creative Interventions with Traumatized Children.* New York: Guilford.

Mason, J.W., Wang, S., Yehuda, R., Riney, S., Charney, D.S., and Southwick, S.M. (2001) "Psychogenic lowering of urinary cortisol levels linked to increased emotional numbing and a shame-depressive syndrome in combat-related posttraumatic stress disorder." *Psychosomatic Medicine 63,* 3, 387–401.

McGirr, A., Diaconu, G., Berlim, M.T., Pruessner, J.C., *et al.* (2010) "Dysregulation of the sympathetic nervous system, hypothalmic-pituitary-adrenal axis and executive function in individuals at risk for suicide." *Journal of Psychiatry Neuroscience 35,* 6, 399–408.

Mehu, M., Mortillaro, M., Banziger, T. and Scherer, K.R. (2012) "Reliable facial muscle activation enhances recognizability and credibility of emotional expression." *Emotion 12,* 4, 701–715.

Mrazova, M. and Celec, P. (2010) "A systematic review of randomized controlled trials using music therapy for children." *Journal of Alternative and Complementary Medicine 16*, 10, 1089–1095.

O'Connor, T.M., O'Halloran, D.J., and Shanahan, F. (2000) "The stress response and the hypothalamic-pituitary-adrenal axis: From molecule to melancholia." *Quarterly Journal of Medicine 93*, 6, 323–333.

Ogden, P. (2009) "Emotion, Mindfulness, and Movement: Expanding the Regulatory Boundaries of the Window of Affect Tolerance." In D. Fosha, D.J. Siegel, and M.F. Solomon (ed.) *The Healing Power of Emotion: Affective Neuroscience, Development, and Clinical Practice*. New York: Norton.

Ogden, P., Minton, K., and Pain, C. (2006) *Trauma and the Body: A Sensorimotor Approach to Psychotherapy*. New York: Norton.

Opthof, T. (2000) "The normal range and determinants of the intrinsic heart rate in man." *Cardiovascular Research, 45*, 1, 177–184.

Oveis, C., Cohen, A.B., Gruber, J., Shiota, M.N., Haidt, J., and Keltner, D. (2009) "Resting respiratory sinus arrythmia is associated wtih tonic positive emotionality." *Emotion 9*, 2, 265–270.

Patel, A.D. (2008) *Music, Language, and the Brain*. New York: Oxford University Press.

Peng, C.K., Henry, I.C., Mietus, J.E., Hausdorff, J.M., *et al.* (2004) "Heart rate dynamics during three forms of meditation." *International Journal of Cardiology 95*, 1, 19–27.

Peng, C.K., Mietus, J.E., Liu, Y., Khalsa, G., *et al.* (1999) "Exaggerated heart rate oscillations during two meditation techniques." *International Journal of Cardiology 70*, 1, 101–107.

Perls, F. (1973) *The Gestalt Approach and Eye Witness to Therapy*. New York: Science and Behavior.

Pesso, A. (1973) *Experience in Action: A Psychomotor Psychology*. New York: New York University Press.

Phelps, E.A., Delgado, M.R., Nearing, K.I., and LeDoux, J.E. (2004) "Extinction learning in humans: Role of the amygdala and vmPFC." *Neuron 43*, 6, 897–905.

Pierrakos, J.C. (1987) *Core Energetics: Developing the Capacity to Love and Heal*. Mendocino, CA: LifeRhythm.

Porges, S.W. (1995) "Orienting in a defensive world: Mammalian modifications of our evolutionary heritage." *Psychophysiology 32*, 4, 301–318.

Porges, S.W. (1998) "Love: An emergent property of the mammalian autonomic nervous system." *Psychoneuroendocrinology 7*, 8, 837–861.

Porges, S.W. (2001) "The polyvagal theory: Phylogenetic substrates of a social nervous system." *International Journal of Psychophysiology 42*, 2, 123–146.

Porges, S.W. (2007) "The polyvagal perspective." *Biological Psychology 74*, 2, 116–143.

Porges, S.W. (2009) "The polyvagal theory: New insights into adaptive reactions of the autonomic nervous system." *Cleveland Clinic Journal of Medicine 76*, 2, 886–890.

Porges, S.W. (2011a) "Music Therapy, Trauma, and Polyvagal Theory." In S.W. Porges *The Polyvagal Theory: Neurophysiological Foundations of Emotions, Attachment, Communication, Self-Regulation*. New York: Norton.

Porges, S.W. (2011b) *The Polyvagal Theory: Neurophysiological Foundations of Emotions, Attachment, Communication, Self-regulation*. New York, NY: Norton.

Porges, S.W. and Furman, S.A. (2011) "The early development of the autonomic nervous system provides a neural platform for social behavior: A polyvagal perspective." *Infant Child Development 20*, 1, 106–118.

Porges, S.W., Doussard-Roosevelt, J.A., Portales, A.L., and Greenspan, S.I. (1996) "Infant regulation of the vagal 'brake' predicts child behavior problems: A psychobiological model of social behavior." *Developmental Psychobiology 29*, 8, 697–712.

Porges, S.W., Doussard-Roosevelt, J.A., Portales, A.L., and Suess, P.E. (1994) "Cardiac vagal tone: Stability and relation to difficultness in infants and 3-year-olds." *Developmental Psychobiology 27*, 5, 289–300.

Rappaport, L. (2009) *Focusing-Oriented Art Therapy: Accessing the Body's Wisdom and Creative Intelligence*. London: Jessica Kingsley Publishers.

Rauch, S.L., Van der Kolk, B.A., Fisler, R.E., Alpert, N.M., *et al.* (1996) "A symptom provocation study of posttraumatic stress disorder using positron emission tomography and script-driven imagery." *Archives of General Psychiatry 53*, 5, 380–387.

Reich, W. (1960a) (First published 1942) "Therapy: Breakthrough into the Vegetative Realm." In *Wilhelm Reich: Selected Writings*. New York, NY: Farrar, Straus, and Giroux.

Reich, W. (1960b) (First published 1942) "Therapy: The Expressive Language of the Living." In *Wilhelm Reich: Selected Writings*. NY: Farrar, Straus, and Giroux.

Reich, W. (1980) (First published 1933) *Character Analysis* (Third edition) New York, NY: Farrar, Straus, and Giroux.

Rizzolatti, G., Fadiga, L., Gallese, V., and Fogassi, L. (1996) "Premotor cortex and the recognition of motor actions." *Cognitive Brain Research 3*, 2, 131–141.

Rogers, C.R. (1961) *On Becoming a Person.* Boston, MA: Houghton-Mifflin.

Rogers, N. (1993) *The Creative Connection.* Palo Alto, CA: Science and Behavior.

Rogers, N. (2011) *The Creative Connection for Groups: Person-Centered Expressive Arts for Healing and Social Change.* Palo Alto, CA: Science and Behavior.

Rothschild, B. (2000) *The Body Remembers: The Psychophysiology of Trauma and Trauma Treatment.* New York: Norton.

Sapolsky, R.M. (1992) *Stress, Aging, and the Mechanisms of Neuron Death.* Cambridge, MA: MIT Press.

Sapolsky, R.M. (1996) "Stress, glucocorticoids, and damage to the nervous system: The current state of confusion." *Stress 1*, 1, 1–19.

Sapolsky, R.M. (1998) *Why Zebras Don't Get Ulcers: An Updated Guide to Stress, Stress-Related Diseases, and Coping.* New York: W.H. Freeman.

Sapolsky, R.M. (2003) "Stress and plasticity in the limbic system." *Neurochemical Research 28*, 11, 1735–1742.

Sapolsky, R.M., Romero, L.M., and Munck, A.M. (2000) "How do glucocorticoids influence stress responses? Integrating permissive, suppressive, stimulatory, and preparative actions." *Endocrine Review 21*, 1, 55–89.

Scherer, K.R. (2000) "Emotional Expression: A Royal Road for the Study of Behavior Control." In A. Grob and W. Perrig (eds) *Control of Human Behavior, Mental Processes, and Awareness.* Hillsdale, NJ: Lawrence Erlbaum.

Schore, A.N. (2000) "Attachment and the regulation of the right brain." *Attachment and Human Development 2*, 1, 23–47.

Schore, A.N. (2001) "Effects of secure attachment relationship on right brain development, affect regulation, and infant mental health." *Infant Mental Health Journal 22*, 1–2, 7–66.

Schore, A.N. (2002) "Dysregulation of the right brain: A fundamental mechanism of traumatic attachment and the psychopathogenesis of posttraumatic stress disorder." *Australian and New Zealand Journal of Psychiatry 36*, 1, 9–30.

Schore, A.N. (2003a) "Early Relational Trauma, Disorganized Attachment, and Development of a Predisposition to Violence." In M.F. Solomon and D.J. Siegel (eds) *Healing Trauma: Attachment, Mind, Body, and Brain.* New York: Norton.

Schore, A.N. (2003b) *Affect Regulation and the Repair of the Self.* New York: Norton.

Schore, A.N. (2009) "Right-brain affect regulation: An essential mechanism of development, trauma, dissociation, and psychotherapy." In D. Fosha, D.J. Siegel, and M.F. Solomon (eds) *The Healing Power of Emotion: Affective Neuroscience, Development, and Clinical Practice.* New York: Norton.

Schore, A.N. (2012) *The Science of the Art of Psychotherapy.* New York: Norton.

Schore, J.R. and Schore, A.N. (2008) "Modern attachment theory: The central role of emotional regulation in development and treatment." *Clinical Social Work Journal 36*, 9–20.

Segerstrom, S.C. and Solberg-Nes, L. (2007) "Heart rate variability reflects self-regulatory strength, effort, and fatigue." *Psychological Science 18*, 3, 275–281.

Shamay-Tsoory, S.G. (2009) "Empathic Processing: Its Cognitive and Affective Dimensions and Neuroanatomical Basis." In J. Decety and W. Ickes (eds) *The Social Neuroscience of Empathy.* Cambridge, MA: MIT Press.

Siegel, D.J. (2003) "An Interpersonal Neurobiology of Psychotherapy: The Developing Mind and the Resolution of Trauma." In M.F. Solomon and D.J. Siegel (eds) *Healing Trauma: Attachment, Mind, Body, and Brain.* New York: Norton.

Siegel, D.J. (2007) *The Mindful Brain: Reflection and Attunement in the Cultivation of Well-Being.* New York: Norton.

Siegel, D.J. (2012) *The Developing Mind: How Relationships and the Brain Interact to Shape Who We Are* (Second edition). New York: Guilford.

Southwick, S.M., Vythilingam, M., and Charney, D.S. (2005) "The psychobiology of depression and resilience to stress: Implications for prevention and treatment." *Annual Review of Clinical Psychology 1*, 1, 255–291.

Steele, W. and Malchiodi, C. (2012) *Trauma-Informed Practices with Children and Adolescents*. New York: Taylor and Francis.

Taylor, J.B. (2009) *My Stroke of Insight: A Brain Scientist's Personal Journey*. New York, NY: Plume/Penguin.

Thompson, B.T. and Andrews, S.R. (2000) "An historical commentary on the physiological effects of music: Tomatis, Mozart, and neuropsychology." *Integrative Physiological and Behavioral Science 35*, 3, 174–188.

Treadway, M.T. and Lazar, S.W. (2009) "The Neurobiology of Mindfulness." In D. Fabrizio (ed.) *Clinical Handbook of Mindfulness*. New York: Springer.

Vacharkulksemsuk, T. and Fredrickson, B.L. (2012) "Strangers in synch: Achieving embodied rapport through shared movements." *Journal of Experimental Social Psychology 48*, 1, 399–402.

van der Kolk, B.A. (1994) "The body keeps the score: Memory and the evolving psychobiology of post-traumatic stress disorder." *Harvard Review of Psychiatry 1*, 5, 253–265.

van der Kolk, B.A. (2003) "Post-Traumatic Stress Disorder and the Nature of Trauma." In M.F. Solomon and D.J. Siegel (eds) *Healing Trauma: Attachment, Mind, Body, and Brain*. New York: Norton.

Wiener, D.J. (ed.) (1999) *Beyond Talk Therapy: Using Movement and Expressive Techniques in Clinical Practice*. Washington, DC: American Psychological Association.

Wilner, K.B. (1999) "Core Energetics: A Therapy of Bodily Energy and Consciousness." In D.J. Wiener (ed.) *Beyond Talk Therapy: Using Movement and Expressive Techniques in Clinical Practice*. Washington, DC: American Psychological Association.

Woldt, A. and Toman, S. (2005) *Gestalt Therapy: History, Theory, and Practice*. Thousand Oaks, CA: Sage.

Yehuda, R., Giller, E.L., Southwick, S.M., Lowy, M.T., and Mason, J.W. (1991) "Hypothalamic-pituitary-adrenal dysfunction in post-traumatic stress disorder." *Biological Psychiatry 30*, 1031–1048.

Yehuda, R., Southwick, S.M., Mason, J.W., and Giller, E.L. (1990a) "Interactions of the Hypothalamic-Pituitary-Adrenal Axis and the Catecholaminergic System in Post-Traumatic Stress Disorder." In E.L. Giller (ed.) *Biological Assessment and Treatment of PTSD*. Washington, DC: American Psychological Association.

Yehuda, R., Southwick, S.M., Nussbaum, G., Wahby, V., Giller, E.L.J., and Mason, J.W. (1990b) "Low urinary cortisol secretion in patients with post-traumatic stress disorder." *Journal of Nervous and Mental Disease 178*, 6, 366–369.

Ziadel, D.W. (2005) *Neuropsychology of Art: Neurological, Cognitive, and Evolutionary Perspectives*. New York: Psychology Press.

Appendix 1

Resources

Basic Mindfulness Exercises

Insight Meditation

This has been adapted by Joel Gluck from Theravada Buddhist teachings.
For the full-length version of this four-step process, please visit: www.insightimprov.
org/Resources.html.

1. Arriving in the Meditation—Relaxing—Noticing What is Present

In a quiet room, find a comfortable place to sit. Allow the body to relax. If you find it helps, close your eyes. Spend a couple of minutes simply arriving in the present moment.

Without changing anything, notice what is already there. Notice the body, the points of contact with the cushion or chair. Notice the energy in the body, the "feeling tone" or mood. How do you feel today, right now? Notice tension and relaxation. Purposely breathe into any areas of tension and let them go on the out-breath. Let go of any unnecessary holding or stiffness. Sit in a relaxed but alert way.

2. Cultivating Mindfulness of a Single Object (*Samadhi*) using the Breath (*Anapanasati*)

When you are ready, notice your breathing. You may notice the belly rising and falling with each breath, or you may be aware of the sensation of breathing in and out of the nostrils. Pick one area to focus on. Do not try to change or control the breath, just notice it.

If you find yourself thinking, about anything—past, future, judging, planning, fantasizing, etc.—just notice you are thinking (you can say "thinking" in your mind), and then return to the breath. It is normal to think—do not judge yourself for this— but simply return your awareness to the breath. This constant returning to the object of the meditation (in this case, the breath) is called "mindfulness." With each in-breath, each out-breath, notice the details—how does the body feel, what changes are there, is the breath deep, shallow, rough, smooth, fast, slow? Become fascinated with the breath.

Meditate in this way for 5–15 minutes, before transitioning into *vipassana* (Number 3).

3. OPENING TO CHOICELESS AWARENESS (VIPASSANA)

Now, instead of choosing a single object for our meditation, we are going to open to all the channels of awareness, letting the objects choose us. Throughout this meditation—if you find yourself distracted or overwhelmed—you can return to your breath anytime, using it as an anchor.

In preparing for *vipassana*, it can be helpful to visit the six "sense doors." First, open up to an awareness of your whole body. Notice any bodily sensations that are prominent. Also become aware of the overall energy and feeling-tone of the body. Next, open to your other senses one at a time: sounds, smells, tastes, and the visual sense. If you find yourself thinking about a sensation, getting lost in thought, return to the present moment and whatever the next sensation is, noticing its immediate features—for example, receive a sound as a sound (pitch, volume, timbre, etc.). Finally, take a minute to open to the sixth sense door: mind objects. Notice thoughts, voices in the head, images in the mind.

Now let yourself open to *vipassana*: rather than consciously choosing what to pay attention to, notice whatever is arising in the field of awareness. This may be a sound, a smell, a pain, an itch, a thought, an emotion, etc. Notice this object arising; notice how it changes, if at all; and notice how it passes away.

If it helps, feel free to label the channel of awareness in which the object is arising: "sound," "body sensation," "smell," "mind object," etc. This can help you maintain moment-to-moment awareness and not get lost in thought.

As *vipassana* deepens as a practice, you may notice more and more not only the objects arising in the field of awareness, but the nature of the awareness itself.

Meditate in this way for as long you like: 5–10 minutes if you are new to meditation; longer for experienced meditators.

4. PRACTICING LOVINGKINDNESS (*METTA*)

The purpose of *metta* practice is to take the qualities of mindfulness and openness cultivated in the first parts of our meditation, and use them to develop our capacity for lovingkindness, compassion, sympathetic joy, and equanimity—for ourselves and for others.

Begin by sending *metta* to yourself. Open your heart to these messages, as you say them silently in your own mind (also feel free to find your own words if these do not work for you). Repeat any one of these phrases as many times as necessary to really feel it and take it in:

- May I be well and happy.

- May I be at ease in my body and in my mind.

- May my heart be filled with lovingkindness—with love and kindness.

- May I let go and be free.

- May I live in peace.

Then take a few more moments to send any other messages of *metta* you would like to send to yourself—these could be messages specific to what you feel you need right now or today.

Next we send *metta* to another person or being. (If you have sufficient time during your sitting, this part of the *metta* meditation is traditionally performed in three steps—sending lovingkindness to a loved one, a neutral person, and a challenging person. If you are new to *metta* practice, it is helpful to begin by sending *metta* to someone it is easy to send to.)

Imagine one person in your mind's eye, and picture them receiving your lovingkindness with an open heart:

- May you be well and happy.

- May you be at ease in your body and in your mind.

- May your heart be filled with lovingkindness—with love and kindness.

- May you let go and be free.

- May you live in peace.

Take a few moments to send any additional messages of *metta* you would like to send to this person.

Finally, we send *metta* to all beings—imagining we can send our lovingkindness out into the world, to all people, animals, plants—particularly those around the globe who are suffering from illness, poverty, hunger, injustice, or ignorance—and out into the universe wherever there is existence:

- May all beings be well and happy.

- May all beings be at ease in their body and in their mind.

- May all beings' hearts be filled with lovingkindness—with love and kindness.

- May all beings let go and be free.

- May all beings live in peace.

- May there be peace. May there be peace. May there be peace.

End by taking a few moments to send any additional messages of *metta* you would like to send to all beings today. Then gently transition from the meditation into the day—taking these qualities of mindfulness, openness, and lovingkindness into your interactions with others.

Other Mindfulness Exercises

Exercises 5, 6, and 7 are based on the teachings of Thich Nhat Hanh. They have been adapted by Laury Rappaport. (Excerpts from Rappaport (2009) *Focusing-Oriented Art Therapy: Accessing the Body's Wisdom and Creative Intelligence.* London:

Jessica Kingsley Publishers. Guided audio CD: Focusing for Wellbeing available at: www.focusingarts.com).

5. MINDFUL BREATHING

Bell: As you hear the sound of the bell, allow yourself to enjoy your breathing.

Begin by taking a few deep breaths into your body, feeling the support of the chair, the earth, and sky. As you breathe, notice the in-breath and your out-breath as you silently coordinate these short phrases with your breath:

> "Breathing in, I know I am breathing in
> Breathing out, I know I am breathing out."

Repeat several times.

> "Whatever thoughts are on your mind, just notice them and allow them to pass by like the clouds in the sky."

After some time, the internal phrases can be shortened to the words "in" and "out." Additional words or phrases can be substituted, such as "Breathing in calm, breathing out peace." Thich Nhat Hanh (2001) also teaches ways to work with difficult emotions: "Breathing in, I am aware anger is in me; Breathing out, anger is leaving me." I tailor the *gathas* (short phrases) to match the client's needs.

6. WALKING MEDITATION

Begin by taking a few deep breaths into your body, noticing the in-breath and the out-breath. Bring awareness to your breath and to each foot as it lifts up, travels through space, and makes contact with the ground. The pace is slow. Short *gathas*, or phrases, are silently repeated in coordination with the breath and a particular foot:

> *Left foot:* Breathing in, I am aware of breathing in.

> *Right foot:* Breathing out, I am aware of breathing out.

After a few repetitions, you can shorten the phrases:

> *Left foot:* In, aware of breathing in.

> *Right foot:* Out, aware of breathing out.

Different phrases can be substituted. For example, to transform difficult feelings you might use the following *gatha*:

> *Left foot:* Breathing in, I'm aware that anger is in me.

> *Right foot:* Breathing out, I'm aware of anger leaving me.

(Substitute feelings such as anxiety, fear, loneliness, etc.) After some time with this *gatha*, it often feels natural to bring in peaceful and calm feelings:

> *Left foot:* Breathing in, I feel calm.

> *Right foot:* Breathing out, I feel peace.

Shortening the phrase:

Left foot: In, calm.

Right foot: Out, peace.

7. PEBBLE MEDITATION

Rocks or stones are placed in the center of the circle.

Bell: A bell is sounded, and clients are intvited to enjoy their breathing as they hear this sound.

Each person takes four stones. Each rock represents a different element: flower, mountain, water, and space. The therapist invites the group members to pick up one rock at a time, to hold it and to breathe mindfully. The therapist recites aloud the following phrases two to three times, as the clients repeat them silently to themselves:

First rock: Breathing in, I see myself as a flower.

Breathing out, I feel fresh. (*Place the rock to the side.*)

Second rock: Breathing in, I see myself as a mountain.

Breathing out, I feel solid. (*Place the rock to the side.*)

Third rock: Breathing in, I see myself as still water in a pond.

Breathing out, I see clearly. (*Place the rock to the side.*)

Fourth rock: Breathing in, I see myself as space.

Breathing out, I feel free. (*Place the rock to the side.*)

Option: After the meditation, notice how you feel and express your felt sense through the arts.

8. BODY SCAN FORMAL PRACTICE

This has been adapted from Kabat-Zinn (1991, pp.92–93) by Patricia D. Isis. (CD available at www.MiamiArtTherapy.com.)

Find a place to lie down that is quiet and comforting, letting your feet fall out from the center, and your arms lie relaxed by your sides, with your hands flat on the floor or resting on your belly uncrossed. Assume a position that invites stillness and wakefulness. Notice that you are breathing. Letting the breath breathe itself. Not trying to change anything or get anywhere. Dwelling in the awareness of each full inhalation and each full exhalation without changing the rhythm of the breath.

When you are ready, using your breath as your anchor, focus on both of your feet. Allow the breath to come into and go out of both feet. Open and allow any sensations that emerge in your awareness of your feet, including the toes, the spaces between your toes, the soles, and tops of both feet. Picture the breath coming in through your shoe, sock, or stocking. Invite the breath into your skin, bloodflow, bones, ligaments, tendons, and joints that make up your feet. Allow any sensations that emerge in your awareness whether pleasant, unpleasant, or neutral.

Let your focus shift to your legs, bringing the breath in through your ankles and moving up through the musculature, bone structure, and blood flow of the lower legs, knees and knee caps, as well as the upper legs, and back down through the ankles. Noting any sensations such as heat, coolness, itchiness, dryness, moisture, tension, numbness, pain, or the absence of any sensation. Simply let your breath anchor your kind awareness to your legs as you experience them completely right now.

Now, gently turn your attention to the pelvic region of your body. Bring your breath into and out of the clothing, skin, bones of the pelvic cage, and the reproductive organs and genitals, as well as the glutimous maximus and anus. Notice with hospitality all the emotions, sensations or lack of each in this region of your one wild and precious body. Open and allow all of your awareness whether wonderful, horrible, or ordinary.

When you are ready, let your breath and attention settle on your spine and back. Feel the breath move up through the bottom of your spinal column saturating each vertebrae and emanating out throughout your back in its entirety. Put out the welcome mat for all that you encounter in your awareness with your breath as your guide. Shift your focus to your abdomen. Invite your breath to come into and out of your belly, touching all that you are stomaching and digesting in your life and body here and now, like it or not. Just allowing all, simply because it is apparent in this region of your body in this moment. Now, focus on the thoracic region of your body, allowing your breath to come into and go out of your clothing, skin, and rib cage bathing the vital organs within. You might notice your heart beat, and carefully note the experience of full and empty lungs without judgment.

When you feel ready, let your focus move to your hands and arms. Bring your life force into the finger tips down through each finger, and the spaces between the fingers as well as the whole hand, wrist, forearm, elbows, and top of the arms. Experiencing the breath as it travels through skin, joints, bones, large and small muscle groups and blood flow, ligaments, tendons, veins, and arteries. Just notice with tenderness and compassion, all that is there or not there.

When you are ready on the exhale, settle your breath on your shoulders, breathing into and out of your entire shoulder region, the blades in the back and the shoulders themselves. Note all that you encounter with lovingkindness and equanimity. And when ready, let the breath come into and out of the neck. Note any heat, tension, pain, darkness, lightness, openness, or closedness. Whatever you discover, allow it simply because it is there already.

When ready, shift the breath to your face and cranium (skull). Let the breath flow into your whole face penetrating the skin, forehead, temples, eye sockets, and eyes, cheekbones, nasal and oral cavities, ears, and chin. Expand the breath to move into the cranium through the hair follicles and into the brain and out. Note all that you experience, pleasant, unpleasant, or neutral in this region of your body and hold it all tenderly in your awareness.

When you are ready, imagine a blow hole at the top of your head, much like a whale has. Breathe into that imaginary hole at the top of your head and send it through every region of your body linking all of you into one complete whole. Bringing the breath into the cranium, brain, and face, into the neck, and shoulders, down the arms, hands, and fingers, and into the chest and stomach, back, spine, pelvis, legs, feet, and out through the toes. And back into the toes, and feet, legs, pelvis, back, spine, stomach, chest, hands, arms, shoulders, neck, face, cranium, and out through the imaginary blow hole at the top of the head. Reinforcing your wholeness, and completeness just as you are right now. Return to your breath coming in and going out naturally. Gently begin to wiggle your feet and toes. When you are ready, turn on your side and gently transition to a pose that allows for sharing your experience.

Music Resources (Van Dort and Grocke ©2013)

The following selections of music are suitable for music and imagery sessions, with shorter selections designed for initial sessions, and longer selections once a group is familiar with the music and imagery process. (Note: duration timings will differ between different recordings).

Composer	Title	Duration
Bach	Suite No. 3—Air	5:15
Bach	Brandenburg Concerto #6—Adagio	5:29
Bach	Christmas Oratorio—Shepherd's Song	5:55
Beethoven	Piano Concerto No. #5—Adagio	7:45
Beethoven	Romance #2 in F major	9:47
Bizet	Carmen Suite #1—Intermezzo	2:32
Butterworth	On the Banks of Green Willow	6:07
Dvorak	Czech Suite—Romance	4:32
Elgar	Serenade for Strings—Larghetto	5:49
Elgar	Sospiri Op. 70	4:31
Faure	Pavane	7:44
Faure	Requiem—In paradissum	3:17
Gluck	Orfeo and Euridice—Dance of the blessed spirits	2:44
Grieg	Peer Gynt Suite—Morning Peer Gynt Suite #2—Solveig's song	4:00 5:00
Grieg	Holberg Suite—Air	5:44
Grieg	Cradle Song	4:07
Grieg	Two Elegiac Melodies Op. 34—Last Spring	5:55
Holst	Planets Suite—Venus —Neptune	8:07 7:01
Korngold	Much Ado bout Nothing—Garden Scene	4:38
Liadov	The Enchanted Lake	7:58

Mascagni	Cavelleria Rusticana—Intermezzo	2:59
Massenet	Thais—Meditation	5:47
Massenet	The Virgin —The last sleep	3.55
Mozart	Eine Kleine Nachtmusik—Romance	6:03
Pachelbel	Canon in D	7:07
Puccini	Madame Butterfly—Humming Chorus	2:46
Rachmaninov	Songs Op. 34—Vocalise	6:51
Ravel	Pavane	6:16
Respighi	The Birds Suite—The Nightingale —The Dove	4:30 4:30
Respighi	The Fountains of Rome Villa Guilia at Dawn Villa Medici at Sunset	4:28 5:45
Saint-Saens	Carnival of the Animals—The Swan	3:07
Stamitz	Cello concerto No. 2 in A—Romance	6:51
Tchaikovsky	Romance in F minor	5:46
Tchaikovsky	Andante Cantabile Op. 11	6:44
Vaughan-Williams	Rhosymedre	3:58

Longer Selections (approximately ten minutes or longer)		
Albinoni	Adagio for Strings and Organ	11:46
Debussy	Afternoon of a Faun	10:30
Dvorak	Romance in F minor	12:46
Chopin	Piano Concerto 1 in E minor—Romance Larghetto	9:19
Haydn	Cello Concerto in C—Adagio	9:45
Mozart	Concerto for Flute and Harp—Andantino	9:40
Mozart	Piano Concerto 20 in D minor—Romance	9:00
Mozart	Piano Concerto 21—Andante	7:15
Part	Spiegel im Spiegel	10:41
Ravel	Introduction and Allegro for Harp and Orchestra	10:17
Vaughan-Williams	Serenade to Music	11:40

Appendix 2

Contributor List and Biographies

Pat B. Allen, Ph.D., ATR, HLM, is a writer, artist, and art therapist who connects to the creative source through art and writing. Her two books – *Art Is a Way of Knowing* (Shambhala 1995) and *Art Is a Spiritual Path* (Shambhala 2005) – explore the borders between art, psychology, spirituality, and social action. Her present work includes exploring the natural world via art, writing in Ojai, California. Her training in the field of permaculture and body-based exploration informs this work. Dr. Allen is a co-founder of the Open Studio Project in Chicago and currently assists with the training of certified Open Studio Process facilitators. She is at work on a book about dissolving dualities via the creative process.

Zoë Avstreih, MS, LPC, BC-DMT, NCC, the founder and Director of the Center for the Study of Authentic Movement, is a Board Certified Dance/Movement Therapist, a Licensed Professional Counselor in the State of Colorado, and a Licensed Psychoanalyst and Creative Arts Therapist in New York State. Zoë is the Coordinator of the Dance/Movement Therapy Concentration in the Somatic Counseling Psychology Program at Naropa University in Boulder, CO and a Professor in Naropa University's Graduate School of Psychology. She was the founder and former director of the Dance/Movement Therapy Program at Pratt Institute. As a pioneer in the development of Authentic Movement, Zoë lectures and teaches internationally and has published widely in the field focusing on Authentic Movement as both a form of therapy and a body-based awareness practice.

Nancy Beardall, Ph.D., BC-DMT, LMHC, CMA, is an Associate Professor in the Graduate School of Arts and Sciences, Expressive Therapies Division at Lesley University, Cambridge, MA. As a Dance/Movement Therapist, consultant, Certified Movement Analyst, and educator, Dr. Beardall's work has focused on cognitive, social-emotional, and relational development using dance/movement and the expressive arts in the public schools. Dr. Beardall has developed curricula for middle and high school students focusing on the prevention of bullying, sexual harassment, and teen dating abuse, promoting gender respect, decision-making skills, healthy relationships, and making a difference in the school community. Her community-building programs through the arts have involved students, parents, and community members.

Fiona Chang, REAT, RSW, M Soc Sc, is the founder and Program Director of the three-year Expressive Arts Therapy Training Program hosted by the Centre on Behavioral Health of the University of Hong Kong. She is the Vice-chairperson of "Art in Hospital," the President of the Expressive Arts Therapy Association of Hong Kong, and former executive member of the Hong Kong Association of Art Therapists. She supports several organizations as advisor, including "Art Therapy Without Borders," South Western College in Santa Fe, the Mind–Body Department of the Five Branches University in California, and the Ragamuffin Project in Cambodia. She is now the Co-chair the Regional Committee of the International Expressive Arts Therapy Association. She has integrated multimodal expressive arts processes in counseling and group therapy for nearly 18 years in a variety of settings. She is an international trainer, amateur artist, photographer, and full-time mother. She is interested in the blending of Chinese metaphors in the Western model of expressive arts therapy in body–mind connection to actualize the self-healing potentials of each individual for a holistic wellness.

John Fox, CPT, is a poet and certified poetry therapist. He is adjunct associate professor at the California Institute of Integral Studies in San Francisco. He teaches at John F. Kennedy University in Berkeley, The Institute for Transpersonal Psychology in Palo Alto, and Holy Names University in Oakland. John is author of *Poetic Medicine: The Healing Art of Poem-making* and *Finding What You Didn't Lose: Expressing Your Truth and Creativity Through Poem-Making,* and numerous essays in a range of books on education, writing, medicine, and healing. His work is featured in the PBS documentary, *Healing Words: Poetry and Medicine.* He contributed two chapters to *Whole Person Health Care,* a three-volume work published by Praeger/Greenwood. John presents in all kinds of settings throughout the U.S., including medical schools and hospitals such as Stanford, Harvard, Shands Hospital in Gainesville, University Hospital in Cleveland, Ohio, Fred Hutchinson Cancer Center in Seattle, Washington. He has taught in Ireland, England, Israel, Kuwait, South Korea, and Canada. John is President of The Institute for Poetic Medicine. Find out more about his work at www.poeticmedicine.org

Michael A. Franklin, Ph.D., ATR-BC, is the Coordinator of the Graduate Transpersonal Art Therapy program at Naropa University. He is also the Director of the Naropa Community Art Studio, an intentional learning environment to study and research service as a spiritual practice, cultural empathy, and the roles of the socially engaged artist. Prior to Naropa, Michael practiced as a clinician and directed the Art Therapy programs at the College of St. Teresa and Bowling Green State University. Michael is an international lecturer and has published numerous papers on various subjects including aesthetics, self-esteem, AIDs iconography, interpretive strategies, community- based art therapy, and contemplative approaches including yoga, meditation, and applied empathic methods. Michael's current research as an artist and writer focuses on integrating the relationships between art therapy, social engagement, yoga philosophy, and meditation (see artisyoga.com).

Jürgen Fritsche was born in Münster, Germany. He is currently pursuing his Ph.D. in Art Education at Munich University. He studied History of Art, Japanese Studies, and Slavic Studies, in Münster, Moscow, and Hamburg; Fine Art at the State Academy of Fine Arts Karlsruhe; and Art Therapy at the Academy of Fine Arts Munich (MA equivalence). He has been working and exhibiting in different countries including Germany, U.S., Brazil, Switzerland, Luxembourg, and Spain. His experience as an art therapist includes art therapy with psychiatric and psychosomatic patients, people affected with HIV/AIDS, cancer patients, patients with chronic pain syndrome, children and unaccompanied minor refugees. He has been teaching Art Therapy at the Academy of Fine Arts Munich, the University of Munich LMU, the Institute of Art and Therapy Munich IKT, the University of Granada—Faculty of Fine Arts, Spain, and soon the Sigmund Freud Private University Vienna, Austria.

Jürgan had been practicing Vipassana/Insight Meditation for over 20 years, beginning with the teachers Joseph Goldstein and Sharon Salzberg. Since 1996, he has been following the Vipassana tradition taught by S.N. Goenka. Monastic retreats in Thailand have deepened his practice.

Bonnie Gabriel has worked in the art therapy profession for the past 13 years after obtaining her Master's degree from Pratt Institute in Brooklyn, New York. She worked at Memorial Sloan-Kettering Cancer Center for 10 years as an assistant to Dr. Paola Luzzatto as well as with patients diagnosed with cancer. She was a member of the professional team that organized and facilitated the "Creative Arts Retreat" for people dealing with cancer in Italy. Her work history also includes working with severe mental illness.

Joel Gluck, M.Ed., RDT, is a drama therapist, meditator, theatre artist, and executive coach who offers individual and couples therapy, workshops, clinical training, and coaching for performers and professionals throughout the world. His writings on drama therapy include "Insight Improvisation in Thailand: Drama Therapy Meets Vipassana Meditation" in the forthcoming book *The Heart and Soul of Psychotherapy* edited by Saphira Linden (Trafford), and "Insight Improvisation" in *Interactive and Improvisational Drama* edited by Adam Blatner with Daniel Wiener (iUniverse, 2007). Joel is a Registered Drama Therapist accredited by the North American Drama Therapy Association (NADTA). He has used theater and drama therapy in his work with ex-convicts, inner-city students, tsunami survivors in Thailand, school teachers in rural India, people with borderline personality disorder patients, and the elderly. Joel has served 20 years as an executive coach and leadership trainer, working extensively with Harvard Business School and other top executive education programs, and with the leaders of some of the largest companies in the world. Joel received a Master of Education degree in Drama Therapy Studies from Lesley University, with a special focus on Buddhist psychology and peace-building. He lives in Cambridge, MA, with his wife, Orapin, and their two children.

Denise Grocke, Ph.D., RMT, MT-BC, FAMI, is Director of Guided Imagery and Music training at the University of Melbourne. She is co-author of *Receptive Methods in Music Therapy* (2007), and co-editor of *Guided Imagery and Music: The Bonny Method and Beyond* (2002). She has numerous book chapters and articles in refereed journals on music therapy and Guided Imagery and Music. She was a co-founder of the Australian Music Therapy Association (1975), and the Music and Imagery Association of Australia (1994).

Daniel Herring, MA, LMHC, has been practicing mindfulness meditation since 1977 when he met Larry Rosenberg (Larry Rosenberg and David Guy *Breath by Breath: The Liberating Practice of Insight Meditation*, Boston, MA: Shambhala Publications, 2004) while studying acting at Emerson College. He has done many intensive silent retreats since then at Insight Meditation Society and other centers. An Expressive Therapy graduate of Lesley College, he has been treating persons with acute and chronic mental illness since 1982 while raising five children and maintaining a daily meditation practice. His mission has been to integrate mindfulness and expressive therapy into mainstream mental health care. Daniel currently practices independently in Haverhill, MA, teaches Supervision and Psychopathology at Lesley University in Cambridge, MA. He lives in New Hampshire with his wife and youngest son.

Patricia D. Isis, Ph.D., LMHC, ATR-BC, ATCS, has a Ph.D. in the expressive therapies with an emphasis on art therapy. Dr. Isis is a licensed mental health counselor in Florida and a Registered Board-Certified Art Therapist, credentialed art therapy and LMHC supervisor. Since 1980, Patricia has practiced mindfulness medititation and art psychotherapy in South Florida. Currently, she provides art therapy services full time in the public schools, maintains a part-time private practice, and provides mindfulness-based stress reduction (MBSR) classes and mindfulness trainings. Patricia is a popular presenter locally, nationally, and internationally. More information is available on her website www.MiamiArtTherapy.com

Debra Kalmanowitz, MA, RATh BAAT, HPCReg, has worked extensively in the context of trauma, political violence, and social change, locally, internationally, and in countries of conflict. Currently living in Hong Kong, Debra is a Research Postgraduate in the Department of Social Work and Social Administration and an Honorary Research Associate at the Centre on Behavioural Health, University of Hong Kong. Debra works with refugees and asylum seekers, continues to co-direct ATI (Art Therapy Initiative, www.atinitiative.org), and to work in her own studio. Debra is the co-author of the edited books *Art Therapy and Political Violence: With Art, Without Illusion, Art Therapy in Asia: To the Bone or Wrapped in Silk* and co-author of *The Portable Studio: Art Therapy and Political Conflict: Initiatives in the Former Yugoslavia and South Africa.*

Jared D. Kass, Ph.D., is a Professor in the Division of Counseling and Psychology, Graduate School of Arts and Social Sciences, Lesley University, in Cambridge, MA. Dr. Kass directs The Study Project on Well-Being, conducting research on the causes and effects of a resilient worldview. His courses integrate the neuroscience of resilient and destructive coping, trauma psychology, mindfulness, therapeutic use of the arts, and multicultural social justice perspectives into clinical practice. He was a staff member of the Person-Centered Approach Project (1975–1981), working closely with Dr. Carl Rogers, and Visiting Lecturer at Harvard Medical School (1985–1991), investigating the health effects of meditation with Dr. Herbert Benson. He has served as a Center Associate of the U.S. Department of Education's Higher Education Center for Alcohol, Other Drug Abuse, and Violence Prevention (1999–2001). Most recently, he has developed a curriculum that mentors social-emotional learning and psychospiritual development in higher education. He is a member of the Association for Contemplative Mind in Higher Education and the Phi Beta Kappa Society.

Anna Lagomaggiore, is a Dance-Movement Therapist, Psychologist, Art Psychotherapist, Certified Movement Analyst (Laban Institute, New York), supervisor and teacher for Art Therapy Italiana, Vice-president APID (Italian Professional Association Dance Movement Therapy), Deputy EADMT (European Association Dance Movement Therapy), Founder of the Associations INDACO and LO STUDIO VERDE, for Dance Movement Therapy and Art Therapy (Genova, Italy). Since 1990, she has worked with patients with genetic disorders (CePim, Genova) and privately with children and adults with eating disorders, anxiety, learning problems, and dyslexia. Anna has published a number of articles in professional journals, and chapters including, "Il terreno che non c'è. Il Contributo della Danza Movimento Terapia al disagio infantile contemporaneo. APID Conference Proceedings, 2011"; "Uovo dentro: sono io! La Danza Movimento Terapia con bambini e adolescenti affetti da Sindrome di Down," in A. Di Quirico (ed.) *Lasciar parlare il corpo*, Magi, 2012; and "Sul filo dell'acqua: modulazione corporea e immagini controtransferali nelle fasi iniziali del processo terapeutico in Danza Movimento Terapia," in I. Bolech and C. Macagno (eds) *Trent'Anni di Arte Terapia e di Danza Movimento Terapia*, Ananke, 2012.

Paola Luzzatto, Ph.D., Registered Art Therapist (U.K., U.S., Italy), Art Therapy teacher, and supervisor, trained at Goldsmiths College, University of London and specialized in Psychoanalytic Psychotherapy (Tavistock Institute, London), and Supervision Techniques (Westimster Pastoral Foundation, London). She worked for ten years in the field of Psychiatry at St Thomas' Hospital, London, with a special interest in Substance Abuse and Eating Disorders; and for another ten years in the field of Psycho-oncology at Memorial Sloan-Kettering Cancer Center, in New York. Paola Luzzatto received the 2004 Prize for Clinical Art Therapy from the American Art Therapy Association. She has published two books for children, a number of articles in professional journals, and two books: *Arte Terapia: una guida al lavoro simbolico per l'espressione e l'elaborazione del mondo interno* (Assisi: La Cittadella, 2009) and *Susanne Wenger, Artist and Priestess* (Firenze: Maremmi, 2009). She now lives in Florence, Italy.

Shaun McNiff, Ph.D., ATR, is founder of the first integrated arts in therapy graduate program at Lesley University in Cambridge, MA. He is a painter and the author of *Art Heals: How Creativity Cures the Soul; Trust the Process: An Artist's Guide to Letting Go; Art as Medicine: Creating a Therapy of the Imagination; Art-Based Research; Depth Psychology of Art; Integrating the Arts in Therapy; Art as Research: Opportunities and Challenges;* and many other books and writings which have been translated into Chinese, Japanese, Spanish, Portuguese, Russian, German, and other languages. A past President of the American Art Therapy Association, McNiff has received various honors and awards which include the Association's Honorary Life Member Award and citations from the Commonwealth of Massachusetts House of Representative and Senate for founding the Expressive Arts Therapy profession. In 2002 Lesley appointed him as its first University Professor.

Lucia Minerbi is a trained architect and later obtained a degree in Art Therapy at the Institute National de Formation du Personel Psychiatriques (INFIPP) in Dijon (France). She has worked as an art therapist in the Italian National Health Service for nearly 15 years, in a specialized semi-residential center for recovery from drug addiction, leading a weekly art therapy group. She has been teaching art therapy at the Lecco Art Therapy Training School, Italy. In 2002 she attended a full immersion course on "The Creative Journey and other art-therapy interventions" at the Memorial Kettering Cancer Center of New York. She has been a regular team member of the Silent Creative Retreats organized in Assisi for oncology patients and their relatives. She has published several articles in Italian professional journals and the chapter "Arte-Terapie e tossicodipendenza" in the book *Arteterapie: I fondamenti* edited by Carola Palazzi Trivelli and Alberto Taverna (Stampatori s.a.s., Torino 1998).

Ellen Mullin followed her training as an art therapist in London with a silent retreat at a Buddhist monastery in Thailand. This experience led to her interest in the dimension of silence as part of a therapeutic process. Her involvement in the creative silent retreats with colleagues from different professions has been a rich and fulfilling experience. She has found collective silence to be challenging but ultimately a time of important reflection, as well as a powerful connection with others; with timeless resonance. She was involved with retreat participants from the point at which they expressed an interest in attending, to welcoming them on their first day.

Gemma Oldrini graduated in Mathematics and Physics from the University of Genova, Italy. She has been a life-long teacher of Mathematics in one of the top higher secondary schools in Genova; she has also been active at a National and International level in the Girl Guides organization. On behalf of the Italian Ministries of Education and of Foreign Affairs Dr Oldrini has served on the examining Board of Italian schools in USA, India and Africa, where she has also traveled extensively on her own. Dr Oldrini is now retired as a teacher, but she is still active in Voluntary Associations and in numerous educational activities. Dr Oldrini has been the main administrator of the Assisi Retreats held from 2001 to 2010.

David K. Payne, Ph.D., is Instructor of Psychology, Wallace Community College, Dothan, Alabama. Up until 2004 he spent over a decade working with the psychological needs of cancer patients as a Clinical Assistant Psychologist (dual appointments in Department of Psychiatry and Behavioral Sciences and Department of Integrative Medicine) at Memorial Sloan-Kettering Cancer Center (New York) and as Assistant Professor of Psychology in Psychiatry at the Weill Medical College of Cornell University, New York. In this academic medical setting, he provided clinical care to patients facing end-of-life issues as well as providing supervision and training to post-graduate psychologists and psychiatrists in the assessment and treatment of psychological distress related to life-threatening illness. He has lectured and written extensively on cancer, pain, palliative care, coping with death and dying, and the use of integrative medicine interventions such as mindfulness and other behavioral techniques with patients facing chronic or life-threatening illnesses. He holds both a

Master's and Doctoral degree in Clinical Psychology from the University of Louisville. Currently he teaches Psychology at Wallace Community College where he is involved in training nurses and in teaching stress management techniques to students.

Caroline Peterson, MA, ATR-BC, LPC, a Board-Certified Art Therapist and Licensed Professional Counselor, is the founder of Springboard Studio in Philadelphia where she is in private practice, teaches Mindfulness-Based Stress Reduction (MBSR) programs, and hosts providers of community-based programs in Yoga and the not-for-profit Springboard Meditation Sangha. Her innovative work with Mindfulness-Based Art Therapy, beginning in 2000, was the focus of two NIH-funded research studies in Oncology from 2003–2010. Caroline is currently a clinician with the Supportive Care Team at the Joan Karnell Cancer Center at Pennsylvania Hospital/Penn Medicine where she has developed programs for persons with cancer and their care partners, including a new Mindfulness-Based Art Therapy program, Walkabout, that integrates mindful presence on outdoor walks using digital photography with collage-making, emphasizing the attitudinal foundations of mindfulness practice. Most recently, Caroline has developed a mindfulness skills training program for employees at Philadelphia Gas Works, the largest municipally owned utility in the U.S. Caroline received advanced training to teach MBSR at The Center for Mindfulness in Medicine, Health Care and Society at the University of Massachusetts Medical School; she received her graduate degree as an art therapist at Hahnemann now Drexel University in Philadelphia.

Laury Rappaport, Ph.D., REAT, ATR-BC, MFT, received her doctorate in Psychology and Spirituality in 1987 and has been teaching expressive arts therapies for over thirty years. She has served as a Professor at Five Branches University where she designed a Mind-Body Department, an Associate Professor at Notre Dame de Namur University, and a long time faculty at Lesley University where she was the Academic Coordinator of the International Expressive Therapies program. Laury is a Certifying Focusing Coordinator and Trainer with The Focusing Institute in NY and the founder/director of the Focusing and Expressive Arts Institute in Santa Rosa, CA. She is the author of *Focusing-Oriented Art Therapy: Accessing the Body's Wisdom and Creative Intelligence*, numerous chapters and published articles, and an audio CD: *Focusing for Wellbeing*. Currently, Laury is on the faculty at Sonoma State University, is an Integrative Psychotherapist with Sutter Health Institute for Health and Healing, and trains people nationally and internationally in Focusing-Oriented Expressive Arts. She has been a meditation practitioner for over 40 years—with roots in Hinduism and Buddhism. Her current teachers are Thich Nhat Hanh and Jakusho Kwong-roshi.

Merryl E. Rothaus, LPC, LMHC, ATR-BC is a Licensed Psychotherapist and Board-Certified Registered Art Therapist in private practice in Boulder, CO. A Transpersonal, Somatic Art Therapist, Merryl works with a diverse set of clients, and has created an innovative method of creative healing and growth, integrating her training in the mindfulness-based Hakomi method of Experiential, Body-Centered Psychotherapy with Art Therapy. Merryl is also an Art Therapy educator, having been Visiting Core Faculty at Antioch University, Seattle, and Adjunct Faculty at Naropa

University in Boulder, CO She is also a clinical supervisor for art therapists and mental health counselors worldwide. Merryl can be contacted at www.merrylrothaus.com

Lori Schwanbeck, MFT, is a mindfulness-based psychotherapist whose work is based on Dialectical Behavior Therapy (DBT), Hakomi Body Oriented Psychotherapy and the healing power of nature. Lori developed Sense and Sensibility, a sensory-focused mindfulness treatment for emotional regulation that she teaches internationally. Lori is an adjunct professor at J.F.K. University, teaches in the Mindfulness and Compassion program at California Institute of Integral Studies and leads workshops at Esalen. She is co-founder of San Francisco-based Mindfulness Therapy Associates.

Janet L. Surrey, Ph.D., is a clinical psychologist and a Founding Scholar of the Jean Baker Miller Training Institute at the Stone Center, Wellesley College. She is on the faculty of the the Andover-Newton Theological School. Dr. Surrey has been consulting and teaching Relational Cultural Theory nationally and internationally for over 20 years, and has been working to synthesize Buddhist and relational psychology. She has co-authored or co-edited a number of books, including *Women's Growth in Connection* (Guilford Press), *Women's Growth in Diversity, Mothering Against the Odds: Diverse Voices of Contemporary Mothers* (Guilford Press), *We Have to Talk: Healing Dialogues Between Women and Men* (Basic Books), *Making Connections: Building Community and Gender Dialogue in Secondary Schools* (Educators for Social Responsibility), and *Bill W. and Dr. Bob: The Story of the Founding of Alcoholics Anonymous* (Samuel French).

Jennifer Frank Tantia, Ph.D., BC-DMT, LCAT, is a Dance/Movement Therapist and somatic psychotherapist in New York City. She serves as a research advisor at Pratt Institute and teaches developmental and somatic psychology at Adelphi University. Former Program Director of the NY state chapter of the American Dance Therapy Association, Jennifer currently serves as Research Chair for the USABP and is the U.S. representative for the European Association for Body Psychotherapy. Jennifer leads Authentic Movement groups and works in private practice in Brooklyn and Manhattan, where she integrates Vipassana meditation into the treatment setting. Her research on Authentic Movement and the Autonomic Nervous System has been published and presented in both the U.S. and Europe.

Sidney M. Trantham, Ph.D. is an Associate Professor in the Division of Counseling and Psychology, Graduate School of Arts and Social Sciences, Lesley University, in Cambridge, MA. Dr. Trantham received his doctorate in Clinical Psychology in 1999 from the University of Florida, Gainesville. His doctoral work focused on exploring the impact of early childhood sexual experiences on the psychological functioning of adult males. He was a Harvard Clinical Fellow (1996–2000), where he completed his clinical psychology internship and neuropsychological post-doctoral fellowships as well as engaged in research identifying early cognitive markers of HIV-related dementia. Currently, Dr. Trantham maintains a private practice where he provides integrative psychological, neuropsychological, and gender assessment as well as psychotherapy with children, adolescents, adults, and families. Areas of expertise include working with gender variant children and adolescents.

Carolyn Van Dort, MA (Creative Arts Therapies), Grad Dip Guided Imagery and Music, Grad Dip Music Therapy, B Mus., is a music psychotherapist working in private practice. Mindfulness principles together with her music therapy training support her therapeutic work. Carolyn is an endorsed trainer for Guided Imagery and Music (GIM) training courses under the auspices of the Music and Imagery Association of Australia, and she is a clinical practitioner on the Psychotherapy and Counselling Federation of Australia, PACFA, register. Carolyn regularly conducts community workshops in music-based mindfulness. She can be contacted at www. musicpsycotherapy.com.au

Karin von Daler, Pscyhologist, MA, MFT, REAT, is an expressive arts psychotherapist, supervisor, and artist in private practice in Copenhagen. Educated and trained in the U.S., Switzerland, and India she teaches worldwide. Karin is the co-creator of the method Creative Mindfulness which she developed on the basis of her experience with meditation, the arts, and Dialectical Behavior Therapy.

Gabriella Ventrella has a degree in Humanities from Naples University (Italy) and she has worked in Naples for 15 years as a secondary school teacher. During this time she published fairy tales and essays, and a collection of short stories (Papadon, Marotta, 1984). She was also an active member of the Neapolitan Center of Semiotic Studies. Later on she trained at the Institute for Person-Centered Rogerian Approach to Listening. Between 1996 and 2001 Gabriella was in Paris and completed a formal training in Creative Writing at the Elisabeth Bing School, after which she attended further training in Creative Writing at the Aleph Atelier. Between 2001 and 2010 she was part of the team of the Silent Creative Retreat for oncology patients and their relatives. Since 2002, up to the present time, Gabriella has organized Creative Writing workshops and seminars, in public libraries and cultural associations, in Naples, where she lives.

Emily Tara Weiner, MA, MFTI, is a registered Marriage and Family Therapy Intern and holds a Masters degree in Marriage and Family Therapy and Art Therapy from Notre Dame De Namur University in Belmont, CA. Emily completed training in Dr. Laury Rappaport's Focusing-Oriented Arts Therapy (FOAT) Levels I-IV. Emily has been practicing meditation since 2004, primarily within the Korean Zen tradition, and lived and trained extensively for a year and a half in several Zen monasteries in South Korea (2006-2007). Emily is a Certified Mindful Schools Instructor, having completed and assisted with a year-long Mindfulness in Education Certification course with Mindful Schools (2012-2013). Emily is the founder of the Mindful Art Program for youth, and specializes in working with children and adolescents. Emily piloted her Mindful Art workshop in the summer of 2012 at the Omega Institute's, Omega Teen Camp, near Rhinebeck, NY, and has since offered her Mindful Art workshop at Inward Bound Mindfulness.

Subject Index

Author Index